More praise for *The Railway Man*

"*The Railway Man* is a dispatch from a territory of human existence about which most of us know little if anything. . . . It is painfully instructive and, in its way, heartening. . . . His is a story of human individuals rather than warring nations."

—*The Washington Post Book World*

"[An] extraordinary story of reconciliation. . . Perhaps the best World War II memoir since Sidney Stewart's great account of the Bataan Death March, *Give Us This Day*."

—*The Cleveland Plain Dealer*

"Profoundly touching. . . Lomax is the kind of hero who doesn't recognize that he is one. But his heroism has shown itself as much in his journey of personal reconciliation and forgiveness, as it did when he refused to confess to the 'hateful little interrogator' he now calls, in his book, his 'blood brother.' "

—*The Christian Science Monitor*

THE RAILWAY MAN

A TRUE STORY OF WAR, REMEMBRANCE, AND FORGIVENESS

ERIC LOMAX

BALLANTINE BOOKS · NEW YORK

http://www.randomhouse.com

Library of Congress Catalog Card Number: 96-96520

ISBN: 0-345-40668-0

Cover design by Ruth Ross
Cover photograph courtesy of the Imperial War Museum

Manufactured in the United States of America

First Ballantine Books Edition: September 1996

10 9 8 7 6 5 4 3 2 1

for
Elizabeth Sutherland Lomax
(1877–1942)

and her grandchildren, Linda,
Eric and Charmaine,
who never knew the story.

And for my wife Patti
without whose support
the story would never have been told.

This book owes an immeasurable debt to the creativity and skill of Neil Belton. His invaluable contribution to the final text far exceeded the usual relationship between author and publisher. It is true to say that without his help I would not have been able to give final form to so much that I have reflected on for the past fifty years.

I am alive, and was dead . . . Write therefore
the things which thou hast seen.

Revelation, I, vv. 18–19

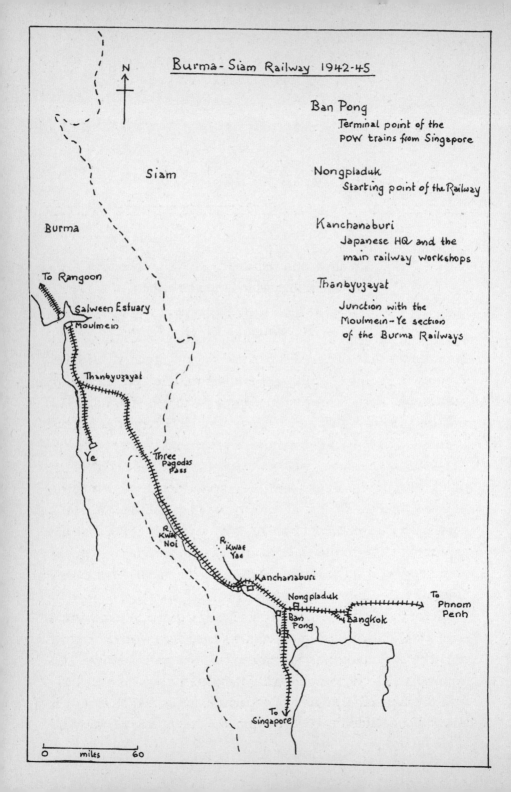

Burma - Siam Railway 1942-45

Ban Pong
Terminal point of the
POW trains from Singapore

Nongpladuk
Starting point of the Railway

Kanchanaburi
Japanese HQ and the
main railway workshops

Thanbyuzayat
Junction with the
Moulmein-Ye section
of the Burma Railways

N

Siam

Burma

To Rangoon

Salween Estuary

Moulmein

Thanbyuzayat

Ye

Three
Pagodas
Pass

R. Kwae
Noi

R. Kwae
Yae

Kanchanaburi

Nongpladuk

To Phnom
Penh

Ban
Pong

Bangkok

To
Singapore

0   miles   60

CHAPTER ONE

I HAVE A PAINTING in the hallway of my house in Berwick-upon-Tweed, by the Scottish artist Duncan Mackellar. It is a large work set in St Enoch Station in Glasgow on a dusty summer evening in the 1880s. A woman in late middle age, dressed in dark and modest clothes and carrying a parasol, is standing tense and distraught, looking out beyond us, oblivious of any other presence. Behind her the high smoke-grimed glass and wrought-iron walls of the station rise up. She is gazing off the edge of the platform at a vanishing train, so that we see her through the eyes of a receding traveller, and she has the flat restrained face of a person who has learned to swallow grief. Her sudden loneliness is captured as she strains to keep an image of her child, or so we assume, who is on the train heading for the emigrant ship or a colonial war – India, Afghanistan, the Gold Coast.

Although it is a conventional image, it is genuinely moving. I have always loved it. Railway stations have always attracted me, not just because trains are there, but because they are also ambivalent places, echoing with completed journeys and shrill with the melancholy noises of departure. Mackellar's painting is about the inevitability of separation, the cost of journeying. And we have never created any sound so evocative of separation as the whistle of a steam locomotive, that high note of inhuman relief as vaporized water is blown off and meets the cold air.

Once in the 1970s I went to St Enoch and stood on the platform at the spot that Mackellar's painting creates for the viewer, and the back of the great shed, like an enormous Victorian conservatory, seemed hardly to have changed. The station was not yet quite disused and silent, though a few years later it was destroyed, like so many of the other steam cathedrals. That age is gone now, finally, but the reality of grief, and the consequences of grief, of which Mackellar caught something in his painting, are not so easily banished.

The passion for trains and railways is, I have been told, incurable. I have also learned that there is no cure for torture. These two afflictions have been intimately linked in the course of my life, and yet through some chance combination of luck and grace I have survived them both. But it took me nearly fifty years to surmount the consequences of torture.

★ ★ ★

I was born in 1919, the year the World War formally ended, the year that Alcock and Brown drifted down out of the rain over the Atlantic and landed their frail bomber in an Irish bog. I remember being told about this feat of aeronautical engineering and skill at a very young age, and thinking about the two intrepid pilots as I was walked along the grey promenade of the seafront at Joppa, to the east of Edinburgh. 'Joppa' is the name of the biblical town where Jonah went when he was fleeing God, and from which he took ship. I discovered soon enough, though it was a long time before space on that scale meant much to me, that this sea was a sheltered inlet, the Firth of Forth, and that even though the distant Fife shore could only be seen in fine weather there were worse seas out there behind the fog and wind.

John Lomax, my father, was a quiet, disciplined, serious man who knew what was best for his wife and child and was unused to taking no for an answer in his own house. Until the age of fourteen he worked for a pawnbroker in Stockport, on the fringe of industrial Manchester, and then in 1893 somehow got into the Post Office, an institution he stayed in until his retirement almost half a century later. He started as a 'telegraph messenger', the most junior post then available and even lower than the entry grade which he would choose for me when I was sixteen. By the time I was born he was a middle-grade civil servant, a manager of staff in the Edinburgh General Post Office, a stable and trusted official.

My father moved to Edinburgh, a city of politics, law and services in 1909, but all his life remained a child of the industrial revolution, full of vivid memories of coal, smoke, smog and steam power, of great mill engines and railway locomotives and the Manchester Ship Canal. It is hard to explain to young people born in countries that have almost forgotten heavy manufacturing just how awe-inspiring the very processes that shaped our lives could be; for my father, and for me later, great machines were not fearful or distressing but things to be celebrated, as fascinating as the natural world, creatures made by men.

By the time I was able to notice such things, he was part of a reading circle of fifteen or so, men and women, who would visit each other's houses and read papers on such topics as the novels of Arnold Bennett, which my father devoured as the nearest thing he could find to a literature of his boyhood world, or the Edinburgh of Sir Walter Scott. My father was also the regional editor of the *Journal of the Institution of Post Office Electrical Engineers*, to which he contributed local news. And, like all dedicated believers in improvement and discovery, he read H.G. Wells. He had a little library of such books. On his shelves I remember Oliver & Boyd's *Edinburgh Almanac* from the 1830s, some books on popular science and Samuel Smiles's *Lives of the Engineers*.

I also remember my father's copy of Hendrik Willem Van Loon's *The Story of Mankind*, which came out in 1931. It was an inspiring narrative of achievement and progress, and as a child I absorbed its tale of optimism and invention, each new breakthrough seeming to promise more speed and ease and excitement. One of the most intense events of my childhood was finding the secret chart of 'The Great Discoveries' hidden inside the decorative dust-jacket of Van Loon's book. I was convinced that there were thousands of readers who had never looked at the back of the jacket, and that this wonderful branching tree of human ingenuity was for me alone.

My first memory of a world beyond my infant needs was not of an animal or a park, but of a strange mechanical assembly. One of my father's frequent destinations on those walks beside the sea was the Joppa Tram Terminus, which was situated where the historic main road from Edinburgh to London touched the Firth of Forth. On one of these walks, when I was a very small child, we rounded the corner of Di Rollo's ice-cream parlour and found Joppa Road blocked by a huge barricade of tram cars, a wall of maroon and white metal. Each tram was an elegant two-storeyed coach-house, with delicate looking wooden frames surrounding the windows, and each was two-headed, its end windows arranged in a five sided prism. The trams had open platforms at each end from which right-angled stairs disappeared tantalizingly into the open upper decks. They were waiting to take the crowds coming from a race meeting in nearby Musselburgh back into Edinburgh. I stared at this herd of machines. I didn't know there were so many trams in the world.

Joppa was, unfortunately for my awakening fascination for vehicles that ran on rails, a tram heaven. It was a terminus on one of the last cable tram systems in the world, its cars attached to their bases by ropes of steel wire up to five miles long running in a conduit between the rails, the cables paid out by big stationary steam engines in the depots. Soon after the revelation of the massed tram cars, my father took me to see an oily trench below the surface of the roadway at the Joppa terminus. This chamber was the cable pit, and in it was a large flanged wheel round which a steel hawser revolved, pulling in the car from Portobello, the nearest suburb to the west. Every few minutes a tram would arrive, detach itself from the eastbound cable and, after gripping the westbound cable, head back to Edinburgh at a stately twelve miles an hour.

There was something infinitely reassuring in the predictability of this system: the heavy double-decked trams drawn through the streets, moving widely but never randomly around the town, cruising steadily through the mill of bicycles, horse-drawn delivery wagons and pedestrians. It was as though the trams laid down an orderly grid on the chaotic life of the city.

The antiquated cable vehicles gave way, soon after I became aware of them, to electric trams. When I was about four, I was with my mother on the promenade when she pointed out what she told me was the first electric tram heading for Edinburgh. The big steam engine in the local depot shuddered to a halt late at night about a month later. My father told me about it the following day; I could tell that to him this was a solemn moment, the end of something, and that it made him sad.

As children we loved playing on and riding the trams, learning the personalities of the conductors, some of them not exactly friendly to boys, and discovering that the drivers now had personalities too, for the fixed jogging pace of the old cable trams was a thing of the past and some of the drivers put the handle down and ran their sparking wagons like demons. A tram one day jumped the rails on the curve of King's Road in Portobello, broke through the wall of Portobello Power station yard and ended up hanging over the railway line that fed the power station with coal. It was a sight, that big green tram car poised so weirdly out of place: a hint that orderly communication between one place and another could be violently interrupted, that the world could be a dangerous place. Still, electric trams were progress, and every advance was greeted in those severe and frugal years with more acclaim than regret. We were entranced by progress, in a way no-one now is. Little did I know where it was taking me.

My mother was not so taken with mechanical wonders, which is not surprising in someone who grew up one hundred and fifty miles from the northern Scottish coast, in the Shetland Islands. She was a very gentle woman, with a dignified manner and a visionary quality that I've always associated with her growing up in a community which still spoke a dialect of Norse. She was the fifth of eight children. No greater contrast with my father's background can be imagined. Generations of her family had gone to sea in small fishing boats. Her father had built up a substantial fish business, had come south and was a prosperous man in Leith, Edinburgh's port, by the time he died in the year before my birth.

My mother's dreams and traditions were also very different from my father's. She talked about lonely crofts, herring fishing, peat fires and the never ending sound of the sea; she described a summer daylight that lasted twenty-four hours, hay-making, banks of sea-pinks on the white mica-sand beaches; and the ferocious winds that rip everything but the most twisted and flexible forms of life out of the ground in the winter months. Her family, the Sutherlands, had their own chronicle of disaster: her ancestor John Sutherland was one of 105 fishermen drowned in 1832 when eighteen open boats were overwhelmed in a July storm; and two more Sutherland men were lost in another Shetland summer storm in 1881. The family lived close to death in a way that city people could not understand. My mother nurtured the romanticism of a person displaced from a hard rural community, though she knew there was no going back. For all that, she was probably homesick throughout her life in Edinburgh.

She gave her child a sense of mystery. Even the place-names of Shetland seemed intangibly beautiful: where else were there islands with names like Vaila, Trondra, Balta and Unst? My mother had modest literary ambitions, and wrote what she called 'essays' and poems; she read a lot of books. The dour realism of Arnold Bennett could not do justice to the extremes of an island imagination, and my mother's favourite reading was probably the work of Jessie Margaret Edmonston Saxby, Shetland's most famous writer, who she knew, and who was already in her late seventies when I was born. She would still be alive in the first year of the Second World War.

My mother cared for me deeply, and was probably over-protective of me, and a little possessive. I had a demanding streak, loved making lists, writing things down, collecting cuttings from newspapers, and my mother tolerated and encouraged all this and kept up a supply of stationery for me. She called me 'The Peerie Professor': 'peerie' was Shetland dialect for 'little'. I loved her, but perhaps the kind of world into which I was born did not encourage identification with her nostalgia for the past; something harder bit into me and led me into my father's world, and after all this was what was expected of boys in the 1920s.

One lasting effect of my mother's influence was the situation of the house I was born in, on a terrace in Joppa that offered a magnificent view of the Firth of Forth. I think she wanted to be near a stretch of water that had no visible landfall, most of the time, and from our terrace you could look out the window over the sea, which was usually grey and cold. Its short restless waves sent a bracing chill into our bones, reminding us that we were lucky to be on firm ground, never quite allowing us to relax into the illusion that we were in command of the earth.

Childhood was a time of stern affection. I was sheltered by serious and old-fashioned people who cared for their 'only child', the term implying a slight misfortune, as though single children were deprived, the lucky product of some fault in the hereditary material. I may have been a surprise to my parents. And I've often thought that it was just as well there was only one of me.

My father had a carefully organized routine and I still have an image of him leaving the house each morning to catch the No. 20 electric tram to the GPO in Waterloo Place in Edinburgh. He was meticulous about timetables and journey times, a trait I have inherited, a need to know that I can arrive and depart predictably.

He took us on holidays, to places like Aberdour in Fife and Glenfarg in Perthshire, crossing the high and wide span of the Forth Bridge in a carriage drawn by one of the beautiful Atlantic locomotives of the former North British Railway. To be trundled across that bridge was to be moved through a rattling world of steel and cold air, the high cantilever towers soaring above us and the water far below, visible through the metal struts. The bridge was a greater wonder than the Pyramids, the most wonderful bridge in the world: as every Scottish boy knew, it was about a mile long, contained eight million rivets and employed twenty-nine men full time just to paint it.

When I was still very young, my father took us to Shetland. This was a real expedition, a five-hour train journey to Aberdeen for a night crossing by steamer to Lerwick. The steamer was called the *St Sunniva*, the pride of the sonorously named North of Scotland and Orkney and Shetland Steam Navigation Company Limited. It was an elegant vessel, a converted cruising yacht, well able for the North Sea.

I think my mother must have known the chief engineer, because when we were out to sea I was taken to the engine room, from which I was extracted only with considerable difficulty. It was another of my childhood epiphanies: a rapture of hot oil, of enclosure in vibrating energetic metal, the loud rhythmic thunder of the pistons in their cylinders, the warm vibrating air, the smell of burning coal, the ingenious swimming movement of the rods as they moved back and forth. If this was a machine, I wanted to be near one again soon.

We stayed in the Shetland Islands for a month. I remember falling into the sea, and running around half-naked all afternoon while my trousers were spread to dry on a rock in the sun; and playing on a beach at Lerwick and skipping flat stones over the water. One stone was a piece of bottle-glass, which ripped open the end of my finger. But it was all perfect, the stiff transparent sheen of salt on hot skin and the seaweed smell of the sea. The high ceremonial point of the holiday was the visit to Great Uncle Archibald, who was no less than the Clerk to the County of

Shetland. He lived at Lystina House, considered the best address in the whole of Shetland. My mother was immensely proud to be the niece of the top local government officer in the islands, while my father, and I myself, were rather more impressed by Great Uncle Archie's stamp collection, which was quite magnificent.

My curiosity nearly killed me even then. I was taken out with my father by a couple of fishermen in a rowing boat on the Loch of Spiggie, in the south of the island. Insatiably inquisitive, I pulled out the bung in the boat's hull and held it up. 'What's this?' I asked. I was aware of a spasm of anger and a sudden controlled urgency about the adults' behaviour. I had done something dangerous. The oarsman pulled for shore, his boat slowly sinking under us.

* * *

Shortly after that first visit to the Shetlands in 1924, I was made to attend the Royal High School in Edinburgh. So far as I could make out, the choice of this school was based not on its 800-year history but solely on the convenience of the new electric tram service and its door-to-door linkage of our house with the school.

For all my later interest in technology, the school did nothing to encourage it: not even physics was taught properly. Our subjects were Maths, English, Latin, Greek and French. It was a deeply traditional academy, and it was difficult to shake it out of its obsession with the classics.

I did not feel that I was a particularly isolated child, but perhaps the habits of the only child made me more aloof, gave me some element of self-sufficiency that others did not need or simply lacked. I avoided organized sports and games, for example, with stubborn determination, a non-conformity regarded as eccentric at a time when team spirit was the key to manliness. I went to a football match, once; I think I played rugby about as frequently; and I occasionally played cricket. On the other hand, I discovered that I could swim exceptionally well, particularly in the sheer hard slogging of long-distance events. I never really discovered what my limit was, but I could swim several miles without pause. This was a solitary and dogged skill, and I loved the drugged rhythm of drawing myself through the water, that strange anaesthetic called stamina sustaining the ache of tired muscles. I was immensely proud, despite being a loner, of the Portobello Amateur Swimming Club badge, even if the regulation colours of brown and yellow made one look like a wasp. This did not save me from persistent pressure, from masters and even other boys, to conform and to put my obvious fitness to use in the rucks and scrums of the rugby field. I would offer to discuss the question over a mile or two in the water, which had a way of silencing my critics.

Because it became with hindsight a premonition of other events, I remember one consequence of slackening my resistance to team activity. I joined the Owl Patrol in the 12th Edinburgh Royal High School Scouts, and wore my brown uniform along with all the other boys. We met weekly in the school gymnasium. One evening in the early 1930s, we were being taught by our scoutmaster to use long staves for crowd control – a most un-scout-like activity, some echo of the General Strike of 1926, or maybe just another of those hints that the world we were about to enter was a place so full of conflict that even games had to be made a preparation for it.

Towards the close of the evening the scoutmaster decided to give us a demonstration. We were lined up as a kind of human barrier, our poles at the ready, while certain other scouts were struck off to impersonate a mob. They were unleashed at us through a suddenly opened door, charging at us wildly in a licensed free-for-all, young bodies crashing into others with good-natured brutality. We could not control them and our troop leader had lost control of all of us. The crush of the attackers caught me with my hand flung out. I can still feel my right arm being bent further and further backwards until it snapped. There was a moment of sheer panic and disbelief, then the shocking pain of the break.

The scoutmaster, resourceful to the last, turned his failed experiment at crowd control into a first aid demonstration. It was not every day that he could show his troop a real broken arm. He snapped a yard-stick in two to make a pair of splints, found some bandages and called for a taxi. When I reached the emergency department of Edinburgh Royal Infirmary I had to wait only briefly before being wheeled into the operating room where I was given a very inadequate anaesthetic: the chloroform barely dulled the crushed nerves. I felt my arm being stretched and manipulated to get the sheared bones back into position. It is strange how easy it is to remember pain.

* * *

I did not like the school, and even though I achieved first place in some subjects in my early adolescence – once scoring 100 per cent in a Latin examination – I found the syllabus intolerably dull. Gradually, I lost interest in academic results. I became enthralled by subjects that the Royal High School found it difficult to endorse.

Like many schoolboys, I collected things as a way of making sense of the world's confusion. In August 1926, my father took my mother and me to Inverness for a few days' holiday while he was doing some work in the Post Office there. We stayed in the Glen Mhor Hotel on the south bank of the River Ness. He bought a large packet of mixed foreign stamps in the Inverness market to keep me amused. This was a good pacifier of a curious and restless child, but it started the first of my collecting passions, that of philately, which has not left me yet. Later this mania expanded into coin collecting, cigarette card collecting, then the collecting of picture postcards. Fortunately other boys were similarly inclined; fortunately too the raw material was cheap, so building up collections was not a problem. This hunger for all the little circulating tokens of an industrial economy could take in anything, and with us it extended to railway tickets, matchbox covers, autographs and marbles. Compared to the temptations open to children today, ours were not dangerous compulsions, and those parents who tried to wean us off this acquisitive mania would be shocked to see these schoolboy collections now selling for small fortunes.

But these were minor pastimes, mere flirtations, compared to the discovery I made one warm evening in the autumn of 1932 when I was out walking with my mother in the Portobello district. I even remember the precise date: 12th September. We were crossing Park Bridge, a long foot-bridge that spanned a wide cut in the ground between a golf course and a residential neighbour-hood. I stopped on the bridge, on an impulse of no importance, and looked down – into a new world. Below me was a shiny heavy web of iron and wood, dead straight parallel lines of metal suddenly curving and merging smoothly into other sets of tracks; ladders fixed to the earth, climbing into the distance. They were spread out and branched off beyond the bridge; close up I could see the worn silver of the rail surface and the dark steel of the chairs and the wood of the cross-sleepers. In the dusk the tracks looked like lines of mercury on the oil-stained timber and gravel.

I was looking into Portobello Goods Yard, one of the largest and busiest rail freight yards in the country. It wasn't empty even on that quiet late summer evening. There were two steam engines working near the bridge, shunting engines pushing trains and empty independent wagons further back into the yard. I read the engine numbers: 9387 and 9388. They were solid machines, their lines unflattering, with large tanks flanking and obscuring the curve of the boiler, but they were gorgeous. Each had a tall chimney, shaped like the stove-pipe hat worn by Isambard Kingdom Brunel as he posed against the giant paddle wheel of his *Great Eastern* for that famous photograph. I was not surprised he looked so confident, if he could create machines like these. Their six driving wheels turned slowly but irresistibly against the tons of rolling-stock in front of them; I heard the crash of straining metal as the couplings took the weight and tension; I smelled again the combination of hot oil and coal smoke that I remembered from my visit to the engine room of the Shetland steamer. A grey column of smoke billowed gently out of the chimney of the squat shunting engine, with little feathers of steam drifting back over the length of the tubular boiler and around the polished brass safety valves in their dome like a fixed bell set in front of the cab. I didn't know it at the time, but I was watching a well-run engine in the hands of a good driver.

On the bridge, I felt suspended amidst the working engines, the branching rails and signal gantries, the station platforms and the brick warehouses. Anyone who has not seen a great railway junction on a sunny evening in the steam age cannot imagine the fascination of it. For a boy – for me – it was an animated, mysterious, mechanical paradise.

Further back in the yard several larger, more powerful-looking engines were drawn up, their giant spoked wheels connected by coupling rods that looked as big as the foot-bridge's girders. There was an awesome potential in those linked wheels, rods and pistons – power at rest. A little way beyond Portobello one of the engines was drawn up beside a blackened wooden shed, and from a high door in its side a wooden chute hung out over the tender behind the engine. A man wearing a waistcoat and cloth cap was filling the chute from a big bucket of coal, and the lumps clattered down on to the black heaps which another man, dressed in a rough blackened grey jacket was shovelling and levelling into place.

That was the start of my incurable interest in railways. From that day onwards I spent a lot of time on Park Bridge, and soon became aware of other boys with similar interests leaning out over the engines as they slowed down on their way into the goods yard, or cruised at speed further out on their way up the East Coast main line between Edinburgh and London. For Edinburgh was a rail centre, and I lived at the eastern end of a great loop of lines punctuated by stations, depots, tunnels, repair yards and goods terminals. I could watch the flagship engines of the London and North Eastern Railway rush by, a long procession of carriages drawn after them as they headed for Edinburgh Waverley – the company's very own station and a mecca for train lovers – or catch the smaller, older engines at the head of suburban and country trains. They were all trains, and that was enough for now.

★ ★ ★

It was like love, my fascination for those huge, noisy machines that were already near the end of their golden age. They moved with such magnificent purpose. They were alive, they had steam, smoke and the smell of minerals; they burned energy without concealment, and you could see their fire. They raced against themselves, losing more heat than they used, running by burning their own cargo of coal; but there was something very human about the need to keep fire going by hand, shovelling and watching, never for a second being able to forget responsibility for the journey and the work. Their waste didn't have to be buried in lead-lined coffins, it was exhaled as carbon, sulphur and nitrogen, or swept and scattered as ash, the unburnt particles of coal settling gently on our clothes and hair.

Some things that humans make transcend their function; instruments can be magical. That explosive, rhythmic sound we call puffing says more to us about getting under way, about departure, than a petrol-driven snarl can ever do; perhaps it has something close to the beat of our pulse. Even if we were using up and heating the earth too much, and no-one knew that at the time, it would have been worth making an exception for steam engines. They were beautiful machines; the most beautiful machines produced in the industrial revolution.

The Reverend Awdry, author of the railway series of children's books that attracted millions of infant readers long after their parents had forgotten the age of steam, once said that railways 'touch' people, make us seem eccentric; and yet we discover that they have the same effect on almost everybody else. I have certainly felt a little eccentric at times; but I suspect that we are all railway lovers, at some deep level.

The honest power of a steam engine is overwhelming – most of its important parts are on display. You see the great cylinder with cranks and mechanisms outside it, you see the ingenious connection of levers and rods to the enormous wheels and you have already understood that this combination of things will work, and you might even see how. Unlike a motor car or a nuclear ship, there's no secrecy about a steam engine's force. What engineers call the 'motion', the linked shafts and pistons and wheels that drive the engine, is as fascinating as the movement of a watch. And almost as jewel-like, for the couplings and connecting rods were often still chipped and filed smooth by hammer and chisel, after they came off the milling machine. Hands still made parts of these engines, and it is no surprise that drivers spoke of them as individuals. But essentially, the engine was a boiler held in heavy frames on a set of steel wheels.

The simplicity of it fascinated me. Coal burnt in a furnace surrounded by water created steam; steam confined in a cylinder pushed a piston, and linked to wheels by rods that turned the straight thrust of the piston into rotatory motion, the engine moved and worked. The idea that hordes of people and commodities could be carried at such shakingly powerful speeds by a sort of articulated kettle, in which the water could never be allowed to fall below the top of the furnace or there would be an explosion, seemed amazing to me. What made it all so different from today's electric railways, which run at set speeds, was the need to be aware at every moment of the perilous balance of fire and water, which also gave the possibility of going a little faster if the engineman was good, or of disaster if he was incompetent.

Like everything else we make – like firearms, for example – the simple idea could be endlessly refined, developed and decorated. I discovered trains in their heyday, when steam under pressure had achieved astonishing things. Libraries of books were written on the improvement of Watt's basic idea. More sophisticated valve gears gave more subtle control of pressure; steam could be superheated to get more pressure out of it; more yards could be added to the labyrinth of copper firetubes inside the boiler to give a bigger heating area, and therefore more heat and steam. But it was the way it all worked together that mattered, in the poetry of great engines, their appearance, speed and mystique.

★ ★ ★

I learned to distinguish machines, to love some more than others. There were, for example, the imposing Atlantic engines, the most powerful Scottish engines of the early century, their four big driving wheels half hidden by 'splashers', like great mud-guards, and their lesser wheels chunky with thick spokes. One of these engines, up close, seemed monstrous, the vast tube of the boiler painted a solid dark green, the front a glossy black, resting on its 20-foot long iron frames. One of the driving wheels would dwarf a boy, who might come a little higher than the silver boss at the centre of its ring of black-painted spokes. The linked piston rods were as massive as one of the rails on which the wheels they drove ran so heavily. The rocking levers of the outside valves looked like swimmers' arms frozen in mid stroke. Above were the pipes, flues and stanchions of polished brass and copper running the length of the boiler, and higher up still the top-hat of the chimney.

By the late 1930s, this mighty engine began to look a little archaic, a little steamroller-like, as the last and most fabulous of the dinosaurs matured, running faster and longer than all their kind. These were engines like the Pacifics, which ran on the express route from London to Edinburgh, so heavy and powerful that they needed four smaller wheels in front of their six great driving wheels and two behind, just to balance their own weight. They were epic creatures; machines that looked as though they could drive through the world. Perhaps only the sight of a rare eagle to a birdwatcher can compare to the surge of excitement I would feel when one of these Pacifics, the pride of British engineering, swept by me, its slipstream battering me against the frame of my bicycle.

Even these leviathans could be improved. In the mid-Thirties, some were streamlined. The cylindrical boiler disappeared beneath a sweeping aerodynamic form painted two tones of grey, its steel adding a third richly military colour to the 'Silver Link', which could do the London–Edinburgh run in six hours, often at more than 100 mph. This made it one of the fastest engines in the world. The curve of the wing lifted over the wheels, a whale showing its teeth. It was like an enormous grey knife blade adhering to the rails, cutting a slice out of the landscape with over a hundred tons of metal. To feel this as it tore past was to be carried away into the future.

Of course, the first photograph I ever took was of a Pacific, the most famous of them all: the 'Flying Scotsman', on the opening day of the summer season of its London-Edinburgh run. I pointed my Box Brownie at the line and hoped that its lens would somehow capture the thundering displacement of air that was about to be unleashed on me. The snap came out, like most railway photographs, as a grainy black and white travesty of the real thing.

But what mattered was being there and having seen it. My hobby had grown into an obsession by the time I left school in 1936. In fact, steam engines occupied most of my free hours between 1933 and the moment when I volunteered for the army in 1939. I read histories of engineering, of companies that were long gone even then, haunting the second-hand bookshops around George IV Bridge in Edinburgh and finding beautiful old books on railways that I could buy for a penny each. Occasionally I would reach out and spend a few pence on some real treasure: a handsome set of Smiles, a book of Victorian photographs.

I had become what is known nowadays as a 'trainspotter', though that is not a word I would use and I do not recognize myself in the lonely boys in anoraks who haunt British railway stations noting the numbers of passing trains. For me this was almost a scholarly passion, a 'subject' as valid as mathematics or French, and I took it just as seriously as any specialist. In any case, the standardized and predictable high-speed engines of the monopoly railway company cannot compare with the magnificent variety of machinery on the iron roads of the 1930s.

I didn't just sit and dream about trains, but travelled to look and see, waiting on cold embankments and cuttings in the hope of catching a glimpse of some rare and famous locomotive. I thought nothing of riding fifteen or twenty miles on my bike to watch an engine hammer past on a rural line, and turning around to ride back to my parents' house as happy as though I had seen a girlfriend.

Until 1923 there had been 120 railway companies in Britain, but then they were grouped into four great combinations. The local combine in East Scotland was called the London and North Eastern Railway. The engines in Edinburgh were different from those in East Anglia, and no engine from Cornwall would penetrate as far north as Newcastle. An engine could sometimes run on a foreign system of track, but it was not always easy: Great Western engines were risky outside their territory for they were wider than others, and could clip a bridge or a platform in alien country, with disastrous results. Locomotives from the north east of England would often decouple from trains at Berwick; the border was a technical as well as historic boundary. A Scottish engine would then haul the train northward.

But now the engines evolved in isolation were infiltrating each other's territory, and you could see some exotic from the far south nosing on to the buffers at Waverley Station. The incredible varieties remained: the old companies' engines were still in use, locomotives developed in the time of Victoria still working in the age of aircraft. I was among the last witnesses to this overlapping, inefficient and utterly wonderful chaos. I felt like Darwin on the Galapagos.

And just like species in their habitats, these creatures with their gleaming layers of paint and elegant steel and brass mountings had often still to be tracked to their native ranges. We talked the language of birdwatchers: rare engines were 'elusive' or 'difficult'. The world of railways was as surprising and complicated as the natural world: there seemed to be more kinds of locomotive than there were different birds in the Lothian Hills. There were at least 28,000 steam engines in Britain on the main lines; and several thousand more in private employment, cast-offs and survivors from the big lines working for breweries, mines, ironworks. The LNER, my local railway, had been built up from great lines like the North British Railway and tiny local companies like the East and West Yorkshire Union Railway, four battered engines lugging coal between some pitheads and the sea.

I rescued the most obscure railway in the British Isles from oblivion by writing a little article about it for *Railway Magazine* when I was sixteen. On Unst, the most northerly of the Shetland Islands, I found some overgrown tracks of a tiny 2-foot gauge running from chromite quarries in the island centre to the nearby pier. Stocky little ponies were pulling ramshackle wagons full of the chrome-iron ore in hot July sunshine. In another part of the island I found more lines radiating out from another chromite pit, the workings completely derelict. The tracks were covered in rough grass and nettles and dockweed; the rusty side tipping wagons were lying in the positions in which they had been abandoned by the side of the track. I felt I had reached the *ultima Thule* of the railway world.

For me it was a question of mapping and understanding that man-made world, of tracing the genealogies of engines, designs and companies. My habits of precision and of needing to know where I was, which may have attracted me to the spider's web of railways in the first place, would later get me into the most awful trouble on the worst railway in the world, but that need to locate myself and to imagine ways of escape would never leave me. And I was drawn to the railways so much that they have been a backdrop to almost every turning-point in my life, and have led me into unhappiness and torment, as well as some of the only real contentment I have ever known.

* * *

Railways are an intensely personal mania, but I was always aware that mine was not exactly a secret passion. Train study was one of the most popular pastimes in Britain. There were always other boys, standing stiffly alert, taking notes and photographs, on platforms, on sidings, at level crossings out in the country. Guardedly, we traded information. We would hear of curious sightings, of locomotives straying out of their areas like big birds blown off course by a storm. The storm was an economic one, homogenizing the local railway systems in the face of the world slump; for the moment, the Depression and all it brought with it was our opportunity. We didn't hear the storm coming closer.

We got permits to visit engine sheds and workshops; saw still, silent herds of the great locomotives in sidings on Saturday afternoons or Sundays. There was a fine illicit thrill about climbing aboard the platform of a steam engine, nine or ten feet off the ground, and standing in front of the wall of instruments, the gleaming levers, throttles and stopcocks that regulated so much power.

We thought of ourselves as being involved with these smoky vehicles of change, we never saw ourselves as just standing on the ends of platforms crossing numbers off a list. We didn't tolerate frivolity, or drinkers or the unserious. But machines don't make good companions, and it is true that I spent much of my youth alone, cycling between stations on roads that could be grey and wet in autumn and winter, with often only a distant relationship to my fellow enthusiasts. It isn't much wonder that I was so easily recruited into the Chapel – but that was later.

Meanwhile, attendance at the Royal High School became more and more of a penance. Many of the boys delivered by tram on the 1st October 1924 continued to be unhappy ten years later. The attitude of many teachers towards pupils was deplorable. They seemed to regard us as something of a nuisance and an interruption to their daily routine; collectively to have been unaware that children and their interests had any connection with the employment of teachers.

There were exceptions. One devoted history teacher came up with a scheme by which any pupil who discovered a genuine error in any history text would be awarded an extra 1 per cent in the term examination. The enthusiasm with which his pupils combed their texts for mistakes was impressive, though there were rumours that their parents had been drawn into the research. Inevitably, a market economy developed around this precious information. Confident boys placed suspected errors on the market, charging rates that varied with the probability of acceptance. It was good practice for life, of a kind.

The school's emphasis on classics was less useful for the world we were about to enter. By the time I was fifteen, my father had to ask the Rector to make special arrangements to allow me to study history and geography instead of Greek. But as the final examinations approached, I knew that my prospects of formal academic success were slim.

On holiday in the autumn of 1935, my father saw an advertisement for a Civil Service competition for a single appointment as a sorting clerk and telegraphist in the GPO in Edinburgh, and announced that I should apply. Sons in those days did exactly what their fathers told them to do, or at least I did, so at the age of sixteen I sat the examination. I took first place in the city, to my own astonishment and my family's, and on the morning the brown envelope came my father told me that I could leave school that day.

I went to the Rector's office and told him that I was going. The Rector, a very elevated person named Dr King Gillies told me in omniscient tones that I was being very foolish, that I could expect only to become a butcher's delivery boy – the ultimate social disgrace. I spoiled his day by showing him the letter from the Civil Service Commission. And so my formal education ended.

I still think I would have made a reasonably good butcher's boy.

Early in January 1936, I started to study at home for the next grade of the Civil Service. I had a couple of months before I started work. I also began to explore the Lothian Hills and the coast, cycling to small harbours and old docks, to obscure sidings that were said to contain interesting survivors of early locomotive classes. These were rehearsals for later marathon rides around the kingdom on my brief holidays from the Post Office. I thought that I might never have so much completely free time at my disposal again. I was right.

In the year of the Popular Front in France and of the Spanish Civil War, the year Japan began its assault on China, I was going on even longer excursions. In 1937, on my annual holiday from what was then a not very fulfilling job, I cycled all the way to the English Channel and back – a 1000-mile round-trip down the west coast, and back up the east coast via Newcastle and Berwick. I did it completely alone. I was barely aware of what was happening thousands of miles away in Asia. I had no politics; I was an only child.

It is strange, looking back now, to think of those boys at school to whom I was never really close. Men born ten years after me could speculate idly about their schoolmates, but that option was closed to me by events in China and Central Europe while I was growing up. I know exactly what happened to each of my contemporaries. Of the twenty-five of us in our final year at school, only four survived the war. But there is no justice in statistics, and by some arbitrary chance not one of the twenty-two young men in my officer class at Catterick was killed.

★ ★ ★

You had to start at the bottom in the Post Office, just as my father had done nearly forty years before. I became a sorter of mail, and after a week's training I was put on the lowest rung of the Civil Service ladder, from which I was destined to become successively Senior Sorter, Postmaster and so on.

A worker called Bobby Kinghorn, who I would later meet under very different circumstances, took me in hand and showed me how to survive without working too hard, and I put his good advice to use on the main shift from 7.30 in the morning until 3.30 in the afternoon, six days a week.

I had to open parcels from overseas so that customs could inspect them, then laboriously tie them up again. They also assigned me to the football pools section, where a dozen sorters filtered millions of coupons being sent out to the punters who were hoping to get rich from their predictions of the scores of the coming Saturday's soccer matches. All this waste paper, victim of the laws of probability, would have to be sorted, bundled and bagged for movement to Waverley Station, where it would be loaded on to trains heading out to towns in the borders and further south.

I was now drawing a big circle around Edinburgh of places to which return journeys could be made by bicycle on early summer evenings, and I'd escape to some point on it every afternoon. So many miles, so many lonely sightings of worked metal and quiet satisfaction at another unusual entry into my orderly classification of the world. Ordnance Survey maps helped you to identify half-forgotten branch lines, perhaps some colliery where there might be a couple of engines whose identity and even whose existence would be unknown to anyone outside the colliery itself; but some of the sidings were so obscure that they did not appear on maps, and there was no alternative but to search them out.

I learned in the Post Office that obsession can take many forms. One much older man became something of a special friend. He had been unemployed for most of the previous five years and had become a communist. He became obsessed with our ignorance of the names of places to which the pools envelopes were being sent. His need for order and his conscientious devotion to the job drove him to make, in his own time, over a period of weeks, a card-index of every British place-name he could find, as an aid to sorting the pools mail. Anything less like the behaviour of a communist militant is difficult to imagine; but perhaps this innocent card-index man would have found a different outlet for his obsession if the circumstances had been different.

Some flavour of the austerity and discretion of the workplace in the 1930s remains with me in the memory of a colleague called Wendy, from whom I took over duties in the motor transport section after I passed the clerical officer's examination in late 1936. One lunchtime she failed to return to the office. Such was our respect for punctuality that I began to imagine that she had had an accident, or been kidnapped. In a manner of speaking she had suffered both fates: she had used her lunch hour to get married.

My job was now to maintain the records for the Post Office Telephones' vehicles all over the south east of Scotland. We had to watch out for things like excessive fuel consumption, breakdowns and accidents. This was my future now: the minute administration of Post Office machinery, counting and accounting in careful detail for the public's means of communication and the people who kept it running.

The life that awaited me if I had not broken from it can be guessed at in the story of the file on expanding shelter for our vehicles in the Edinburgh area. I wrote minutes, memos, drew up lists of suitable premises. In 1948 I went back briefly to the Post Office after leaving the army, after a war in which millions of people had died cruel and pointless deaths, in which I had been shattered psychically and physically. On my first day back in civilian employment the file on garage accommodation was solemnly handed to me. It had not been opened for almost a decade. Time had stopped in this fusty government office while for me it had accelerated beyond reason.

Some inkling of dread must have percolated into me back in 1936, because I decided to make another move. I realize now, looking back, that for all my conformity I was looking for something more satisfying, more wholly absorbing than the set lines of my life could offer; in my own way I was very ambitious. I decided to take evening classes in telegraphy and telephony. My father thought that this was most irregular, wanting to switch from the office grades to the technical, from the supervisory to the practical. We were staff, we did not work with our hands. But with that stubbornness which I would later learn much more about, I went ahead.

CHAPTER TWO

I GREW UP IN a world in which tinkering and inventing and making were honoured pastimes. My father, though he was not a telegraph engineer, liked to experiment with technical equipment. In the early 1920s he and his friends Mr Weatherburn and Mr Patrick were building a wireless, which they kept in Weatherburn's house.

It sat on a table in a room cluttered with glass valves, flex, pliers, copper wire, soldering irons and screwdrivers. There was a strange burning metallic smell, a smell of glue and oil. I could touch the dark rolls of thick sticky tape, but was warned not to touch the big black dials with their pointers turned to the brass buttons set into the wood panel. Three beautifully-milled brass cylinders, detectors for those mysterious waves that I couldn't see as they rolled into the lighted room, were set into the polished mahogany of the box. The front panel was studded with protruding, fragile looking valves, switches and dials, and polished brass terminals. I could see the delicate metal in the bulbs of the valves. The whole apparatus looked at once ridiculous and awesome. It was like an unfinished toy, but also an engineered aesthetic tool, something crafted and heavy. Its front sloped back like the stand used for the big Bible in church.

My father placed a pair of heavy headphones around my ears, and I heard, through the hiss and buzz of far-off energies, a disembodied human voice. Somewhere a long way away a man was sending his words into space and they were somehow being collected here and narrowed through my ears alone.

In the worst times, much later, when I thought I was about to die in pain and shock at the hands of men who could not imagine anything of my life, who had no respect for who I was or where I had come from, I might have wished that my father had had a different passion. But after the First War, technology was still powerful and beautiful without being menacing. Who could have thought that radio telegraphy, a simple channelling of ethereal lines of force, could cause terrible harm? It was a wonderful instrument by which people could speak to each other, and I knew that up on the hill in Edinburgh Castle there was a station of the BBC speaking calmly and authoritatively through educated English voices about the weather, the news and the Empire.

By the time I started my own radio course in 1940 I had already heard Adolf Hitler's voice coming out of my father's radio, an endless rhythmic scream full of strange crescendos. Hitler was not only the most powerful man in Europe, he was also clearly mad. None the less the threat his voice contained seemed as far away as all radio voices.

I got stuck into the electrical rote-learning that the Post Office Telephones arranged for its staff. We had to memorize complicated circuits and patterns of valves. A typical exam question might be 'Reproduce the Circuit for the No. 2A Switchboard', which was a bit of a labyrinth. The radios of the late Thirties were large heavy pieces of equipment, not quite as massive and unwieldy as Mr Weatherburn's home-made wireless, but solid and imposing for all that; and I began to learn how they worked and how they should be maintained. We also learned about telephones, morse signalling and telegraphy. I was moving on, but I can't have been content.

★ ★ ★

My mentor in the Post Office, Bobby Kinghorn, was a friend of the kind that a lonely young man makes in his first job: older, wise to the routines of the office, giving off the air of a vigorous, if slightly mysterious, life outside it. I knew he was interested in religion, and once I lent him my father's copy of Hilaire Belloc's *The Path to Rome*, one of those accounts of conversion that English Catholics delight in. Kinghorn never returned it, to my father's considerable anger. But my colleague had, as it turned out, taken a very different path to Belloc's.

My only vivid religious memory from my childhood is of being a choirboy in the Episcopal Church at the age of eleven or twelve. I remember the music and the division of the choir into *cantoris* and *decani*, and that I was assigned to the *cantoris*. What happened, therefore, came as much as a surprise to me as it did to my parents, who had grown used, if not exactly reconciled to my relentless exploration of Britain for unusual machines.

On summer evenings you could see a great variety of trains at a station in the west of Edinburgh called Dalry Road. It had an island platform in the middle of tracks that ran past it from east to west, and off beyond the tracks were engine sheds and repair works. Sometimes you would see outside its longest shed a string of pre-First-War engines, stubby six-wheeled locomotives of the defunct Caledonian Railway nose to tail with their high steam domes and thin quaint chimneys.

One Sunday, I stood on the island in the warm dusk, surrounded by empty tracks stretching off on either side, waiting for a train that might have some exotic engine at the head of it. The old railway systems were dissolving fast now, and anything might be coming through, a strange engine of the former London and North Western Railway, perhaps?

I was approached by an older man who struck up a conversation about trains and about recent sightings at this very station. He was a gangly clothes-pole of a man, a long coat flapping around his shins. I thought he was simply a fellow obsessive and we talked politely about rare southern birds and dying Highland breeds. He really did seem to know a great deal about locomotives. Then, once he had hooked me, the talk turned to religion, and he was so hypnotically persuasive that the transition didn't seem abrupt. In those days, steam locomotion and the divine were not as far apart in my imagination as they should have been.

Today, a man accosting a youth at a spot like this would arouse suspicions of only one kind, but this man had no carnal intentions at all. He was simply after my soul. His name was Jack Ewart and he belonged to Charlotte Baptist Chapel, a famous independent evangelical church in Edinburgh. He could talk, he could seduce you with talk of love and compassion and salvation, that subtle mixture of flattery and fear that the apostle of any sect learns to use. I found myself, a lonely and impressionable young man, being drawn into the reassuring and comforting world that glowed in his voice. It seemed to offer fellowship and certainty.

Within a few weeks I had joined what was then a fundamentalist Christian sect. I had done exactly as my father told me to do.

I had left school, joined the Post Office and been a good son. Now I was doing something for myself.

I met Bobby Kinghorn at the Chapel. This was his secret life. We were in a kind of cult, it seems to me now, a sect that resembled the Plymouth Brethren or the 'Wee Frees', the rigid schismatics of the Scottish Free Presbyterian Church. It was a powerful magnet for a young man looking for a centre to his life. Looking back, I can recall little except an extraordinary arrogance – the members of the Chapel were better than everybody else, they were saved, they were exempt from normal rules and they were certainly above compassion. I didn't know it, but I was now living in a matchbox with people who thought they could rule the world. This was, after all, a church with but one chapel which financed its own missionaries to Africa and Asia.

The Chapel was famous for the extremity and ferocity of its preaching. The minister, J. Sidlow Baxter, who was a real fire and brimstone orator, reminds me of those tent gospellers who now make fortunes on television channels in the USA. An accountant before he found the Lord, he relished the tabulation of human weakness. He would rant, cajole, pray, threaten and demand; his sermons were the high point of our services, which were otherwise pretty routine affairs with announcements, readings and hymns.

What held me there was a kind of sociability I had not been used to, and a genuine, if transitory, conviction of their rightness. I was utterly fascinated by the sonorous mysticism of the Book of Revelation, as I was by the driving certainty of the narrative in the Book of Genesis. I went to Chapel several times a week: to two Sunday services, and once or twice during the week. There were also sedate social occasions, teas and fundraising efforts. And of course like any sect it had 'policies' about things you could do and a great many more about things you could not, like going to the cinema, to dances, pubs or watching the new medium of television. They would have banned the radio too, but it was too well-established by now and they all listened to it anyway.

The older members were immensely bitter and obsessed with status. If newcomers or visitors occupied a pew which an older member felt that he or she had a claim to, the interlopers were the object of furious resentment. These were petty divisions, petty angers, small minds. But for all that they made me feel welcome. Ewart, my proselytizer, was still my closest contact in the group. I discovered that he made a speciality of recruiting young men and that he was genuinely interested in trains: a fairly unique form of evangelism.

The Chapel, however, inevitably cut into my profane pleasures, my expeditions around the country and my collection of industrial information. And my membership further strained my relations with my parents, who were desperately upset and worried about it. It was as though my intensity of commitment to almost anything I did was bound to alienate those who loved me.

All this time I was living at home, expected to be in at certain times and to behave properly; this was a disciplined Scottish family. My parents had never liked me swinging off on my bicycle, my disappearances in search of railway engines, my quiet intensity. My bonds with them were thinning by 1939; we could never talk easily, and the distance between us now grew. I felt boxed in at home, and resented my father's timetables the more I boxed myself into the tiny world of the Chapel.

Apart from Chapel, I had little social life. I had no girlfriends; there were very few women of any age in the Post Office, for girls went into nursing or catering, and in the Civil Service as soon as a woman married she had to give up her job. There had been a girl called Caroline Jordan, a neighbour's child who I helped with maths and Latin. I think her father had me in mind for her, but nothing came of it.

Instead, I met a young woman in the Chapel, the daughter of two members of its congregation, and we began to see each other in a decorous way. Her mother was a formidable woman, of intransigent virtue, but her daughter and I walked out together, avoiding the temptations of the city of the world. Dances and films and similar occasions of sin were out of the question for us; we visited each other's houses, took long walks in the country and busied ourselves with Chapel affairs.

I am aware that I missed a lot in my childhood. I did not know things I should have known, my education was curtailed; my emotional education was still very rudimentary before it was almost snuffed out a few years later in a prison yard. I was pitchforked into work straight from school; from work into the army; from the army into hell.

In a way, though I feel very distant from the young man who was so easily drawn into that sectarian embrace, the moral conviction of being saved, that I really had found God, helped me to survive what came later. I was still very committed and religious when I went to war. A rearrangement of personal authority took place during the three and a half years of our imprisonment. Under those terrible pressures a private might emerge as a leader, and his standing would simply be accepted. I must have seen it in very pure Protestant terms, as though we had somehow returned to the conditions of the Old Testament. I even felt myself gaining some moral authority, growing in a human way despite starvation and misery and dirt. I never felt that I was owed any particular status, but some others acted as though it were there. Some of the traditional leaders, on the other hand, some of the senior officers, sank without trace. If I can be grateful to the Chapel for anything, it is for helping me build that armour of stubbornness that got me through.

* * *

I was not a politically-minded young man, and I could lose myself in my religious and mechanical enthusiasms. The drastic nature of the world in the late Thirties didn't really sink in until my father confirmed the worst predictions. Out walking on the promenade at Joppa one afternoon in the spring of 1939, he rebuffed my polite enquiry about holiday plans by saying with adult finality that since there was going to be a war, he very much doubted if there would be much scope for holidays that summer.

Once conscription was introduced later that year, I decided to take, not exactly evasive action, but action to optimize my position. I joined the Supplementary Reserve of the Royal Corps of Signals, which recruited men from the Post Office Telephones. Until war was declared, my only duties would be attendance at the annual 'camp' of Scottish Command Signals.

So it was that on 4th May 1939 I became 2338617 Signalman Lomax E.S., based in Edinburgh Castle. Mills Mount barracks was inside the north side of the castle, with a magnificent view for miles across the city and out over the Forth to the hills of Fife. The 'camp' that summer consisted of me and a young man named Lionel.

Few people can have had a stranger introduction to the British Army. There was no induction into a depot or drill hall; no weapons training; not even a sergeant-major to humiliate us. I was simply told to sit at a typewriter and to turn out letters; Lionel was shown how to fill up quartermaster's returns. An insurance clerk, he couldn't stop referring to Scottish Command Headquarters as 'Head Office'.

Gradually, in this unmilitary atmosphere we learned the harder business of the Royal Signals. A corporal called Moore tried to turn us into efficient signallers, making us see how our work was important to the string of coastal defence batteries on the north coast of Scotland and in the Orkneys, where the great naval base of Scapa Flow was located. We learned about the importance of precise information so that the guns in their remote emplacements out on the cliffs wouldn't fire blind, and to understand the importance of accurate communication between the different parts of an army. Later I would wish that some of our teachers had learnt their own lesson a little better, but for now war was still only a word.

After this genial brush with the army, I spent the rest of the lovely summer of 1939 perfecting my scheme for improving and expanding the garaging arrangements for the Telephones vehicles in the city, swimming, hunting classic engines and going to Chapel.

On 24th August 1939 I received my mobilization papers, went to work as usual and closed my file on Garage Requirements. After saying goodbye I took the No. 23 tram up Hanover Street and the Mound and walked up the Lawnmarket to the Castle. Lomax had gone to war.

* * *

Mills Mount was now a crowded and hectic base. Royal Signals reservists from all over the country were turning up, short of beds and equipment, and I found myself sending out more mobilization orders to other reservists. I was issued with full battledress, all rough cloth and webbing – except for the trousers. There was a shortage of trousers. The guard commander, like most of his kind in Scottish regiments, couldn't share our joy at walking around centaur-like in civilian pants.

I was sent down to the Assembly Rooms in George Street in Edinburgh to take charge of the confused lines of would-be signalmen of all ages and classes who were trying to enlist. Some had been sent by the BBC, the Post Office, the private electronics companies; they were to be the technical elite of the army. I was struck by how effective a single man in uniform, confident of his authority, could be in maintaining order over several hundred men unsure of their position.

Each night I would go back up the Mound, and walk inside the old black walls of the castle which dominated the city like a crouching beast, as it does to this day. It is difficult to imagine it now as anything other than a tourist attraction. Times change, and so do buildings. Changing people is harder, or so I have found.

In the barracks we had radios on all the time, as you would expect. At 11.00 am on 3rd September, we heard Arthur Neville Chamberlain say in his exquisite reedy voice that we were now at war with Germany.

Fifteen minutes later, the air raid sirens sounded throughout Edinburgh. From Mills Mount I could look down into the main streets of the city. On Princes Street, the trams came to a standstill; every motor vehicle stopped where it was. Passengers walked with a swift nervous urgency, making for the air raid shelters in Princes Street Gardens, through which the main railway line was sunk. It was empty and silent now. Within minutes the streets were deserted except for the immobilized vehicles, some with their doors open, stretching away down Princes Street. A hand had swept over the city, stopping its heart: the war came in this silence.

Nothing happened; there was no raid. I had tangled up the straps of my gas-mask, and had to be rescued by a company sergeant-major called Dennis Bloodworth, who really was as strong as he sounded. We went back to preparing ourselves for real battles.

Equipment now began to arrive in earnest. We already had a 'Wireless Set No. 3', a big and seemingly powerful thing, with controls on the vertical front; it was made of stamped grey steel with none of the ornamentation of domestic sets. This was a machine for keeping open a channel of communication between Edinburgh and London, in the event of telephone lines being broken, and it did not hide its function of grabbing electro-magnetic waves as brutally as it could. Everything about it spoke of war and emergency. It was noisy to operate, it gave out heat, and I had to sleep next to it before I wangled a bed in the barrack block at the West End of the Castle. It was an austere place but at least I could sleep. I was learning that you have to survive not only in the face of the enemy, but also within your own army.

With this in mind I applied for a commission, and appeared before an interview board in the building owned by the *Scotsman* newspaper on the North Bridge. Washed and polished and eager to please, I was told by the major who interviewed me that the average expectation of life of a second-lieutenant on active service in the Great War had been two weeks. I said I wished to persist.

★ ★ ★

While I was waiting for my application to be processed, I volunteered to go to the Orkney Islands, where the battleship *Royal Oak* had just been sunk, in its base at Scapa Flow, with almost a thousand casualties. This was the first real shock of the war, and might have taught us more about the vulnerability of gigantic gun-platforms. People could hardly accept that it was enemy action that had sunk such a dreadnought; it must be sabotage, or some fault of our own. But of course it was a German submarine. In any case, our signals work clearly needed improvement.

We sailed from Scrabster Harbour, near Thurso on the north coast of Scotland. After the worst sea journey I could remember, a day of icy wind and pitching seas on a fifty-year-old steamer that lacked any suitable covering for the North Sea in late autumn, we arrived – Sergeant Ferguson and his squad of twenty, including me – in Stromness. We settled in and helped to control the local signals traffic, by radio, telephone and telegraph. We were part of the North Signal Section, one of His Majesty's more remote garrisons.

I liked it on the cold, bleak island, working methodically every day in a requisitioned hotel. What I thought of as my developing gift for survival and adroit moves in large organizations made me the entrepreneur of the group. I did a deal with one of the cooks in the hotel by which she provided fried egg rolls and tea and I sold them to the men in the middle of the morning. I was much in demand.

On an island, you noticed people's isolation more. When I distributed the mail for our little squad, I saw that some of the men could never conceal their distress when letters failed to arrive. And a couple of them looked almost terrified if mail did come for them.

I had considered volunteering for Shetland, but the thought of a 115-mile trip still further north by trawler in mid-winter through one of the worst stretches of sea in the world was too much even for me. The attraction of that Viking outpost was strong; my mother's voice spoke whenever I remembered its harsh moorland and its ocean light. But the other voices were insistent, and I missed the chance that might have kept me marooned and safe on a little archipelago while the deluge lasted.

Orders arrived, in March 1940, instructing me to report for preliminary training before I could go to a Royal Signals training unit for officer cadets.

Sergeant Ferguson and I left Stromness on a fine March morning, and the *St Ola*, the same awful steamer that had brought us to Orkney, chugged out of the harbour into Hoy Sound where the wind, rain and sea ripped into us. In the huge sheltered bowl of Scapa Flow, with huddled islands all around the horizon, the weather was bearable, but once out of its shelter and into the Pentland Firth, the gale threw the steamer around like a toy. Ferguson and I settled down in the lee of the funnel, where there was a memory of warmth and shelter, and before long we were soaked through, frozen stiff and nauseated. I was violently sick over my sergeant's greatcoat, but he didn't seem to mind; he was in another world.

I had made my choice; I was to be an officer.

★ ★ ★

For two months I sat with a fellow NCO in an upstairs room in a drill hall in Edinburgh being given intensive personal tuition in radio work by a lieutenant in the Royal Signals. Our text was *The*

Admiralty Handbook of Wireless Telegraphy, a theoretical tome in two volumes. Each radio set also had its own manual, and we worked hard, hard enough to satisfy our conscientious instructor. By the middle of May I was on my way to Catterick Camp in Yorkshire, the headquarters of the Royal Signals.

I arrived at the Marne Lines and was promptly stripped of my rank. I was now a cadet, my white shoulder tapes and cap bands telling the world that I was neither officer nor man. It had all been too much for one boy: I had barely arrived before I was turned out on parade with the other 250 cadets for a funeral. A cadet on an earlier course had shot himself after being told he was 'RTU'd', the worst humiliation: being returned to your unit.

With this sober beginning, we settled down to seven months of training intended to turn us into effective Royal Signals officers. It was the most demanding and intense period of study I have ever undertaken; the Royal High School seemed child's play by comparison, and of course it was. We learned about radio, telegraphy and telephony to a level beyond the Post Office's dreams, and were taught about military organization, how to use quite heavy machine tools and even about intelligence work.

In June 1940 the British Army was evacuated from Dunkirk, and for the first time the war began to touch us. We were told to expect troops and refugees, and prepared beds and mattresses in halls, gymnasiums and every large building where there was room. After a couple of weeks the emergency passed; the army had retreated in surprisingly good order and it survived. A cloud lifted. Our beds were not needed, the evacuees went elsewhere.

The war then made another stealthy, silent leap in our direction, like a storm threatening to come in off the sea. It was feared that the Germans would follow up their advantage and invade, catching the exhausted troops who were the core of our army at their weakest. That summer, I spent a lot of nights on a little platform at the top of a very high wooden tower, with orders to keep watch for enemy parachute landings. I forced myself to stay awake, looking up at the fields of stars and hoping that I wouldn't be the one to see drifting silk crossing them. But once again the war stayed away, withdrew beyond the coast; nothing happened.

In fact, the worst that happened to me on this marvellous course was pulling an extra drill for my entire class by attempting to poison the company commander. Captain Knowles was a stickler for inspections, and liked to check things in turn; bootlaces, rifle barrels, the insides of hats. One day, he decided to inspect the No. 13 Course's kit. There we were, shaved and washed, loaded with rifles, gas-masks, haversacks and water-bottles, and he ordered us to present the bottles as we would our firearms. He pulled the cork out of mine and took a deep whiff, and staggered backwards into the arms of the company sergeant-major, who was unfortunately an exceptionally small warrant officer. Dignity was not maintained.

It was not a happy situation, and it resulted from my desire not to leave anything behind that could be useful, a habit that I would have unlearnt then and there if I had known what it could bring down on me. On an exercise out on the moors, I had been appointed cook and at the close of the exercise I had not wanted to waste the leftover milk, so I poured it into my water-bottle. I strongly recommend stale milk, fermented for three weeks in a British Army canteen, as a harmless substitute for gas.

Weathermen talk about an area of low pressure, the cold air pushing out the warm, the threat of rain and winds of enormous force. I was living all the time now on the edge of such an area. The war kept coming closer, and not content with knowing it was out there, I went out to meet it. Towards the end of 1940, a notice appeared in Daily Orders, inviting volunteers for service in India.

I volunteered, not without thought, but I broke the old soldiers' rule for a second time, and have wondered about it since.

The army can be inscrutable and it was to be some time before I learned whether I was going to India. Meanwhile, the pace quickened. Late in December 1940 there was an urgent demand for more signals officers, apparently even including young and inexperienced ones. No. 13 Course was brought to a swift close, lopping off the last two weeks. We got into our new uniforms and kit and were sent into the world as officers. I was now Second-Lieutenant Eric Lomax, No. 165340, allocated for the time being to a base at Great Leighs in Essex. We were taken to Darlington Railway Station, climbed into blacked-out trains and were dispersed throughout Britain.

* * *

After a few weeks in a unit of Scottish Divisional Signals, under a vigorous Glasgow businessman turned colonel, who was an excellent commanding officer, I felt that I was becoming a real soldier, helping to protect the east coast of England immediately north of the Thames; but the War Office unfortunately hadn't forgotten my rash enthusiasm and I was soon sent to a holding battalion in Scarborough – the first step in the long journey to India taking me back up to the north of England. Such are the ways of armies.

Our battalion was responsible for the defence of this vulnerable seaside town, and while I was on duty one evening the war finally made its leap across the coast and put out a finger for me. I was speaking to a policeman on the edge of a public park, and the familiar air raid warning and drone of aircraft engines – which always turned out to be ours – was suddenly augmented by a high whistling sound I had never heard before. The policeman and I were equally quick, and when the bombs dropped around us we were flat on the road. Not quite: I was flopped across a sandbag, my bottom a few inches in the air. And that was enough for the lethal blast of air, travelling just above the earth, to give my behind a blow that felt like a whack from a giant oar. The policeman had to inspect my rear, which he did with great kindness, before I would believe I was not seriously damaged.

I was lucky, probably saved by a couple of inches and some quirk of air-pressure. The people in a large block of flats nearby were buried under the rubble of their building. The storm was no longer a report on the radio now, it was filthy weather all around me.

My parents came down to Scarborough, and we could so easily have died together. They had taken a room in a house run by a Miss Pickup, and I took meals with them when I could. One evening, the three of us were sitting in Miss Pickup's lounge when we heard a loud rattling, like a box of tools falling over in the attic two storeys up, and then a crash. The ceiling over our heads burst open and a small cylinder fizzing viciously with flames and giving off frightening heat fell on to the landlady's carpet. I knew enough to recognize that it was a magnesium incendiary bomb, and that it would burn the house down and us with it. I dashed out into the back garden, found a large spade, ran back inside and scooped the bomb up and ran for the garden again. In those few seconds, just as I got outside, the incendiary burned through the steel blade of the shovel and fell near my feet.

This devilish firecracker tossed carelessly into a harmless

parlour was a new twist. I can still hear the dry rattle it made as it hit the roof and worked its way through the thin ceilings towards me and my parents. Luck, perhaps some fault in the bomb, saved us. A neighbouring house received the same kind of hit and was ablaze, so fiercely that when two or three other men and myself tried to put out the fire we had to retreat, with minor shocks from wet electrical fittings.

* * *

Plans for the movement of the battalion to India began to take proper shape. Perhaps inevitably, I was put in charge of the baggage arrangements, which consisted of working out how many covered goods vans we would need when we pulled out of Scarborough for the port from which we would embark. We were not told the name of the port; I simply made my calculations and hoped we would get the wagons we needed.

In the middle of March 1941, we finally assembled late at night in this blacked-out Yorkshire resort. The battalion filled a street in front of silent hotels and the boarded-up shops. An army trying to be quiet, we made a hushed rumble around the war memorial, young men in heavy boots, laden with canvas and metal, glancing seriously at the monument to the dead of the last war.

The movement was supposed to be secret, but in the dark streets crowds of townspeople had come out, as well as parents who had come from all over England, mine among them. They stood smiling, even laughing, but doing it with the tense hilarity of people who are determined to be remembered well and know that they are now playing against frightening odds with their love for their children. My mother stood there in the crowd, and I suppose she waved. She looked distraught. I never saw her again.

We marched to the station through the darkness, the NCOs barking orders in stage whispers. A special train had steam up, exhaling its gases carefully, the distinctive sooty smell of steam-raising Welsh coal penetrating as it burned with the smoke into our nostrils and uniforms. The carriages had black blinds drawn over the windows; in front of the carriages, the three goods vans I had ordered were drawn up.

When we had disposed of ourselves in the coaches, and stowed all the kit in the string webbing of the luggage racks, the engine got under way, taking a mighty pull on the hundreds of tons of vehicles and humans as the driver swung his long regulator handle and released steam into the cylinders, the pistons thrusting back and forth, and hot gas shot along the copper intestines of the boiler and up the chimney.

As the train moved out of Scarborough into the total darkness of the Cleveland Hills, all we knew was that we were going north. I guessed that we were on the east coast main line. In the middle of the morning, stiff from a night in a crowded and heated carriage, I looked out the window and recognized Joppa Station, a quarter of a mile from my home. My mother and father were two hundred miles to the south. The moment felt very empty. I knew then that our final destination would be the Clyde, where our ship would be waiting.

I was about to leave Britain to go to a war in Asia, defending the eastern borders of the Empire. I thought I had learned so much and that I was ready for anything, but before leaving Scarborough I had done one last thing. I got engaged to S., the young woman from the Chapel in Charlotte Street.

She came down to stay at Miss Pickup's; my parents arrived, and found the engagement a fact they had to live with. They did not approve, but accepted it as my final declaration of independence. My fiancée was all of nineteen, I was twenty-one. We were children, emotionally, though the Chapel gave us a false sense of rigid maturity. I felt that it was the right thing to do. We were so young; we barely knew each other.

CHAPTER THREE

THE TRAIN TRUNDLED on through Edinburgh Waverley and later that morning the southern outskirts of Glasgow, running past sidings and factories. That afternoon we slowed into Greenock, on the eastern end of the Clyde estuary.

Out on the water, in the chill wind of late winter, lay a great armada of ships. I felt part of a heroic expedition, seeing those vessels strung out down the estuary. There were four splendid P&O liners, a captured French passenger ship, the *Louis Pasteur*, several destroyers and two battleships. These looked immense, even at the distance I was standing from them on the dockside. I remembered going to see HMS *Hood* when it came to the Firth of Forth in 1938: the awesome power, decks as long as fields, the grey gun turrets the size of houses. It made you feel small and safe to have this weight of firepower on your side.

After the usual milling and shouting, and the unpacking of my goods wagons, we formed up on the quay in the deceptively casual disorder of armies on the move. But we knew we were highly organized; we felt our power. Tenders came to take us to the ships, we embarked quickly and soon we were slapping through the choppy water towards the long line of vessels. Our tender pointed through the spray to one of the nearer ships, a big P&O liner which we discovered was the *Strathmore*.

Most of us would never have imagined that we would ever step aboard this floating country house. It was an imposing environment, all polished wood and brass, but its spotless decks and its cabin windows seemed deserted, as though the diplomats, the administrators and the gilded travellers who normally used it had abandoned ship at the sight of these boyish invaders in rough khaki. Feeling like pirates, we were soon allocated to cabins or mess decks by our senior officers and by the crew.

Although this was a military adventure, we were still guests of the ship. The Captain was still very much the captain; we were passengers. All our activities had to fit in with his organization of the ship. So on this strange peacetime basis, we set about our warlike duties.

The following day, our convoy of about twenty ships drew up its anchors and with a minimum of noise, no ceremonial blasts on the sirens or crowds on the harbour walls, headed out into the open sea. We were not told where we were going, and after we had left the Firth of Clyde, running out into the north channel between Ireland and Scotland, we hadn't much idea where we were – except that we were sailing roughly north west into the Atlantic. It was difficult to be sure even of the number of ships in our company, because the convoy occupied such a large area of the ocean. Nor were we told the names of the grey warships that occasionally glided up out of the fog.

In this state of official ignorance, our time was filled for us. Every morning hundreds of young men would be out doing PT exercises on deck. After the first few days the deck grew hot under the thin soles of our gym shoes, and the sun higher in the sky. We were no longer sailing north west, and had turned south. Somewhere off to the east lay the coast of Africa.

The Signals contingent went over to a training routine, keeping ourselves and our men busy by organizing courses and reminders about how to keep an army's communications clear and efficient. In the evenings we tried to run entertainments, using whatever talent we had available: songs, revues, mild ribaldry, but all held in check by the total absence of alcohol. And of course there was not a single woman on board; even the nurses were male.

We were setting off to sail around the scarlet map of the Empire, and we talked endlessly about where we might end up. As it turned out, we were preparing ourselves to face the wrong enemy. Our assumption was that we would have to defend the north-west frontier of India against a German attack through Persia; no other enemy seriously crossed our minds.

I shared a cabin with a friendly young fellow signals officer, Alex Black, and got on well with him. We talked about the business of what we were doing, as all colleagues do, and gossiped about men and officers. Enforced companionship can be a hell for some people, but these years were made bearable for me partly because of the comrades that the war chose at random for me. I vividly remember eating green ginger for the first time in my life aboard that ship, and sharing it with my cabin mate.

The warmth of the weather was now tropical, damp and intense. The day came when it was announced that we were about to put in at Freetown, in Sierra Leone. This was a real event for us; young people from the backgrounds that most of us came from had never been 'abroad' before in our lives. We were now well and truly travelled, if sitting on board a liner in the bay at Freetown counts as abroad.

Unfortunately only very small ships could be accommodated at the Freetown quayside, so most of the convoy had to anchor a long way out. But not so far that I couldn't see and even smell the land, the docks, the palm trees just back from the harbour, the damp jungly smell coming out on the breeze, like rotting vegetables in the dusty green heat. I saw a very distant train heading up-country on the far side of the city. I knew that this was the famous 2 foot 6 inch gauge main line railway, probably the only one of its kind in the entire British Commonwealth. The little white drift of smoke from the engine seemed to hang in the hot air.

It became oppressive on board ship, hotter and more humid each day. The exercises and routines became exhausting; the coast more tantalizing, the smell more disgusting because we could not move around the city that was generating it. We were not sorry when the entire convoy resumed its journey. Our immediate destination could now only be South Africa.

About five days later I was detailed as Paying Officer for the Signals draft as we sailed along the South African coast towards Cape Town. So when the spectacular docking of so many big ships was accomplished, I was below decks handing out cash to men eager to get ashore.

Cape Town was a festival of goodwill. Soldiers were taken to people's houses, were celebrated and had drinks bought for them. After four weeks at sea it was quite an experience. But I wandered off one afternoon and headed, inevitably, for Cape Town railway station, an addict hoping for a surprise. As no other member of the ship's company or the troops seemed to share my interest, I was on my own. I certainly got my surprise. On a plinth in the station was an ancient locomotive, a small tank engine built by Hawthorns & Co. in Leith in 1859. It was the first locomotive ever to work in the Cape Colony, and was probably the oldest surviving Scottish engine in the world.

If it seems odd to find solace in an old steam engine after a month at sea, on the way to God knew where and in the middle of a world war, all I can say is, well, you weren't there and didn't see it, and I had my passion to tend. It was a lovely old tank engine, a beautiful piece of machinery on fragile ungainly wheels with surprisingly delicate coupling rods. It looked almost too danger-ous to drive, a mad inventor's toy. I admired it in the middle of that hot African station for a long time.

* * *

Two weeks later we were in Bombay, and I felt for the first time the shock of the East. Six weeks before, I had been in cold grey Scarborough. The intense dry heat, bustle and colour of India were overwhelming. Within yards of the air-conditioned hotel where I was billeted there was utter poverty. I saw hundreds of sleeping bodies each night in the streets. I could barely absorb the sensations with which I was bombarded.

Before I could get settled into Bombay and get used to walking on the Malabar Hill, amid the splendour of official British India, I was despatched on an epic train journey of my own. The Frontier Mail, the flagship of the entire railway system, took me on a trip of almost 1400 miles up the subcontinent to Rawal-pindi, near the foothills of the Himalayas at the angle made by the plain of the Punjab and the mountains of Afghanistan. The stops were a wonderful litany of the Raj: Ratlam, Nagda, Kotah, Bharatpur and Muttra; Delhi, Chandigarh, Amritsar, and Lahore; and from Lahore, the final 180 miles up and across the Punjab to Rawalpindi. My main concern was not losing my revolver, a precaution drummed into us as soon as we arrived in India, for there were revolutionaries on the loose. If you lost your gun you as good as lost yourself. Yet I never felt threatened, despite this fear of rebellious subjects, travelling on my own in a train full of hundreds of Indians. Our dominion seemed so secure.

I settled into a passable imitation of the Indian Army officer's life in Rawalpindi, with its old buildings, its seemingly unchanging way of life. I had a bungalow normally occupied by a colonel, and they gave me a bearer and a *dhobi*. As the freshest graduate of the Officer Cadet Training Unit, I was up to date with the latest radio practice and became a lecturer in telecommunications to my brother officers and men.

I also had to learn to ride, for the Indian Army still travelled on horseback. Their old army radios, especially, were transported by troops of horses and mules, and we used the heliograph, a tripod with mirrored discs, anywhere you could get a visual line between two points in sunlight. I felt that I was slipping back gently into an older way of military life.

One of the Indian Army's most agreeable traditions was that it allowed a great deal of leave. When mine came, I decided to go to Kashmir. I sat beside the driver of a 'bus', which turned out to be a lorry with very unforgiving suspension – this was the 'first class' seat – for 200 miles as we ground up into the hills, up the great U-shaped bend of the Jhelum Valley and into Srinagar. I had come to the most beautiful place in the world.

The mountains were unbelievable masses of rock and snow merging with the sky, and the Vale of Kashmir seemed to this child of northern Europe like a fertile garden of Eden: the luxuriance and accessibility of fruit I had never even heard of, the abundance of trees and flowers. I booked a small house-boat at the southern end of the Dal Lake and for a week lived in an idyll, eating well, walking in the Shalimar Gardens and at night sitting out on my boat alone under the sky which was dense with layers of stars.

I rode as far up into the mountains as I could from Pahlgam, which is itself 7500 feet above sea level, with a party of English missionaries. We were mounted on horses with mules carrying our baggage. Beyond us were the Karakorams and Tibet. For two days we pressed on up the Lidar Valley until on the second evening we reached Shisha Nag, a magnificent isolated sheet of water more than two miles above the sea. The valley above us was blocked by a glacier. I remember the sun, the cold, the enormous river of ice in the air above me glittering as I ate hard-boiled eggs and boiled ice for water.

In the early morning, the snow on the mountain peaks was caught by the sun, turning pink before the light penetrated to the valley floor. Then there was the silence. I do not think I have ever before or since heard such peace and deep silence. There were other kinds of silence later, but they were tense and sick with anxiety and violence.

Kashmir filled my mind. Later, it went some way to keeping me whole. If I had had no idea of perfection, I don't know if I would have come through.

★ ★ ★

My orders, when they came, were to take charge of the signal section of the 5th Field Regiment, Royal Artillery, then stationed at Nowshera, eighty miles away on the north-west frontier. The regiment was being built up for 'tropical service'. There was one

Scot for whom India seemed quite tropical enough, but I was now a loyal cog in His Majesty's machine.

The regiment was an old-established one, and had expected to stay on guard at the Empire's most romantic outpost for a while yet. Instead it was hastily mobilizing, under strength with its sixteen 4.5 inch howitzers, and deficient in all kinds of equipment. Soon after I got to Nowshera, the regiment took delivery of brand new tractors for its guns, Karrier KT4 'Spiders', which were ordered to be painted green. Knowing officers predicted that we were headed for Malaya.

On 11th October the guns and vehicles left Nowshera for Bombay in three special trains. Mobilization took a lot of trains, and the innocence of railways, if not of the machines themselves, was complicated for me by realizing more and more how essential they were to the conduct of war. Then, on 17th October, General Wakeley, the commanding officer of the 7th Indian Division, took the salute at a farewell parade on the huge square in front of the barracks.

In the course of the parade Wakeley announced that we might have to fight the Japanese. No senior officer had ever suggested this in public to his men before, in my experience, and it gave a frisson of excitement and aggression to the occasion.

General Wakeley went on to say that we should try to fight the Japanese at night, as they suffered from night blindness.

When the band of the Lincolnshire Regiment played us out of the siding at Nowshera the following day on our special military train, we did not know that we were very nearly blind ourselves, being led by the blind.

* * *

At Bombay harbour a few days later we saw an imposing liner approaching the quay. It was the Orient Line flagship *Orion*, another wonderful example of the democracy of war: our travels were now all on special trains and requisitioned luxury cruisers.

I was the last to board the ship, after midnight, and the captain didn't want me even then. I had in my charge several crates of carboys of neat, undiluted, full-strength sulphuric acid which we needed to keep our radio batteries topped up, for if they were less than fully supplied they gave less than full power. The captain needed this particular Jonah in the way that he needed a Japanese torpedo. But our regimental commander somehow persuaded him that the security of the entire British Empire in the Far East depended on me and my acid, and eventually, watched by the entire cheering regiment, my crates were swung inboard in a net by the ship's derrick.

After a brief stop at Colombo, the main port of Ceylon, we sailed eastwards, suspecting that we knew what our mysterious 'tropical' destination was but in fact kept properly in the dark. On 6th November, green hills, jungle-clad from their summits to the sea, appeared to starboard, our southern side, and we could make out a similar coast to the north. We were clearly sailing through a bight between substantial masses of land: the Straits of Malacca. Singapore it had to be.

The *Orion* docked at Keppel Harbour, in the south of Singapore Island. If our journey had been a secret, our arrival certainly was not. A band of the Manchester Regiment was waiting on the quayside playing 'There'll Always Be An England' and other tunes with gusto, the trumpets and tubas and cymbals making their huge summery brass noise. It was triumphant and joyful. A crowd of dignitaries was there: port officers, civil servants, officers. Someone pointed out Lieutenant-General

A.E. Percival, the General Officer Commanding Malaya. He was the man in charge of The Fortress, and we had come to help him defend it.

* * *

A month later I was living in a khaki canvas tent in a camp by the edge of a road on the east coast of Malaya. It was a pleasant sandy area full of coconut palms, half a mile from the beach. Behind the camp stretched endless regular acres of rubber trees with their thick glossy leaves.

The fine rain was constant in the warm heat, and almost soothing. This cluster of guarded tents was our Regimental HQ, and the thirty signalmen were the heart of the camp. We had our radios set up, their low hum a constant background noise. A man was always sitting in front of each set, headphones to hand, ready to receive or transmit. We were at work. The place was called Kuantan.

We were waiting for an assault by the Imperial Japanese Army and Navy, which we knew were out there on the sea over the horizon, for we were now formally at war with them.

Early on the morning of 8th December I was sleeping in a trench when a messenger woke me to show me a message with the ominous priority 'O ii U'. This was the code for the highest possible priority signal. The Japanese had attacked all over the Far East; a dreadful attack on Pearl Harbor in Hawaii, all the US battleships destroyed, an air raid on Singapore, and at Kota Bharu two hundred miles to our north, near the border of Malaya and Siam, they had stormed ashore from small boats and landing craft.

The scramble was immediate. Messengers and radio signals

went out to all the gun positions, extra men were sent to the observation and guard posts. The urgency and tension were extraordinary, and yet the war still seemed a long way away from this deceptively peaceful tropical camp. It was as though it was taking one last breather before finally pouncing, after all those false starts and premonitions.

I could not see any guns from the camp. They were scattered around the area, among the pawpaws with their heavy yellow gourds and the flame-of-the-forest trees, a mile between each gun so as not to be vulnerable to a massed Japanese naval barrage. I could go out of my tent and walk for a mile, or ride a motorbike even further, and almost forget our deadly business, enjoying the illusion that I was alone in this beautiful place, surrounded by the splendour of its plant life. Then you would come on a single howitzer with sandbags around it standing silently in the forest, the men edgily fingering their rifles.

We kept in touch with them as best we could. Like much else in warfare, signals theory was one thing, jungle practice another. Those cumbersome radios didn't generate a lot of wattage, when it came to it, and a lot of energy was lost in the surrounding trees, electromagnetic waves soaking into the trunks and leaves, distorting voices, drowning messages in static. We resorted to sending wireless signals down the phone lines, an ingenious improvisation which we christened Line Assisted Wireless, by setting up our aerials a few feet below the overhead wires: the outgoing signals were attracted to the wires and another radio further down the line of wire could capture the signals. We were discovering that our army was part of a connected system, that machines had only limited power. They still needed our voices and our eyes to give them intelligence.

We were forced to rely more and more on our land lines,

telephone wires strung around the area, to talk clearly to each other. Our old-fashioned switchboard lent a touch of civilian absurdity to a command centre from which a terrible artillery bombardment could be called down on an enemy; with its plugs and jacks it looked as though it should be in some provincial hotel.

Our troops were mostly Indian: Sikhs to the west of us, Garhwalis to the east. We were halfway up the peninsula of Malaya, which dangles the island of Singapore from its foot, and Singapore was the only reason for our presence on this coast. The island was the 'Fortress', the 'impregnable fortress' as it was always called in official descriptions, on which the defence of the Empire in Asia depended. The citadel of the fortress was the celebrated naval base in the north of the island, from where the great ships of the Royal Navy could sail out to dominate the South China Sea and the Gulf of Siam. Huge 15-inch guns looked out from the southern shore, for that was the way the enemy would come: from the sea. We hoped that our battleships would now be moving out from their base to search for and destroy a Japanese invasion fleet. We were merely guarding an airfield a few miles inland which was part of a chain of defences on the landward side of the island. It had finally dawned on our leaders that the Japanese might attack Singapore from the rear, and perhaps not at night, and from the rear it was anything but impregnable.

I remember precisely, only hours after I arrived in Singapore, a Signals staff officer, some hopeless decent man, telling me that the Japanese could not attack through Malaya. He said 'there is nothing there. It's just solid jungle, all the way up. They will not come that way.'

Now it must have been obvious to the staff in Singapore and

certainly to my colonel and to every private soldier, that we were, despite the tranquillity of our surroundings, trapped and desperate. We had seen a lot of Malaya since we disembarked in Singapore, from Ipoh in the west and right across the waist of the country to where we now were, and it was not solid jungle. It was intensively cultivated, rich land, with good and plentiful roads for traders – or for soldiers.

The one place in the country that lacked roads was Kuantan. If the Japanese drove down on us from the north, there was only one road out for us, to Jerantut, which was about sixty miles inland behind us. East of that town was the river Pahang, a wide fast stream crossed by a ferry. This obstacle course was bad enough, but Kuantan too had its river, a mile west of the town, and it was a horrible sight to military eyes. The river was wide and brown and sluggish, its ferry made up of two rusty barges fastened together, which were moved by winching a cable that stretched from shore to shore: a primitive watery version of the system that worked the old Edinburgh trams would have to rescue us if things went wrong. It spelled massacre and disaster; bad ground and bad water. It was hard for us to imagine who had chosen this spot for us to make a stand, and what good we could do except to die at our posts. Our orders were, indeed, more or less to do just that: to defend the airfield to the last man. The Garhwali troops had to defend eleven miles of beaches and the little town of Kuantan with a pitiful total of four companies. The Sikhs had equally few men. There were no troops at all to defend the coast to our south; and none for the main road out of the trap.

But we were soldiers, part of a great tradition, so we tried not to think about our leaders' vision and prepared to fight. Besides, the Japanese did not seem a formidable enemy. They had surprised the Americans, we thought, but we were forewarned.

The Japanese first came the day after I had been rousted from sleep by that sensational signal. Early that morning we heard a new engine note in the sky, different from the Hudson and Blenheim bombers which we had grown accustomed to hearing take off from the airfield. In a clear sky, I saw waves of twin-engined planes with rising sun emblems on their wings, three neat waves of nine each, like migrating geese. They passed and repassed over the area where we knew the airfield to be, and dropped bombs that looked so small and black in the distance. The explosions were mingled with the crack and rattle of light machine-guns and cannon as the Sikh company shot up at them, but the bombers calmly and methodically went to and fro over the earth, walking their bombs around in it, then turned and flew away.

In the afternoon we heard our own planes take off one by one, wheel around and head south. In the sunlit silence that followed we thought we heard the sounds of road vehicles through the trees, lorries moving away from us. Major Fennell, our second-in-command, took me and a small group out to the airfield to investigate.

We drove on to the long spacious runway that had been dug and levelled out of the forest. It was empty apart from a few wrecked planes, and so silent that you could hear the birds and the insect sounds from the forest. I walked towards the trees. The huts for accommodation were in there, the radio shacks hidden further back. It was spooky, as though there were rifles pointing at us from the dark under the trees. But the huts were empty, scattered clothes all over the floors, photos of women and children strewn among the vests and jackets. In the radio rooms, the equipment had been wrecked, wires trailing out of smashed panels, the glass of valves crunching under my boots. Out on the runway, there were cold mugs of tea half-full by the aircraft on which mechanics had been working. I picked up a blue flimsy envelope with an Australian postmark. It was unopened.

The place for which we were supposed to sacrifice our lives had simply been abandoned, without explanation. Our headquarters had told us nothing; the local air force commanders had not consulted us before fleeing. We were left on this awful ground with no air cover.

From then on, the probabilities began to look harsh and unfavourable to us. Very late that same evening, an observer on one of the beaches reported that he had seen Japanese landing craft moving towards a village further up the coast. As darkness fell, I transmitted an order from Colonel Jephson to the guns. Within seconds of speaking into the mouthpiece and hearing the squawked acknowledgments from the batteries, I heard the deep flat blast of a howitzer firing, immediately followed by several more. All that night the guns slammed like bolts on a massive door being pushed heavily back and forth. We could see quick flashes occasionally, a patch of rubber trees reversing out of the darkness for a second, but nothing more. I knew the shells would form a shifting pattern, moving across a square of sea and beach like a flail, and that landing craft and soldiers would burst and drown in the geometrical figure drawn on the gunnery officer's map.

Dawn broke. We had fired over a thousand shells. There had been no response to the night long barrage, and when observers went out they reported that Colonel Jephson had been scourging the empty sea. There were no landing craft.

Later that morning I walked down to the beach. I had been up most of the night, on duty with my signalmen. These beaches were incredibly beautiful; they had coconut and nipah palms, fine clean sand and the warm green of the sea. I stood beneath the trees admiring the way the waves came in. It was so peaceful, standing on a mile of deserted sand with a long line of palms at my back. I felt I was waiting for the Japanese, at that moment, completely alone. Then the loud rumbling started again, a deeper and more distant version of the night's barrage, like thunder but obviously not thunder, drifting in from the sea. It went on for about an hour.

I had heard the British Empire begin to fall, if I had but known it. Out at sea, just over the horizon from where I stood, the two mightiest, most invincible battleships in the world, the *Prince of Wales* and the *Repulse*, and their escort destroyers, were being attacked by swarms of Japanese torpedo bombers. They had no air protection; like the land dreadnought of Singapore, like us, they were playing tragic roles in an outdated military drama. Their day was done. I remember myself as I was then, hearing the huge cracks of the explosions as my comrades, the radio men, were trapped at their posts under the bridges of the great ships.

We had seen these ships as our salvation. We lost hope when it was confirmed over the radio that they had both been sunk within a couple of hours off Kuantan. Admiral Phillips had turned his titanic weapons towards us because he also believed that we were being invaded; he too had heard that Japanese troops were storming ashore in our sector: our own panicky observer had helped unwittingly to bring a strategic and historical era to an end. It was absurd. The weak, shortsighted, nightblind Japanese had destroyed our ultimate deterrent. For the first time, we began seriously to consider defeat.

On 10th December we received reinforcements: some armoured cars and the remnants of a Frontier Force Regiment battalion arrived, tough Sikhs who had withdrawn from the north of Malaya; and although we no longer had an airfield at Kuantan, we at least acquired a chaplain, a nice man called Pugh. Percival's orders to the Frontier Force soldiers and to all the others in the north had been to fight, to 'impose delay' on the Japanese, retreat and fight again all the way down the peninsula. We were about to discover that a leapfrogging, fighting retreat is easier to imagine than to carry out.

We had watchers out on the tracks to the north, organized by a civilian from the Malayan Forestry Service who knew the area well. We got reports of mysterious parties coming through the jungle; every day, we expected a fight. There were false alarms, and a permanent screwing up of tension. Two weeks passed like this. We celebrated Christmas, Padre Pugh conducting impressive and well-attended services at our camp and out among the batteries in the forest. We killed a lot of local ducks and ate well.

Our unit's particular orders were still to stand and fight in defence of the now derelict airfield. We accepted this task stoically, wondering what Percival would say if he could see the jungle reclaiming the landing strip. But two days after Christmas, we were ordered to withdraw immediately and regroup west of the river. A sudden retreat on this scale would cause chaos, our commanders felt, and Brigadier Painter, who was in overall charge of our immediate area, protested vigorously to the major-general above him. The previous orders were reinstated. I dutifully relayed these contradictory messages between my superiors.

While their debate was going on, one of our forward posts phoned in to say that it had been attacked by Japanese troops, and some of our vehicles had been destroyed. We were now in a battle zone without doubt, and the Japanese wished to keep us there. They tried to destroy our ancient ferry by bombing it, but it survived.

The first of my friends to die was Lieutenant Taffy Davies, an artillery officer, a friend since Nowshera. He and two signalmen called Cartwright and Howe drove off on their motorbikes alongside a truck that was delivering some ammunition to a battery. I discovered later that he and Cartwright set off to return on their own. We found Taffy's body a few hours later on the road beside his wrecked machine, machine-gunned and bayoneted, and stripped of his boots, puttees and equipment. Cartwright's bike was there, but he had disappeared. Further along the same road, thirty Garhwali troopers lay dead among their burnt out lorries.

Our orders were changed again, for the third time in three days. All guns and vehicles were to be withdrawn across the river.

The ferry was a nightmare. The bottleneck was even worse than we had predicted: a line of vehicles a mile long waited to cross it. Relays of men tugged and strained on the old cables, floating artillery pieces two by two across the turgid brown stream. I sat on a motorbike at the back of this line, hoping the truck in front would move; I remember the mortal fear that a passing Japanese bomber would sight this dense column of targets.

At three in the morning, on the first day of 1942, in a darkness lit by oil lamps and electric lights run from truck batteries, the last of the Kuantan garrison crossed the river.

We had a roll call as soon as we had completed the crossing; I was horrified to find that one of my sections of three men in a radio truck was missing. We searched for the men, hoping that they had come over in another truck, but they were not to be found on our side of the river. A sergeant called Watson and I went back across the ferry on motorbikes to look for them. Once on the far side, we started the motors. Without lights we drove back towards Kuantan, Watson keeping 200 yards behind me, the growling engines sounding shatteringly loud in the moonlight. I hoped that Japanese hearing didn't compensate for their poor night vision. In the clearings to the side of the road, in the huge rubber plantations beyond them, there wasn't a sound, no sign that we had ever been there except for the odd wrecked vehicle and the tracks of our tyres in the dark clay beside the tarmac. I could sense rather than hear the sea as we roared through this abandoned landscape. I knew that just ahead of us the enemy was moving with his tanks and bicycles. I had still not seen a Japanese soldier, alive or dead. That night I was lucky, and although I failed to find a truck in working order or my missing men, I also failed to meet the Japanese.

We went back and were pulled across the ferry for the last time. Some hours later the missing section appeared, having assembled in the wrong place; they expected the worst, but words failed me. We withdrew to the airfield, about six miles away, after blowing up the winches and pontoons. Two hours later the Japanese were at the ferry, and two days later the airfield was under fierce attack from all sides. By then I was on the road to Jerantut, part of a slow-moving column of tractors, guns and trucks. Behind us we could hear relentless firing and shelling. The outnumbered Frontier Force Regiment, under their commander Lieutenant-Colonel A.E. Cumming, was fighting a heroic rearguard action to allow us to get away.

* * *

The retreat was confused, three- or four-day marches followed by a sudden halt, an order to emplace the guns, to fire in support of an infantry counter-attack somewhere off behind us, and then the regiment would move on again. We knew that we were heading out of one trap into another, a gigantic plug-hole, and we knew that the big guns, where we were going, pointed out to sea, away from our enemy.

Once I was in a truck, driving down a long straight road through a rubber plantation, reflecting that when you have seen one rubber tree you have seen them all, and feeling how depressing acres of them looked to a retreating soldier. Ahead of us there appeared a plane, coming in our direction, flying very low. It looked silver against the sun. We pulled over and jumped down into a gouge in the stiff black mud beside the rubber trees. He dropped a few bombs, one nearly on top of us. Again I felt the violent invisible blast of the shock. This was my second infinitesimally close shave, and I was saved this time by geology: the nearest bomb sank deep into the mud before exploding. Harder soil would have killed us.

We reached Singapore a week before the causeway linking it to Malaya was blown up. We had to press through crowds of frightened Malay and Chinese villagers who the Japanese had driven in front of them, and on the island the streets and roads were full of these refugees. They lived in tents, under trees, in the fields. No-one knew how many of them there were: someone told me half a million. Soldiers lived in the vehicles they had driven down the peninsula. There was a pervasive smell of decay, ordure, anxiety: the smell of defeat.

Yet there were nearly a hundred thousand of us, well-armed and ready to fight. For my part I was sent to Fort Canning, General Percival's headquarters in Singapore City, in the south of the island, where they needed signals officers. This was the 'Battlebox'. I went in and didn't come out for three weeks. The siege of Singapore for me was a series of clipped shouts for help over the radio and terse bulletins of disaster.

I spent most of my time underground in the Battlebox, hearing and relaying orders, passing on information, sending out instructions for desperate recombinations of units to try to stop the collapse. On 8th February the Japanese guns opened up all along the Straits of Johore; at dawn on the 9th I heard that they were ashore in the north west. Most of our troops were in the east. Within three days the Japanese had pushed down through the island and taken the village around the big hill of Bukit Timah, ten miles to the north west of us. Up around the naval base on the north coast there were huge supplies of oil, and for the last couple of days of the battle the hill, which dominated the island, was overhung by black clouds of smoke. It looked as though it had erupted.

Not that I saw daylight much: we worked eighteen hours a day, and slept on the floor of the command centre among the radios and phones. Our offices were a series of connecting rooms, so that runners and despatch riders were always coming through and stepping over tired bodies. We saw nothing until the very end, and what we heard was confused. We knew that the Japanese had taken the reservoirs and turned off the taps; we could hear their unchallenged planes bombing and strafing every day. The big ships were leaving Keppel Harbour with civilians; troops were deserting and wandering around the city. Towards the end the commanders couldn't even give sensible orders because there was so little information coming in. I saw General Percival a few times, walking in a corridor of the Fort or through our signals centre, a gaunt, tall figure looking utterly dejected and crushed; he was already a broken man. He was about to have his name attached to the worst defeat in the British Army's history.

On Sunday 15th February 1942 I was told by another officer that he had heard we were about to surrender. Early that evening a dead silence enveloped the old fort. In the signals rooms everybody went to sleep, depression and exhaustion flooding in, as we collapsed on mattresses laid on top of cables and land lines. The spring of tension that had kept us going for weeks had been broken.

I slept for ten hours. The following morning I stepped outside and saw four cars moving slowly up the hill, small rising sun pennants fluttering on their wings. Their occupants sat bolt upright, arms stiff by their sides. They drew up outside the main entrance and a group of Japanese officers got out, long swords in black scabbards hanging from their dark green uniforms. They were the first Japanese troops I had ever seen. They strode confidently into the Fort.

These people now ruled Malaya, dominated the seas from India to Polynesia and had broken the power of at least three European empires in Asia. I was their prisoner.

CHAPTER FOUR

THE DAY AFTER I saw our conquerors, the British forces left in the city were ordered to walk to Changi, site of a prison and a settlement around it, in the extreme east of the island. Changi was fifteen miles away.

We set off from Fort Canning, carrying whatever we could in backpacks and the few vehicles we were allowed. Our long column stretched for more than half a mile and as we walked out into the open we could see other lines of soldiers, marching in strict step, converging from side roads on to the only main route into Changi. Soon we were a dense mass of jostling overloaded men, trying to keep good order and dignity. This was the British Army marching to its humiliation.

A defeated army is a strange thing. Our awesome killing-machine was obeying the orders of an enemy we couldn't even see – there never seemed to be more than a couple of dozen Japanese guards at Changi. When we got there we were allocated living areas, our cooks set up their pots in tiny domestic kitchens in the bungalows of the vanished civilians, food and medicine was gathered in. Keeping the troops 'occupied' became an

obsession, and soon grass-cutting, drain-clearance and gardening became the main activities of fighting men. Small craft
workshops sprang up: I ordered a little wooden case for my
spectacles, one of the best purchases I have ever made. Everyone
knew to whom he was responsible; there was no-one who could
say that he did not know who he belonged to. But the entire
purpose of our mighty collective existence – the defence of the
Naval Base and British power in the Far East – had been snuffed
out.

What replaced our previous motive force was uncertainty,
creeping in and growing stronger day by day, a negative force
feeding on anxiety and fear. Before, we'd had the spring of
aggression to keep us moving; now there was a kind of nervous
elastic pulling us backwards. We still wanted to fight: but our
bitter young energy had to be bottled up. We began to experience
the overriding, dominant feature of POW life: constant anxiety,
and utter powerlessness and frustration. There was no relief
from these burdens, not even in sleep. So we filled the days
organizing ourselves and our men, underemployed and angry.

An eerie peace prevailed for three weeks, during which I did
not see a single further Japanese. There were still a few revolvers
and rifles at Changi, we were still an army, but we shuffled
around harmlessly waiting for our masters to dispose of us.
Almost the first decree they made was to remove the sense of time
by which we lived: they announced that Tokyo time was being
introduced, which meant advancing clocks and watches by 1.5
hours. We therefore had to rise earlier, in the dark. I cared about
time (and found a kind of beauty even in timetables); I needed to
be precise about when things might be done. I hated them taking
time away from us. Time was to become an issue between me
and the Japanese.

I was living for the moment with other Fortress signals men in a little bungalow, with a splendid view out over the sea to the east, an enormous tantalizing space in which we were lost. Here were tens of thousands of Allied prisoners-of-war dumped on the seashore, with not a chance of sailing away.

Our odd kind of normality was shaken one morning on parade when we were addressed by Colonel Pope, the OC of Southern Area Signals. He said that many of us had never seen a Japanese yet, that they had left us entirely alone since the surrender and that this was beginning to give us a false sense of security.

He then said that he had taken statements from a batch of POWs who had just arrived at Changi about what had happened at Alexandra Hospital, the main military hospital at Singapore, when Japanese troops had overrun it just hours before the surrender time. They had massacred the doctors, nurses and patients, even on the tables in the operating theatres. Survivors were dragged outside and finished off with bayonets.

The Colonel had another story that he wanted us to reflect on, told by POWs sent from Sumatra and the islands. Some of the small ships that had left Singapore just before the fall had been loaded with medical staff and wounded men. One of these boats had been sunk near the shore of Banka Island. Among the survivors were a large number of Australian Army nurses, all women, who struggled ashore and were rounded up, ordered to walk back into the sea and machine-gunned in the surf. The Colonel said that his information was that dozens had been killed.

The report about the nurses took us across a threshold into a new area of foreboding. It was still hard for us – there was no reason why we should have been able – to grasp the fact that we might have to explore human brutality to its limits. But nurses are venerated in armies, with a romantic reverence, so the killing of the nurses seemed inconceivable. Colonel Pope's conclusion did not need to be more than laconic. 'We have not seen much of them. This does not mean they are not dangerous.'

Soon after that parade, the Japanese staged a ceremonial humiliation on a vast scale. Every able-bodied prisoner had to line a route which included all the main roads in the Changi area, 50,000 of us standing two deep, strung out for miles around the camp. A cortège of open cars drove past, preceded by a camera crew in the back of an open lorry. They were making their propaganda film for home consumption, and we were the extras. I'm sure it looked impressive, all those men in uniforms which were already becoming a bit ragged, and some men dressed just in grimy shorts and vests, forced to attend to a few Japanese generals as they cruised by in their requisitioned British cars.

It takes time to break an army. Each new tightening of the leash is experienced as a degrading restriction; it all seems slow and insidious, though in retrospect I can see that they reduced us very quickly. In late March, for example, they decreed that Allied officers must no longer wear badges of rank. Instead we were to wear a single star on our shirts, just above the left breast pocket. This was a way of saying to us that our hard-won distinctions were of no interest to them, that we were simply two classes of prisoner.

In fact, as the spring came on they made it plain that prisoners were of interest to them under only one category: labour. Having concentrated us, they now began to pick us off in useful batches. They called for more and more working parties in Singapore, and in early April summoned over a thousand men 'for duty overseas'. This first unwilling regiment of labourers was sent off to an unknown destination under the command of a British colonel.

As if to underline how little we could do about this, or any other insult, on 14th April I was standing outside our bungalow with some signals men when a great fleet of Japanese warships came over the horizon, sailing westwards. In line astern, their guns jutting proudly and their funnels raked, the grey ships passed us on their way through the Straits of Singapore. There seemed to be no end to the line – battleships, cruisers, destroyers and smaller gunboats; an entire battle fleet steaming past Fortress Singapore as though it owned the sea. I remembered how deeply struck I was by the sight of our own ships in the Clyde little more than a year before, how invincible we looked. It felt bitter to have to review this enemy armada from a patch of grass wearing a star sewn roughly on to my worn shirt.

When the Japanese called for a working party for 'a Japanese project' in Singapore at the end of that month, I volunteered. I would keep on breaking the golden rule of soldiering, but I was restless and the unknown was better than the oppressive routine at Changi.

They made us walk twenty miles to a former Royal Navy hutted camp at Kranji, to the north of the city. For the next two months we marched out of our camp every morning, up the Bukit Timah road, past the Ford Motor Company factory where Percival had made the formal surrender of his garrison, and up the side of Bukit Timah Hill.

One morning as we left our quarters we saw, off the side of the road, six severed heads set up on poles. They were Chinese heads. At a distance, they looked like Hallowe'en fright masks; every morning, we marched past them. It was known that the Japanese were carrying out purges of suspected Kuomintang plotters in Singapore, and it is hard to explain now how this display of medieval barbarity did not shock us more. We felt immune to it; these heads were trophies of an inter-Asian conflict, we were British soldiers – and could not imagine that cruelty does not discriminate once it is unleashed.

On the hill, which was covered with dense undergrowth and timber, we had to cut down the trees, clear the scrub and creeper and build a road up towards the summit; then slice the top off the cone of the hill and level it. This was to be their gargantuan war memorial in Singapore, visible from all over the island. I'm glad to say I never actually saw the finished pile, not even a photo of it. It was blown up in 1945. The work gave me eight weeks of relative freedom to move around when I was not showing working parties of men from Bradford how to dig a trench in such a way that they were not up to their ankles in mud. This was far from the worst experience of captivity: the Japanese used the British chain of command, we got things done and they left us to get on with it. But the labour was heavy: ripping up the long roots of tropical fruit trees which dug into the earth like hard matted hair took great bursts of concentrated energy. The edges of cut bamboo opened skin with the ease of razor blades and the wounds went septic very fast. You could damage a lot of men by making them do this kind of work for a long time; it never occurred to us that anyone would try.

I was preoccupied with other things. One night I walked out of our quarters with a former Shanghai police officer called Wyld who had somehow ended up in Singapore in time to be captured. We were going to meet a Portuguese (and therefore neutral) civilian called Mendoza, to whom we had been recommended by Lim, a Chinese boy who sold us eggs. We walked very carefully in the dark through the gardens and plantations of a former European residential area.

Mendoza lived in a fine bungalow on the main road to the hill we were transforming. After some guarded small talk, Wyld put a gold ring carefully on the table in front of him and made our proposal. We wanted to be put in touch with the local Chinese sympathetic to the Kuomintang and to be smuggled to China, or at least the Burma Road, which ran along the top of Siam and Burma into China.

This was a crazy venture, much more dangerous than I could have imagined at the time. But Wyld was a superb linguist, and Chinese was one of his gifts. We thought that this would get us through.

It gradually dawned on us that the boundary keeping us in was as much psychological as it was physical; that we could walk for miles in the pineapple plantations around Kranji without seeing a single Japanese, that we could sell stolen Japanese equipment to the local Chinese traders, but there was nowhere to go to: north of us was the long peninsula, separated from Burma and therefore from India by high mountains choked in forest; south or west were the occupied Dutch colonies of Java and Sumatra; east, nothing but the sea.

Behind our billet was a little hill. One large POW climbed it every evening, just before the daylight failed, in as stately a manner as he could. He hooded his eyes with his hand like a pantomime scout, gazed around the whole horizon with great solemnity and called out in a remarkably loud voice, 'I see no fucking ship.'

If the state of Limbo, which some religions recognize, is characterized by this sort of helpless mockery and despair, and populated by ghosts suspended between human life and hell, I think I will recognize it when I see it.

In June we finished our work of levelling and earthmoving, and were sent back to Changi. We never heard from Mendoza, who now of course had no way of contacting us. I returned to a dwindling camp. In our absence the process of slow strangulation had tightened its pressure. They were now taking huge drafts of men away, thousands at a gulp. Twenty-five covered goods wagons packed with POWs left from Singapore Station; three thousand Australians were sent away by ship; a thousand taken to Japan. Every month more were taken away.

We lived in a world of half-verified information, smuggled news and above all, of rumour. The stories that circulated around the camp added to our pervasive anxiety. Always you wanted to believe that the worst could not be possible.

The rumour coming back now was that these huge work-details were wanted for a grandiose scheme. The Japanese were building a railway. Some inhuman visionary on the Imperial staff in Tokyo had dreamed up a way of avoiding the Allied destroyers and submarines in the waters around Malaya. The Japanese needed, we could guess, a way of getting supplies from Japan to Burma and on to India, which they were surely planning to invade. So they decided to build a railway across the spiky mountain chain between Burma and Thailand, a route so terrible that our British colonial engineers, as I knew from my reading, had rejected it as too brutally hard. I could not believe it; nor could I believe that I had become a prisoner only to be sent to work on a road for the machines that had given me such intense pleasure when I was free.

The final emasculation of the army took place in the late summer. First we were beheaded. Lieutenant-General Percival and the Governor of Singapore, Sir Shenton Thomas, and all officers above the rank of lieutenant-colonel, were removed in a single transport; in all, four hundred top brass disappeared, sent to some mysterious destination.

There were now about 18,000 of us left. A new Japanese commander had been appointed, General Fukuye Shimpei, and he made his mark by issuing an order that every remaining POW had to sign a 'non-escape form'. Only four prisoners signed. To show us that he meant to be taken seriously, Fukuye shot four prisoners on the beach near Changi. Allegedly, they had tried to escape. Of course we heard about all the cruel details; Fukuye intended that we should. He had ordered Colonel Holmes, our most senior remaining officer, to appear on the beach in the late morning of 2nd September with six of his colleagues. The four POWs were tied to posts in the sand; a firing squad of members of the Indian National Army, the renegade nationalist force supported by the Japanese, were led out in a calculated piece of political theatre. British soldiers were to be shot by their former subjects. The first shots failed to kill them; slow volleys finished them off as they lay on the bloody sand.

Less than an hour later, while this story was flashing around the camp, the Japanese ordered every single prisoner to move to Selarang Barracks, near Changi. The order added that anyone not there by 18.00 hours would join our comrades on the beach. In the blazing afternoon we walked two miles, carrying our sick, our heavy cooking equipment and our supplies, to this modern barracks built for a single battalion of Gordon Highlanders.

The barracks consisted of seven three-storey blocks around three sides of a parade ground. There were soon over 16,000 of us crammed into a space designed for 800; and 2000 seriously sick men were still in the big Roberts Hospital. Our discipline and organization meant that every unit was given a place somewhere. Every inch of space was occupied. Bodies covered the entire parade ground; sat hip to hip on the flat roofs, crowded on to balconies, stairwells and barrack-room floors. The latrines filled up. We dug through the tarmac of the parade ground to make more, but nothing could quench the overpowering smell of human excrement piling up, the congestion of sweat and discomfort. Fragmentary pieces of food were passed around. There were no proper cooking facilities, so we began to improvise them; there was one water tap for the population of a town.

On the second night, which was also the third anniversary of the outbreak of the war, the Australians organized a concert. Lit by oil-lamps, their 'choir' stood at one side of the parade ground and sang 'Waltzing Matilda', the lonely anthem of isolated men. Every voice in the square took up the refrain, a chorus of 16,000 sending the wistful, defiant air out past the barrack blocks into the darkness. 'There'll Always Be an England' followed, and the recital finished with a crashing version of 'Land of Hope and Glory'. What would Elgar have made of these thousands of voices rolling out to the beat of his surging march, as Japanese guards paced around the edge of the light with bayonets fixed?

The following day, our situation was clearly intolerable. Our medical officers pointed out the dangers; worse still, the Japanese administration announced that they intended to move all the patients from Roberts Hospital to join us. They were prepared to let loose epidemics among this mass of men and condemn the sick to death. Colonel Holmes issued an order instructing us to sign the piece of paper. We lined up in front of tables and did it. It read: 'I, the undersigned, solemnly swear on my honour that I will not, under any circumstances, attempt escape.'

We walked back to our quarters in Changi. For over a month I regained a measure of freedom and space, but Selarang had been a watershed. It was an important twist in the spiral of capitulation and cruelty. Nothing was ever quite the same again. Then on 25th October, after watching thousands more men leave for what we were now certain was a vast railway project, I joined the exodus myself.

I was ordered into a covered goods van with about twenty-five other men, the big door of the van open for air as we rolled through the vivid green and mud of the fields. Occasionally we would pass through miles of that depressing neatly-planted rubber. We sat on the steel floor or on our kit, talking and dozing. The train rumbled north up the west coast, with occasional stops for what we coyly termed 'essential purposes', and as we crossed over into Siam on the east coast the beaches came into view. Out in the water were chimneys of rock covered with greenery standing erect like great mouldy teeth.

On our slow journey up that neck of land twice as long as England, I read Olaf Stapledon's essay in prophecy *Last and First Men*, written in 1930. Its oratorical flights of scientific fantasy were hard going in that hot, crowded wagon, but Stapledon's vision of global conflict ending in 'a crescendo of radio hate, and war', of Europe destroyed and of a cycle of Dark Ages, was full of strange premonitions. He wrote the book in the person of one of the Last Men, speaking across the ages to us in our chaotic century in a voice of warning, at the moment when the earth is doomed by the radiation of a 'deranged star'. It was easy to imagine apocalypse in those years, but living it was turning out to be painful and squalid.

At Prai station, when we halted for food, I went up to look at the engine and discovered that it was a Japanese class C56 locomotive. I knew a little about it; knew it had been built in Osaka, and that it would have had to be altered to the narrower metre gauge for service on the tracks of Malaya and Siam. The Japanese were clearly here to stay, if they were shifting their trains to their new empire. I found myself, despite my aching limbs and tiredness, despite the grinding uncertainty about where we were going, admiring the quality of the engineering and the finish of the big engine with its smoke deflectors around the front of the boiler, and its six magnificent driving wheels. I couldn't deny my fascination even now.

On a long stretch between Sungei Patani and Alor Star, in the north west of Malaya, I realized that I needed a latrine very urgently. My purpose was becoming extremely essential. We had not got so much as a bucket in our wagon. I told my immediate neighbours, and within minutes I was being held out of the open door of a moving goods wagon by four British Army officers while I relieved myself. I was not a hearty physical person, and this public intimacy was unbearably embarrassing. I still remember it as the most undignified experience of my life.

After a journey of more than a thousand miles from Singapore, the train ran into Ban Pong station. We were ordered to disembark, horribly stiff. I was now a railway man whether I liked it or not.

★ ★ ★

Ban Pong was a big village which had the merit, for the Japanese Army, of being the closest point on the Siamese railway system to the coastal plain of southern Burma, more than two hundred miles away over the mountains. It had become the nub of the planned new Japanese railway system, connecting Singapore with Bangkok and on to Phnom Penh, Saigon, Hanoi and China. All these lines would be linked up to Burma, and ultimately to India. The village was now a boom town, with extensive camps and hutments, its railway station jammed with trains, the river clogged with boats. Nearby at Nong Pladuk there were sidings, shunting engines, strange four-wheeled bogies and a lot of activity around the station.

So much became clear to us as time went on. At first, all we saw were open-fronted shops in buildings made of teak and mahogany, attap huts and stone colonial houses. Children and chickens ran about the streets, small elegant women in bright clothes tended little stalls piled with vivid red and green chillies, mangoes and pawpaws. We passed one such market under some trees near the station. Ban Pong seemed to have one long main street, with some other streets zigzagging off it. On the outskirts were the usual cultivated areas, patches of wild scrub, and the forest.

We were marched along a road for a little way. There was a camp of long, low huts of attap, and it was obvious even from the road that the end of each hut sloped down into a muddy lake of floodwater. The far end of each hut must be a stinking malarial pool. We were allocated among these huts, in which men crowded into the higher parts, their sleeping spaces reduced to a couple of feet, in order to get away from the water. This was named, with deadpan banality, the Wet Camp. It was obviously a lethal place.

After a few days, a group of about a hundred of us were sent a quarter of a mile away to another camp. This turned out be a workshop, staffed by Japanese mechanics and engineers, and we would be assisting them with repairs. It was a respite for us.

There were four officers in our group: Major Bill Smith,

Captain Bill Williamson, a lieutenant called Gilchrist and myself. There was also a senior warrant officer, Sergeant-Major Lance Thew of the Royal Army Ordnance Corps.

We were not an especially well-knit group. Smith and Gilchrist were much older than us, members of the Straits Settlement Volunteer Force, raised from among the planters and merchants of Singapore and their employees. Many of them played brave parts in the fighting, but there was always a certain reserve between them and the regular army, a feeling that their enjoyment of the good life had made them careless about the defence of Singapore, and I never found much in common with these two with whom I was now forced to share a hut.

Major Smith had been a low-grade Colonial Service officer and was the kind of character whose lack of intelligence is cruelly punished in extreme conditions. A tall, angular figure, he had difficulty understanding what was happening to him, and was excluded instinctively from any decision-making. We took to calling him 'Daddy'. Gilchrist was a very small person in his fifties, and had no worthwhile military experience or other skills; he was one of those men who in the harsh conditions of captivity could quickly and unfairly be judged not much good at anything.

With Bill Williamson I hit it off much better. He was a pleasant, unassuming and very competent person, and acted as the camp adjutant. He got things done, and when I saw he was learning Japanese I knew we could get along. He lent me his Japanese grammar and helped me to identify some of our gaolers' basic vocabulary as they walked past our hut or shouted at us in the open areas of the camp. I made sure that Williamson and I were in adjoining bed-spaces.

Sergeant-Major Thew was an extremely capable technician, for whom the army was merely another outlet for his lifelong passion for mechanics. He had a little radio shop back in Sunderland, and he made and repaired radios for the Ordnance Corps before his capture. He was well built, a powerful looking man, and had a scarred face, but he had acquired the scar in a wartime accident and the streetfighter's appearance belied his other-worldly character. He loved the craft of radio telegraphy, and dreamed of radios as I did of trains. He was an extraordinary and luckless man.

Our single long hut could hold about a hundred men and was little more than ingenious tents made from local vegetation: bamboo and attap, a big leaf-palm, tied together with a rope-like creeper. The floor was trodden earth, which became hard and solid, but under each bed-space was still raw clay, which sprouted even in the dark and weedy things poked up through the planks of the bed. The cool dark spaces also sheltered wriggling and crawling life, of which the most terrifying were scorpions and snakes. Williamson and I used to walk around the camp, talking about books and languages, and I once idly tugged on a creeper hanging from a tree; the snake I found myself holding was luckily some harmless python.

For nausea, little could surpass the big hairy centipedes which seemed about a foot long, if you could imagine them ever lying still and straight enough to measure instead of undulating and trembling. Lesser creatures we learned to take in our stride: cockroaches scurried like metal mice and if you stepped on one with a calloused bare foot it burst with a sound like a plastic bottle. The thatch was riddled with beetles, ants and spiders, dropping on to our sleeping bodies at night.

Since Nong Pladuk was the point of origin of the new railway, the yards were full of track-laying equipment which needed constant repair at Ban Pong, given the breakneck speed at which it was being used. The equipment consisted of road-rail lorries, which could run on flat road surfaces or on railway tracks, and what at first looked like long low wagons on which rails were stacked. In fact these wagons were a couple of four-wheeled bogies held together by bolting in position two ordinary steel rails. This created a rigid eight-wheeled wagon body on which rails and sleepers were loaded, and pushed up the line behind the tracklaying gangs. When they had emptied it, they would dismantle the two rails holding it together and lay the bogies by the side of the track, and the inexorable tractor would push up another wagonload until all the wagons were empty. The bogies would then be replaced on the track and pulled back to Nong Pladuk for the next load.

The pace of work was intense, the prisoners driven by Japanese guards under a hot sun on a patchy diet that was just about adequate in Ban Pong, where food was relatively easily available outside the camp, but got progressively poorer the further up the line you went. The tracklaying gangs were thus unknowingly working themselves to death.

A flat-bottomed steel rail weighed about 70 pounds per yard, and usually came in 24-foot lengths. A rail is therefore a massive thing for hungry men to lift and manoeuvre into position, and one rail followed another relentlessly on this criminal folly of a line. The steel rails were spiked directly to the wooden sleepers by hammering in big steel nails. This is brutally heavy work: exhausted and ill-fed city boys and dragooned Asian labourers did not have a chance. Rest periods were rare, and any slackening was met with abuse or violence.

Railways have always broken the bodies and spirits of their builders, I knew that already: the Panama Railway cost the lives of one in five of its workforce; the railroads across the Rockies had demanded appalling sacrifices; the Alpine tunnels were considered to be death traps, even for the well-fed peasant boys who built them. Yet the Burma-Siam railway was unique; to a mind haunted by images from biblical times it recalled the construction of the Pyramids; it was not only the last cruel enterprise of the railway age, but the worst civil engineering disaster in history.

Of course I write this in retrospect, but even when I reached Ban Pong I knew there was something careless and therefore evil about the project. Though my own luck still held: all I had to do was to help repair the lorries, the bogies and the engines. We were working for Japanese railway fitters, turners, welders, most of them humane men interested in getting a job done, and their workshops were not cruelly managed. I could respect them and they let me and my comrades alone.

Some way out of camp, however, you could see the reality of a hand-built railway. Soon after I got there I walked out one day – I had been appointed Messing Officer by Major Smith, or rather by Williamson acting through Smith, so I could move around fairly freely in search of food – and came to a place where a gap had been torn out of a hill. Hundreds of half-naked men were passing the earth in baskets to one end of the cutting, and were using the soil to build an embankment on the far side, one big basket between two struggling men. There was scarcely a piece of machinery among them, they were working with saws and axes and picks. They were clearing bamboo clumps fifty yards wide, feathery bamboo with deep roots that had to be torn out by hand with ropes, and chopping out tropical hardwoods with blunt implements. I knew from Bukit Timah Hill what that was like: a fight with tools. Perhaps some of Stalin's canals were built like this; few railways have been.

In order to keep our group fed, I used some of the ten cents a day we were paid by the Japanese to buy food from the local peasants and traders. Rice, cooking oil, some eggs and bits of fish; fresh vegetables when we could afford them; and sometimes a few ducks or even a pig. Flesh could only be paid for in the wages of theft. I used a 44-gallon drum, with one end replaced by a door, as an oven; we had huge shallow iron bowls for cooking masses of rice.

Occasionally I would have to go down to the town with a couple of men and a Japanese guard. He turned these occasions into an outing for a different kind of sustenance. He would stop us at a coffee shop and hand me his rifle and disappear into the back of the shop. I would stand there in the shade at the front of the store, a prisoner holding my enemy's loaded rifle as he visited a whore. Out in the hot sun, Siamese villagers walked by, the street stretched away to the edge of town. The guard knew and I knew there was nothing I could do with his gun and that I had nowhere to go.

It was at Ban Pong that I discovered an uncanny bureaucratic oddity. Bill Williamson and I were called to the Japanese administrative office one day. The Japanese officer had a huge stack of POW registration forms, several thousand of them, piled on his desk. I saw that mine was on top of the heap. I had been allocated Serial Number 1; the numbers allocated ran well into the 20,000s. It made me feel exposed, important in a way that I would have shunned. In the lottery of war soldiers talk about their numbers coming up and this singularity was an unpleasant joke.

We were surviving, but that was not enough. All that energy which the surrender had stifled was still there, we were rebellious and eager to know what was happening in the war. We wanted to know if the tide had been turned; we wanted to win, even if only vicariously. Since we were young and clever and knew about machines, since most of us had been reared on enthusiasm for popular mechanics and loved the idea of transport and communication, we did the logical thing, and started to build a radio.

Enthusiasts had taken bits of radios from Changi, broken down and scattered among a number of men so that each had only a tiny piece to be responsible for. We also had headphones. But making one was still like assembling a mechanical jigsaw puzzle. We settled on an incredibly modest attempt to build a battery operated set that could receive All India Radio from New Delhi. But even this was a tall order. We had to reinvent wireless telegraphy, scouring a tropical prison camp for the materials we needed. We bartered stolen Japanese tools with a local trader for valves. I worked out the optimum length for an aerial for receiving the correct wave-length of the station; but we could not afford to display a full length antenna, so we had to make do with a 'quarter-wave aerial'. Men would be given strange tasks: to find flat unfolded silver paper, or small pieces of flat aluminium; or lengths of wire of a certain gauge; or quantities of wax. No-one asked any questions; the prisoners' discretion was wonderful.

Thew was our radio maker. He was in many ways a dotty amateur scientist, absent-minded and insensitive to risk. Making a radio at that time required a lot of soldering, and arrangements were made in the cookhouse for the soldering iron to be heated under conditions of great secrecy. But how can you carry a red-hot iron in secret? Thew once solved the problem simply by forgetting where he was. He walked across the main square holding the glowing iron, as though for a prisoner-of-war the most natural thing in the world was to be wandering around with this essential tool of electronics in his hand.

We arranged a security system in the main hut. POWs apparently engaged in reading or doing their woodwork were stationed in strategic places, on the lookout for guards, while Thew worked in his bed-space with assistance from the others. We finished one night, and Thew crawled under his blankets and tuned his primitive detector. He had a pencil in his hand, I remember, and he emerged smiling from ear to ear with some scribbled notes. It had worked beautifully. He had heard the crisply modulated English voice of the announcer cutting through the static.

The radio was primitive, little more than a crystal set, tuned to a single frequency and incapable of sending a signal; it was also a simple masterpiece. It was about 9 inches long by 4 inches wide, and fitted snugly into a coffee tin with a false top, which we filled with ground nuts. It sat there innocently by Thew's bed, a rusty silver tin can hiding the valves and condensers.

The routine was the same each evening. Prisoners would be detailed to stand around the camp and warn us about the approach of any Japanese, many of them not even being told why they were doing it. Thew would couple the set to the aerial, which was hidden in the rafters, switch on the apparatus and burrow down under his blanket with the headphones on. He was always the operator, since he was by far the best person to deal with any tuning problems if the signals were lost or distorted. The news bulletin took about ten minutes, and he would note down the main items with his pencil as he listened. The precious scrap of paper was handed around a small group afterwards, as Thew dismantled the set and placed it back in its hiding place. I still remember his strong, careful handling of the crude little machine, the tenderness of the true craftsman.

We were stealing back information from our captors. We

heard about the victories of the Solomon Islands, of New Guinea and Guadalcanal, and that the Germans had been stopped in Russia and driven back in North Africa. From November 1942, when our radio started operating, we felt again that we might eventually be liberated, that we were on the winning side.

Lance Thew could be a hair-raising innocent. We were free to ramble around the area, and often came upon small Siamese settlements. Thew had stumbled on an 'empty Buddhist temple', as he put it wonderingly, with a small gold-leaf-covered statue of Buddha in a dusty niche, and a few dead flowers around the image. He helped himself to the statue: a nice souvenir of Siam. When we discovered it in his bed-space, we ordered him vehemently to return it. We were afraid of some frightening chain of repercussions; less rationally, we dreaded the fixed smile of the deity and the feeling of bad karma that grew around him. I wondered later, and not idly, whether what happened was a kind of punishment for this blasphemy.

Perhaps what Thew did was just another symptom of our devil-may-care attitude, our defiance of the Japanese and of imprisonment. We still felt invincible. Surrender hadn't brought weakness and submission.

All that winter, however, the long trains kept coming to Ban Pong station, a mile to the west of our workshop. Covered goods wagons packed with filthy, hungry men were pulled from Singapore and unloaded their freight of captive labour. The chugging Japanese and British engines had to use, in place of coal, the local wood, which sent up a characteristic thin and aromatic smoke, and at least twice a week we would see trails of it drifting over the trees when the noise of an arriving train had died away and the locomotive would be standing in the station, quietly expiring. The railway was burning men.

CHAPTER FIVE

THE OFFICIAL MEDIATOR between gaolers and prisoners at Ban Pong was a young Japanese interpreter with an American accent, whom we called Hank the Yank. He was a friendly enough man, and when early in February 1943 he came and told us that we should be ready to move the following day, the instruction caused no more than the usual spasm of anxiety.

At least we knew where we were going: Kanchanaburi, a town about thirty miles to the north west of Ban Pong on the new railway's route to Burma over the Three Pagodas Pass. We were now pretty certain that the railway was destined to reach Moulmein in Burma, where the river Salween empties into the Gulf of Martaban. Relieved, therefore, that we were not being sent much further up the line, from which horrific rumours were already coming back as the work parties went deeper into the wild hilly country of Kanchanaburi Province, we packed our gear with aggressive good humour. We had our cookhouse equipment, our medical stores such as they were, and our bits of furniture – the odd stool or home-made table, a little unit of shelving made from discarded boxes: things we had scavenged and put together over the past few months to make our huts orderly and bearable.

We were cocky, taking risks and laughing at our captors because we did not yet fully understand the nature of the risks we were running. Life could still seem the kind of game it always becomes when young men are cooped up together and before they discover they are trapped. We almost flaunted our stolen goods. I had a saw strapped to the outside of a canvas bag which I had acquired before leaving Changi; we had whole workboxes of tools hidden in our baggage: chisels, hammers, screwdrivers, that soldering iron . . . If it had been a matter of cutting through bars to escape this prison, we would have flown away long ago.

We piled into a lorry driven by a British private soldier. I sat in front, with a Japanese guard between me and the driver. A small convoy of vehicles turned westwards out of the camp, leaving the bamboo fence and the long hut behind us. Halfway to Kanchanaburi, or 'Kanburi' as it was universally known among the English prisoners, our driver slipped his foot on the clutch in the sticky heat and bumped into the lorry in front of us. The Japanese guard went berserk, screaming incoherently at the driver, pushing him out of the cab. I got down carefully on the other side, keeping my distance but looking at the guard intently.

This was a man full of rage and fear and resentment. No older than me, and outnumbered by his prisoners, he nevertheless had absolute power over us and now he was close to losing control. Retribution would be his, no matter what we did. He went on berating the driver. I thought about the stories, about the nurses' bodies in the surf at Banka Island. He gripped his rifle so that his knuckles paled under the olive brown of his skin. But he calmed in time, and no blow was struck. He ordered us back into the cab and the lorries moved off again.

Until now, all our contact with Japanese violence had somehow been at second hand, for even the severed heads of the poor Chinese back in Singapore were not a direct threat to us as British prisoners. I had never, until that moment, seen any fellow prisoner threatened with assault, though of course the tracklaying gangs were being grossly abused simply by the nature of their work. It is true that I had seen men forced to stand hour after hour in the full blaze of the sun for some infringement of camp discipline; but no direct physical attack. I felt now that I had come very close to violence that morning. It was hard to tell if this was one unstable man, or whether his nerves were fraying because of some larger calamity; perhaps a foreknowledge of eventual defeat. This weird confrontation on the road, with the green of the big mango trees and nipah palms for a backdrop, seemed a step further towards danger, and away from the shreds of civilization and comfort we were still clinging to. Milepost zero of the railway was just east of Ban Pong. I began to fear that the higher numbers would be negative ones, measured on a brutal new scale.

At first, we seemed to have landed on our feet again. Kanburi was then a little town surrounded by the remains of a defensive brick wall. Within it was a main street, with the river Mae Klong parallel to it on the far side of the walls. There were shops here, and some substantial wooden buildings, corrugated-iron huts and patches of overgrown waste land. Some buildings backed on to the river, their yards running down to its banks, which were high above the muddy brown flood.

A little way outside town was the main 'Airfield Camp', as the Japanese called it, and to the south lay the railway workshops where our technical knowledge would once again shelter us from the worst. The workshop camp was known to the Japanese as the

'Sakamoto Butai', meaning the camp under the command of Major Sakamoto. It consisted, as usual, of a series of bamboo huts thatched with attap which were used as workshops, stores and offices, similar quarters for the prisoners in a separate compound, and a small group of better huts for the Japanese. Between each hut was a space about a hut's width. The latrines were at right angles to the hut: deep trenches (though never deep enough) with planks across them and sheltered by a bamboo and attap cabin. A not very convincing bamboo fence ran around the entire site, with a guardroom at the main entrance near the road. One bored guard stood at the other side of the camp perimeter, a few hundred yards from the railway.

Sidings had been laid out near the town; closer in, there was a locomotive yard with a wooden water tower and a huge firewood dump. All of these engines burned wood, and steam engines are voracious consumers of timber. Once again, our camp was a repair-shop for the construction gangs' tractors, the road-rail lorries and, as time went on, the locomotives themselves.

Our group was joined by officers and NCOs from other camps. Fred Smith, a sergeant in the Royal Artillery, was one of them; a regular soldier, a first-rate technician and a person who combined stoicism and good humour with immense physical toughness. Later I would realize that he was one of the most impressive men I was ever likely to meet. Here too were Major Jim Slater, a textile machinery manufacturer turned artilleryman who immediately superseded Bill Smith as our senior officer and whose droll and unquenchable pessimism made him the camp Jeremiah; Harry Knight, an easygoing Australian engineer from one of the Malayan mining companies, a useful and trustworthy man; and Alexander Morton Mackay, another artillery officer, who had been born in Scotland but spent a lot of time in Canada.

He was in his early forties, vigorous and companionable, more youthful in spirit than his age seemed to allow. Of all my fellow-prisoners 'Mac' or Morton, as he was usually known, was the one who became closest to me.

Two other men in our hut at Kanburi can now only be thought of together, though they had nothing in common at all: Captain Jack Hawley and Lieutenant Stanley Armitage. The latter was a quiet studious Irishman; Hawley was his polar opposite, a smooth and showy character who modelled himself on romantic film-stars like Ronald Colman – a man who enjoyed the clubs and the ease of pre-war Singapore, where he had worked for the British American Tobacco Company.

* * *

In the workshops, we found subtle ways of keeping overworked lorries in apparently good mechanical condition, but with an unfortunate tendency to break down a week after they left our hands. I was learning the arts of subterfuge and quiet resistance, and I was becoming a competent thief.

I took on the job of unofficial camp carpenter, making wooden paths so that the frequent rain would not force us to wade through liquid mud. I found that by far the easiest way to acquire materials and tools was to walk into the workshop stores in broad daylight and to walk out again with the goods prominently displayed. I was never challenged. Little did I know that I was profiting by their carelessness, and that it had another darker side to it.

The Japanese were already making us conform to Tokyo time, which meant that we usually rose in the dark. When they also declared that officers had to work, they made me timekeeper and signwriter. My job was to sound the gong in the main workshop as the signal for starting and stopping work. This gong had to be sounded eight times a day, and the clock that was supposed to guide me in issuing my reverberant signals was a small Japanese timepiece perched on a shelf by the generating plant.

I soon realized that the working day could be ten hours long, yet contain less than ten hours. I conformed carefully to the official starting and finishing times in the morning and evening, but in between them I began to fiddle with the clock and as each day passed, each intermediate starting time got later, while the intermediate finishing times got earlier and earlier. Now we were stealing time as well as information from our gaolers. This was a popular and revolutionary approach to labour control, and even some of the Japanese mechanics approved of it. Unfortunately, I was found out, and a Japanese soldier was given my job. My only punishment was to be told to stick to signwriting and painting.

More than anything else, we wanted to delay them, to hinder their efforts, to do shoddy work in such a way that the origin of the nuisance could not be traced back to one man or group. Even people who were working on tasks like stonebreaking – which was considered a 'light' job – would work unbelievably slowly, giving the absolute minimum of co-operation. I think every prisoner became a slacker, a saboteur, and of course some of us are doing it to this day, having spent so much time creating quiet havoc in our early manhood.

We could not surrender the hope of escape. The country was, in a sense, a vast open prison, and we thought that there might with luck be a way out through the north of Siam. But in order to go anywhere after the first couple of miles, information would be vital – information in the form of a map.

It was always very important for me to know where I was, to locate myself precisely on a grid: to record, list, and categorize the world around me as far as possible. It was a way of creating certainty in a world now robbed of all certainty. Of all of us in the camp, it was characteristic of me to make the map. As official signwriter, I had access to pencils, and there was always paper for mechanical drawing in the workshop. I took a large sheet of plain paper, over two-feet square, from the chief engineer's desk. In the storehouse I noticed a small atlas that included much of South East Asia and Siam; I 'borrowed' it and slowly copied the relevant pages with a pencil, working on a scale of about 50 miles to the inch. It was too small for practical purposes really, but it gave me such hope as I filled in details gleaned from POW lorry drivers who had been some distance up the railway, and memorized topographic facts from Japanese plans and documents left lying around the stores.

The map also showed the route of the railway, which I was able to work out as we had a chain of informants all the way up the line. The track hugged the river for a considerable stretch, and if we stayed close to both we might be able to scavenge food more easily if we made a run for it. But mapping the railway had its own intrinsic pleasures.

This was a clandestine piece of artistry, but at the time the secrecy was instinctive, an expression of prisoner's caution rather than any real awareness of the risks I was running. No-one had told us not to make maps, yet it was so obviously a deadly business that I took great care to conceal mine. I kept it in a bamboo tube and hid it lovingly. It was covered in neat pencilled place-names, the boundaries of Siam and its rivers drawn as elegantly as I knew how. The paper took on an antique texture, softened, with wavy edges from my handling of it and the moisture it absorbed from the humid air.

* * *

If anyone wanted to walk out of the camp, there was very little to stop them, and we had soon explored the whole area. Dense feathery bamboo covered much of the ground; big fruit trees were so abundant we hardly knew what to do with the fruit – mangos, durians, pawpaws. Beyond us to the north and west you could see broken and densely-green hills.

Kanburi and its markets were less than a mile away. We had permission to buy food in the town, so we did not starve, even if the staple diet was still rice and a basic stew. We sometimes bought Siamese delicacies like a fried banana concoction made by peasant women over a pan of hot oil, or dried fish.

It was becoming clearer all the time that the Japanese engineers had decided to take a most difficult route for the railway, and that they were going to stay as close to the river Kwae Noi as possible; this allowed them to supply the labour-gangs by boat. This also meant that they were imposing terrible demands on our comrades, for the limestone hills came right down to the river along this part of its meandering course, and the prisoners and labourers would have to hack through them. Viaducts and cuttings and trestle bridges would be needed to support the track, and would have to be built with axes, saws, spades and hands – and nothing else. We were not sorry to be where we were.

We could still find humanity among our gaolers. In Kanburi there was a very reasonable officer called Ishi, a Cambridge graduate by his own account who, whether or not he had ever been near the fens, spoke excellent English. He liked to talk engineering with us, and even to argue about the war. We could ask him what was happening, and he would give us some official version of events in New Guinea, though he admitted that they had already lost the island of Guadalcanal in the Solomons. One day he said in his anglicized drawl that if we were really so interested in the war why didn't we take out a newspaper subscription? Thinking that we were victims of some deadpan sense of humour different to our own, we gave him the money he asked for – saved out of our 'pay'. Within a week, we were taking delivery of the English-language *Bangkok Chronicle*, by post. This paper was now a Japanese organ, full of disinformation, but by reading it critically we could still learn a lot. One stirring article told how German forces were 'advancing westwards' in North Africa, which was a strange way for Rommel to fulfil his objective of capturing the Suez Canal. In this way we followed, with increasing pleasure, the Axis retreats in Russia, Africa and Asia.

But we should have been much, much, more careful than we were of an increasingly cornered and baffled enemy. At the workshop camp the Japanese with whom we came most into contact were reasonable men. But not all of our captors were decent human beings caught up despite themselves in a war which had taken them thousands of miles from home. We had a pet kitten in the camp, a seductive black stray, and we doted on it. It was a creature more helpless than ourselves that we could look after. One day it was playing in the dust of the compound when a Korean guard was passing. He unslung his rifle with its long fixed bayonet and skewered the little animal, as though he were going to toast it.

* * *

We had a radio working again, and the set now had a few refinements. Fred Smith had become our second radio maker. He had stolen an old mains radio from a house on the Bukit Timah road in Singapore and repaired it back at Changi with a few valves which he had also somehow acquired, and before he was sent up the railway had taken his improvised set to pieces and hidden it to evade the Japanese searches. Lance and Fred were using a modified buzzer from a field telephone set with an old battery as a power supply, and after many hours of tinkering they could tune the set to the right frequency and damp down the sound so that the BBC voices were intelligible.

It was still the same ritual every night: the tense guard around the hut, Thew huddled under his blanket, the earnest discussion of the news afterwards. Unfamiliar names on hazily remembered maps: Kharkov, Kursk, the Trobriand Islands. Lines of victory as well as lines of defeat were now connecting us to the world at war.

The news was passed along by trusted men, through hundreds of different mouths, around the workshop compound and up the miles of railway track to the real death camps. We made sure that one reliable man, Gunner Tomlinson, was placed on the ration train going up the line and briefed him on what to tell the men suffering there. It was difficult for them and for us to distinguish truth from rumour, to know how much to believe. Who knows how the news was distorted as it went along, how truth became legend and vice versa; but having these scraps of information was a wonderful boost to our morale and to our sense of connection with the world we had lost. The radio meant more to prisoners than anyone can imagine: it literally gave meaning and normality to our lives; now we felt we knew what we were living for.

Reading was an important part of that normality and dignity. I had a Bible, an Authorized Version, which I read constantly. Later, I swapped it with an Australian called Harkness for the Moffatt edition of 1926. I still have it: the book survived everything. The once-black boards are worn down to soft grey fibre, with smudges of black ink traceable on it; the spine board is gone. It was underlined almost throughout by Harkness in blue fountain-pen, meticulous neat small capitals annotating every column of every page of every book of the Bible. The widow pages at the end of each book are covered in the same tidy blue script. My own Bible in Ban Pong and Kanburi was annotated in the same way as I read the New Testament consecutively through with a bookmark, again and again.

The Book of Revelation continued to exalt me. 'I am Alpha and Omega, the beginning and the ending . . .' Its vision of apocalypse and of last things, of a world falling apart only to be recomposed in light and happiness, had been at the heart of the Chapel's belief and of those long sermons at Charlotte Street. Nothing since my arrival in Malaya had persuaded me that disaster could not strike; that empires could not disintegrate; or that human beings could not find themselves helpless in extreme situations.

Perhaps only prisoners held at an enemy's pleasure, without fixed term or rules, can understand Job's bafflement with his God:

I am full of confusion; therefore see thou mine affliction; for it increaseth. Thou huntest me as a fierce lion; and again thou showest thyself marvellous upon me. Thou renewest thy witnesses against me, and increasest thine indignation upon me; changes and war are against me.

We could not talk about many intimate things together, but we could talk about religion, even though most of my fellow prisoners were members of the Church of England and I was a member of a Baptist sect. I recall exchanges of passionate letters between young men in the camp exhorting each other to greater spiritual effort. It was a way of encouraging the best in our humanity, and it all helped us to survive.

I still wanted to learn, to improve. I remember making careful notes on Hindustani on green scrap paper, neat columns of vocabulary and tenses; and even collaborating with my friend Williamson to learn some Japanese. We mastered a bit of basic vocabulary, enough to help us catch some of what the guards were saying.

The year 1943 wore on, the balminess of spring giving way to the ovenlike temperatures of summer. We grew almost accustomed to the humidity, the rains, the rich black mud which they created, and we maintained our elusive inner life which the Japanese couldn't touch. We were now used to walking around half-naked, our thin bodies browned in the sun, and to the permanent itch and rawness of ingrained dirt on the skin that comes when there is never enough soap to go round.

The camp at Kanburi was uncomfortable and oppressive; on the whole, however, it was a 'good' camp. Almost all the work was skilled; there were few calls on us for outside work, and relatively little hard labouring; the Japanese in charge were, as at Ban Pong, engineers rather than professional Imperial Army soldiers, some of whom were ideological fanatics, or Korean camp guards who took out on their prisoners the contempt with which they were themselves treated by the Japanese; and we could get to Kanburi and its precious food markets in half an hour.

Others were not so well situated. One evening in April, I noticed some filthy, depressed and tired British soldiers collapsed against their packs outside the main gate of the camp, on the road to the north. As I walked out, I realized that there were hundreds of them. They lay around with the unmoving stillness of men who are already in a bad way, and know that there is worse to come. One of the men told me that they had just walked thirty miles from Ban Pong with no food and very little water, driven by aggressive Korean guards, and that they were supposed to keep walking up country. None of them knew how far, or what awaited them when they got there.

This ragged army of neglected soldiers scattered around the grass by the side of the road was a stark reminder of the Japanese Army's capacity for that carelessness which is really an indifference to, a crime against, humanity. These exhausted men formed the advance guard of 'F' and 'H' Forces, sent from Singapore to Ban Pong in special trains. The trains from there to the higher reaches of the Burma-Siam line, which was now nearing completion, were filled night and day with new rails and equipment, so these men – 'on loan', one of them explained, from the Japanese Malayan Administration – were expected to hump themselves and their equipment to their work stations in the hills.

For the next two months, columns of bedraggled men passed the front of the workshops at Kanburi. We did what we could, sharing food and water with them, but they were already lost. Through some crazy oversight, they were never transferred to the Japanese Siamese Administration which, accordingly, did not feel obliged to look after them. Those responsible for their feeding and care sat in offices in Singapore, a thousand miles away.

I have tried not to anticipate, to use hindsight too much in my telling of this story so far, but the fate of these already half-addled men deserves recording here. 'F' and 'H' Forces had the highest casualty rates of all the POW drafts on the railway. They were to give the work a final boost, to complete the line earlier than planned – a kind of expendable shock force. Some of them would walk two hundred miles up into the hills; one in three of them would die, and many of the rest be crippled for the rest of their lives by illness or injury.

We speculated even then that there may have been some cruel method in this madness. Admiral Yamamoto, the strategist of the attack on Pearl Harbor and probably the greatest naval commander in the history of Japan, was shot down over Bougainville Island in the Solomons on 18th April, just before 'F' and 'H' Forces were sent out to walk to the end of the railway. Was what happened to them some demented form of mass punishment? Did the death of their leader provoke in the Japanese a desire for some further vast humiliation of their prisoners? These were the kinds of questions with which we tormented ourselves, and to which I still have no answers.

The men passing the camp would spend the night in the open, with no protection from the mosquitos that plagued us after dark. When they walked on, they left bits of kit behind them to lighten their loads. How much would they have left, I wondered, by the end?

At about the same time the first of the civilian labourers arrived. At first there were thin columns of Asians, Chinese, Indians, Malays, Indonesians, straggling along the main road from Ban Pong towards Kanburi. Later on there was a flood, a tide of unhappy men, and sometimes even women and children, streaming towards the upper reaches of the Kwae Noi and the most distant camps on the railway route. Like the POWs, they had been summoned to accelerate the completion of the railway. Unlike the POWs, however, the labourers had no organization. They were individuals, or families, with no structure or chain of command.

It was possible even then, with my small knowledge of the scale of events overtaking all of us, to guess that these pathetic labourers would die in enormous numbers and be the biggest victims of the railway.

Yet even here, in a prison camp close to men responsible for organized cruelty on this huge scale, and capable of unthinking, spontaneous cruelty to individuals, I was still able to take pleasure in the machines I loved and to which I was now so unwillingly close. We retain more innocence than people imagine, even when death is yards away. One day, soon after the departure of 'F' and 'H' Forces, from the direction of the new Burma line, a column of smoke and steam rose up. There had not been a locomotive on these new tracks before, and I was immediately aroused. The train, which was a small one of three or four stores wagons, came right into the camp. It was propelled by one of the most amazing steam engines I had ever seen. It was a beautifully preserved, turn-of-the-century machine built by Krauss of Munich, its origin described on a magnificent brass plate. I remember the joy of its sudden appearance on that dusty and degraded siding under the palm trees. Its cowcatcher stood out proudly beneath its high waisted chimney; its gleaming black boiler and brass trim brought with it ghosts of journeys between spa towns, perfumed goodbyes and lives gambled away.

* * *

My time as an involuntary professional railway man came to an abrupt end in August 1943.

Whether we were betrayed, or the Japanese just got lucky, I will never know; I have spent many nights awake, in the past half century, piecing it all together, trying to trace the leak. Perhaps someone boasted in the hearing of a guard about an Allied victory; perhaps some fool was keeping a diary of the news passed to him by the drivers who were our couriers. It mattered desperately, once upon a time, to know who had betrayed us, for in our eyes he was as much a traitor as if he had informed on us knowingly. After the war, the survivors would have gone after him with deadly intent – if we could have been sure. But all we had was the endless, painful uncertainty, rubbing like sandpaper on tender skin.

On 29th August 1943, instead of dismissing us from the normal early morning roll call, the Japanese guards kept every POW standing at attention in the assembly area. It was still half dark, quite chill in the strengthening sun. A group of them walked back into the huts; the rest, unusually alert and aggressive, surrounded us with fixed bayonets. We could hear them moving around inside the huts, at first with no great energy or purpose; then something happened to set them off. A crescendo of pulling, clattering and dragging began.

An hour passed. The sun was now high and hot, but we were forbidden to move. Over a hundred of us stood rigidly in our vests and scraps of uniform. The search went on and on, belongings piling up behind us as they threw and carried things outside the hut. I couldn't see very much, but soon there was a small haystack of objects. And a lot of activity seemed to be centred near Thew's corner of the long hut.

After about three hours Thew was called, a Japanese guard

shouting his name. He went into the hut. We were dismissed, and turned to see piles of motorcar batteries, dynamos, boxes made of wood and tin, and an incredible variety of tools – all of them Japanese, and the remnant of what we had already sold to the local Siamese and Chinese villagers through the camp fence. A lorry drove up, and the whole heap of contraband was taken away. Thew was allowed to return to us; his shock was dreadful to behold. The guards had found the radio.

One of the men had been standing so that he could see inside our hut. The search party had seemed to take the whole business fairly casually, at first. They walked down the entire length of the dark space, picking up only a few odd articles. One Japanese, passing Thew's bed, saw something in the folds of a dark blanket. It probably looked like a tiny triangle of white paper, as small as a postage stamp in that weak morning light, but it must have stood out against the neatly-folded wool of Thew's bedding like a coy invitation to mischief: a little paper something out of place.

The guard, still possibly all innocence, flicked it with his finger and pulled. It was a small sheet of paper, and I knew it well. On it was a rather nice hand-drawn map of the Solomon Islands. We had copied it from an illustration in a Japanese newspaper which we had lifted from a guard, in order to help us follow the references on All India Radio to the savage fighting on Rendova, Munda and New Georgia in the Solomons. The blanket was whipped off the bed and there, stark and unmistakable, lay a pair of wireless headphones, the green canvas webbing and the black steel of the earpieces curled like a small sleeping animal.

In the ransacking they found, as we knew they must, not one but four small wireless sets in various stages of completion. We had kept busy, and lavished much care and attention on replicating our first success. Like the original one, the new sets were also neatly and beautifully made and fitted into coffee tins. The bottom of each tin was detachable and formed the bottom of the radio. It all fooled the casual observer, but these observers had now become sharply focused.

When we got back inside the huts, we found them in chaos. Every man went to look for his particular cache of forbidden goods, and found it barren. Every bag and box had been turned over; every sleeping space inspected. Even the passion-fruit creeper outside the officers' hut had been pulled off the wall and torn apart.

The day had turned black. The pessimists, Jim Slater their gloomiest spokesman, said that the entire camp would be exterminated. The optimists hoped that the discovery by itself might satisfy the Japanese, but they looked haggard as they said it, and the camp went to work that day in fear and silence. Thew was the centre of a great fog of helpless sympathy as he worked, unsmiling and tense, on a diesel engine in the shop. There was very little sleep in the hut that night. Whispered speculation ran among the bed-spaces like the bugs as they dropped on to the wooden floor from the roof thatch and scurried away.

Early next morning Thew and one other soldier, who was found to have more stolen Japanese stores than most of the others, were summoned by the Japanese Camp Commander and after a brief time inside his hut were seen to emerge into the sunlight, which was now 100 degrees in the shade. They stood to attention, a guard posted near them, and were still there a few hours later. This was standard punishment, we knew, and could last for a whole day or longer.

That afternoon, Thew disappeared for a little while, but reappeared carrying a heavy iron sledge-hammer. He was stationed out in the open again, far from the nearest shadow, beside a great block of wood and began to swing the hammer down on to the block, over and over again, blow after blow, hour after hour. The dull thud of metal on wood could be heard all over the camp, underneath all the other sounds, as men walked to and from the workshops. It was like a drum beat announcing some terrible, nameless event.

Thew was not a weak man, but none of us were fit, and certainly not fit for this kind of mindless mortar-and-pestling of a dead log. In the evening the officer in charge of the Japanese guards sent to the POW cookhouse for some food for Thew. The cooks did him proud: they prepared meat and vegetables representing rations for a number of men, raiding our meagre stocks of protein, and packed them into a large mess-tin, completely covered with a heap of innocuous boiled rice. The commander inspected the tin and passed it: the sticky white mass must have looked like additional punishment. Thew got his meal.

Late that night he was released, blistered, bruised and exhausted, and very burnt by the sun. How we saw so clearly that this was not the end of it I can't be sure – some instinct of foreboding, some accumulated knowledge of the Japanese habit of referring serious matters to new levels and departments, with each handing out its response – or punishment. This system, we thought, must now be in operation.

It is impossible to describe the emotional state of POWs at a time like this, as retribution gathered momentum. Work and feeding went on as if nothing had happened, but there was everywhere a desperate haunting fear, superimposed on the normal perpetual uncertainty which filled the mind of every prisoner. Little groups of men sat in odd corners of the huts or out in the yard, endlessly chewing over grim alternatives.

The first move was against Bill Williamson. He was summoned and told to accompany a party of men being sent up the railway. At the time it seemed he should be envied: the Japanese had clearly decided he was not important to our enterprise. He had been a good friend, but partings in wartime had to be conducted according to rules that averted too much emotion. Reticence was safer.

A week later Thew was taken away from the camp with all his kit. Though he had been allowed to go on working after the first round of punishment, he never for a moment imagined he was off the hook.

Two days after his removal a messenger from the main camp at Kanburi, about a mile away, came to the officers' hut. It had started, we heard, as soon as Thew got to the camp; a long interrogation followed by a terrible beating. He was then made to come to attention, barely able to stand, and forced to hold this position for fifty hours outside the guardroom, all day and all night for two days.

On 10th September, Fred Smith followed Thew to the airfield camp. He was not attacked violently, but he too was forced to stand to attention – for no less than four days, falling over asleep, kicked awake, and dragged upright again and again. Smith was an incredibly tough man, physically, but one hundred hours of agonizing forced alertness is more than any body can bear.

As always, this information came back in second- or third-hand form, made worse by distance. What we could not see with our own eyes took on dreadful proportions. The possibilities twisted off like threads into the future, each one more painful than the last, a maze in which there could be no good outcome. I have written of the uncertainty that eats at a prisoner's mind and fills his days with anxious tension: those three weeks were the hell of uncertainty – the only sure thing was that we were on the edge of the pit.

Any feeling of security was utterly false. We imagined them doing their paperwork, telephoning each other, wondering what to do next. It was like being on death row without a formal sentence. And in all this time, their curious mixture of carelessness and obsessive attention to detail revealed itself: there were no further searches. For all they knew, we had other radios and could easily have disposed of them during those weeks.

Nor could we forget the stories about Pomeroy, Howard and Kelly. In February two escape parties, one consisting of Captain Pomeroy and Lieutenant Howard, the other of three men led by a Sergeant Kelly, had left the railway near Kanburi. The two officers got quite far, but they would have had to walk through rough limestone country, stumbling over creepers, dense rough grass and thickets of bamboo. They probably did not have even a map as good as mine: what chance did they ever have?

Sergeant Kelly's group was the first to be recaptured, followed by Howard and Pomeroy. All six officers and men were then murdered, without any form of trial or court martial. We heard that they had been shot out of hand; we heard that they had been killed slowly, bayoneted to death one by one after being made to dig their own graves. No-one knew what to believe.

Day after day the officers in their hut in the Sakamoto Butai wondered and worried, inventing and cancelling different versions of the worst. I have often wondered why, under these circumstances, I kept my own map. It was now rolled up in a hollow bamboo tube in the back wall of our latrine behind the hut. It represented, I suppose, a slim chance – a remote glimmer of hope. It was the only carefully drawn general map of the area in the hands of any prisoner, as far as I knew, and I kept it in case we needed to run for it, in case we needed to set out on that thousand-mile walk to the Burma Road. And it was a beautifully drawn map.

On 21st September we found out what they intended for us.

Early in the morning four unshaven and untidy Japanese soldiers filed into the officers' hut. I recall that one of them was fat. One of the others said they were here to remove five officers to 'another camp'. There were nine officers living in our hut, and it so happened that seven of us were there when they came. This was what we had been waiting for; the end was coming with a group of squalid, indifferent camp guards. We did not need to speak among ourselves to feel intensely of the same mind about what was happening. I sat down. The fat Japanese read out the names of those he wanted: Major Smith, Major Slater, Major Knight, Lieutenant Mackay and Lieutenant Lomax.

As he spoke, a truck drew up outside. In the background, Captain Hawley and Lieutenant Armitage sat still. They said nothing for there was nothing that they could say or do. The Japanese gave us instructions to pack up at once and to get into the truck waiting outside. Beyond the reference to another camp we hadn't a clue where we were going.

The next few minutes were quiet panic. I dismantled my battered mosquito net and my old canvas camp bed and rolled them up. Everything else went into my kitbag, with some clothing and smaller things in a big shoulder pack and a haversack. The fragments of furniture made and collected over such a long period were discarded in the space of a moment; the rickety table, the bamboo stool, the clothes line and hooks and shelves: they had all become useless. The only thing of interest now was survival.

While bustling about I had to do some very quick thinking, which is not always good thinking. Since we were now in very great danger the prospects for us were poor, if the initiative was left in the hands of the Japanese. I knew that there was a good chance of a firing squad or hanging party at the end of the road they would bring us down. I considered – if you can call such an impulsive decision considered – that if we were going to make a break for it and head northwards, up country towards the Burma Road, then we would be better off with a map than without one. I decided to carry it with me, wherever we were going. It was my talisman of certainty; it gave a sense of direction to the blind steps we were now taking.

I asked permission to use the latrine and walked back to the attap and bamboo shelter around the hole in the ground. In my shirt pocket I had my 'diary', notes on books and incidents since the fall of Singapore written in minute script on small pieces of toilet paper, and I thought about throwing it down the latrine; but it seemed a pity to lose it, and it was so harmless. I could not think straight. After peeing for the sake of appearances, I reached into the hollow bamboo in the back wall where I kept the map. It came out without difficulty, and with it a black scorpion, very irritated, darting and wriggling. I shook it to the ground from the folded edges of the paper and it lunged at nothing with its venomous tail. The black ones were more dangerous, I'd been told. I have often wondered what would have happened to me if I had been stung by that insect.

No one saw me retrieve the map, which I tucked into my shirt. When I returned to the hut I slipped it into a Royal Signals instrument mechanic's leather bag in which I kept the smaller items of my kit. The scruffy guards kept a little way off. Their lack of interest in us screwed the tension up even further. It was as though we were being called by some large and slovenly organization for a job interview.

The five of us boarded the truck and sat on our untidy heaps of baggage. Japanese guards came and sat very close to us; they made us understand that any attempt at escape would have fatal consequences. The truck banged into gear and pulled off.

POWs moaned and groaned about everything, all day and every day; probably the whole British Army complained endlessly. It was a way of getting through the boredom of warfare and the worse tedium of captivity. Our men were nevertheless very much aware that their officers did the best they could, and that officers often had to take real risks on their behalf in standing up to the Japanese camp administration, and of course they knew about the discovery of the radio. When something went wrong, and they knew that something had now obviously gone very wrong, the 'other ranks' closed firmly behind us and gave us unshakable support. All the prisoners in the vicinity of our hut waved us off. Some saluted raggedly; some saluted us magnificently. Most of them never saw us again.

We were driven quickly out past the guardroom, the hard wooden seats of the lorry jolting us around, and then to the right, along the main Kanburi road. Driving panic and tension seized me; you feel as you approach extreme danger a throbbing in the head and a heaviness in the limbs, the impulse to flight being held down by a weight you can't shift. We barely spoke to each other; we barely had time. After a mile we were driven through the entrance to the main camp at Kanburi, where they had taken Thew and Smith. This main camp held several hundred men and the Japanese military here were in charge of all the POW camps on the lower stretch of the railway.

The truck pulled up just inside the main camp entrance, near the guardroom. We were ordered down and our kit was dumped on the ground. They told us to sort it out, and we gathered our pitifully shabby belongings and took responsibility for every piece of baggage. After a long delay some Korean guards searched our kit, but there was now little left which would be of interest to even the most diligent searcher – except for one thing. The Korean who rummaged through my kit failed to find it.

The guards conducted the five of us to the main guardroom where we were brusquely ordered to stand to attention, a few feet in front of the building and well away from any shade or protection from the sun. The guardroom was a flimsy three-sided wood and thatch structure, open in the front, with a table across the gap. A guard stood at attention on the side nearest the camp entrance; a few more were seated behind the table. Among them was a large, fat and rather elegantly-dressed white-haired man, who now proceeded to address us in fluent American English. He ordered us forward. His attitude was aggressive, sneering and hostile as he checked our identities, making contemptuous references to Western duplicity and cowardice throughout the short procedure.

He ordered us back into the sun. There we stood beside a long ditch, neatly spaced like five telegraph poles along a road. The time was ten o'clock in the morning.

The morning and afternoon dragged on, every minute almost an hour. When you are forced to stand stiffly to attention in a blazing hot sun you have nothing to do but think; yet thought is a process that should be directed by the will, and under extreme stress thoughts spin away on their own, racing faster and faster like a machine out of control, one that has lost the touch of a human hand.

There was nothing we could do about it now: we stood there,

knowing it was coming. The wretched little guardroom was no bigger than a domestic living room, and the few guards sprawling inside it or on guard behind us controlled the lives of several hundred men. So few to hold so many.

We stood for twelve hours with our backs to that hut. The nerves and flesh of the back become terribly sensitive and vulnerable when turned to an enemy. At any moment I expected to feel a rifle-butt on my spine, a bayonet thrust between my shoulder-blades. All we heard was their talk, their occasional rough laughter.

The intense heat of the sun, the irritation of flies and mosquitos feeding on sweat, itching skin, the painful contraction of eyes against the light and even the fear of violent death had been superseded, by the evening, by the even more powerful sensation of a burning thirst. They gave us nothing to drink, all day, but they allowed us occasionally to go to the latrine. On one of these visits I regretfully disposed of my diary. The flimsy pages covered with neat notes on books, on grammar, on lists of collectible stamps fluttered into the stinking trench.

As dusk fell the five of us were moved into a closer and more compact group in front of the guardroom. The darkness came on with singular abruptness. We were lit by a weak light from behind us in the guardroom. A time signal was heard as a noisy party of Japanese and Koreans approached through the dark from the direction of the camp offices. They looked like NCOs, their uniforms dishevelled, one or two of them unsteady on their feet. All of them carried pick-helves. They stopped to talk to the guards, as though exchanging ideas about what to do with us.

Major Smith was called out in front of our line, and told to raise his arms right up over his head. His tall, gaunt figure, his thin arms held out like a scarecrow's, looked terribly weak and pitiful. He stood there on the edge of the circle of light. I thought for a moment – a last gasp of hope – that this was the beginning of an advanced form of their endless standing to attention. A hefty Japanese sergeant moved into position, lifted his pick-handle, and delivered a blow across Smith's back that would have laid out a bull. It knocked him down, but he was trodden on and kicked back into an upright position. The same guard hit him again, hard. All the thugs now set to in earnest. Soon little could be seen but the rise and fall of pick-helves above the heads of the group and there were sickening thuds as blows went home on the squirming, kicking body, periodically pulled back on to its feet only to be knocked down again. Bill Smith cried out repeatedly that he was fifty years of age, appealing for mercy, but to no avail. The group of attackers seemed to move in concert with their crawling, bloodied victim into the darkness beyond the range of the miserable lighting from the guardroom, but the noises of wood on flesh continued to reach us from the dark of the parade ground.

They were using pickaxe-shafts: like solid, British Army issue handles, and perhaps that is indeed what they were. The guards behind us did not move. There was no expectation that we ourselves would move, intervene, run away: merely the slack, contemptuous knowledge that we were trapped. That first blow: like a labourer getting into the rhythm of his job, then the others joining in, a confused percussive crescendo of slaps and thuds on flesh and bone. They kept kicking him, getting him up, putting him down – until he stopped moving altogether, unconscious or dead, I could not tell. Nor could I tell how long it all took. How does one measure such time? Blows had replaced the normal empty seconds of time passing, but I think it took about forty minutes to get him to lie still.

The gang came back out of the night. My special friend Morton Mackay was called forward. I was next in line. As they started on Mackay and the rain of fearful blows commenced I saw to the side another group of guards pushing a stumbling and shattered figure back towards the guardhouse. Smith was still alive; he was allowed to drop in a heap in the ditch beside the entrance.

Mackay went down roaring like a lion, only to be kicked up again; within a matter of minutes he was driven into the semi-darkness and out of the range of the lights, surrounded by the flailing pick-helves which rose and fell ceaselessly. I remember thinking that in the bad light they looked like the blades of a windmill, so relentless was their action. In due course Mackay's body was dragged along and dumped beside Smith's in the ditch.

The moments while I was waiting my turn were the worst of my life. The expectation is indescribable; a childhood story of Protestant martyrs watching friends die in agony on the rack flashed through my mind. To have to witness the torture of others and to see the preparations for the attack on one's own body is a punishment in itself, especially when there is no escape. This experience is the beginning of a form of insanity.

Then me. It must have been about midnight. I took off my spectacles and my watch carefully, turned and laid them down on the table behind me in the guardroom. It was almost as if I was preparing to go into a swimming-pool, so careful was the gesture of folding them and laying them down. I must have had to take a couple of steps backward to perform this neat unconscious manoeuvre. None of the guards made a move or said a word. Perhaps they were too surprised.

I was called forward. I stood to attention. They stood facing me, breathing heavily. There was a pause. It seemed to drag on for minutes. Then I went down with a blow that shook every bone, and which released a sensation of scorching liquid pain which seared through my entire body. Sudden blows struck me all over. I felt myself plunging downwards into an abyss with tremendous flashes of solid light which burned and agonized. I could identify the periodic stamping of boots on the back of my head, crunching my face into the gravel; the crack of bones snapping; my teeth breaking; and my own involuntary attempts to respond to deep vicious kicks and to regain an upright position, only to be thrown to the ground once more.

At one point I realized that my hips were being damaged and I remember looking up and seeing the pick-helves coming down towards my hips, and putting my arms in the way to deflect the blows. This seemed only to focus the clubs on my arms and hands. I remember the actual blow that broke my wrist. It fell right across it, with a terrible pain of delicate bones being crushed. Yet the worst pain came from the pounding on my pelvic bones and the base of my spine. I think they tried to smash my hips. My whole trunk was brutally defined for me, like having my skeleton etched out in pain.

It went on and on. I could not measure the time it took. There are some things that you cannot measure in time, and this is one of them. Absurdly, the comparison that often comes to my mind is that torture was indeed like an awful job interview: it compresses time strangely, and at the end of it you cannot tell whether it has lasted five minutes or an hour.

I do know that I thought I was dying. I have never forgotten, from that moment onwards, crying out 'Jesus', crying out for help, the utter despair of helplessness. I rolled into a deep ditch of foul stagnant water which, in the second or two before consciousness was finally extinguished, flowed over me with the freshness of a pure and sweet spring.

I awoke and found myself standing on my feet. I do not recall crawling out of that ditch but the sun was already up. I was an erect mass of pain, of bloody contusions and damaged bones, the sun playing harshly on inflamed nerves. Smith and Slater were lying on the ground beside me, blackened, covered in blood and barely conscious. Mac and Knight were in a like state a few yards further away. We were only a few feet from the guardroom, close to the point where we had been standing the previous night. Slater was nearly naked; a pair of shorts and some torn clothing lay on the ground behind him, mud-stained and blood-stained.

The guards simply ignored us. They stood in front of a barely moving, battered pile of human beings under the fierce sun and acted as though we were not there.

By the middle of the morning I must have felt brighter because I began to wonder why I should stay standing up when the other four were lying down. I sagged at the knees and sprawled out beside Smith and Slater. There was still no response from the guards.

About noon, the large American-speaking Japanese interpreter sauntered over from the camp offices, squatted down beside us and inspected us with a critical eye. He sent a guard for a bucket of tea, which he offered to each of us from a mess-tin. Vague stirrings of life from the others; bodies in various horizontal postures managed to drink quite a quantity of tea. I was sitting up. I tried to take the tin, only to find that my wrists and hands were so swollen and useless that they couldn't hold it. The Japanese interpreter solved the problem by pouring warm tea down my throat. I gagged on the acid lukewarm liquid, but it was a huge relief to my dreadful thirst.

The Japanese man lectured us, his sneering voice triumphant over our heads. He told us that Thew and Smith had been through his hands a little while before, that it had been necessary to give them a certain amount of 'treatment'; that they had told the story of the manufacture of the wireless sets and the reception and distribution of the news, that the Japanese knew the extent of our involvement and that we would shortly be questioned. He said that we might get off lightly if we made suitable full confessions, but that if we were difficult or obstructive in any way there would have to be, regrettably, a repetition of the previous night's 'incident'. Then the interpreter looked at us in a strange half-respectful way and said with considerable dignity: 'You are very brave men; yes, indeed, you are very brave men.'

He moved away and we collapsed again. The sun was now high and we had no protection. Slater told me afterwards that he felt himself naked in the burning sunlight, unable to move, and felt someone trying to cover him with a scrap of shirt and some shorts. I remember scraping them up somehow with my broken arms and pushing them towards his body: his nakedness looked so vulnerable. He didn't betray any interest at the time and appeared to be in a kind of coma. We lay around in that state until late afternoon, when the guard commander, suddenly inspired by the thought that we had had enough rest, shouted at us to get up. He became quite violent, his voice screaming at us, full of petty vanity and anger, so we tried to respond. Slater and I managed to rise but the others continued to lie there mutely. The guard commander ignored us again after that. We remained outside and at the side of his hut throughout the afternoon, evening and night of 22nd September.

Early the following morning the main POW workforce in the camp gathered into squads and prepared to march out on to the railway and towards the bridge they were building over the river.

Every squad which marched out of any camp was required by the Japanese to salute and to give an 'eyes right' or 'eyes left' to the guardroom as it passed. It was always a matter of pride with every POW that this should be done in as slovenly a manner as possible, often with an outbreak of coughing or sneezing as a detachment neared the guards.

That morning, the leading squad looked just as a POW detail usually did, a group of half-starved and angry men wearing the weirdest of garments; some wore ragged shorts, some what we called G-strings; some were in dirty shirts, or army-issue string vests, and most of them had old hats or home-made headgear against the vertical sun. They shuffled along preparing to express the usual defiance. This time, however, the man in charge of the squad called out 'Eyes Right!' as his men approached the five of us, before they even reached the guardroom. The shuffling bunch of malcontents disappeared; every man marched past stiff and erect; each man gave his 'eyes right' with faultless precision. Sandhurst cadets could not have done any better. Each successive squad took the hint. Can any group of officers anywhere ever have had such a tribute?

Later that morning we saw what appeared to be a small funeral procession approaching. It stopped at the guardroom. Up close it showed itself to consist of a POW with a red cross on his sleeve, two teams of stretcher bearers and a Japanese guard. This guard spoke to the commander, the stretcher parties lifted up the two bodies which looked worst, while the rest of us were told to follow on foot. The POW with the red cross introduced himself as a Dutch doctor from the Netherlands forces in Java. He took us to the camp hospital and told us that his instructions were to repair us.

The 'hospital' was a small attap building with an earthen floor, a central passageway flanked by low bamboo platforms down each side of the hut. The quiet medical orderlies helped us up on to one of the platforms and laid us out like sardines. The remains of our clothing was stripped off and they washed us gently from head to toe with warm water. They gave us freshly-made lime juice to drink, and we had to be prevented from slaking ourselves to the point of nausea. Nothing has ever tasted so refreshing.

When most of the dirt and blood had been removed it was possible for the doctor to assess the damage. For my part, both my forearms were broken and several of my ribs were cracked. One hip was clearly damaged. There did not seem to be any skin on my back. What astonished even the doctor was that there was not a single patch of white skin visible between my shoulders and my knees, down both sides of my chest, hips and legs. Most of the skin was in place, but it had turned a uniform blue-black, swollen and puffy, like velvet in texture. I was in such pain I could not begin to locate its source. The four others were in as bad a condition; everyone had broken ribs; but by some chance I was the only one with fractured limbs.

The medical staff soon had us bandaged up, while the doctor himself set the broken bones in my arms and put them in splints. There was no anaesthetic, but the additional pain hardly seemed noticeable. It struck me that this was the second time my bones had been reset without the muffling of drugs. That scoutmaster in Edinburgh had not known the half of it.

We tried to settle down and sleep for the remainder of the day, sipping lime juice whenever we wished, but we were half-paralysed with pain. The astringent fruit juice was almost the only medicine that the doctor had in his little hospital. Somebody meanwhile must have gathered up our scattered kit from around the guardroom and brought it over to us. My spectacles and watch were still intact.

The Japanese, we learned, had ordered that under no circumstances was anyone to talk to us except the hospital staff and that even this contact was to be confined to discussion of our wounds. So of course we spent hours talking to that wonderful doctor. We heard how Smith and Thew had been treated, and how they had now vanished. The beating they gave us was premeditated carefully: the Japanese had given instructions that no-one in the camp was to leave his hut that evening, and that anyone doing so would be shot on sight. All that night armed guards had patrolled the camp boundaries and the lanes between the huts.

When the beating started, the doctor had begun to prepare for us. He sat up all night listening in order to gauge what our condition would be if and when we were handed over to him. He had counted the blows of the pick-helves, and counted nine hundred strokes by the time the beating ended just before dawn.

I woke up in the afternoon to be told that there was again a little group of officers standing outside the guardroom and that they had come from the Sakamoto Butai. From their descriptions it was obvious that it was the turn of Hawley, Armitage, Gilchrist and an officer called Gregg, who I did not know well. They stood there all day, the medical orderlies coming back with unchanging reports of their stiff, flyblown discomfort in the sun. Once again, at about ten o'clock at night the squad of thugs went into action.

We could see nothing, but we heard a lot. We listened to the dull sounds of wood on flesh, to the tramping of heavy feet on the ground, to the roars and screams of anguish, and to the shouts of the drunken NCOs. It went on and on; we lay awake for hours.

Early the next morning the doctor was called out by a guard. He was gone for a while, and when he returned he said that two of the men were in trouble and that he would do what he could for them. His voice was tense, and even in our pain we could see he was holding something back. We kept expecting our four friends to be brought into the hut, but no-one arrived.

There was nothing our Dutch medical man could do for Hawley and Armitage. He saw a squad of Japanese soldiers carry away the broken and lifeless bodies and drop them down a deep latrine in the Japanese section of the camp.

Gilchrist, possibly because he was so small, possibly because of his advancing age, or possibly because of that inexplicable capriciousness of the fanatic mind, was not touched at all. Gregg, the fourth man, also escaped a beating. The doctor had again sat up late at night and counted the number of the strokes. This time he reached four hundred before being called out.

For two or three days we lay in our refuge, too stiff and sore to move, but with thoughts racing through our heads, idea succeeding idea until we were sick with mere speculation. We could tell that they were not finished with us. Lying there, unable to move, we expected them to come and finish us off. Suspense became a cruel insult added to physical injury. We knew that there was a whole sequence of steps; that each one of them would be unpleasant and that we could not look ahead, could not say to ourselves 'that's the end of it now, we have reached some kind of sanctuary'. All we had was the agony of fear of worse to come.

Our food was very good, the best the camp could supply. Many little delicacies were smuggled to us by the other POWs, and we drank gallon after gallon of lime juice. With each passing day we felt better. We each found that our skin was losing the intense black of the bruising; pale patches began to show up as our bodies mended themselves. The physical healing happens so fast; it is the rest that takes time.

One morning a party of smartly-turned-out Japanese officers walked without warning into the hospital hut. Among them was the foppish white-haired interpreter. They inspected us aggressively, made a remark to the doctor about there being no permanent damage and swept out again. We were, evidently, still very much on their minds.

When I went through my kit with the help of Mackay and Slater, I found only one thing missing: my hand-drawn map of Siam and Burma showing the route of the railway.

CHAPTER SIX

A T FOUR O'CLOCK in the morning of 7th October 1943 the five of us were roused from our sleep. Three or four figures were standing quietly in the shadows at the door of the hospital hut. I caught glimpses of them as they paced about. The insignia on their collars was unfamiliar to me, but it was unmistakable for all that; these were men whose presence was more terrifying than any number of drunken sergeants running amok. They represented something colder, more calculating, an organization that lurked on the edges of the worst imaginings of all the prisoners on the railway. The Kempeitai's reputation was like the Gestapo's; worse, for us, because we knew more about what this Japanese secret police unit had done in China during the 1930s.

A lorry was waiting outside. I was the last out. I tried to pack such kit as still survived, the long splints on both arms making every small task painful. Mac helped me to get my things together, as he had been doing for days now. I joined the others outside and we climbed on to the truck. As dawn was breaking we were driven swiftly through the main gates of Kanburi POW camp. We thought that this could easily be our last journey, and the cold light was perfect.

The truck again took us only a very short distance; we were moving tortoise-like through their circles of punishment. We found ourselves being driven into the town of Kanburi itself and along a narrow street parallel to the Mae Klong River. The street consisted of a long row of sizeable buildings, the houses of Siamese and Chinese merchants. I had seen it many times in daylight. The ground floors were normally used as shops, warehouses and offices, and the upper floors as living accommodation. We stopped at one of these merchant's premises, a tall building which had a special protective wall built out on to the street, with an armed sentry at the narrow entrance. We were not aware until then that the Kempei had a local headquarters. Our war had suddenly become one in which secrecy, suspicion and paranoia were weapons.

We were quickly hustled out of the truck and through a gloomy passage into the yard at the back of the building. The yard was a long narrow one which ran as far as the river bank. Although we seemed so close to the broad slick expanse of muddy water, the banks were high and the river far below us. The left-hand side of the yard was bounded by a wall; and along part of its length there were blocks of little hutch-like cells or cages. They resembled drawers in a filing cabinet. We were each ushered into one of these cells through a small, low door about two feet square. The front of each cage was made of bamboo lattice-work; each cell was about five feet long, little more than two and half feet wide, and less than five feet high. The top was solid, a flat surface presenting itself to the sunlight like a hot plate.

We were allowed to take into our box one blanket each, a drinking cup or mug and the shirts and shorts which we happened to be wearing. The rest of our kit and our footwear were removed. They had taken away the last shreds of our dignity and caged us like animals.

The little doors were locked and we were left to our own thoughts. I lay down on the floor, diagonally across the cell; I am over six-foot tall, and I had to lie cramped, my arms held up to prevent my own weight crushing the unset bones; but there didn't seem to be anything else to do. The cumbersome wooden splints and bandages were desperately constraining, and there was no point in crouching upright under the roof. The heat was suffocating after the sun came up and it seemed to suck the air out of the cage.

We couldn't communicate with each other – shouting was certainly out of the question, as there was a hard-faced sentry in the yard, the long spike on the end of his rifle casting a shadow across the ground in front of the cells. In the forenoon, they gave us a small bowl of heavily-salted rice formed into leaden balls. There was another helping of this dehydrating mush in the evening. I was very suspicious of this and I ate as little as possible of the rice; I thought it might be a way of making us ragingly thirsty and of breaking us down; but two bowls of intensely salty rice daily was all we got for the rest of our stay in that place. I felt more and more hungry, and was thirsty all the time.

At least I was supping with the Japanese with a very long spoon. One of the medical officers in Kanburi camp had made me a spoon fastened to a wooden handle so that the whole thing was about eighteen inches long. This was the only way I could feed myself, since I couldn't raise my arms enough to use a normal spoon, and the Japanese wanted me alive enough to let me keep my special utensil.

The cell became literally an oven by the afternoon, an enclosed box containing heat. Ants, vicious large red ones, crawled all over it and over me; the immobility of my arms in their splints was a fierce frustration, preventing me from sweeping away insects from my legs and back.

It is impossible to account precisely for the next few days; I could not even account for the normal interchange of night and day and my mind was confused, sometimes even to the point of oblivion.

I think that there is no doubt that one full day and night elapsed before the interrogation started, but after that time became a blur. Sometime early in the morning I was taken by two guards into the main building. I passed some of the other cages and was able to see dim figures reclining inside, but they did not stir. Once in the house I was pushed towards the front, and into a room constructed entirely of wood, a dark tropical hardwood that gave the chamber a permanent twilit atmosphere. Across a plain narrow table, also made of dark timber, two Japanese were seated.

One of them was a large, broad, muscular, shaven-headed man wearing the uniform of a Japanese NCO, his face and thickset neck full of latent and obvious violence. The other figure, in an ordinary private's uniform, was far smaller, almost delicate. He had a good head of very black hair, a wide mouth and defined cheekbones, and looked very unmilitary beside his rounded and thuggish colleague. There was no ease between them; it was obvious who was in charge.

The smaller man opened up, speaking a heavily-accented, uncertain but quite fluent English. He introduced himself as an interpreter whose job was to assist the NCO of 'the special police', as he put it, in his investigation into the 'widespread anti-Japanese activities' which had been occurring in the POW camps in the neighbourhood. They knew, he said, that these illegal activities were being directed by officers in the Sakamoto Butai.

The NCO then spoke, or rather shouted in a series of short barks, and the small man began his task of translation. Their styles of delivery were, and remained almost to the end, very different: the NCO relishing his own aggression, assuming my guilt and utter worthlessness in the contemptuous way he put his questions, the younger man speaking like a mechanical conversational voice doing its duty, with almost no inflection of interest. He seemed to be a little afraid of the NCO – or perhaps I just hoped that he was even a little as afraid as I was. He now interpreted a long speech in choppy, menacing segments. This introduction was more or less to the effect that 'Lomax, we have already examined your colleagues Thew and Smith. They have made full confessions of the extent of their activities in making and using wireless sets in the Sakamoto Butai. They have fully admitted circulating news sheets. Lomax, they have already told us all about the part you have played, about the collections of money to buy parts from Bangkok for the radios and about your passing on the news to other camps. We are satisfied you are guilty. Some of your fellow POWs have used wireless sets before and they have been caught and executed. Lomax, you will be killed shortly whatever happens. But it will be to your advantage in the time remaining to tell the whole truth. You know now how we can deal with people when we wish to be unpleasant.'

You will be killed shortly . . . A flat neutral piece of information, almost a conversational remark. I had just been sentenced to death by a man of my own age who looked as if he were a little detached from his surroundings, and who seemed completely indifferent to my fate. I had no reason to doubt him.

I knew that I was the only Royal Signals officer for miles around Kanburi and it had already occurred to me that with my obvious knowledge of communications, they would be particularly suspicious of me; so the indictment delivered by the interpreter was as unsurprising as it was unanswerable.

The questioning started. They wanted to know about my family history: detailed and precise questions about my grandparents and other relatives, my mother and father and their occupations. The room was close, and I was already very tired and sore. The pointlessness of what we were doing began to overwhelm me. Here I was trying to explain the migrations of my Lancastrian and Scottish ancestors to a couple of uncomprehending Japanese men in a Siamese village.

They wanted to know about my work before the war, my schooling, my war record up to the capitulation of Singapore in February 1942. From that date my movements were questioned in really minute detail; when they finally placed me in the Sakamoto Butai, after several hours of halting progress, I had to account for almost every hour of my time.

They also asked about my spare-time activities before the war. I tried to explain my interest in trains and railways, tried to make them understand some of the fascination of living in the country that had started the industrial revolution. The young interpreter's face was a cold mask of bafflement. They exchanged staccato comments about my response, but moved on.

They moved to larger and, given the circumstances, more abstract questions: Who is going to win the war? Why? Where will the Allied landings be? Then they would shift suddenly to specifics, asking me why we wanted to get the radio news, demanding to know why we could not accept the news given in the English-language Japanese bulletins and in the local news-papers. There would be a banal question like 'Do you enjoy eating rice?' And so on, and on, and on again.

Their real interest was anti-Japanese activities in the camp, and still more in any contacts we might have had with resistance forces or agents outside it. They hammered away at this endlessly, and I could see that for them I was a piece in some crazed jigsaw puzzle that linked Singapore, Malaya, Thailand and elsewhere – wherever they were having trouble or there was resistance to their occupation. I knew that to give even the appearance of having such contacts would be absolutely fatal; and of course we had none.

They tried to cross-check whatever they had already got from Smith and Thew, which was not much, so they wanted to know the date on which we first received the radio news, what the items were, and how often we worked the set. I tried to be vague, non-committal and prolix all at the same time. Then, once, the interpreter let slip that Fred and Lance were in fact still being kept somewhere in the building. It was a brief surge of hope to know that they were still alive.

Where I knew they knew something, I gave them straight-forward corroboration, but of course this in turn allowed them to produce a list of apparent discrepancies between my version and previous versions of events, and so it started all over again.

I thought during one suffocating, endless session – it may have been in the afternoon of the second day, though I had lost all sense of time by then – that introducing a diversion might be a good tactic. There was something earnest and studious about the young interpreter, something in the way he seemed to relish – or was I imagining this? – our exchanges about British life and culture. I found it hard to tell because I loathed his endless singsong questions, his dreadful persistence and smug virtuous complicity with what they were putting me through; I was beginning to feel that he and I had been in this room for months. But I asked him anyway to tell me something about the Japanese educational system during some exchanges about my own education, to which they had returned, as though the clue to the crumbling of their imperial ambitions could be found in the teaching of the Royal High School. He volunteered some account of his own schooling, and we had an interesting little chat about language teaching. At that moment, and there were others, he became a hated intimate, a sort of lifeline – simply because we could share a language and a moment of curiosity about each other.

The Kempei NCO slowly became suspicious and began to interrogate the interpreter, who reminded me that it was he who was supposed to be asking the questions. The interpreter was simply meant to be a channel of communication, and when it got blocked or distorted the NCO would shout at him too. Although I felt that the interpreter was in some way a human being like me, I hated them both; hated the interpreter more, because it was his voice that grated on and that would give me no rest.

They were obsessed with radios, of course, but waited a long time before introducing the subject of transmitters. Then they went at me. 'Did you have a transmitter? Tell us how you would make a transmitter. What materials would you need? If you made a receiver why didn't you make a transmitter? Lomax, could *you* make a transmitter? You made a transmitter. Tell us what you transmitted.' It was in these questions that they revealed their extreme ignorance about radio equipment in general, wanting to know how a simple receiver could be converted into a transmitter, for example – which can't be done.

Answering these questions was easy enough, but trying to make them understand the truth I was telling was a different matter. I was floundering in the gap between their knowledge and mine, and was suddenly the victim of my whole upbringing and culture; for my interrogators were from a relatively backward society. It is hard to imagine this now, after half a century of astonishing technological development in Japan, but in 1943 the Japanese Army was a technically primitive organization, reflecting in this the partly feudal state of its homeland. The two men sitting across the table from me simply did not know enough to judge what I was telling them, which was that the technical problems of making a transmitter were too great, and that no group of prisoners with the pathetic materials available to them could work a miracle.

At some point they brought in a different NCO, the first one having failed to get the answers they were looking for. So far they had not laid a finger on me, but the endless disorienting abuse relayed by the impassive young man, the barrage of ludicrous questions and the deprivation of sleep were bad enough. I sat hour after hour balancing my broken arms on my thighs, longing for rest. It all became a featureless blur, eighteen hours a day from what seemed like early in the morning till well after dark. Once or twice they woke me at night and brought me to the room. The endless wearisome repetition wore on and on. There was so little inflection in the interpreter's voice, it filled my dreams with its flat repetitive questions.

I thought that I must be the first English person he had spoken to, after his training. His first interlocutor in another language a person he is helping to break down: would this make him feel proud? I hated him more and more. He was the one asking the questions, driving me on. I was sick of the sight of him, I would have killed him for his endless insistence, his boring mechanical curiosity about things I thought he would never understand.

I remembered all that POW talk about the moment when you are absolutely doomed and you take one of them with you. It was easier said than done with two broken arms, but it came to me all the time now and I wanted to do it. It was the interpreter I would have tried to kill.

I could not spin them a yarn, of course, or go into complete fantasy because I feared their violence when they found me out. I did not know for sure what they knew, only what they wanted to know; my task was to give them sufficient information to satisfy them without incriminating any other person. You have a fraction of a second in which to think up answers and I felt so close to disaster all the time, through one careless word. They wanted to know who our contacts were, how the information was sent up the railway, who we were buying parts from, so I would say that it was a man who wore a shirt without insignia so we could not tell what unit he was in; that it wasn't me who passed on the information, it was another soldier in another hut whose name I didn't know; that we left a note outside our hut and never saw who picked it up.

I was trapped. I did not think at the time that there was anything heroic about refusing to give information, or the names of my friends, but I was certainly stubborn, and perpetually vigilant. I had to say something, and yet if I had given the slightest indication of the membership of the wider network they could have rolled it up, torturing each man to reveal his contacts. Gunner Tomlinson would have been forced to reveal the names of the men to whom he gave the edited news-bulletins, and these innocent listeners to the BBC at fourth hand made to suffer. So far, I seemed to be the only one in our group being questioned in such detail: I was in the net because they thought that the Royal Corps of Signals was the organizer of all communicative evil.

It is a strange feeling, being sentenced to death in your early twenties. It made me feel relaxed, in a strange way, to know that I was living on borrowed time. Yet day after day the psychological torment continued. With Pomeroy and Howard in mind, I did not expect any other outcome except – at best – a few Japanese soldiers facing me in the forest, being tied to a post, then a volley. It occurred to me that my family would never be able to find my grave.

They left me my imagination, and it was a worse tormentor than they could ever be. I expected death, but had no clear image of an ending that would make sense to me. I was now living in a world without rules – they could make up their own, and there were no grids or points of reference at all. The world I knew was one in which regularity was almost sacred, a world of predictable and marvellous organization; arrivals and departures were significant, but ultimately controllable events. Mine was a world in which all kinds of communication were revered and I had become dedicated, in my own way, to improving and under-standing it. All this had been burst apart by violence. Communication and movement between places had fallen into the service of horror in the place where I found myself.

When I was not being questioned I lay in that cage. We had not been allowed to wash or shave since we arrived here, and I was now filthy. My cage was worse. I was not allowed to visit the latrine at night, and we were living on a rice diet. I think it was Slater, in the next cage to mine, who was not being interrogated very much, who badgered the little interpreter as he passed his cage and persuaded him that it was not good for them or us that we should have to foul our mugs and cages. We were eventually given closed lengths of bamboo to pee into during the night. But I never saw the interpreter outside that hot wooden room. Slater and I could not compare notes because of the constant presence of the guard; in any case, the less we told each other the better we knew it would be.

There was no light at night and I just lay across the floor of the cell, unutterably depressed. I tried to keep count of the passage of time by making scratches on the wall of the cage with a fish bone which I found in the rice. Squadrons of mosquitos from the river droned all round and over me during the hours of darkness and the only possible sanctuary from them was inside the blanket, but that was so suffocating that I had to endure the bites of the insects instead.

In the nightly delirium I had weird exalted visions, lying there in my shorts and shirt with my long-handled spoon for company. My mind was turning into a machine that produced texts, words and images, cutting them up and feeding them to me in disconnected and confused snatches, slogans, scenes, fantasies. I became a screen with bits and pieces unfolding across me. Sometimes the messages had a sound, quite loud; sometimes they were intensely visual. Most of them were religious, or at least came full of immense and comforting majesty; they were based, mainly, on the most exalted literature I knew, which was that of the Protestant seventeenth century: phrases like

Behold I stand at the door and knock
if any man hear my voice, and open the door, I will come in to
him . . .

lives there who loves this pain . . . break loose from hell

How many miles to Babylon?
Three score and ten
Can I get there by candlelight
Yes, and back again.

I am Alpha and Omega the beginning and the end the first and the last and did those feet in ancient time walk upon England's mountains green. O for that warning voice which he who saw/ The Apocalypse heard cry in Heaven aloud. Yet man is born unto trouble, as the sparks fly upward.

At the worst moments time became completely separated from my inner world of pain and sleeplessness. Once I came out into the yard, after what I thought was an all-night interrogation and saw the dawn light oiling the river at the end of the yard, filling our cages with luminous shadow. Then suddenly it went dark and I realized that I had been watching the sun set.

They brought back the first NCO. He would bang on the table with a big wooden ruler, waving it threateningly to get my attention. 'Lomax, you will tell us.' He was becoming more and more aggressive.

One morning I was taken into that room and there on the table, spread out carefully, was my map. It looked so fine, so neatly done. The NCO and the interpreter stood at the window with their backs to me. The room was silent. They left me standing there for a long time.

Then they turned and from both of them came a storm of fake anger. They had obviously known about it all along, but were now trying to shock me. This is a very good map . . . why did you make it? From where did you steal the paper, where did you get your information? There must be other maps from which you got your information . . . Where are they? Were you planning to escape on your own? With others? Who are they? And then they kept returning to one thing: who we were planning to meet up with, whether there were villagers who had promised to help us, whether we received instructions by wireless, whether any villagers had radios. Were you in contact with the Chinese? And so on.

The young interpreter was now getting deeper into his role as interrogator, as though he were enjoying it. They were really worked up. I could feel their frustration at being sent around in circles by my stubborn refusals. There was a violent electricity in the air.

They wanted to know why I had drawn the railway on my map. I tried to convince them that I was a railway enthusiast, that I had made the map so that I would have a souvenir of Siam and the railway, and know where the stations were. They could not imagine that this was partly true: I had not lost my instinct to record and list and trace. I spoke to them about trains, loaded them up with information about British standard gauge and how interesting it was to see a metre-gauge railway in operation, and the problems of exporting locomotives designed for one system to countries with different systems. The interpreter struggled to find the right terms, about gauges and boiler sizes and engine weights.

He kept saying to me: 'You are railway mania?', meaning, I think, 'maniac' or 'fanatic', his voice expressing genuine, angry puzzlement, and then he would try to explain this incredible excuse to his colleague, who looked darker and more brutal by the minute.

Suddenly the NCO grabbed my shoulder and pulled me out, half stumbling, the relentless force in his powerful arm, his fingers pinching my flesh where he grabbed my shirt. I remember seeing the yard, and the river bank, and the wide brown river flowing past as we stood there. I remember seeing the cages, and noticing Major Smith and Mac and Slater, and seeing that Thew and Smith were now in cages too. But I was told fifty years later, by someone who should know, that I was first taken to a bathroom, and that there was a big metal tub in it, full of water, and that my head was shoved under the water again and again. I believe my informant, but to this day I can't honestly say I remember this. Nothing: a strange selective filter allows us to hold some thing back from ourselves. But I do remember the rest.

A bench had been placed out in the open. I was told by the interpreter to lie down on it, and I lay on my front to protect my bandaged arms by wrapping them under the seat. But the NCO quickly hauled me upright again and made me lie on my back while he tied me to the bench with a rope. My arms were loose. The questioning recommenced. The interpreter's voice: 'Lomax, you will tell us why you made the map. You will tell us why you made a map of the railway. Lomax, were you in contact with the Chinese?'

The NCO picked up a big stick, a rough tree branch. Each question from the small man by my side was immediately followed by a terrible blow with the branch from above the height of the NCO's head on to my chest and stomach. It is so much worse when you see it coming like that, from above, when it is slow and deliberate. I used my splinted arms to try to protect my body, and the branch smashed on to them again and again. The interpreter was at my shoulder. 'Lomax, you will tell us. Then it will stop.' I think I felt his hand on my hand: a strange gesture, the obscene contrast between this gesture almost of comfort and the pitiless violence of what they were doing to me.

It is difficult to say how long the beating lasted, but for me it went slowly on for far too long. The NCO suddenly stopped hitting me. He went off to the side and I saw him coming back holding a hosepipe dribbling with water. From the facility with which he produced it and the convenient proximity of a water tap I guess he had used it before.

He directed the full flow of the now gushing pipe on to my nostrils and mouth at a distance of only a few inches. Water poured down my windpipe and throat and filled my lungs and stomach. The torrent was unimaginably choking. This is the sensation of drowning, on dry land, on a hot dry afternoon. Your humanity bursts from within you as you gag and choke. I tried very hard to will unconsciousness, but no relief came. He was too skilful to risk losing me altogether. When I was choking uncontrollably, the NCO took the hose away. The flat, urgent voice of the interpreter resumed above my head, speaking into my ear; the other man hit me with the branch on the shoulders and stomach a few more times. I had nothing to say; I was beyond invention. So they turned on the tap again, and again there was that nausea of rising water from inside my bodily cavity, a flood welling up from within and choking me.

They alternated beatings and half-drownings for I know not how long. No one was ever able to tell me how long all this lasted, and I have no idea whether it finished that day, or there was more the following day. I eventually found myself back in my cage. I must have been dragged there.

After dark – perhaps that same evening, or was it some other evening? How can I be a reliable witness about time? – the Kempei NCO made a special journey to my cage and handed through the bars a mug of hot milk, made from sweetened condensed milk. This was an incredible delight, but even at the time I knew it was not an act of kindness: it was a way of maintaining ambiguity, of keeping a prisoner off-balance.

The interrogations stopped. One morning, without warning or explanation, our cages were opened and the small interpreter took charge of us. Our kit was brought out of the building and into the yard. All seven of us were told to pack one bag, for we were moving again. This was a further shrinkage of our belongings and of our humanity. We asked a lot of questions, but there were no replies from the young translator-interrogator. A truck drove up, with a number of guards on board.

We had to show the interpreter what we were packing. I showed him my Bible, and he nodded. Then I displayed a mounted photograph of my fiancée. He decided that space was at a premium, carefully tore the photograph from its mount, threw the frame away and handed me back the photograph.

Then Slater asked: 'Can we take money with us?' I was too disturbed to work out whether he meant it satirically or not. The interpreter replied: 'You won't need money where you are going.'

As I was climbing aboard the truck, with Mac's help, the interpreter walked up close to me and said gravely: 'Keep your chin up.' He stood there in the yard, a tiny figure standing among the larger regular soldiers. The truck pulled away.

During the journey we were able to speak quietly beneath the noise of the engine as the guards spoke among themselves. We spoke about our interrogations; I told them about my treatment with the hosepipe. Their warmth, and the solidarity of their anger, was worth so much. There was an extraordinary urgency about this whispered conversation: we were sure that this time we were about to die. Slater's incurable hopelessness seemed the right attitude to all of us.

But instead we were taken to Ban Pong station, thirty miles away, back to the beginning of the railway, and got off at the east-bound platform. It looked as though our destination must be Bangkok.

A train arrived quite soon, an ordinary local passenger train, full of Siamese civilians. Seats were easy to find: local people moved rather than sit next to the Kempeitai.

The train moved off eastwards. After a while we passed the big camp at Nong Pladuk, on the north side the line, which was one of the largest POW camps in Siam. On the south side were the extensive new railway yards, with rows of wagons, flatcars and shunting engines, and a large number of Japanese C56 steam locomotives. I had first seen one of these at Prai, on the way here, but that seemed a very long time ago. The presence of all this machinery could only mean that the Burma-Siam Railway had been completed in record time. The engineers must have felt proud of themselves.

I wondered whether many people who travelled through to Burma on that line across the viaducts cut into the hills by hand would know what it had cost; and I wondered how long it would remain intact.

Despite what had been done to us, most of the information about the construction and operation of the radios, and our lines of communication for distributing the news, and even the purpose of my map, remained our secret. Silence was the only reprisal we could take. Now, apart from the assumption that we were on a train on our way to the royal capital of Siam, we had no idea what was facing us.

CHAPTER SEVEN

AT THE MAIN railway station in Bangkok the Kempei agents led us out on to the platform, among the Siamese travellers in their vivid sarongs, and handed us over to a squad of soldiers. Their numbers and their attitude of alert defiance, as though challenging us to try to escape, signalled our importance to some security-obsessed bureaucrat further up their hierarchy. My six companions were immediately handcuffed, while I had a rope tied around my waist, with one of the guards holding the loose end. They paraded us through the midday throng, in which life was hurrying along to its normal imprecise schedules. The civilians barely glanced at us, or studiously ignored us, for the sight of a man with his arms held out in front of him in splints being led like a donkey on a rope, accompanied by six bruised wretches in handcuffs, was not something to notice too openly. We moved through that crowded station like ghosts.

A Japanese truck was waiting for us. We were driven away, and it was a strange feeling to be in one of the few motorized vehicles on the streets. War had subdued this city, leaving it practically no traffic except bicycles and the occasional cart. The quiet was oppressive as our truck roared through banging its gears and trailing dirty fumes. We passed the German Embassy, a big stone building picked out by the fire-engine red of the swastika flag fluttering on its roof. For a while we ran parallel to one of the electric tramway routes, with elderly single-deck tram cars clanging slowly along. They made a homely noise.

We reached a large nondescript building, with guards standing to attention outside it on an entirely empty street. The Kempeitai ran this place, judging from the uniforms of the men who took us inside and led us to our cells. I was separated from the other six and put into a cell packed with desperately frightened Siamese and Chinese civilians, some of them in tears. I noticed that the cell was square, and this seemed very strange; later I realized that most cells are oblong. I was reduced already to noting the smallest changes in the small spaces in which I was imprisoned wherever I now went.

I have never been able to discover where that building was. Next day all seven of us were reassembled and moved again, this time to the grounds of a grand house, some other requisitioned mansion in the Japanese Army's secret estate. There were various outbuildings in the grounds, and one of them had been turned into a large cell with a walkway for a guard along the front of it and bars through which he could see and speak to us. We were hustled inside and told to sit; when we did, the Japanese officer shook his head and demonstrated the posture he wanted us to adopt: he was determined to make us sit cross-legged.

We occupied that cell for thirty-six days, sitting with our knees spread and ankles locked, from seven in the morning until ten at night, with the exception of a bare hour of daily exercise in the yard. They did not expect us to move or to talk during those hours in the cell. We suffered the cramps and rigors of unsupple muscles forced into this unfamiliar position. You discover the weight of your own body in surprising ways: the crushing pressure of your leg on your heel becomes unbearable, for example, and comfort is a minute shift of position that gives momentary relief before the new alignment begins to ache. My hips were still very painful, and I had to hold out my broken arms and rest them on my knees, so that is how I sat – like a caricature of a praying Buddhist.

Major Smith, so much older than the rest of us, could not manage the position at all, and his distress was acute, his knees splayed out at the weirdest angles and he was constantly in such pain that he was ready to risk the guards' anger and abuse by sticking his legs out straight in front of him. After a while even the guards gave up trying to bend him into the shape they desired and allowed him to sit as he normally would. In this as in all other situations, poor Smith was the most vulnerable of us.

Some of the army guards who had to enforce these absurd secret-police rules of deportment were better than the average run of men doing prison duties. One of them tried to talk to us in English, which was not only a welcome relief from sitting cross-legged in depressed silence, but gave us hope that we could get information from him. He was a 'Gunso', a sergeant, a regular army professional with no interest in petty cruelty. He asked us questions about the British Army, and about our food and climate, and we tried to pump him about what was waiting for us in the big house. He couldn't say, and probably had very little idea himself; I wondered whether he would be a member of our firing-party, if it came to that.

One of the guards told us one day that the previous occupant of our cell had been a POW, a Scotsman named Primrose. He described his uniform as though it had a skirt, and said that he had been charged with the murder of a fellow-prisoner. We were deeply curious about this Scottish soldier in his kilt and probed our guard as much as we dared. The story that came out was one of those legends that later circulated around the network of prisons and camps, a rumour that was so strange it could be true. Primrose was a lieutenant in the Argyll and Sutherland Highlanders, and in the middle of 1943 had been in a camp far up the railway. The Japanese sent in a huge labour force of Tamils, who were as usual treated like atomized slaves, starved and brutalized and dying in handfuls every week. Cholera broke out in the Tamil camp, and the Japanese railway administration found a novel way of containing the epidemic: they shot its victims.

When a single British POW caught the disease he was moved to an isolation tent on the outskirts of the camp, to await 'disposal'. Primrose happened by the tent in time to see two Japanese guards carry the feverish soldier out to a tree. One of them prepared to shoot him, from a considerable distance; the guard was clearly nervous and incompetent, and would almost certainly only wound the prisoner, prolonging his agony needlessly. Primrose grabbed the rifle and shot the man himself with a single round to the heart. And for this he was charged with murder.

I wondered what had happened to him: had they already killed him for his act of loving violence? For years I remained fascinated by what Primrose had done, his decisiveness and compassion. It seemed so symbolic of what they had reduced us to, that he should have to kill one of his own men out of kindness.

The days dragged slowly by in mindless boredom and discomfort. Apart from our more humane guards, we had no distractions or stimulation of any kind. They fed us rice with some nondescript fishy sauce, and lukewarm tea. Apart from our trips to the toilet hole, we squatted on the ground.

Thew muttered under his breath once: 'I can't think of anything to think about.' Fred Smith hissed back: 'Have you thought about *everything* already?' 'Yes,' said Thew. 'Well, start again,' Fred suggested. But after a time recycling your memories is beyond a joke, and the mind chews itself painfully over and over, cud without nutrition.

The exercise period was always a relief because there was plenty of water, and we could wash out there in the sun. They even gave us a hosepipe, which in that yard had almost certainly seen some strange uses, and the others would turn the gush of water on to me because I could not lift the hose with my bound arms. The cold water swilling over me washed out some of the sweat and a little of the tension.

On the morning of 22nd November we were abruptly told to smarten ourselves up. They gave us what was left of our kit and we had to get into uniform, as far as that was possible any more, an instruction that rattled us. This sudden formality was disturbing, as change of any kind had become to us in our helpless situation.

We were taken into the main building and into a large room with long windows. Several Japanese officers sat along a table with their backs to the light. They clearly formed a court martial. The president of the court appeared to be a lieutenant-general, wearing the most remarkable whiskers I have ever seen, drooping down far below his chin. Our reception at the railway station was indeed intentional; we were a prize catch.

There was an interpreter, but his English was more halting than my interrogator's had been at Kanburi. He read out the charges. The prosecuting officer wished to make it clear to the judge that the seven tattered characters standing in front of him were the most dangerous anti-Japanese group they had ever had to deal with, that the group was experienced in and had been involved in subversion, sabotage, secret radio-operation, illegal trading with Siamese civilians, organization of escapes, theft, dissemination of British propaganda – and so on. The ultimate accusation was read out with great melodramatic expressions of indignation: we were, collectively, accused of being a 'bad influence'. This catalogue was flattering, and had we not felt sure that they were about to shoot us we would have enjoyed the compliment even more. A stenographer carefully recorded the prosecutor's speech.

An officer representing the defence, who was a complete stranger to us, gave a rather half-hearted address which seemed to be to the effect that we were sorry for our anti-Japanese activities and had not intended to cause trouble. The defence speech was not recorded for posterity.

The presiding general asked us if we had anything to say. Jim Slater spoke up, with considerable courage, and suggested to the court that whatever conclusion they might come to, we had surely been punished enough already. The judge asked what he meant. Slater attempted to describe quickly and neutrally the beatings at Kanburi, pointing to my broken arms and our still visible cuts, and my torture by the Kempeitai. If the judge had not been aware of our treatment before, he certainly betrayed no interest now.

After conferring with his colleagues, the judge pronounced sentence, his whiskers lending the moment a suitably farcical air of gravity. Thew and Fred Smith, ten years' imprisonment each; Bill Smith, Slater, Knight, Mackay and Lomax, five years each.

We were taken back to the cell, and resumed our cross-legged squatting. Our relief was so intense that it amounted almost to joy. For the first time since the discovery of the radio in Thew's bed at Kanburi, the imminent threat of death had been lifted. We sat there no longer like condemned men, and Slater's elation at our reprieve was almost palpable in the stuffy air of the cell. For the first time, we began to think that for us the physical and mental ill treatment might be over.

* * *

A few days after our trial, the radio party was told to get itself ready for another move. The guards did not tell us where we were being taken, but they ordered Thew to stay behind, and no amount of pleading and questioning would make them explain his detention to us. This was the second time he had been separated from us, our radio buff, and we were desperately afraid for him. Fred later told me that Thew had blandly informed the white-haired interpreter at Kanburi that he needed a radio because he worked for the BBC. The man had beaten Thew around the head with the flat of his sword. He might have annoyed them too much, once too often; or perhaps they had singled him out again for additional torture and questioning; or they felt he was, after all, too dangerous to keep alive. It was dreadful to have to walk out of that cell and leave him sitting there alone.

We were put into uniform again; my five comrades were handcuffed; my arms were still in splints and the guards decided that I was sufficiently restricted without the cuffs. Yet another truck rolled up and we were driven back through the dead streets of Bangkok to the railway station. Our weird group once more attracted a certain amount of attention as we were taken to a waiting train. As I walked along the platform I remember looking with pleasure at a perfectly ordinary, shabby passenger train and hoping that we were going to be allowed to sit on seats, like ordinary travellers, now that we were convicted subversives instead of battered prisoners. Instead we were shoved into the guard's van, which was at least empty and spacious – an improvement on the foul covered goods vans in which we had travelled from Singapore to Ban Pong just over a year before. The escort told us to sit on the floor with our backs to the end of the van. We spread out our kit and settled down. Slater thought we would be taken to Japan; others assumed we would serve out our sentence working, under closer supervision, back at Kanburi or somewhere else on the railway. One of the guards settled the question of our destination by saying: 'Shonan.' Singapore. We were starting all over again.

Singapore is 1200 miles from Bangkok, and there are more comfortable ways of travelling between the cities than sitting on the steel floor of a luggage van for three days and nights. But this was a better journey than most in our experience as prisoners, even though my five companions were handcuffed for most of the way. For once, the Japanese administrative arrangements worked well. Food appeared miraculously at certain stops, and it had obviously come from Japanese cookhouses. We ate exactly the same food as the guards. It was among the best we had eaten for two years.

Bill Smith's frailty singled him out yet again for embarrassment, or perhaps we were simply a little embarrassed by him. He clearly had a slight bladder problem and the regular stops were not enough for him. There was, as usual, no latrine on board to which we were allowed access, and Smith was once in real discomfort. The rest of us immediately began to calculate the speed of the train, the time to the next stop, whether we could risk holding him out the door – a manoeuvre I suggested reluctantly, remembering my own humiliation on the way to Ban Pong – but the train was moving too fast and the other four were afraid of dropping him. Smith interrupted us with great suppressed urgency and begged for a more immediate solution. He could not bear to foul his mug or mess-tin, so someone suggested that he use his footwear. So it was that the poor man urinated into his own boot, which was large enough and watertight enough for the purpose: there was no leakage at all. It is the strangest tribute to the quality of British shoemaking that I can think of.

The journey was monotonous and uneventful, perhaps because we were so exhausted by letting go the tension and uncertainty that had gripped us since our arrest at Kanburi. The guards kept us sitting against the back wall of the coach, so we saw almost nothing of the view, only the occasional glimpse of forest at a sharp angle out of the open door. We tried to sleep as the wagon swayed and rolled, pounding the metal of the rail with the metal of its wheels in that smooth, lunging rhythm of train travel. Unless some violent force intervened, we were as trapped as those flanged wheels on our own iron road.

We reached Singapore railway station on 30th November, in the afternoon, and were picked up by an unusually strong force of guards. We still did not know where we were going. Once the truck was on the move, however, Bill Smith, who had spent years in and around the island and knew the city well, said quietly that he thought we were heading for Outram Road Gaol.

We pulled up outside high, grey gates set in massive, mock-gothic walls and waited. It looked from the outside as British and as Victorian a prison as any in London or a provincial English town, a reassuring and solid symbol of legality and justice. The huge doors swung open from the inside, the truck drove in and the doors boomed shut. Little did we realize that we had left all justice behind.

CHAPTER EIGHT

T HE SIX OF us were led into a reception area where there was
an obviously well-practised routine. We were told to strip,
and stripped totally of all our miserable things, clothes, books
and pictures. All I was allowed to keep was my long spoon and
my pair of spectacles, which had survived everything, though
hardly intact; they were held together with surgical tape and
gentle handling. I always treated them as though my life
depended on it – which it did, in some ways, for semi-blindness
added to what I had gone through would surely have been the last
straw. At least I could trust the witness of my eyes, at a time when
what I heard was often humanly incredible.

I was still wearing my splints, but a warder inspected my hair,
which was now long and tangled, along with all the others', and
our ears. I never found out what strange information he was
expecting to find in men's ears, though presumably he was
checking for hacksaw blades in our anal passages when he poked
around in there.

We were each given an extremely small pair of shorts, a shirt, a
cap and a so-called towel, which was not much bigger than the
shorts. Each of these items had been worn out, patched and worn

out again, as though a whole company of men had slept in them. We felt ragged enough when we walked into that prison, but these clothes made us look like castaways. They took away our shoes; of washing materials and toothbrushes we had none. I wondered whether our kit would truly be kept in store for when we were released in five or ten years' time.

Finally we were told that our names were abolished and that we were to have new identities. Mine was *rokyaku ju-go*, which sounded splendid but translated merely as No. 615. The former Prisoner No. 1 was slipping fast. They made us memorize and repeat our numbers over and over again until we got them right, and all of us managed except the hapless Bill Smith, who could never cope with even a single word of Japanese. The warders gave up on him.

These gaolers appeared to be Japanese military prison service men, wearing white epaulettes to distinguish them from their regular colleagues outside. Others, including many of the warders, it would turn out, were ordinary Japanese soldiers convicted of disciplinary offences. Even to be a warder in Outram Road was a punishment.

The initial ceremony of degradation over, we were marched outside. We headed in a line out of the reception area into a cell-block. I noticed a large letter 'D' at the entrance. As we came into that long gloomy hall, with iron stairs stretching before us and galleries up above us in what seemed like level upon level, I was aware of a total silence. Our bare feet and the guards' boots were the only sounds in that high arcade. There were cell doors on each side, and another floor of cells above that, but I was too agitated to notice properly whether there was a third floor. The hall looked more or less as I imagined a British Victorian prison would look, on the inside, with cliff faces of cells opposing each other across empty space. The air in the hall was close, as though it were a morgue rather than a place that held living men.

Fred Smith and I were put into Cell No. 52; the others into Nos. 53 and 54. The guards told us, with menaces, that talking was forbidden, even between men sharing a cell, and that attempts to communicate between cells would be punished severely. The door was then shut, and we looked around our new home. It was totally empty: a stark oblong space, about nine feet long, six feet across and with a very high ceiling. The walls were peeling, had once been thickly painted in white and were utterly blank. The door was solid and steel-clad, with a rectangular slot like an English post-box. There was a small window, very high up in the end wall, through which we could see the sky. It seemed to be a nice day outside.

We were very, very tired. The anti-climax of the trial and our survival was still having its effect and we wanted to rest and to be left alone. I could not remember when I had last slept in a real bed, so I lay down on my side on the bare cement floor, and immediately went to sleep.

Fred and I were woken by the door banging open; a guard handed in a set of three wooden planks and a strange wooden block and a blanket for each of us, followed by a wooden latrine bucket with a lid. We were puzzled by the wooden blocks, until we realized that these were our pillows. Our cell was now fully furnished.

Later in the evening there was a rattling at the cell door; the slot was banged down and a bowl of rice, a small saucer of tea and a pair of chopsticks for each of us were handed in through the slot. Even on our first day, the complete absence of colour, of sound and variation were such that the arrival of this wretched meal was an event. We tried to make it last as long as possible, but eating a bowl of overcooked rice can only take so long.

The first day ended like that, with barely enough food to keep us alive and nothing like enough to dull the appetite. I thought I already understood hunger, but this was a new level of craving. Fred and I spoke in whispers, trying to make sense of our deprivation, wondering whether they seriously intended to leave us in this condition for our entire sentences. We were waiting for sleep, expecting to be switched into darkness when the electric light bulb high above our heads was turned off; but it stayed on all night, and we fell asleep in the glare of our empty cell.

★ ★ ★

No-one had told us where we were; indeed had Bill Smith not identified the place as Outram Road we might have been left wondering where we were for a long time. All we knew was that Outram Road had been the main civil prison in Singapore until the new gaol at Changi was opened late in the 1930s. It was now clearly being run as a punitive military prison, an extreme version of what the British Army would call a 'glasshouse'.

We were kept in our cells almost all the time. The only interruption to this incarceration was that on most days, at different times, the cell doors were opened for a form of roll call. We were each required to call out our numbers, and we all managed this except Bill Smith. Sometimes someone else would call out his number for him; sometimes he would reply 'Twinkle, twinkle, little star', which the warders seemed to find acceptable.

The main events apart from this were the delivery of the so-called meals three times a day. Each consisted of rice and tea, or at least a quantity of slightly discoloured hot water which looked like tea. This was our main fluid intake for the day, and thirst usually preceded it by many hours. The rice came in a large aluminium bowl, the tea in a small enamel dish. The other big moment was the handing out of the latrine bucket to a squad of prisoners supervised by guards, and the return of the bucket, emptied and washed, later in the morning.

One morning, at last, Fred and I were taken out of the cell apparently for some purpose other than the roll call. When we reached the open yard at the end of D Block we realized that we were here for exercise, but what we saw was a glimpse of the underworld. In the yard were about twenty prisoners, most of them apparently unable to walk. Some lay flat out; some were crawling on their hands and knees. Several were totally naked. Almost all had one thing in common: they were living skeletons, with ribs and bones protruding from shrunken flesh. Since we had not seen ourselves in a mirror or looked objectively at each other for a long time, it was a terrible shock to realize that we must look like these damned creatures – or soon would. One man was blown up like a balloon, his face so inflated that his features were unrecognizable. This was what advanced beri-beri looked like, while others seemed to have the disease in earlier or less severe forms, but still with dreadful body swelling. Their skins were raw, pustular and peeling; some men were covered in angry scabby patches. We thought these tragic figures must be British and Australian, but they were almost beyond recognition.

Fred and I were told to join a small group of nearly naked prisoners, who were being exercised by a Japanese soldier. The exercises consisted only of standing still and waving our arms about, by number, in response to the instructions 'ich, ni, san, shi, go, rok, shich, hach', and periodically walking around in a circle. The six of us from Kanburi were in better shape than those

POWs who had been any length of time in Outram Road, and we hardly felt robust. Very occasionally, when we were out in that yard, we were allowed to have a wash. There were taps in the walls of the yard; there were buckets, but it was forbidden to touch them without orders. So these filthy, scabrous men walked or crawled within a few feet of the water that could have cleaned and eased them even a little.

Without my cellmate, a sight like this might have destroyed me. But Fred Smith was an absolute hero, and I have never forgotten him. I can still quote his army number from memory: 1071124. He was an incredibly fit, strong man, shorter than me but very sturdy, and he survived the cumulative mistreatments astonishingly well. He could never understand why, although he had been interrogated three times at Kanburi, he had not been tortured or beaten. So certain did it seem that he was going to get what Thew had been given that Lance had passed him his short puttees, and he had wrapped the strips of cloth around his body under his shirt to make a thin barrier against the pick-helves; but perhaps because some Japanese officer decided that a mere artilleryman could not be central to the conspiracy of signals and ordnance officers which they had imagined for us, Fred never had to test his cotton armour.

Fred was a good and considerate companion. His father had been an engine driver – the irony was lost on me at the time – at Stewart's Lane rail depot in south London. He had grown up around there, and just before being posted to Singapore had been assigned to the Coastal Battery at Pembroke Dock, in West Wales. Because he was an artilleryman, a regular soldier with experience of coastal guns, he had been sent to help man the mythic 15-inchers on the southern coast of Singapore Island. He would talk about his wife and son, and his worries about his wife's neglect of his son, and I detected some bitter suspicion of his wife's fidelity beneath the coded language men used in wartime about their loved ones.

Fred was an uneducated working-class man, a 'rough diamond' in the language of the day, but in the situation we found ourselves in rank and class counted for nothing. Character, decency and loyalty counted for more than previous good fortune or the possession of a commission. Fred was simply a good man. (Only once, in all my time at Outram Road, did I ever pull rank. I told two characters to stop arguing with each other, afraid that they would draw down the Japanese guards and pay heavily for their irritation and boredom. They ignored me. It would take more than an officer to put a lid on the anger these men were forced to swallow every day.)

We looked after each other as best we could, and watched each other's physical deterioration carefully; but the only physical weakness that I can remember Fred ever revealing, despite the thin starvation rations and the filth, was a terrible boil on his back, below his shoulders and out of reach of his hands. It got so bad that I kept showing it to the guards, and it became a huge angry red swelling threatening to poison Fred's blood. One day, without warning, a Japanese man came importantly into our cell clutching a naked razor-blade, the kind used for shaving. This was the medical orderly. He looked at Fred's back with as much interest as he would have devoted to a cockroach and ordered him to lie flat on his stomach. With a swift gesture he cut an X into the abscess. Blood and pus spurted on to the wall and floor of the cell. Fred didn't make a sound.

The worst new enemy which we faced, even compared to the dirt and hunger, was perhaps the most formidable of all: silence. It was often absolute. There could be a sick, deadly hush throughout the entire prison, so quiet that you could hear the metallic twisting of a key in a lock echoing up the levels to the long roof. A warder's boots would make a booming sound on the stone floor, and I would be afraid that the sound of a whisper would carry all the way along to him.

For they were serious about their decree of silence. It seemed particularly sadistic to make us share a cell and forbid us to speak to each other and at the same time deprive us of books and distractions of any kind. There was precisely nothing to do in that room.

Sometimes the slot would fall open when we were talking quietly and a voice would shout at us in Japanese to shut up; at other times the door would be thrown back and a guard rush in, his sheathed sword whipping down on our heads and shoulders like a hard rod, the shock worsened by fear that the blade of the sword was only a thickness of leather away from slicing us apart.

By listening to the sound of the warder's fading footsteps or hearing their voices we could tell when we were more or less safe for a few minutes, and talk in low tones. We worked out what the arrangements were for warders' shifts and meal-breaks, and learned to tell where they were from the strength of the sound their feet made on the floor. Our hearing seemed to grow more acute in the silence. Before long, we were able to identify each warder by his footsteps. We seldom found out their names, instead identifying each by some nickname: Horseface, or Mary – a guard who we thought effeminate for his very quiet feet, who we hated. He was one of those who wore rubber-soled boots to deaden the sound of his coming.

We were here because we had broken a taboo on listening to forbidden words, and their ban on talking had an obscene aptness about it, whether they were aware of it or not. We had survived two years in the camps only by endless talk; and our need to know what was happening around us was now greater than ever.

When we were taken to work we were usually on different squads, in different areas, and so Fred and I could swap notes of the snatches of whispered conversation we had had, and talk about what we had seen. Everyone on these work-details was trying as hard as possible to talk to everyone else, and the regime of silence was undermined by these countless small dialogues.

Our conversation was necessarily about our most immediate surroundings. Who has been moved into the cell down the corridor? What are people being made to work on now? Who are those new arrivals? Is Bill at death's door? Why is a prisoner sitting bolt upright in a bath out in the yard at the end of the block?

Piecing together information, very slowly, very gradually, was like rubbing at a dirty window with a tiny rag, making blurred peepholes that allowed us to catch glimpses of the world outside D Block, but also confirmed to us how bad our situation was, how dangerous it was to be in Outram Road at all. We did not know what the death rate was, but we knew that some people had got out and had never been seen again. Nobody knew where they went to, whether there was an even worse cell somewhere – underground in the dark, perhaps – or whether they were murdered. All we knew for certain was that we were living with risk day after day in this vast tomb.

By the middle of December 1943 we had established that Outram Road consisted of parallel blocks, and that the military section occupied two of them, Blocks C and D; beyond a very high wall were the other blocks, which were being run by the Japanese Army as a prison for civilians, for what crimes we could not then imagine. As far as we could tell, there were about thirty prisoners in our block. The infallible indication that a cell was occupied was its inclusion in the list for a latrine-bucket visit in the morning. Everyone in the block seemed to have been convicted by Japanese court martials of 'anti-Japanese offences' ranging from escape attempts and sabotage to more spectacular crimes. The rumour was that one man was here for attempting to steal an aircraft and fly it towards Allied territory.

We also discovered that in the past some men in our block had become so ill that they had died quietly in their cells, from a combination of disease, brutality and starvation. And still the most tantalizing information was that occasionally prisoners who were on the point of death were sent away from the gaol altogether. The best rumour was that they were sent to Changi, to a special hospital there. The other rumours came to seem less important, remote probabilities compared to the certainty that nothing could be worse than where we were.

* * *

If it seems absurd to send prisoners to gaol, what our captors were in fact doing was consigning us to a lower circle of hell. This was a place in which the living were turned into ghosts, starved, diseased creatures wasted down to their skeletal outlines.

But as always, whether on the railway or in the camps, there were people who were humane enough to take risks to help us. Some of the Japanese prison staff tried to do nothing to add to our squalor and unhappiness. I remember that the same Gunso who had guarded us before our trial in Bangkok ended up in Outram Road shortly after we arrived, and that he personally removed my splints when the bones of my arms seemed to be set, and took away my long spoon but only after I had assured him that I could manage without it. But some of his colleagues were bored, slovenly and brutal Japanese private soldiers. They were randomly abusive, and could beat us at will for minor or imagined infractions of the rules. There was a good deal of this casual violence.

Among the warders, we were astonished to discover that there were two men who appeared to be English. Before long they identified themselves in whispers through our door-slot as Penrod Dean, an Australian Army officer and John O'Malley, a British signalman. They had been among the first POWs to be sent to Outram Road and had been nominated by the Japanese as *tobans*, or trusties. They collected food from the kitchens, making deliveries to the cells and collecting the empty dishes. So far as was practicable they looked after the interests of the prisoners, slipping us extra rations or insistently bringing illness to the attention of the indifferent guards, at least making it more difficult for them to ignore us. I saw O'Malley carry paralysed men into the sunshine of the exercise yard in a desperate attempt to keep them alive, cradling those frail creatures of skin and bone in his own emaciated arms.

But there was very little a toban could do in the face of such systematic neglect. We had no toothbrushes, for example; my teeth were ruined by the middle of 1944. We were allowed no shaving kit either. A month or so after we arrived we were taken for a haircut. A Japanese barber set up outside a cell on the ground floor and every prisoner in turn was ordered to sit in front of him. He grasped my neck in his left hand and took up a large set of clippers in his right, and started snipping the hair on the nape of my neck, working the clippers around and up and across my head in a single movement, down my sideburns to my beard which showered its wirier hair on to the softer filaments of my head, never lifting the clippers once. I could feel the cold metal bumping on my exposed skull, which felt as fragile as an egg. It was like being shorn by a skilful, rough sheep-farmer. That shave was the only regular hygienic attention we received.

In return we were expected to do irregular work. There was no pattern to it, because I think that they wanted us to spend as much time as possible in blank isolation. The work could involve floor-washing, gardening, carrying firewood to the cookhouse or – the task we dreaded most – cleaning the Japanese toilets. The condition of those rows of holes was appalling. There is something unbearably sickening about cleaning other men's ordure.

Or else they would ask us to shift 100 kg sacks of rice, which was crippling work for men in our condition. But the most bizarre task was one that allowed a group of us to stay together for a while in the sunshine out in the yard. The guards produced a great heap of rusty and extremely dirty army equipment which we suspected had either been stored in the open or had been salvaged from a ship. There were mess-tins, and buckets and containers of all kinds, caked in rust and dirt. Our job was to clean all these and restore them to pristine beauty. The trouble was that the only tools we were given were large rusty nails, bits of wire and handfuls of earth. With these primitive resources the Japanese expected sparkling results.

A dozen prisoners were gathered in the open, sitting on concrete under a lean-to attap roof that deflected the fierce heat a little. We sat cross-legged, hunched over the filthy utensils. If somebody looked sideways instead of down, a guard would lean over and punch him in the face.

Even under these circumstances we managed, with care, to

talk. I had always been close to Mackay, and we sat beside each other while we scraped junk metal with wire in the hope that gleams of steel would start to appear beneath the grime. For much of the time we worked naked, partly to try to get fresh air around our unwashed and itching bodies and partly because we had very little to wear anyway. One day I noticed that Mac, who had been a well-built man, had become so thin that his anus stuck out like a short pipe.

I then discovered that I could close my hand around my own upper arm and that my stomach was very close to my spine; there seemed to be no solid body on me anywhere. My ribs were sticking out. I asked Mac how I looked, and he said that I looked like a skeleton with skin stretched over it. I had become one of the living dead who had so frightened me when I first came to Outram Road. I knew then that I was close to death, and that I had to get out of Outram Road at all costs.

It wasn't only the decline in my physical condition that led me, eventually, to take the risk of making myself deliberately worse so that they would have to move me. The balance of probabilities seemed just to be in favour of the assumption that they were not quietly murdering the sick prisoners, and I convinced myself that the percentage prospect of survival if I stayed was virtually nil; but this rationalism was beside the point: beyond reason or calculation, I wanted out of this place.

Certain events weakened me, but toughened my resolve. Early on, on Christmas Day 1943, I was given a fish head with my evening rice. I ate the head, but I could not manage to eat the eyes. They lay on my plate, little tough jellies staring up at me. I longed then for the winter feast of northern Europe, for my family and for my mother in particular, and the contrast between my memories of them and this tropical black hole was acutely depressing.

I found a definition for 'hunger' when I was sent on a rare errand without a guard to take an empty pan to the cookhouse, and as I was walking through the main hall I saw a single grain of rice on a cell doorstep. I went over and picked it up and ate it.

Then there was the itch. We were used to diseases of the skin, which were rampant in the camps because of the lack of soap, but this was an itch the like of which neither Fred nor I had encountered before. The slightest touch on one's skin produced an urge to scratch savagely. To succumb to this temptation was disastrous, and made the itch worse than ever, so we sat motionless with our skins on fire.

The itch developed into a horrible skin condition, perhaps an extreme form of scabies. Each of us in turn found little pimples appearing on our skin. To begin with they were clear and transparent; then the clear liquid turned into yellow pus, the pimples burst, erupted and the fluid dried into horrible yellow scabs. Picking them off meant losing a patch of skin. I myself lost every inch of skin on my body with the curious exception of the skin on my face and the tips of my fingers and toes. Worse still, as fast as one picked off the scabs new eruptions appeared. Those men who were too ill and weak to move and were unable to do anything for themselves gradually became encased in a brown-ish-yellow crust of pus, a spectacle that still wakes me at night, the nausea still fresh.

O'Malley and one or two others voluntarily took on the task of cleaning up the most helpless men by patiently picking off the encrusted scabs and washing their bodies in cold water. What they did deserves the adjective 'heroic' as much as bravery under fire.

Partly as a result of their efforts, the Japanese began to take note of the disease. A liquid which they described as 'creosote' was brought into the block in large containers, and they produced a few metal tubs. Those of us who were badly infected were allowed to have what was almost a bath, our first in several months, though still without soap, in the yard outside the block. I sat in a tub for hours. It did not noticeably improve my skin, but the feel of the water lapping around me was worth the pretence.

When the 'creosote' did not work, the Japanese administration gave us a paste or ointment which looked suspiciously like saddle-soap. We were told to strip and to coat every inch of our bodies with the ointment, telling ourselves that at least it might suffocate the tiny maggots or whatever it was that was causing the trouble. Perhaps it did; or perhaps the epidemic had run its course, for the disease slackened off soon afterwards.

By the end of April 1944 my three British fellow-officers, Bill Smith, Jim Slater and Morton Mackay were all seriously ill, and Harry Knight, the Australian major, looked no better. When I caught glimpses of them I was terrified for all of us. Only Fred Smith seemed to retain some strength despite the starvation diet. The guards sent a stretcher party one day and removed three of the others, but left Fred, Harry and me. The fact that we could totter across a yard must have excluded us. I was now the only officer left in the entire block, apart from Knight.

The old anxiety and fear surged back with renewed force. Although we had a sentence, we could not imagine this term of imprisonment coming to an end. The uncertainty was gross and desperately stressful. We didn't think we could survive years of this, and even if we did there was no guarantee of being 'released' into anything but a larger and perhaps relatively more humane prison camp. We were prisoners within a world that was itself a prison. That larger sentence of servitude was completely indeterminate, for who could say when the war would end? And if the Japanese won it, what would they do to us?

I found this uncertainty particularly difficult. I was afflicted with the strange combination of a vivid imagination and a need to locate myself exactly, to be sure of where I was and where I was going – I had the character of a mapmaker, a listmaker, of one who knew about dates and classes and varieties. Being thrown into the pit and not knowing whether I could ever find a ladder to climb out of it did me no good at all. Without reading, writing or bearings of any kind I felt that I was living through the end of whatever time had been given to me; the delirium of the last days was closing in.

We could not measure time, let alone occupy it. Our time was now entirely theirs. We could identify Sundays because the guards took time off on Sundays, and O'Malley or Penrod Dean could sometimes identify the hour or date for us, but that was never enough. When the evening came, there were twelve hours of utter emptiness to get through. Outside it was dark; inside, the electric light was on continuously. During those long nights I sharpened my desperation to get out, even though it felt like jumping from a window in the dark, not knowing where I might land. And in the end, I used time itself against them.

* * *

They gave me my chance when they took the unprecedented step of separately identifying extremely sick men and classifying them as 'byoki'. They were then placed in a group of cells on the ground floor furthest from the door of the block.

I had discovered that I could drive up my pulse rate by deep and accelerated breathing, so producing a state that frightened my cellmate and even me; and that there was one exception to our complete lack of any means of measuring time. In very still and very quiet conditions the faint chimes of a clock somewhere in the distance could be heard, though it was a long time before I was aware of it. I imagined it as a public clock on some tower, for it struck the quarters as well as the hours.

I disciplined myself to count the little beats of blood in my wrist for fifteen minutes at a stretch. It was not that hard, really; what else did I have to do? Forcing myself to concentrate on nothing but my pulse – the effort alone probably put me into a kind of agitated trance, and I was already near hallucinating from starvation and weakness. They had taken all sense of normal, filled time away from me and I focused my panic in on myself in a fever of self-control.

I would count carefully all the time I was doing this and divide the resulting figure by fifteen, giving the pulse rate per minute. The normal rate is about 76; I got mine up to a figure which was so high that I could not count properly and I was confident that I could repeat this whenever I wanted to do so.

One day, when I was lying down and there was a warder within earshot, I worked my pulse up, cried out and twisted and clutched myself. My performance had an effect: the warder took a look at me and had me carried down to one of the 'sick' cells. And so I lost sight of Fred Smith, who seemed resigned to survival in Outram Road and whose extraordinary resilience could not be disguised long enough even to pretend weakness. He had supported me to the hilt and told me I was doing the right thing, but I hated leaving him alone in that horrible bare cell.

In the sick cells the doors were left open during the day, which was a slight improvement, and you did not have to take part in work squads. I was joined in the cell by an Australian called Stan Davis, who was not officially sick – he was supposed to look after me, and save the therapeutic energies of the medical orderly. Stan probably knew as much about medicine as that individual, in any case, and when we were able to talk we plotted the best way for both of us to get beyond the sick cell to the hospital at Changi – if indeed it was not a dangerous mirage. Stan was another radio man, even luckier than we had been. A private soldier in a motor-transport company, he had been part of a group operating a radio in the POW camp in Sandakan, in British North Borneo, and planning an escape. This group really had been in subversive communication with local civilians. The Japanese shot his officer, Captain L.C. Matthews of the Australian Army Signals.

Stan and I agreed that I would eat all the food which came into the cell other than rice and that Stan would eat all the rice, and nothing but rice, and we swore that we would stick to our diet until the end, whatever it might be. My resolution was not as suicidal as it may sound because by May 1944 the food had improved slightly, and the rice now came with a few soya beans or fragments of fish, but I very quickly became even thinner while Stan got more and more bloated, and looked as though he had real wet beri-beri.

We each made exaggerated shows of trying to move about, taking care to fall over or otherwise to collapse whenever we left the cell, and so after a while we were spending twenty-four hours in the cell with nothing but determination to drive us on. We had nothing to distract us from our self-destructive will to live, and only the faint chiming of that mysterious clock to mark the passing of time.

Stan and I exchanged anecdotes of the campaigns in Malaya

and life in Borneo, the fall of Singapore and the early days of captivity. He had been brought up a Catholic in Western Australia and entertained me with stories of the fierce angry discipline handed out by the Christian Brothers, a religious order that specializes in teaching poor children; and he spoke about distances I could barely imagine, deserts taking weeks to cross and farms measured in square miles. I tried to find a way of explaining lowland Scotland to this hard man of the outdoors, for whom life in these cells must have been terribly constricting; we compromised by reciting poems like James Henry Leigh Hunt's *Abou Ben Adhem*, which seemed to declaim something beautiful and defiant to us:

'What writest thou?' – The vision raised its head,
And with a look made of all sweet accord,
Answered, 'The names of those who love the Lord.'
'And is mine one?' said Abou. 'Nay, not so,'
Replied the angel. Abou spoke more low,
But cheerly still; and said, 'I pray thee then,
Write me as one that loves his fellow-men.'

I tried to sleep as much as possible, but it was difficult to find a comfortable position. When the body is so thin that your prominent bones stick out like handles there is no ease to be had on three wooden planks, and my hips were still in poor shape. I would drift into a kind of coma, full of dreams and hallucinations and waking impressions that were clear and completely unreal. As at Kanburi after the beatings, my mind was churning and spewing disconnected fragments of learning and memory; bits of rage at our treatment at Kanburi came up, the cages, the beatings, the repetitious stupid refrain of 'Lomax you will tell us' and the little interrogator with his thuggish friend. I felt I had been dead, I had been sentenced to death, 'Lomax, you will be killed shortly', I was suspended between life and death in my delirium. Often it was a brain fever spinning out automatic rhymes and strange biblical nursery verses. One of these at least I wrote down later:

> At the beginning of time the clock struck one
> Then dropped the dew and the clock struck two
> From the dew grew a tree and the clock struck three
> The tree made a door and the clock struck four
> Man came alive and the clock struck five
> Count not, waste not the years on the clock
> Behold I stand at the door and knock.

There were non-stop, intensely tactile visions, so real that I could smell and see the places they presented to me: a procession of ocean-going ships slipping down the Clyde past Greenock; the unbelievably delicate evening light of the West Highlands; a summer lake in Kashmir, with vast snow mountains above it. My mind wandered back along the roads I had cycled in my search for steam engines, but it was a jagged, confused and chaotic reprise of those long journeys. I walked with S.'s hand in mine on an Edinburgh street past dark high buildings with glimpses of steps plunging down into old courtyards.

I had one vivid and frequent dream with a scene that seemed utterly perfect and unattainable, a vision of impossible beauty. It was the image of an old English garden in summer, near a cathedral, with banks of honeysuckle and roses under oak and willow trees, the cathedral spire rising above them. It seemed so entirely real, and at the same time a romantic painting of such a scene, as though I was looking at it from the side so that the smooth lawn swept away from me in a great green triangle. There was an old brown-red brick cottage hidden in the trees; it felt like order and wealth and safety.

The visions became more frightening and grotesque. One evening, the long wall of the cell began to dissolve. The cracked cement and the brickwork melted away. Far away was an immense figure, standing erect with many waving arms, emerging from a heaving sea of flame and smoke, and growing larger, until it seemed to fill the entire view. It seemed to be standing above a lake, and the surface changed into distinct waves, and then into human figures tiny against the mass of the giant. They seemed to be worshipping, chanting, praising, calling out 'Kali, Kali, Kali'. I felt sheer terror as the figure's eyes looked down directly at me, the terror mounting like choking until I woke up to find myself looking at the bare light bulb and the cell walls.

★ ★ ★

After two months of dogged persistence in our dreadful routine, and by then we were both in a bad way, I made another attempt to frighten the warders by working myself into a crisis, my pulse racing and my body shaking – and this time the symptoms hardly needed to be simulated. It's not too difficult to feign imminent death when you already look like a corpse. Stan called a warder, who looked at me, and then called someone else. He may not have wanted a death on his watch without checking with a superior.

Usually, they shut the cell door at night, but that night they left it open and a warder looked in several times to check on me. I acted up enthusiastically whenever I heard him coming. The following morning there were sounds of an unusually large group walking towards our cell. It turned out to be a stretcher party. I was bundled on to the stretcher, calling out for Stan to be taken too, but they stumbled out of the cell without him. Once again I was leaving a friend.

I kept my eyes shut, but could tell that we made our way down the central hall, across the sunlit yard and into the administration offices, where I was dumped on the floor. My kit was loaded on top of me and the stretcher was lifted again, out into the open air. I could hardly believe it when I realized that I was being put into the back of a vehicle, an open truck of some kind. I was about to learn what happened to the men who had gone out of here before me, and take the consequences of my leap in the dark. The truck drove off.

I could look up through half-closed eyelids and see the sky, and smell the air of a city again. The sun was warming and the vault of blue looked imponderably beautiful and limitless. I heard Chinese voices, Malay voices when the truck slowed, even women and children's voices – the first I had heard for a long time.

The truck seemed to leave the traffic and traffic noises and drove through what smelled like countryside. I was beyond fear, but I hoped dully that I was not being driven to some lonely execution ground. After about half an hour there was a silent length of road, then a right-hand turn, another short road, a near stop, another right-hand turn which interrupted the sunlight – and then, an English voice. Almost immediately, the stretcher was lifted off the truck, I was transferred to another stretcher and carried away.

I opened my eyes fully for the first time. I was still a prisoner, and around me I saw the functional and naked walls of a modern gaol. But this was what I had been trying to achieve for months: I was inside Changi at last.

CHAPTER NINE

IT IS UNLIKELY that many people have regarded a notorious POW camp as heaven, but I felt that that is where I had arrived within a few hours of being at Changi.

When I finally opened my eyes, with almost superstitious caution, I did not see a single Japanese soldier. I was surrounded by the concerned and grinning faces of ragged British and Australian prisoners. My stretcher was the centre of caring bustle and activity and after a few minutes I was carried into the ground floor of a two-storey block which my bearers called HB. I was in the safest possible hands, in the care of sympathetic and supportive British and Australian servicemen. Then I began to cry, an uncontrollable cascade; tears of relief and joy.

I was given a bed, a real iron bed with a mattress, sheets and a pillow. The bedding was hardly needed, given the sweltering atmosphere of a Malayan summer, but the feel of cotton on my filthy skin was beautiful. Someone brought me some real tea. Then they began to appear around my bedside, bags of skin and bones I was half-convinced had been dumped by the Japanese on some city rubbish heap: Bill Smith, 'Mac', Slater, explaining that they were in the upstairs ward and that HB was one of the two hospital blocks inside the gaol and was reserved for us, for men from Outram Road. I would be moved upstairs shortly, they said. It was an astonishing coming-together, and I felt a calming wave wash over me, knowing that we had all survived so far.

A man called Jim Bradley introduced himself. I thought I had not met him before, until he explained that he had been in solitary confinement in Cell 41 in Outram Road and had been carried out on a stretcher just before Christmas. I remembered the stretcher which had been carried through the main hall of Outram Road that day, bearing a stick figure with a huge matted black beard, as though the hair had grown wild as the body wasted. Bill Anker also came up, and Ian Moffatt and Guy Machado, who had all been carried out of solitary cells, in each case with their faces lost in a mass of hair and beard. No-one was allowed to cut the hair of those in solitary confinement. There were more petty levels of cruelty than I had imagined.

At first no-one bothered about medical attention for me, but I didn't feel neglected: being in Changi was the best psychological lift that a body could wish for. My bed was just inside the ward, near the entrance; it was a little like being in bed on a railway-station platform, with crowds and movement to and fro. Yet I slept well that night, from utter exhaustion, and from the effort of talking loudly and freely to so many people.

HB was run by an Australian Army doctor from Hobart called Bon Rogers. He was an outstanding and truly dedicated man, remembered by thousands of POWs who passed through Changi.

When he examined me in the morning, the first thing he did was to weigh me. I was put on an old scales and discovered that I weighed 105 pounds, about 60 pounds less than my normal, pre-war weight. Rogers gave me a course of vitamin pills, and prescribed milk and even the occasional egg for me. This was a really rich diet: the food that came into the hospital was the best that Changi could provide, but it was still mostly rice.

Just being there was the real cure. With the relative peace, the predictability of the routine, a little extra food, the cleanliness, the kindness of the male nurses, and the comradeship and support from the other refugees from Outram Road, I slowly but steadily began to gather strength and to put on a little weight.

The Japanese had, I discovered, restored my Bible to me. They were as meticulous about prisoners' property as they were careless of their bodies. I even got my watch back. But when I tried to reawaken the spirituality I had always experienced in reading that sonorous seventeenth-century prose, I found that I had nearly forgotten how to read, and the page was a blur; my eyes could not focus properly. I had not seen a single word of print for over seven months. My acquaintance with language had shrunk to the letter 'D'.

I was reduced to spelling out the captions and garish headlines in a bound volume of *Lilliput*, a gossip and pin-up magazine of the day, and later a children's spelling book, from which I slowly copied out simple words. I had lost my mind, and spent days digging about for some memory of script. To my intense relief, the skill of reading came back fast.

After a few days I was moved upstairs to HB2. There were ten of us in that ward, five on each side of a central passage. At the end furthest from the door were the nursing staff and, equally important, the shower heads. I luxuriated in the abundant, clean, cold water that came on twice a day, for there were times in Outram Road when the stink of one's own body and its rotting covering seemed ineradicable. Just to stand with water pouring over me was lovely. In the ward there were also, at the entrance, two lavatories, real WCs with flushing mechanisms that actually worked.

Despite the cramped conditions and our shattered emotions we got on extremely well; there was never so much as an outbreak of bad temper. We had all travelled a very long way along the valley of the shadow of death and we had all emerged, so we had no time for small irritations. Some of us had taken extreme measures to get out of, and extreme boldness had put some of us into, Outram Road.

Jim Bradley, for example, had escaped from Song Krai, a camp at the very top of the railway. He was among ten prisoners who had walked into the jungle and into Burma, where high ridges ran at right angles to their line of march to the sea. It must have been like stumbling up and down through uncurbed bush on the sides of steep rocky trenches. Five of the party died in the wilderness; the survivors were captured. They were about to be shot out of hand at the prison camp, but Captain Cyril Wild, who had been Percival's interpreter at the surrender of Singapore and had been banished to this last ditch of the prison world, addressed a passionate and eloquent appeal to Lieutenant-Colonel Banno, the local Japanese commander. Jim was only alive thanks to the fluency of Wild's Japanese.

Jack Macalister's life was even more charmed. He was the Australian flyer we had heard about at Outram Road. Shot down over Timor, he had attempted twice to steal a Japanese plane, with the help of the local resistance; on each occasion he hadn't succeeded in taking off. Escapers, radio spies, stealers of planes: crucially for our harmony, we knew we were all still in extreme danger. The prison chiefs at Outram Road would never forget, or be allowed to forget about us. As far as they were concerned, we were simply in Changi to gain enough strength to be recalled to finish our sentences, and we were thus in a strange conflict. Bon Rogers wanted us to regain our health, and so did we, but the last thing we wanted was to be well enough to return to Outram Road. We were ghosts on holiday.

There was in any case a limit to what could be achieved in the hospital at Changi. Some of us could not get our limbs to work properly. My arms were in bad condition, as I discovered for myself when I tried to write or move my fingers quickly without lifting my arms high. Some men's eyes had been weakened dangerously: those who had lost their glasses suffered from near-blindness. Stomach illnesses were endemic. Slater had appalling dysentery. Nevertheless, slowly, our physical condition improved.

Bon Rogers came around every morning in the best hospital tradition, exuding authority and reassurance, and he took the closest personal care of us. The nurses gave us whatever medicine was available. I was given an enormous daily dose of rice-polishings in a kind of broth. These are the fibrous husks of rice, removed in the normal processing of white rice and contain vitamins and roughage. They were difficult to consume, so light and dry that they floated in a heap on the surface of water. However, I packed the ticklish flakes down diligently.

On his rounds, Dr Rogers also began to give us snapshots from the war. Since we had been in Outram Road the English and Americans had landed in Europe, the Russians had forced the Germans back towards Warsaw and the Japanese were being wiped out in the Pacific and pushed back in Burma and China. This was exalting news, but it was not unmixed with fear. Only if the war came to an end quickly had we any real chance of survival, but even then we were worried about the vengeance the Japanese might exact if they saw defeat on the horizon in the form of an invasion fleet. Even if the Allies started bombing Singapore in earnest, there might be reprisals on prisoners, and on convicted criminals among them first of all. The best we could do, therefore, was to live a day at a time, but no matter how hard we tried, and no matter how soothing our friends at Changi tried to be, we could never throw off the permanent burden of continuous fear that the warders from Outram Road were liable to appear at any moment to conduct their own so-called medical examinations.

It was clear to us, though we were careful not to ask or learn anything we did not need to know, that Bon Rogers was not getting his victory bulletins from obliging Japanese guards. Where the radio was and who was operating it were interesting secrets, but we prayed that the group running it would be more careful, or just luckier, than we had been. It was one more proof of how hard it is to shut down speech.

In the afternoon we tried to read and to rest. There were enough books in Changi to provide an amazing and eclectic library, endlessly circulating until the books fell to pieces: religious tracts, Victorian novels, the works of Hugh Walpole, Somerset Maugham, the Powys brothers and Arnold Bennett, moving from hand to hand in a hot, sweaty prison-city. For the population of Changi never fell below about 3000, and frequently rose to 5000, and because the Japanese allowed the POWs to run it internally more or less at their own discretion, there was more cultural activity here than in most small towns.

Changi had stamp-collecting clubs, debating societies, literary circles, even a dry land yacht club for commodores nostalgic about the sea. Everyone was using memories to support themselves and entertain each other.

Up on the second floor of HB, we could not take part in

debates about the shape of the post-war world or the meaning of evolution, but we certainly had books. There was a book bindery at the prison, and the tattered volumes were kept together with heavy, home-made gums made from rice and water or stewed bones, and patched up with cannibalized prison records, of which there were reams. Charge sheets for Indian privates written in copperplate in happier colonial days became the endpapers of works by Bunyan, Blake or Defoe. The adhesive still feels solid, heavy, and crude, but also very strong; I have some of these books with me now. They are the most well-thumbed, eroded books I have ever seen, worn to a softness and fragility, and made compact by sheer use, but they seem indestructible.

One of the books I still have is a Gibbon's stamp catalogue for 1936, *Stamps of the British Empire, Part One*. I remembered how not long ago I was spreading out hundreds of these stamps on the floor of an Edinburgh house with a young friend. The thought of the order and beauty of these franked bits of serrated, squared paper was extraordinarily comforting to me: there was once a world of regularity, punctuality and neat categories. I made careful pencilled notes on African and Malayan stamps, columns of different prices, colours, devices and monarchs' heads. It was a therapy of lists; it was a way of forgetting arbitrary, unpredictable hell.

It was during this time in Changi that I swapped my Authorized Version of the Bible for the Moffatt translation which I still have, because I was curious about this new and celebrated edition, and so Harkness got my tiny marginal commentaries and underlinings and I got his. Between rereading the Bible, learning Hindustani – which I was also trying to do, from a grammar – and classifying things in order to remember them, the afternoons and the months passed quickly for me.

Bon Rogers told us that as a safety measure we must never go out in daylight, but he allowed us out for walks around the gaol after dark. It meant we were still in a prison within a prison, but the restriction was worth it. There were no Japanese inside Changi – except when they came in to seize a prisoner or negotiate with the senior officers – so Bradley and I made slow circuits of the complex while we looked up at the night sky and breathed the air of our heaven. Outside the walls thousands of Allied prisoners were living at Selarang, at Kranji and in other makeshift camps, but we were dangerous, so we were in the prison itself. Our favourite walkway was the road between the inner and the high outer walls, because it was so secluded; it made a blank concrete channel, and it was like walking along the bottom of a drain. The Japanese were at the main gate, but not on the walls, and we walked unmolested for hours.

For many prisoners, Changi was a dreadful place: only Outram Road made it seem homely to us. I was relieved to see the shockingly swollen figure of Stan Davis, ill with beri-beri, arriving at Changi soon after my own arrival; and Harry Knight was carried in on a stretcher one day. This reminded us that we were on leave from obscenity. He was at rock bottom; barely recognizable, his frame reduced to weak bones in loose pale skin, his eyes sunk in his head. Rogers had him moved immediately to another hospital wing inside Changi, but within ten days Harry was dead.

Jack Macalister thought that his own recovery had gone far enough to be dangerous. He talked to one of the medical officers, quietly and privately, and one day they put their plan into operation. It was all done calmly, as though the MO were about to give him an injection. Jack sat on a chair and held a length of 2-inch steel pipe vertically over his left foot. The other man lifted a big hammer and smashed it down on the open top of the pipe. Macalister was in bad pain as the MO wrapped his foot in plaster, but he had bought himself an extra few weeks of companionship and humane treatment.

Knight's death prepared me all too well for leaving what Macalister was determined to keep. The POWs on duty at the prison entrance would instantly send a message to HB if any of the Japanese from Outram Road appeared, so that we might have at least a few minutes' warning in which to arrange ourselves. On 25th January 1945 the blow fell, and the warnings were useless. A party of Japanese, including one who we thought might be a doctor of some kind, came without warning into the hospital block. Their medical officer, accompanied by Bon Rogers, walked around every bed on both floors and looked closely at the occupants. Dr Rogers outlined each person's medical history and listed their various ailments and demonstrated their disabilities. Unfortunately, I was betrayed by my own cursed vitality. I was looking quite well that day, for a sick prisoner, and the Japanese officer decided that I was well enough for Outram Road.

Within a matter of minutes I had to pack my kit, say goodbye to the fortunate ones and climb on to a truck where, for the second time, the Imperial Japanese Army Prison Service took charge of me.

We drove quickly into Singapore and headed straight for Outram Road. I had expected this for weeks, but the thought that my clean, relaxed body would shortly be reduced to scrapings and dirt, and that my time at Changi was about to pass away like water was unutterably lowering. The truck drove up to the huge doors, they opened like the jaws of a beast and shut with me inside.

⋆ ⋆ ⋆

I knew the routine; stripping off, laying small items on a table, handing everything over for storage, and being inspected and examined in every orifice.

They allocated me a new number. This time I was No. 540, otherwise *Go-hyaku yon-ju*. I wondered what had happened to the last 540, whose number had come and gone. Then we were taken across to D Block. I knew the way. I was allocated a cell almost opposite No. 52, my old address, and found that I was sharing with a young Indonesian from the island of Celebes, or Sulawesi.

We communicated haltingly, for his English was not good, but we got on well together. He was the first Asian person I had ever been close to as an equal, and so my forced education in other ways of life continued. He had been a Dutch East Indies soldier in Sumatra, and the Japanese had suspected him (rightly, as it turned out) of membership in a resistance group. He was lucky to be alive at all. He talked about his village, about the fishing and farming his people lived off. I told him about the Shetlands, of which his island seemed a tropical reflection.

Some things had changed for the better in Outram Road. Cell doors were now open nearly all day, although this meant that we had to be even more careful about talking. The food had improved a little. The worst of the diseases which we had had to suffer a year earlier seemed to have been eradicated. Meals were now taken in silence at a long table in the middle of the main hall. Most prisoners were out of their cells for a good part of the day.

Presumably the Japanese had suddenly realized that in D Block they had a potential labour force which was not only docile but which did not have to be paid. About thirty or forty men were taken out on most days in trucks to excavate tunnels in a hillside some miles away, preparations for some suicidal resistance to invasion. We did not feel good about those tunnels.

They also enlisted us as gardeners. There was now a high-ranking officer in Outram Road, a Colonel Parker of the Indian Army. He and I were assigned to the care and manuring with our human dung of the vegetable gardens which ran down the outside of the blocks, and supplied the kitchens. The smell of faeces was overpowering in the heat as we watered and hoed and pulled up vegetables. The stink permeated our clothes as I moved doggedly along the rills with this senior, rather patrician figure by my side.

They once took us to the potato garden and told us that we could help ourselves, but the potatoes were not ripe and we contented ourselves with eating the tops, which someone later told me are poisonous. They did not seem to do our stomachs much additional harm. Parker remarked that we must be the first British Army officers to be turned out to graze a potato patch.

The sheer horror of the prison had only diminished. It was still a ghastly place. The daily routine was still composed of near-starvation, brutality, frustrating and heavy work, lack of medical attention and confinement in our cells for fourteen hours a day. The psychological burden of living under an arbitrary regime was still too heavy for comfort. The slight improvement in health had created a new problem: the prospects of getting out on grounds of illness were drastically reduced.

I was determined to do it again, for all that. I loathed the thought of dying in this cesspit and began to consider alternatives. Escape over the wall was probably feasible, but a half-naked, ragged and crazy British prisoner on the roads around Singapore would be extremely conspicuous.

I tried to plan rationally, to list the attractions of various possibilities and eliminate the unattractive options. The basic problem was information, or rather a lack of it. Despite the usual chain of whispers, serious communication was out of the question. It was still nearly impossible to find out who was in the gaol; new prisoners would appear and familiar faces disappear without warning.

It was very unusual to be ordered to go on an unsupervised errand. One day I was told to go to the next block to pick up some buckets and as I turned a corner there was Lance Thew, similarly unaccompanied. We stood in that silent yard in amazement at each other's presence. The fluke of meeting without guards allowed him to tell me quietly that the Japanese had kept him behind after the court martial to repair their radios, in a fairly comfortable workshop where he could probably have seen out the war tinkering with radio receivers and transmitters, but he didn't fancy that and had escaped. After 'taking a look around Bangkok' he realized that his chances of getting further were not very good, and gave himself up. Thew was a man who didn't just tempt fate, he thought he knew its frequency and could tune in to it, but now he too was in Outram Road.

* * *

I decided that one of the best steps I could take towards escaping once more would be to get on to the Binki Squad. The squad consisted of six or eight men who were called out from their cells every morning, and collected from a store the broad wooden stretchers on which they carried the latrine buckets, and then opened up a manhole in the yard outside D Block. On a command, the squad broke up into pairs and set off, visiting every occupied cell on their routes. While prisoners were supposed to set their buckets on their doorsteps, they did not always do so, and with three or four pairs of prisoners on the move simultaneously and only one guard, there were opportunities for quick spoken exchanges. The binki men had access to water, and information, and they had mobility.

I told one of them that I would like to join the squad, and a few days later I was called out and told to join the group just going on duty, apparently replacing someone who was ill.

I got used to the smell of full latrine buckets swinging on the stretchers around my shoulders. Over the next few weeks I slowly and patiently established from my brief conversations with prisoners, bending down over their stinking buckets of waste, that there was no scope at all for getting out through sickness, but that one or two people had been taken away following accidents at work.

I also discovered that there was something up on the first floor which was off limits to other prisoners. We were never allowed to go up there, except on latrine duty. The cell doors there were shut all the time. In the silence you would have expected small sounds to betray the presence of other men, but even though the guards were heard to go up the stairs we never heard so much as the rattle of a bowl. Yet somewhere up above us, we were convinced, were comrades of ours undergoing a punishment even more extreme than the one that applied to us.

I had almost nothing to do but think, and so I thought about escape all the time; it became the single overriding concern of my life. But for a long time nothing useful came to me.

I kept thinking about the stairs. At the end of the main hall, furthest from the main door, was the large iron staircase leading up to the first floor. No prisoner had ever mounted them during my first period in Outram Road, but now there were those mysterious and very special prisoners up there. Only one pair of binki men was needed to collect their latrine buckets, empty and return them. I arranged to have a place on the first floor gang.

For several days I examined the stairs closely. The treads were made of iron, English cast iron, but there were no backs to the steps. I counted the steps obsessively as I walked up and down, and checked my arithmetic to make absolutely sure. I needed to know the exact number of steps, as though the numbers held some promise in themselves. I came to the conclusion that if I were to trip or fall on the 17th step from the ground, which was almost at the top of a straight run of steps, I would have a long way to bump down to the bottom, which might do enough damage to make an official accident without killing me. Then I thought that if I were to include the stretcher and the latrine buckets in my fall, the accident would be much more impressive. In my desperate urgency to escape I was quite prepared to stage the fall on the way down, which would leave me awash in foulness. I decided, however, to arrange the accident on the upward journey, with the load of cleaned empty buckets.

I nerved myself hard. I planned it, as I liked to do with everything; for several days I rehearsed loading empty buckets on the stretcher so that there would be as much weight as possible at my end at the right moment; getting behind the stretcher, stepping on the first step with the right foot, counting the steps, then, while putting my weight on my right foot on the 17th step, putting my left foot through the open back of the step and falling.

One morning I woke up and decided that I was going to throw myself down the metal prison stairs that day. As we left the yard, I wedged my spectacles as securely as I could behind my ears, jammed my cap on tight to protect my ears and the glasses, and entered the block. I told the man in front of me not to hold on to his end of the stretcher too tightly and to let go altogether immediately he felt it being pulled out of his hands.

We moved sedately through the main hall and came to the bottom of the stairs. I counted as we went up, then as we neared the turn of the stairs, with my right foot on the 17th step I lifted my left foot towards the 18th, shoved my leg through the open back and pulled the stretcher down on top of me with its load of empty buckets and lids.

The noise of crashing wood and metal in that huge silent gallery was frightful. I roared with pain and relief, and sprawled out at the bottom mixed up in the heap, trying to look as contorted as I could. My spectacles survived even this, and were still wedded to my nose. I was hurting, but I could not take the risk of checking how much damage had been done.

I heard both Japanese and English voices. Willing and gentle hands, obviously English or Australian, picked me up and carried me off to my cell. My bearers laid me out on my planks. I did not want to move but I wriggled just enough to check that I could move my fingers and toes, and they seemed to be in working order; I had been terrified of damaging my spine. I was badly and painfully bruised, but even my ribs still seemed to be in the right places. I had got off very lightly – perhaps too lightly for my own good.

Guards came in to have a look at me. I kept my head still. One of them took my pulse and poked about my chest and legs.

Another figure arrived, out of range of my eyes deliberately narrowed to focus on the blotchy ceiling. I lay there, ignored the evening meal and remained semi-conscious for most of the night. I was determined not to move; lying motionless became steadily more and more uncomfortable.

Days and nights followed each other. It is incredibly difficult to remain in a single position for so long, but I was waiting for the Japanese guards to start imagining strange paralyses wasting my body until I was beyond suspicion of malingering. My Indonesian cellmate was magnificent, attending on my rigid figure uncomplainingly, helping me to eat and drink. I asked for the latrine bucket to be brought to me, since it would be unwise to be mobile enough to stagger to the other end of the cell. Sometimes he washed me down, when he could get some water.

Two weeks passed, miserable and difficult weeks; I was beginning to find the near-starvation difficult, especially as I was deliberately rejecting food that I could see and smell. Sometimes I ate a little, just to keep my shut-down faculties alive. But nothing eased the abrasion of bones on skin without fat – I felt encased in a paper-thin membrane irritated and chafed by the very act of lying still. The urge to move was unbearable. All that time I wore the same shirt and shorts, which became dirty rags congealed to my body.

As a step towards forcing the issue I allowed my rice bowl to drop with a clatter one evening, spilling the white grains over me and the floor. I lay on my back and tried to urinate. It isn't that easy to foul yourself voluntarily; but eventually and degradingly, persistence was rewarded and a large puddle expanded across the floor.

The guard on that shift must have noticed something, for after only a few hours the medical orderly appeared. He nudged and pinched me and then walked away.

The following morning a stretcher party picked me up and brought me to the administration block. I was dumped on the floor. The medical orderly appeared at my side. I was careful not to turn my head, lying in profile like a lanky mummy. A metal instrument tinkled as he picked it up, and then I felt sharp pressure and a prick inside my mouth, a needle jabbing into my gum. It felt like a long needle piercing my jaw. I could feel it forcing through on to the bone, filling my face with iron. As this was clearly the medical examination I had to remain deadpan for another few minutes; if I had reacted I would have ruined weeks of plotting.

He drew out the needle, and soon my kit was dumped on me, as before, and I was moved on to the stretcher and loaded on to a vehicle. Once again there was the long run past Kallang, the right-hand turn, the slow run of about a hundred yards and another right-hand turn. When I heard a Scottish voice say 'It's Lomax again!' and recognized the speaker as Robert Reid, late of 5 Field Regiment at Kuantan, the voice of the Angel Gabriel could not have been more welcome. Within minutes I was among friends in the hospital block.

* * *

The physical and psychic relief was once again immense. This time I was determined that I would leave Changi as a free human being or not at all. I discovered that the date was 10th April 1945.

Bradley and Macalister were still there, Bill Smith, Alex Mackay and Jim Slater too. But the malevolent shuttle between the two prisons kept working right to the end. Macalister, despite his terrible preventive measures, was taken back to Outram Road four days after my arrival for the second time at Changi.

Bon Rogers was as calm and dedicated as ever, a man living out his medical oath. He put me on a grass diet. I did not actually have to chew the stuff, but had to drink at least a pint of grass 'soup' each morning. It was a revolting liquid, but like everyone else privileged to receive it, I drank it down.

They also gave me the hot bath treatment. In the open yard a domestic bath was set up with an attendant who went back and forth fetching hot water for each new bather. His task in my case was to help me remove some of the near-solid scum and dirt which I had again brought with me from Outram Road.

I got back into the routine of HB2, reading and talking. Sometimes in the evenings the Australians Russell Braddon and Sydney Piddington came into the ward to talk. They were experimenting with telepathy and asked for volunteers to attend their demonstrations. It was eerie, in a darkened prison block, to see them guess the contents of a prisoner's pockets or the name of a man's wife, calling up invisible energies as mysterious as radio waves had been to me as a child. We were probably appallingly credulous, but what they did seemed to us real magic in those last months of the war, as the tension mounted towards a barbaric last stand by the Japanese military rulers.

Bon Rogers told us that in Europe the Nazi armies were nearly destroyed and Berlin was under attack from east and west. But around the overcrowded blocks and yards of Changi there were rumours of trenches being dug nearby, of preparations for mass murder. When we heard that Rangoon had been captured on 3rd May, our exhilaration was poisoned by fear. Now, surely, was the moment of Japanese vengeance.

As though I had created a gap in the scheme of things, after all

my efforts to fake an accident, I had a real accident that may have
saved me from being returned to Outram Road. The only way we
could get salt was by distilling it from seawater. Every day a party
would go down to the shore, fill up old oil drums and bring
seawater back to camp, which was then distributed among the
blocks. We got a quantity one day in HB2 and I volunteered – I
had learnt nothing, after all – to boil it down to salt. I had an army
mess-tin, and an old electric fire element twisted to make a hot
ring linked up to the mains, and eventually I had a tin
threequarters full of semi-liquid salt and assorted grit.

Sitting on the edge of my bed, I was adjusting the apparatus
when I caught my arm on the long handle of the tin and tipped it
off my makeshift electric ring. It landed neatly on my right knee.
The salt sludge, which was near boiling point, flowed like lava
down my leg, taking the skin with it. The pain was so intense that
I lost touch with the situation for a while, but I remember Jim
Bradley tenderly dabbing the salt off with warm water, and an
orderly injecting me with morphine, and then floating in the
clouds. It was a long time before they took the bandages off.

One evening early in August Bon gathered us round him on
our beds and told an incomprehensible story, which he could not
credit himself. He said that a new type of bomb had been used
over Japan, that it had destroyed the city of Hiroshima, that it was
a weapon of terrible power developed in secret by the Allies, and
that there was talk of surrender, but none of us believed it. False
optimism was at a premium in Changi by late 1945.

The Japanese medical inspections continued even now. On
9th August eight men were judged fit to return to Outram Road
and that evening the reports from the secret radio spoke of
another bomb of almost cosmic power and another Japanese

city destroyed. I was passed over in the selection.

Six days later Japan surrendered. Four days after that, the gates of hell were opened from the inside and all the surviving Allied prisoners were brought from Outram Road to Changi. One or two of them died a few hours after they arrived. Fred Smith was all right, surviving twenty-two months in Outram Road without a break, his unyielding stamina holding his shrunken body together, his spirit seemingly unbroken. But then we all tried to be patterns of courage to each other, and the price we paid would not be exacted in full until much later.

That same day a radio loudspeaker appeared on the outside wall of Changi Gaol. Suddenly All India Radio was blaring gloriously out all over the compound, excited British voices describing the scale of the Allied victory. Thousands upon thousands of light-headed, delirious prisoners came from the outlying camps and danced under the walls, their hilarity coming as much from hunger as from joy. The Japanese guards stared at the loudspeaker in disbelief. Hundreds of men sat beneath the speaker cheering every item of news and revelling in the sullen depression of the guards. In HB2 we exulted, but we were aware that the real victory for us was to have survived.

Two or three Liberator bombers came over and dropped a quantity of parcels and medical supplies and crates of food. Then a lone bomber dropped three parachutists. We watched them float down, unclip their harness and walk up to the front entrance of the gaol. They looked terribly young to us: a British officer each from the airforce, the navy and the army, with a priggish and bossy air about them of coming to take charge of us. We did not feel helpless or in need of rescue by such inexperienced young men. The army captain was told by a POW that he had been in school when we were first locked up and that if he liked, we would give him lunch, but that was the only co-operation we were going to give him.

The Japanese retired quietly to their barracks, and handed over their arms. More of our troops dropped from the sky and arrived by sea and found our prison-city organizing and feeding itself and reconstituting itself as an army. They let us get on with what we were doing.

As we restored our contact with the army and the world we began to find endings for some of the stories that we'd had to tell each other over and over, never certain of their proper outcome, for the past three years. The Australian nurses at Banka Island, for example: fifty of them had died, even more than we thought, but two had survived. Primrose, the humane murderer of his own soldier, was not executed but returned to the railway, and he had survived. The silent prisoners on the first floor of Outram Road were men who had attacked ships in Singapore Harbour in September 1943 – just after our arrest – and got clean away, and returned a year later, when they were detected; ten officers and men were captured. They were beheaded on 9th July, near Bukit Timah, a bare month before the war ended; they had provided the occasion for my second exit from Outram Road, and I never had the chance to thank them.

I heard about other radios in other camps, hidden in broomheads, in bamboo tubes and water-bottles, and what had happened to some of the men who made them. We already knew that the Australian Captain Matthews had been executed in Borneo. Now I heard that a captain called Douglas Ford had been shot in Hong Kong for the sort of thing we had done at Kanburi. The name sounded familiar; he had been at school with me in Edinburgh. Ford and Matthews had both operated radios and made contact with civilians outside their camps. If the

Japanese had once been sure that we had done the same at Kanburi, we would never have come through.

Lance Thew had disappeared again, removed from Outram Road in May. The Japanese must have been desperate by then for skilled radio men. I never saw or heard from Thew again, though I know he survived. But of Bill Williamson, the calm and competent linguist who had escaped our punishment at Kanburi, there was no trace at all. It was as though he had vanished, somewhere up the railway.

I tried to draw up a full record of prisoners who had passed through the military section of Outram Road, determined to log all the names so that others could account for them. I read the medical records and spoke to all the survivors. I wanted to get the facts on paper and into the hands of South-East Asia Command before we were all dispersed. We were being split up and assigned to different units around Changi in preparation for going home. When I started to type, on an ancient manual machine, I discovered that my right arm and hand would not work properly, so I tapped away very slowly.

I also drew up detailed complaints about our treatment at Kanburi, taking statements from the survivors. Major Slater, as the senior officer among us – suddenly ranks mattered again – signed the statement. The Kanburi Radio Affair, we called it in our statement after we agreed a final version; the designation began to seem a kind of euphemism. We were becoming history, and we could tell how close we were to being forgotten already.

The good can be forgotten as easily as the bad, even more easily, so I also typed out a commendation for Signalman O'Malley, that heroic toban from Outram Road. I described what he had done in the unemotional language of an army memo, but it still recalled him carrying paralysed men into the sunshine, caring for the sick and doing his utmost to ease conditions for the damned.

This meticulous, orderly registration of witnesses and participants and descriptions of the criminals was a wonderful displacement of anger and revenge. It still astonishes me that there were not more spontaneous outbursts of summary justice on the guards, but our normality reasserted itself very quickly, and that did not include lynchings.

I kept copies of all these documents. Today they are almost faded, but not quite. O'Malley's commendation is typed in faint pale violet on the back of an Admiralty telegram form; the complaint against the Kanburi Aerodrome Camp Commander and his NCOs on some heavy green ledger paper, and you can see the jumping keys and how faded the ribbon was. I have a list of some of the civilian prisoners from the blocks at Outram Road which we seldom saw, written on POW toilet paper – a thin, fibrous transparency covered in small pencilled capitals. The typed list of prisoners evacuated from Outram Road to Changi is almost illegible, with neat dotted lines separating the categories, on thin tan paper which once surrounded a toilet roll, the black serifs of the type nearly cutting through it. You can still read the label: 'Red Cross Onliwon Toilet Tissue'.

CHAPTER TEN

THE RANDOM HAZARDS of captivity gave way to the orderly regime of the army. I was once more a serving officer, and I was being sent home. I had not seen my family for over four years; I had been around the world and had witnessed things that had not been dreamed of for centuries in the world I had left behind. My 'unpleasantness', as I often called it, for we survivors almost competed with each other in laconic understatement, seemed to have ended with the surrender of Japan. I was more worried about my physical injuries: my arms, my exhaustion, the skin diseases which I could not eradicate; I still had ringworm when I left Changi. I didn't understand yet that there are experiences you can't walk away from, and that there is no statute of limitations on the effects of torture.

The rush of reorganization, the excitement of departure and the concentration on gathering the evidence for the high command of what had been done to us held other thoughts at bay. The past two years had seen so many fresh invasions of fear and anxiety that it was difficult for the mind to dwell on particular episodes, and although I had had enough angry hours to think about Kanburi, the discovery and betrayal and the

Kempeitai interrogations, I was now almost too busy to remember. Instead there were the latest and the last of the wartime partings from friends I had come to admire. Jim Bradley, who was in the next bed to mine in HB2, was still very ill and was sent to a hospital ship; Macalister rejoined the Australian Air Force; Fred Smith and the others were sent to different parts of the jigsaw-puzzle army around Changi. After we were broken up, many of us never saw each other again.

My 5th Field Regiment, which had been left in the lurch at Kuantan in 1941, was by then in Formosa, but we were expected to be attached to some body of men and to make ourselves useful, so I was sent to help take charge of the Indian troops, of whom there were thousands in the city, leaderless and disorganized. Colonel Parker, with whom I had grazed potato leaves, was now my commanding officer. We organized some big parades, checking names and identities of men who had been used as labourers and survived, remnants of the once-proud Imperial Indian Army. Some of the assembled men had joined the Japanese-sponsored Indian National Army, and could have taken part in the abortive invasion of India in early 1944; these men were denounced by their comrades who had stayed loyal to their original commitment. The INA men were arrested and passed from our hands.

One day I was simply told to get down to the docks with about fifty men and to take them to Calcutta. I said goodbye to Malaya, as abruptly as that. We sailed on a converted liner called the *Devonshire* and reached India in less than a week.

In Calcutta I was sent to a place called Belvedere, a magnificent residence used by the Viceroy of India when he stayed in Calcutta, which had been turned into a reception centre for returning POWs. It resembled an enormous Italianate

English country house, the sweeping staircases and colonnades of the façade rearing massively in the heat of Bengal. The loggias and caryatids of this massive palace were now shrouded in purplish camouflage. The ballroom with its acres of springy wooden flooring had been divided into offices for a paymaster and the Red Cross, a canteen, a bar and a post office. It had splendid rooms, full of heavy English chairs with thick legs, long polished tables and sideboards laden with blue china. The windows were enormous, letting in the afternoon light of an Indian autumn on to young men unable to believe their luck.

It was run by 'lady volunteers', brisk self-confident women used to servants and to getting their own way but on the whole wonderfully kind to us. Most of them, at least. One afternoon a woman joined me and another officer who had been on the railway as we drank tea on the veranda, looking out over the green, watered grass and the rose bushes and still marvelling at our recovery and the sheer pleasure of amenities that made this place a paradise to us. She was a vigorous breezy memsahib, and thought it right to speak her mind, as she would no doubt have described it. She was sure, she said, that as we had been prisoners-of-war during most of the fighting she expected that we would be eager 'to do our bit' now. There wasn't a trace of irony in her voice. In it you could sense her picture of the camps in Siam and Malaya as places full of bored, underemployed and shameful men. We held the sides of our chairs tightly and said nothing. At the time I thought that this was one insensitive civilian, but I soon discovered that you have to have seen things with your own eyes before you believe them with any intimacy, and that there are some things which many people do not want to know.

After a few days of rest I began to feel weak, fainting and generally exhausted. The sudden requirement to do nothing was more than my system could bear. A doctor put me to bed for three days in a military hospital and I slept for fourteen hours a day.

After my brief convalescence I was sent on to Mhow, in central India, where the kit I had left in 1941 had been kept in a store manned by Italian prisoners-of-war. From there I sent my mother a birthday telegram. The prospect of seeing my family again was becoming real, the remoteness of their faces diminishing, but it was still hard to see across the gulf that the war and Outram Road had put between us. I looked forward to my parents' house in Edinburgh as one does to a bracing plunge into a clean, cold pool; it represented normality and the pleasure of an unexciting kindness.

I felt other anticipations too. In Mhow I had a gold wedding ring made for my fiancée. I assumed that she would still be there, and that time would have stood still for her while so much had happened to me. I had no idea how much the world had changed, or how much I had changed – and how little some people had moved from the ruts they had made for themselves before the war.

From Mhow there was a train to Deolali, and a delay while I and other stray officers were allocated to a ship returning to England. We were sent down to Bombay and found ourselves on the *Johan van Oldenbarnevelt*, a requisitioned Dutch ship heading for Southampton.

On board I was approached by some former POWs from Siam who had officers in charge of them who had not themselves been POWs. They were being allocated ordinary ship's duties by regimental officers who had no conception of what these men had been through. My robust lady volunteer back in Calcutta had co-thinkers in the army, it seemed. The ex-prisoners felt that they had done as much forced labour in the previous three years as they wanted to do for a while: they wished these officers in hell. These were broken-down men, ill and in need of rest and great care. I went to the ship's adjutant and argued that they should be treated as passengers, not as working soldiers. He agreed, but carelessly and offhandedly, an ominous sign of the complete ignorance that was being drawn over our experiences like a veil.

Apart from this the voyage was eventless. I read day after day. We reached Southampton on 31st October 1945. The band had played 'There'll Always Be An England' when we arrived at Singapore in 1941, but our landfall was quiet and subdued, in the chill grey weather of the English coast at the approach of winter. Some mail came on board and my name was called. I was handed a letter from my father telling me that my mother had died three and a half years before, about a month after the fall of Singapore. She was sixty-four years old. She had died thinking that I was dead, because I had been reported missing. And my father also told me he had married again.

I knew the woman he had married. She had been an old family friend for years; or rather, a friend of his. I had never liked her much; she had always seemed an insincere and acquisitive person. All the calmly-constructed images of home which I had been nurturing on the voyage back simply vanished. I was so shocked that I could not tell grief and anger apart, sorrow for my mother almost eclipsed by my response to what seemed like a betrayal by my father. It was a quick and brutal indication that I was not returning to anything I would find familiar. I felt exhausted again, physically and emotionally, remembering her seeing me off in that darkened street in Scarborough; remembering all the times I had thought of her, and her already dead. There were things I could probably have told her that proved hard to share with others.

I spent ten hours on the train the next day too numb to plan much. When I got to Edinburgh there was no-one to meet me, and this may have decided my course of action. I did not go home. I couldn't bring myself to turn up as a stranger to find my mother's place taken, and be dependent on that woman and my father, so at the station I took one of the cars driven by women volunteers to my fiancée's family and went down the next day to my father's house in Joppa, my base secure.

My reserve must have been palpable. Over my natural formality was now laid the instinctive caution and blankness of the prisoner used to hiding his feelings. I hardly knew it then, but I had begun the process of shutting down my emotions, pulling back into cold anger at the first sign of confrontation rather than expressing myself. My father and his new wife – I could hardly bring myself to think of her as my 'stepmother' – were welcoming, but I was not. They wanted me and my fiancée to come with them on a holiday to the Lake District, but I evaded the invitation.

I don't mean to be unkind to my father. He was in his sixties then, and retired from the Post Office, and he told me later that his friend had saved his life by marrying him, that he was going downhill fast after my mother died so suddenly. I couldn't grudge him that, but I could not reconcile myself to what he had done, thinking that the second Mrs Lomax cannot have been indifferent to his good pension and comfortable house when she took him on. Within two days I was in a world that seemed cynical and petty compared to the companionship and the seriousness that comes from facing death which I had found in the camps and Outram Road.

Three weeks later S. and I were married. We were as innocent of each other as could be, and I was led into it by my own docility, her eagerness and a romantic idea of her that I had sustained through thick and thin. I was in love, yes, but with what? I was taking a leap in the dark every bit as risky as that jump on the stairs at Outram Road Gaol. I had been six years in another life – in another world, for all she knew – while she had gone on in the quiet certainties of a strictly religious provincial family. Edinburgh had suffered the usual privations of wartime Britain – rationing, blackout, the evacuation of children – but it was not as damaged as parts of London or some of the Midlands towns had been by German air raids, and I could hardly believe that it had been in the war at all.

She was the nearest safe haven I could find from my father's betrayal and the pain that I could not get rid of or understand. I was already living in a world of my own; the privacy of the torture victim is more impregnable than any island fortress. I could not have begun to understand that in 1945, for I did not have the words to describe what I was going through.

Nor did anyone I knew; and certainly not the army. The entire extent of my attention from the British Army after the war consisted of a brief medical examination at an army centre in Edinburgh in November 1945. I could walk across the room, was warm to the touch and had no incurable diseases, so they turned me loose. Get on with your life, the doctor seemed to say, as though it was the easiest thing in the world. The wounds were not on the surface, nor detectable by stethoscope. My rush to marriage was a symptom of their presence.

The prison camp had become a familiar world to me. I had hardened myself to survive in it, and now I was separated from it, burdened with experiences that I could not describe, cursed with the gifts of deviousness, prevarication and impassivity that had been so essential during my captivity, and expected to resume a normal life.

One of the principal difficulties of the ex-prisoner-of-war is finding the strength to resist the force of circumstance, to say 'no' to unwanted suggestions and commands. I think that I had particular difficulty finding the will to dig in my heels, though I also had deep reserves of stubborn energy. But being swept along by events, especially in those first months of freedom, demanded less of my depleted powers. And combined with this negative force was the positive desire to settle, to find an emotional sanctuary as caring as Changi had been of my other injuries in 1944.

Prisoners-of-war don't find it easy to settle. Today, fifty years after the end of the war, I know a man of about my age, who was also a prisoner in the Far East, and who leaves his house each morning and goes walking, walking, walking until it is dark. He cannot sit and relax. He has become a well-known figure in the town where he lives. For years he controlled this agitation with drink, which kept him close to the pub and a kind of peace, but his alcoholism began to destroy him and he sobered up. Work was always difficult for him, but it too provided a kind of anchor. Now that the alcoholic foundation has been taken away and he has retired, he drifts like a boat, always moving on his own secret current. It's as though the restlessness which he has been suppressing all his life since his return from the Far East now has nothing to keep it in check, and it has taken him over.

My experiences had put a huge distance between me and my previous life, yet I behaved – was expected to behave – as though I were the same person. In the legal and civil senses I suppose I was, but that was about all. Here was Eric Lomax playing the part of the newly-wed, pretending he was what he had been in 1941, before he left for the East, when his innocence and much of his emotional life had not been ripped out of him. That young man's life had been mapped out by his obsession with trains and other relics of the industrial age, which were more alluring to him than the history recorded by conventional scholars. The cry of a locomotive had been like an invitation to get away from himself, but the obligation undertaken by that now vanished young man held me in its honourable grip. I had grown up appallingly in the years I had been away. I was much harder, less able to enjoy other people's pleasures easily and certainly less able to sympathize with their smaller misfortunes. Yet I stepped back confusedly into the tide and it carried me away, as it did so many other young men in that winter of 1945.

We were married in the Chapel, of course, and I was as passive about being drawn back into it as I was about everything else. J. Sidlow Baxter was still in command, still denouncing sin and evil with his evangelical bookkeeper's fervour, and he was glad to enter me again on the credit side of his flock. The wedding ring I had commissioned in India turned out to be too small for my bride's finger.

We were happy, at first, as excited as any young lovers can be, but we did not know each other well enough to have signed away our lives together. She was pretty, articulate and gifted with a fine singing voice, but her culture was limited by the nature of her upbringing. Her only world had been that of the Chapel and her parents' friends. She had stood still in the quiet, determined way that people who are sure of themselves, and who have never been exposed to influences from outside their circle, can sometimes do for their entire lives.

It cannot have been easy for her; she really had no idea of what she was taking on. One of the first things she found herself doing was rubbing special cream into my infected skin. Ringworm and eczema were among my contributions to the honeymoon. I can see how hard it was, despite our later estrangement. I was broken down; her own romantic ideas were rubbed up against the reality of this nervous, pale and debilitated young man. She was as much a victim of the war as me.

One of the first unbridgeable distances between us was created simply by our inability to talk. I have spent most of my life unable to talk about my experiences in South-East Asia, but I am pretty sure that in those early years of intimacy with my wife I wanted to try to tell her, to explain to her what it had been like. It was hard for her to be interested. I was expected to behave as though my formative years had not happened. My fumbling attempts to begin a description of the effects of what my comrades and I had experienced in Kanburi, or to talk about the Japanese who had done these things to us, were brushed aside. She naturally felt that she had had a hard time of it too: for civilians there had been the difficulty of getting eggs, the air raid warnings, the waiting in lines. She simply did not know, and I am sure that tens of thousands of returning soldiers walked bewildered into the same incomprehension. It was as though we were now speaking a different language to our own people. The hurt I felt silenced me as effectively as a gag. It was hard to talk, but my wife made it easy not to.

The nightmares began soon after my return. They were usually about Outram Road. I would be left in a cell on my own, with no food or water, starving and suffocating and crying out for release, and in the dream's compression of time months would pass while I was ignored, and I knew I was never going to be released. Or I would be doing something perfectly innocent and would suddenly find myself back in Outram Road, the victim of some arbitrary justice, this time with no prospect of ever getting out again because there was no reason for me to be there. At other times I would fall endlessly and painfully down the iron staircase covered in disgusting sores. They were all the same dream.

In the cold light of day my anger was more often turned to the Japanese who had beaten, interrogated or tortured me. I wanted to do violence to them, thinking quite specifically of how I would like to revenge myself on the goon squad from Kanburi and the hateful little interrogator from the Kempeitai with his dreadful English pronunciation, his mechanical questions and his way of being in the room yet seeming to be detached from it. I wished to drown him, cage him and beat him, to see how he liked it. I still thought of his voice, his slurred elocution: 'Lomax, you will be killed shortly'; 'Lomax, you will tell us'; you remember phrases from encounters that have hurt you, and my meetings with him were cast in a harsh light.

The Kanburi Radio Affair was already a footnote to the history of the war. Lance Thew had been awarded the British Empire Medal and the rest of us – living and dead – were 'mentioned in despatches'. Then one morning I read a small paragraph in the *Daily Telegraph* stating that Captain Komai Mitsuo and Ser-geant-Major Iijima Nobuo had been hanged the day before at Changi Gaol for their part in the murder of two British POWs, Lieutenant Armitage and Captain Hawley. Other people had suffered more than we had – the horrors of the European camps and the scale of the massacre of the Jews were beginning to sink into the minds of an unbelieving population – but that did not entirely explain the relegation of our experience to the bottom of the page. The British public was not very interested in the Far

Eastern war crimes trials, in general, and official policy was to downplay them for the sake of reconstructing Japan as an ally of the West. The Kanburi trial was a very minor tribunal.

But it was not minor and not a footnote, of course, to anyone concerned with the crimes which it judged. I knew that my statements had helped to hang these men, and I felt a cold twinge of satisfaction. The trial seemed infinitely fairer than any judgment they had ever made on us. I regretted that there were not more of them going to the gallows; I felt that thousands of them were guilty. There was unfinished business between me and the Japanese people as a whole, and a few of them in particular. The administrators of Outram Road and the men who coldly worked so many to death on the railway were more guilty than the drunken sergeants who beat us at Kanburi. But most war crimes trials were about cases of actual murder, so I felt satisfied, as far as this one went. Hawley and Armitage were revenged. I was not sure that I had been.

No trace of my interrogator or his brutal superior the Kempei NCO, who had irritated me so personally, was ever reported. I had never even made a statement about them, though I remembered them more than the killers of Hawley and Armitage who to me were simply a faceless bunch of club-swinging thugs; I remembered the faces of the Kempei men almost every day.

* * *

The army was my other safe haven. I signed on for another two years after my return, deferring my life for a while; I was not in a good state to make important decisions. So I applied for and got the post of Signals Officer at the Edinburgh University Senior Training Corps, which would allow me to live at home and continue working in as peaceful a military environment as possible. I spent the next two and a half years teaching undergraduate officer cadets how to operate radio and line communications.

This organization for turning students into officers was an important and active part of the University – Britain still maintained powerful armed forces, the Cold War was beginning and storm clouds were already gathering over Malaya again, as the communist insurgency gathered strength. Most training corps had a full-time army commander as well as a few warrant officers, but I was one of the few signals staff officers in any university. After volunteering for so many things that had caused me so much grief, I felt I deserved this less arduous posting.

It was a genuine respite for me. I lectured the cadets about radio telegraphy, and took them away into the Highlands to teach them how to turn theory into practice when hills intervened between receiver and transmitter, and how to communicate in fog and rainstorms. I put them through it, organizing programmes that gave everybody a chance to discover the joys of cable-laying, switchboard work and despatch-riding. Most of the work revolved around radios now, much more sophisticated versions of the sets with which I had started the war. I could barely recognize them at first, and had to teach myself how to use them from the manuals. No more Line Assisted Wireless for me; and I hoped that these boys would never find themselves stuck in a place like Kuantan as blind and deaf as we had been. Occasionally I took them for a fortnight to Catterick, the Royal Signals headquarters camp, to show them some real army life.

Not being able to share memories was, as I've said, a common affliction among those who returned from the war and I could not talk about what had happened to me with a soul. The single and partial exception was anyone who had been through similar experiences; but in the crush of everyday life there were few encounters with ex-POWs. I became close to one former POW, however, and we could talk to each other, guardedly and euphemistically. I saw in him some of the same traits that I had developed, his capacity for enthusiasm and joy replaced by surface coldness and docility. When I applied for an appointment in the Colonial Administrative Service, he did too. I felt he was drifting, as I was in a different way, and I had become briefly part of the tide that was pulling him along. He was following me passively instead of determining his own fate.

I wanted to enter the Colonial Service because I needed to move, and because it offered variety and excitement, and an expansive alternative to the stultifying routines of office life, which I now dreaded. The Service needed people who were self-reliant, who were good administrators and were willing to learn about different things, and of course it would allow me to see more of the world. I had not lost my desire to escape confinement.

As if to remind me of what life could have been like, I had as a formality to rejoin the Post Office Telephones in 1948. This was the job which had been kept for me since I left it in 1939, and I had to turn up to claim it so that I could be transferred away from it. Such are the ways of bureaucracies. I was there for all of a fortnight; and the first thing that was handed to me was that file, full of my notes and memos on garage accommodation. When the deluge recedes, the most banal things are found drying out in the light.

This brief return to my old life also produced a stain on my character which has not been removed to this day. When I was demobilized I took leave, quite properly, and calculated that I would have to report to the Post Office on a certain day. Their calculations, however, alleged that I was a day late at the end of this 'post-demob' leave. Formally, I stood accused of being absent without leave. Nearly forty years later I asked for a record of my service, and my transgression is still shown on the civil service records: length of service: twenty years; AWOL: one day.

The Civil Service works with deliberate speed and before they would send me overseas I had to spend a year or so in more homely duties. I became an officer of the Department of Agriculture, and attempted to become an expert on diseases of the potato. My only previous experience of the vegetable had been at Outram Road, when Colonel Parker and I became unwilling gardeners for the Japanese. I could confirm now that the green leaves containing solanine are indeed poisonous. I read up on potato ailments, and drafted memo after memo about menaces to the crop. One of my main concerns was to arrange trials of new brands of potatoes to ensure their suitability for making chips. Every new variety of spud had to be registered and assessed. Fish-and-chip shops were where many British people ate their main meal, so the quality of the fried chip was of some concern to the government. One shop in Edinburgh co-operated nobly with us and very august people from the Department would solemnly sit around a table and taste chips made with different potatoes.

Eventually the Colonial Office in London accepted me as an assistant secretary, and told me that I would be assigned to the Gold Coast, the British territory in West Africa now called Ghana. I knew that I was joining the administration of an Empire which was more or less gracefully dissolving itself, in one of the world's more remarkable processes of decolonization. Our task in the Gold Coast was to hang on as long as we could, partly to keep the radical nationalist Kwame Nkrumah out of power as a matter of policy, and to put certain developments in place and prepare the way for an efficient and orderly handover of power to the Africans.

Meanwhile, it had begun to dawn on me that my marriage had been a mistake, for both parties. After our first daughter was born in December 1946, my wife's own mother did not see us or the child for about six years; there was an absolute break. Her family cultivated feuds; she had relatives in the Scottish borders, for example, and few of them would communicate with her. She would often say that people in her family would never let a slight die a natural death. I think this side of her character may have been developed in the Chapel, and it was certainly not discouraged.

The pettiness of the occasions for these vendettas was staggering. Certain of her relatives would not speak to her because when we sent out the traditional little boxes of wedding cake to our friends and relatives at the end of 1945, they went out in two or three batches, and this meant that some people got theirs before others. And the ones who were in the second and third deliveries were infuriated because it implied that the recipients of the first wave of little sugary wedges were considered more important than them. These were people who were not even aware of their own entrapment.

This intolerance over things so surpassingly trivial was very hard for me to take. I had felt less morbid vindictiveness towards the Japanese guards in Changi than these seemingly normal Scottish middle-class people were displaying to their own blood relatives. Marriage can be like incarceration without a key, as I was beginning to find out.

Of course it takes more than one person to create what Milton called 'disconsolate household captivity', and my withdrawals into cold and blank anger in the face of hostility, pulling my shell around me and locking it tight, cannot have made things easier. Confrontation threatened my whole being, triggering flashes of memory that I could not articulate to anyone, and most tragically of all, not even to my wife.

The feeling of claustrophobia was worsened by the Chapel, where fierce feuds, outbreaks of ostentatious remoteness and snorting resentment would break out over the seating priorities. One woman who had been going to Chapel for thirty years complained loudly one day when my wife and I inadvertently sat in what she regarded as her personal pew. I could not help noticing that most of the veterans had done very little in the war; their complaints about how awful firewatching duties had been did not, under the circumstances, engage my full sympathy. I became impatient at their ignorance and their sheer hypocrisy. They would never dream of going anywhere or learning anything new. One couple kept such a tight rein on their unfortunate daughters that these grown-up women had no opportunity to meet young men, and you could see them ageing into enforced loneliness.

The Gold Coast, when I was sent there in December 1949, was in part an escape from an increasingly unhappy existence. It laid the groundwork for my later drift away from that world, Chapel and all. The death of my father soon after I started work in Africa cut other ties with the pre-war past; his second wife went on living in the house overlooking the Firth, and I never went back there.

* * *

The month of my arrival with my wife and young child was the beginning of the most dramatic phase of the independence movement in the Gold Coast. Nkrumah had just launched his 'Positive Action' campaign for immediate self-government; the country was convulsed by mass rallies, riots and demonstrations. Sir Charles Arden-Clarke, the governor, declared a state of emergency in January and arrested Nkrumah in an attempt to break the headlong rush to independence. He spent the next fourteen months in gaol. But the leaders favoured by the British failed to win the hearts of the population, and eventually Nkrumah was released, hailed as the undisputed leader of his people and became our partner in the countdown to the withdrawal of our power.

I was assigned to the Department of Rural Development. We had two main tasks: to initiate the Volta River Project, and the construction of Tema Harbour. The first was a plan to build a huge dam across the Volta, the 1000-mile-long river that runs from Upper Volta, as it was then called (it is now the state of Burkina Faso), to the coast east of Accra, in the process creating the largest man-made lake in Africa and the ability to generate tremendous quantities of hydro-electric power. The electricity would help develop the country and specifically its aluminium industry; there are vast amounts of bauxite in West Africa, and a lot of electric power is used in the refining process. It was a truly gargantuan project. I prepared the first contoured map showing the reach of the water that would flood out when the dam was built, joining up dozens of 1-inch survey maps until they covered the floor of a good-sized room. Many of my colleagues refused to believe the implications of what we were doing, and I saw a look of almost terror on their faces when they saw the size of my map and the predicted spread of the water.

The Tema Harbour Project was intimately linked to the dam, and to the ambitious plans for an aluminium industry. Outside the capital Accra there was an ideal spot for a major port, and we proposed to build one from scratch. I remember how a consultant engineer put a wooden peg in the sand on the beach and announced that this was where the western breakwater of the harbour would start.

I was now part of the industrial revolution that had fascinated me for so long, and was playing a small role in the great post-war wave of industrialization. The work was satisfying, even if it now seems touched with the delusion of the time that chemicals and metals could solve almost any problem. Installing heavy industries in what we now call Third World countries proved more complicated than anyone first thought, and the problems of post-independence Africa still more difficult. But the work was well planned and well organized, and these were pleasures in themselves. I was co-ordinating aspects of the plan for the colonial administration and I met US consultants with experience of the Tennessee Valley Authority and other large projects, which reawakened my old passion for reading about the great railway engineers and bridge builders.

One element of the great scheme was, inevitably, the building of new rail lines. The most ambitious of these was the proposal to build a railway from Kumasi, the inland capital of the old Ashanti kingdom, all the way north to Ouagadougou in French-governed Upper Volta. This would have been a bold chapter in the story of the railway age – 600 miles of track connecting the arid savannah and semi-desert of the upper reaches of the Volta with the tropical regions of the coast, but it never left the engineers' drawing-boards. Rivalry between French and British aims in Africa and sheer pressure on resources killed the project. But there were other new railways, a branch line out of Accra to Tema Harbour, and another to link Accra and Takoradi, respectively the capital and the chief port on the western side of the country. The freight was still construction traffic on these roads; sturdy, small engines hauled wood and rocks for embankments and breakwaters; they had none of the romance of my childhood icons, but they were steam engines for all that.

I loved seeing this little railway take shape under my partial direction, and by the time I left the country some of these lines were in operation – modest 3'6" gauge tracks, only a little broader than the metre-gauge tracks that I had grown so familiar with in Malaya and Siam, with many of the same kinds of engines running on them, for the same Crown Agents bought them for the Gold Coast and our possessions and dependencies in South East Asia.

I wrote to the general managers of 3'6" gauge railways all over the world begging them, if they had any surplus engines, to sell to us because we were terribly short of them. One of the great networks built to this gauge was the Japanese system, but I could not bring myself to write to its management. I had had no contact since the war with any Japanese. I couldn't pretend that I was in a normal trading or business relationship with Japan.

Meanwhile, my wife and I suffered the loss of our son Eric, who died a day after he was born in Takoradi. It was terrible for her, and it led to a deepening of our unspoken estrangement.

I stayed in my post for six years. For the last year I was on the west side of the Gold Coast as Assistant Government Agent in Sekondi, acting more like a traditional, old-fashioned district commissioner. I had my own district, the most important in the whole country at the time because it contained Takoradi, the principal deep sea port. I was a little governor; I was magistrate, deputy coroner, chairman of the board of visitors of the gaol (which looked exactly like a small version of Outram Road) but for all that I did not have the vice-regal powers of an old DC, who ruled his district with absolute power. I was one of the last of the British colonial officers, and we knew we were on the way out. Decolonization was an agreed strategy, so I simply improvised my various roles as best I could. As magistrate I had to assume that everyone's evidence was unreliable, from both claimants and defendants, and sort things out on the basis of common sense. In child custody cases, for instance, I would let the children decide who they wanted to be with.

Kwame Nkrumah was the man of the hour, at that time the most celebrated nationalist in Africa apart from Gamal Abdel Nasser in Egypt. We had accepted his accession to power as inevitable, his popularity in the country invincible. I met him when he came to Sekondi. My superior, who was responsible for the whole of the western side of the country gave a dinner for him, and I was invited. I found him amiable and articulate, but out of his depth; I felt he had no training for the immense responsibilities he was about to take on, like many demagogic MPs in Britain and elsewhere. On another occasion he expressed a desire to go swimming, so I lent him my trunks. This is perhaps the closest I have come to the seat of power!

* * *

We came home, finally, in 1955, with work on the harbour and the dam well under way, the grant of Ghanaian independence only two years off. I took early retirement – I was thirty-six years old – and cast around for something else to do. Since this is not an account of my career, I will record briefly that I went on a personnel management course in Glasgow for a year, my interest in what these days would be called 'human resources' aroused by my experience of marshalling men and materials in West Africa, and then worked for the Scottish Gas Board, with their industrial relations branch. I became interested in the teaching of better industrial relations, and at the end of the Sixties I became an academic, lecturing at the University of Strathclyde and all over the country on personnel management.

I had to behave all the time as if the past had not occurred. I did not think that I was any different from anyone else, despite my terrible nightmares, which I refused to acknowledge as a problem. I wanted to believe that it had all been buried, yet Outram Road kept coming back, night after night. Silence, disease, hunger, fear, above all the intensity of the uncertainty and fear. It was almost always that terrifying scenario of being inside the gaol again after the war, and since there was no reason for my imprisonment, this time there could be no reason for getting out. My wife did her best to reassure me, but the distance between us was hard to bridge. I would cry out at night, wake up sweating as though I had run up a hill with a heavy load and shake with relief when I found myself in the damp heat of Sekondi or the cold Edinburgh night.

Curiously I recognized the symptoms in others, especially in one man in the Gold Coast who had been in Germany as a POW, and was now nervous, defensive, in bad health. But nobody ever spoke about it and I never brought it up. The only way in which 'my war' came up would be around the subject of the Japanese, when I could and would say that I hated them with absolute totality.

It isn't easy to describe the more subtle ways in which Kanburi and its aftermath lived on inside me. I found it difficult to tolerate grey areas in my life, to accept ambiguity or uncertainty of any kind, and I could not easily forgive the mistakes of others, what is euphemistically called not suffering fools gladly. Trifles bothered me, or perhaps it is truer to say I could not be bothered with them, and I would find ways of procrastinating over the small irritations with which life bombards us. For example, while my professional work was extremely organized and I brought real energy and dedication to it – I could organize my thoughts and speak without notes with military precision – I found bills, circulars and, especially, demands for personal information more or less unbearable. They were contingencies, distractions, irruptions of uncertainty into a life that craved regularity. It was better to concentrate on one thing at a time. I would often ignore bills with mistakes, unable to face the confrontations and idiotic bureaucratic obstruction I knew I would have to go through to sort them out.

I was often inward-looking, a victim of a strange passivity that made me absorb experiences like blotting-paper but which made it difficult for me to give; it made me appear slow, yet I was anything but lazy. I felt sometimes like a guest in my own house. When confrontation came, I would resist with immense stubborn energy, revenging myself on the Kempeitai and the guards in every encounter. Although I could not have admitted it, I was still fighting the war in all those years of peace.

I began to worry, a little later, that the sins my captors had sown in me were being harvested in my family in more ways than one. Among Far Eastern ex-prisoners-of-war there is a rumbling of belief that our children are damaged, in some way genetically harmed. It seems to us, when we get together now as older men, that we have bequeathed some strange problems to our children. It is interesting that some American scientists suggest that the notorious 'middle passage' of the slave trade may have caused intolerable genetic stresses which damaged the immediate descendants of slaves. I don't know whether it is good science, but we murmur these things among ourselves, caught between rumour and doubt. Who knows, too, what effects our suppressed feelings may have had on the psychic development of our children?

My elder daughter Linda fell ill, struck by a brain haemorrhage at the age of twelve; to begin with a doctor thought that it was simply a fainting fit, but she did not recover consciousness. She lost the power of her right arm and hand; mercifully, she was left-handed. She had been a promising pianist, with real talent at the age of ten; and now she would never do anything two-handed again in her life.

Linda then had a whole sequence of attacks, nearly dying on several occasions, and she had to live the rest of her life aware of these little bombs always threatening to go off in her head. She achieved her aim of working in a big insurance company, investigating suspicious claims and worked diligently on these cases. Her good humour, so terribly shadowed, could make her friends forget her condition; but she could not escape her congenital weakness. She died at the age of forty-six.

My second daughter was born in 1957. She enjoyed a normal and healthy childhood and became a successful nurse and mid-wife.

My frequent absences on the lecture circuit were a contributory factor, no doubt, to the breakdown of my marriage, but they were also a symptom of its failure. I wanted to get away. In 1970 I moved out for six months, later drifting back, but it was never the same again. In 1981 I left for good.

CHAPTER ELEVEN

WORK AND THE strong pull of the currents that run through everyday life – no matter how threatening they can seem to someone whose memories are bad – give the illusion of sweeping us away from the past. Like many men who went through Japanese prisons, I found I could allow my professional life to crowd out my desire to settle those old accounts.

Although I relived the past more often than I wished and had, again like many of my wartime comrades, accumulated a library of books about the campaigns in Malaya, the Burma-Siam Railway and the camps, I still felt a certain reluctance to confront that past directly. In the 1970s, my friend Alex Morton Mackay – by then living in Canada – found my address through an ex-POW organization and wrote me an affecting letter in which he described how I had been an example and an inspiration to him, with my arms in splints and my specs taped together; but if I recognized myself in his description, I knew it was not the whole story. No one is a hero to themselves. I found it difficult to reply to Mac, but we did eventually correspond and one day, after a service of remembrance for those who had died in the Far Eastern war, we finally met again. Fred Smith joined us for lunch in London. It was my only reunion with these two men who had meant so much to me.

But that past was not easily denied. The need to know more about what had happened to us in Siam was not some idle curiosity, and it asserted itself powerfully whenever I had time to think. After my retirement in 1982, I could put off no longer the need to know, the desire became more intense than ever. I wanted to find out what had really happened; why the Japanese had made the search of our hut on that particular day, and if somebody had tipped them off. I wished to establish the exact sequence of events. I also wanted to find out more about the Japanese responsible for the beatings and murders, apart from those already brought to justice, and above all more about the Kempei personnel who had tortured me at Kanburi. I knew nothing about their units, their names or their fate after the war. The prospects of finding the right men, of finding them alive, even of making a start were so remote; but as the events receded the obsession grew. It was like trying to reconstruct a coherent story from evidence reduced to tattered rags, faded documents, bones and rusty rails. And memories, which are even less durable.

Perhaps I was trying to recover something of what I had been before being sent to war and put to work on an insane railway. I also admit that I wanted to make them pay, pay more than they had already done. The more I thought about it, and thought about it, the more I wished to do damage to the Kempei men if I could ever find them. Physical revenge seemed the only adequate recompense for the anger I carried. I thought often about the young interpreter at Kanburi. There was no single dominant figure at Outram Road on whom I could focus my general hatred, but because of his command of my language, the interpreter was the link; he was centre-stage in my memories; he was my private obsession. His slurred and struggling English; his endless questions; his repetitiveness; the way he gave voice to the big torturing NCO: he represented all of them; he stood in for all the worst horrors.

By the time I had hardened my desire to search out the truth, I had already met Patti. I was still lecturing to audiences about industrial relations around Britain, and one day in 1980 I found myself standing on the platform at Crewe Station, that great and historic railway junction in the centre of England. I should not have been there at all. I had gone to Chester to view a book auction – the old collecting urge was still as strong as ever – and went to the station to take the train back to Manchester, then on to Edinburgh, only to find that the train was cancelled. I am still grateful for that blockage on the line, whatever it was. Instead I took a train to Crewe, where I knew I could meet a train going up the west coast to Scotland. I had not spent a lifetime learning about railways for nothing.

At Crewe I was just in time and as the Glasgow train pulled in at the platform I ran for it and climbed aboard. I had a first-class ticket, so I entered an old-fashioned carriage with a corridor and separate compartments. The third compartment was occupied by a pleasant, good-looking woman sitting alone and that was the compartment I chose. I was suddenly aware that I had let myself become a bit shabby, with my old prisoner's teeth and good but wellworn clothes, even though I looked younger than my sixty-one years. She made me feel awkward, this slim, handsome, dark-haired person who looked at least fifteen years younger than me, a glamorous and confident woman from a different world. Her face, however, had so much trusting kindness in it that I forgot about age and fashion.

She was consulting a little book, *The Observer's Tourist Atlas of Great Britain*, which she balanced on her knee as she traced her journey up the west coast. She was English, and had worked here as a nurse, but had lived in Canada for many years, and this was a journey of rediscovery for her. I was pleased to learn that she had run an antiquarian bookshop in Montreal. She was on her way to visit a friend in Glasgow. I was soon discoursing about the history of the towns we were passing through, hoping that I was not boring her. But there was a kind of instant rapport between us that made me go on.

Two men got in. I refused to move my raincoat off the seat, coldly and stubbornly. The captive's ability to obstruct could be very useful; I did not want an audience for what I now realized was a very important conversation. Three hours later the train drew into Carstairs and I screwed my courage up and asked her if she would have lunch with me the next day in Glasgow. She said yes.

It emerged quickly that we were both living rootless and not altogether happy lives; her marriage was as reduced as mine. We saw a lot of each other, and spent some good time together in Somerset, where she was staying during her British holiday. And then she went back to Canada. There were many letters and long-distance calls after her return. At an age when changes of emotional direction seemed impossible, and when I was already brooding on my vengeful quest, I had fallen in love. And then we were together: she came to live with me in Edinburgh. I was now part of a second extended family, Patti's sons Graeme, his wife Jeanne, Nicholas and Mark welcomed me. They gave me hope for the future. Quick thinking about the movement of trains can have strange outcomes, though it failed to surprise me that my meeting with the woman who would play so great a part in changing my life should take place on a railway.

I did not tell Patti all at once about Malaya and Siam during the war, but it came out slowly. She was discovering for herself that she was living with someone with unusual problems, but meanwhile I carried on with my quest. In January 1985, I published an article in the London 'FEPOW Forum', a news-letter for ex-prisoners-of-war, appealing 'before it is too late' for information about the events at Kanburi in 1943. I asked for eye-witness accounts, for information about the 'American' inter-preter and the Dutch doctor. As for the seven officers, I looked around and they were all dead, Mac having died a few years before, and 'Daddy' Smith, the frailest of all of them, living until the age of ninety before passing away in 1984. And I could tell that Fred was dying: 'My chest has been very bad lately and the cough is getting worse', he wrote to me that year; in the same letter he admitted something which he had always been able to keep concealed: 'My nerves were cracking during the nights, always at night-time.' Fred's heart – that indestructible rock of support – gave out five years ago.

About twenty letters, almost all of them kind and considerate, came back after the article was published. One of them came from T. C. Brown, who had been a sergeant in the Royal Norfolk Regiment:

Your article in Forum brings back horrific memories of that night . . . I remember you all lined up in front of the Guard Room and the night of the bashing the Kempei came rushing to our hut and pulled up the bamboo bridge over the drain to our hut, we thought we were in for a bashing but of course you were the victims, what a night, the cries of mercy was terrible and there we lay not being able to do anything but pray for you, it was dark so we could not see what was going on . . . The following day two of you were missing off the 'parade' outside the Guard Room if I remember right it was the tall slim officer and a small officer in your party . . . After the Japs surrender a Cpl Johnson of the Foresters told me that he knew the two missing officers were buried behind Guard Room, apparently he was on fatigues over the Jap Quarters and found an Officers Cap there soaked in blood . . . Never will I forget the mess you people were in after the bashings, I was NCO i/c Sanitation and saw quite a bit of you on your journey under escort to the latrines.

There were many letters like this, which touched me but gave me no information of the kind I was seeking.

Then a letter came from Henry Cecil Babb of Oxford, a former regular army chaplain who was now almost eighty years old. He had served in Malaya since December 1940 and been captured, like the rest of us, at the end of that disastrous campaign. He arrived at the main POW camp at Kanburi in August 1945 just as the war was coming to an end, and he was told by some junior officers that about two years earlier, two unidentified POWs, who had been involved in the operation of a radio in the railway workshops camp nearby, had been killed and their bodies dumped in a latrine near the guardroom. The officers had asked him if, despite the passage of time, he would conduct a formal service. Babb agreed, and read the prayers for The Burial of the Dead, the first time he had ever done so without knowing the names of the deceased. 'For I am a stranger with thee: and a sojourner, as all my fathers were.' It was good to think of poor

Hawley and Armitage, the ladies' man and the scholar, being commemorated in that squalid place where no-one seems to have remembered them.

I wrote to Babb and told him the names of the men he had prayed for, and when he replied he told me that after the war he had not returned to England immediately, but had volunteered to take part in an official War Graves Commission party which was setting out to travel the entire length of the railway, all 258 miles of it, in a search for rough cemeteries and for the bodies of missing men. The group had been organized by the Allied administration in Bangkok and consisted of sixteen British and Australian troops, together with a young Japanese interpreter. The expedition left Bangkok on 22nd September and went as far as Thanbyuzayat in Burma, travelling on open wagons fitted up with attap roofs, and returned on 10th October 1945 after locating 144 cemeteries – mostly trackside graves in the jungle – and over 10,000 bodies. Babb recalled conducting another burial service, for the entire crew of a USAAF B29 bomber which had been shot down just before the end of the war in the mountains on the Burmese side of the frontier.

Babb had lost touch with all the members of the search party, but he told me that the interpreter had recently sought him out and that he might be able to help me in my search for information. Would I, he asked, be willing to let him make enquiries on my behalf? I asked specifically for information about the identity of the men who had beaten me so meticulously and of the hateful 'American' interpreter who had supervised the beatings; I was trying to tie down the history of the murders first, and I confined the questions which I passed to Babb to that night in the main Kanburi camp. I hardly expected to receive any news from so unlikely a quarter and was glad that Babb was acting as an intermediary. Direct correspondence with a former Japanese soldier would have been impossible for me.

This man was called Nagase Takashi, and he lived in the city of Kurashiki. He wrote to Babb, saying that he could not help him with the information he required, but that he thought the man in question had died soon after the war.

Babb suggested that some of the information I was seeking might be in the Public Record Office in Kew, where records of some of the war crimes trials were now held. In the spring of 1985, I found myself sitting at a quiet table reading fading copies of old documents in File WO235/822, the official record of the trial of those held responsible for the deaths of Captain Hawley and Lieutenant Armitage and for the ill-treatment of my colleagues and me.

It was an extraordinary afternoon. I forgot my surroundings, and entered a kind of trance as I read, visualizing the scene in Kanburi almost as a spectator. There was the guardroom, the Korean and Japanese guards, the wooden table, the drainage ditches, the areas of raw earth, the dust and heat and in the distance the hazy mountains which were a barrier between us and the friendly west; the row of British army officers, beginning to suffer terribly from several hours of exposure to the heat, from the brilliance of the sun and from thirst, still standing to attention with great difficulty, and then from the dark the rabble emerging to beat the men.

I came to myself after several hours of reading and rereading the evidence, including some of the documents I had typed myself, feeling completely exhausted. Perhaps the most remarkable element in this experience was the curious sensation that I was reading something in which I was not personally involved. I was seeking these exact truths on behalf of some person I barely knew.

Babb moved from Oxford to Cambridge late in 1985, and I went to visit him. He was very old and ill, but clear-minded and articulate. I was not surprised to discover that he was, like so many of us, ambivalent about that part of his past. He had destroyed his POW notes and papers in the 1960s, and later regretted doing it; he tried to reconstruct them from copies in the Imperial War Museum. His faith had thinned after the war; he had exchanged religion for the certainties of mathematics, and taught the subject for years, returning to his role as padre only once, on a visit with ex-POWs to modern Thailand.

He gave me some information about his correspondent Nagase Takashi, who claimed to have become active in charitable causes near Kanburi in the post-war years, and who had just built a Buddhist temple close to the railway there. I read about his activities with cold scepticism and found the very thought of him distasteful. I could not believe in the idea of Japanese repentance. He had organized a meeting of 'reconciliation' at the River Kwae Bridge, that too-famous structure which has given so many people such a false picture of POW life through the David Lean film (who ever saw such well-fed POWs?). I had not seen a Japanese since 1945 and had no wish ever to meet one again. His reconciliation assembly sounded to me like a fraudulent publicity stunt.

Padre Babb died in 1987. I might have taken up direct correspondence with his repentant Japanese ex-soldier, but it would have been easier to cut off my arm.

★ ★ ★

It was becoming more and more difficult for the person I loved most to bear with me. The ex-prisoner, even after several decades of 'forgetting', can puzzle and frighten others. It is impossible for others to help you come to terms with the past, if for you the past is a pile of wounded memories and angry humiliations, and the future is just a nursery of revenge. At times my good qualities, which I am self-aware enough to know that I have, could almost be crowded out by sudden triggerings of frightened anger. A confrontational edge to a voice could bring all my shutters down. All of this made it difficult to imagine a way of healing my wounds.

Patti had to suffer the sudden icy rages, the withdrawals of affection and contact, of a man who could not stand being teased even lovingly. My hurt response was never deliberate; it was a way of disappearing into myself, of adopting the impassive hurt features of the victim; I shut down as a way of protecting myself. Patti was bewildered by it. I recall not speaking to her once for almost a week because of some imagined insensitivity. Another time, I woke from an afternoon nap after some wonderful days in which we had been getting on so well, and possessed by the spirit of loving fun I crept downstairs naked, intending to surprise my wife as she prepared dinner in the kitchen. When I appeared like a ghost at the door behind her she turned and, matching my high spirits, threw a wet dish-cloth at me to cover my indecent condition. That harmless gesture pitched me into a frightened remoteness, ruining a delightful piece of hilarious intimacy.

Everything in my world was still printed in black and white. I had become so used to burying the truth, the real pain, that I preferred to hope it would go away: as I thought my torture had, as I fooled myself Outram Road could be made to do. My unreasonable docility was allied to immense stubbornness.

Patti suspected that I had been seriously damaged by my wartime experiences, and that they were at the bottom of our difficulties, and decided that something had to be done about it; neither of us could bear the thought of our relationship breaking down.

I had no idea where to turn. The thought of consulting a psychiatrist or psychotherapist had never entered my head. The ordinary former Far East POW has probably never talked to anyone about the details of his experiences, except perhaps to other ex-POWs. A few have succeeded in writing memoirs, but they are very few. Not talking becomes a fixed habit, a way of shielding ourselves from those years, and this is doubly true for the victim of torture, who most certainly does not talk. I can write this now, but I have come a long way since the moment I first determined to confront my memories.

We found ourselves pursuing parallel lines of enquiry. Patti read an article about the long-term health of former POWs from the Far East by Dr Peter Watson, a Senior Medical Officer of the Department of Health. He had studied a thousand of us, and listed the medical problems that we faced, and reported that over half those he investigated had obvious psychological problems.

She wrote to Dr Watson, and soon I was on my way to the RAF Hospital at Ely, in Cambridgeshire, for a tropical disease investigation, with a special request for psychiatric evaluation. I was going to have to talk at length about Siam and Malaya, more than I had ever done at one time to anyone. I knew that for the treatment, whatever it was, to have any effect, I would have to talk, but I could not bring myself to do it. I solved the problem by writing the story of my misadventures in the form of a Memorandum, which ran to over fifty typewritten pages. I presented this to an astonished Squadron-Leader Bloor, the consultant psychiatrist at Ely. I could not possibly have told him any of it by word of mouth, but the Memorandum gave us a basis for discussion. For the first time in my life, I felt that a barrier was being pushed aside.

After four days in Ely I returned home. In the meantime Dr Bloor called to confirm that Patti had on her hands a straightforward case of psychic damage arising from wartime trauma, a kind of prolonged battle-stress. He may have had a more clinical name for my state of mind, but it did not matter; simply to have the problem identified and named was in itself a step forward.

Meanwhile, I had read an article about the launching of a new organization. It was called the Medical Foundation for the Care of Victims of Torture, and had set up shop in a disused hospital in London. I knew nothing about it, but wrote to its director, Mrs Helen Bamber, and early in August 1987 I was invited to visit them. Helen Bamber received me personally. I can still see myself sitting at the end of her desk with my back to the wall, haltingly describing why I had come in precise sentences that hinted at things I could not say. I still thought that what I was telling her was unique to me, and perhaps I felt a little ashamed of my difficulties; but when she told me that everything I had told her was so familiar to her, from countless victims of torture from many different countries, the most intense feeling of relief flooded through me.

She was utterly unhurried, and this is what impressed me more than anything. She seemed to have infinite time, endless patience and sympathy; but above all she gave me time. It was astonishing simply to know that the pressure of everyday life would not drown out what I had to say. I remembered the half-hour medical examination in 1945, when I was still raw and sore, and there was no interest or time. Half a century later I was still livid with suppressed anxiety and now at last here was someone with the time. Not only that, there was the easing of mind that came with knowing I was not uniquely crippled or mad.

That meeting was like walking through a door into an unexplored world, a world of caring and special understanding.

Helen Bamber is a remarkable woman. A small person, whose stillness and calm presence belie an extraordinary energy for her seventy years, she has spent most of her life working with the victims of cruelty. The Medical Foundation of which she is a founder is probably the only organization in the world whose staff and consultants are expert in the problems of the tortured. Helen entered Bergen-Belsen with the Allies at the age of nineteen in 1945, and stayed for two and a half years. It is an illusion to think that the inmates of the Nazi camps were 'liberated' and went home; most of them had nowhere to go, and it was people like Helen who looked after their tuberculosis, their memories of cannibalism, murder, and the grotesque selection procedures that sent some to work and some to the gas chamber. She learned as a girl in Belsen the importance of allowing people to tell what had been done to them; the power of listening to their testimony and of giving people the recognition that their experience deserves.

For many years Helen worked with Amnesty International, and the demand for special services for victims of torture eventually became so pressing that she set up her new organization. We've learned so little in my lifetime that torture is now a global epidemic: Helen's small group has seen 8000 cases in its ten years of work.

Our first meeting was an exploratory one, but after an attempt to interest my local health service in taking me on – when I was told by a young psychiatrist that ancient history did not fall within her brief – I received an invitation from Helen Bamber to become the first ex-serviceman from the Second World War to be accepted as a patient of the Foundation. This changed my life, at nearly seventy years of age.

I was amazed again and again that everyone in the Foundation from the Director to the newest and youngest member of staff cared enough to observe and to listen, and to listen again. I could hardly believe that I was beginning to talk.

Throughout 1988 and 1989 Patti and I attended this extra-ordinary place every four weeks, making a round trip of 600 miles on each occasion. The doctor assigned to me, Stuart Turner, was a man of infinite tact, and he persuaded me in his 'guided conversations' to reveal more and more, gradually bringing to the surface every fragment of my experiences from early 1942 onwards. He seemed to have wide and painful knowledge of the world's tortures and of their effects on victims. I had never before met a doctor who was so perceptive and so willing and so quick to understand.

I was aware of myself for the first time as a person for whom the idea of torture might hold some answers – why I was such a strange combination of stubbornness, passivity and silent hos-tility; why I was unable to express open anger, and why I found authority so difficult; and why I was sometimes unable even to feel.

Stuart once told me that I was the only patient he had ever met whose face was so inscrutable that he could not tell what I was thinking. I had never heard my mask-like expression described so objectively; it must have slipped on whenever I wanted to hide from his questions for a moment.

While I was learning how to face the past and beginning for the first time in my life to understand what sort of person I had become during the war, I had not forgotten my personal quest for the full truth of what happened in 1943, and yet in the course of these two years, my search changed its character only very slowly. The need to identify the Japanese responsible for these particular cruelties was reasonable enough, but the idea of revenge was still very much alive in me.

*　*　*

One of the men I had found in my belated search for information was Jim Bradley, who had lived in the bed next to mine at Changi in 1944. He published an account of his experiences as a member of the Wilkinson escape party in 1943 and his subsequent mistreatment, and after reading a review of his book I found a copy in which I read a warm tribute to 'the late Eric Lomax'. It was a pleasure to write and surprise Jim with my insistence on living. We met and renewed our friendship. In October 1989 I went to stay overnight with him and his wife Lindy at their home in Midhurst, a village in Sussex on the edge of the South Downs. We had a pleasant evening, talking about the old days, and over breakfast the following morning Lindy gave me a photocopy of an article from the *Japan Times* of 15th August 1989. This is an English-language paper published in Tokyo and not a publication I was ever likely to buy. Lindy had been sent it by a member of the War Graves Commission in Japan, who knew of her extensive collection of cuttings about the war in the Far East, and she thought that this article might be of interest to me because it mentioned Kanchanaburi.

The article was about Mr Nagase Takashi, the interpreter who had helped the Allied armies find their dead along the railway after the war, and Padre Babb's eager correspondent. As I read it,

I experienced a strange, icy joy of the weirdest kind. A photograph accompanied the piece. It was of a slight elderly man, dressed in a dark collarless shirt and leaning back in a chair against a wall full of books, his arms spread out to the side making him look resigned and vulnerable. Behind his right shoulder was a large photograph of the River Kwae Bridge with its distinctive spans in the shape of minor arcs. The face was unsmiling, thin and familiar with pain, the face of an ailing seventy-one-year-old man; but the text with its short paragraphs and neutral prose revealed a younger face behind it.

The article described how Nagase had devoted much of his life to 'making up for the Japanese Army's treatment of prisoners-of-war'; how he had been ordered to join the Allied group trying to locate the graves along the railway, and how, although he had seen trains loaded with POWs leaving Singapore for Thailand in 1943, he was unaware of what occurred on the upper reaches of the railway until he went with the Allied party and saw the corpses in grave after grave in the primitive trackside cemeteries. On that trip, Nagase was quoted as saying, he decided to dedicate the rest of his life to the memory of those who died constructing the railroad.

This was the man I remembered from Padre Babb's account, and about whom I had been so scathing. But there was more. The article described his ill health, his recurrent heart disease, and how every time he suffered a cardiac attack 'he has flashbacks of Japanese military police in Kanchanaburi torturing a POW who was accused of possessing a map of the railway. One of their methods was to pour large amounts of water down his throat. "As a former member of the Japanese Army, I thought the agony was what I have to pay for our treatment of POWs," Nagase said.'

I did not say anything in the Bradleys' kitchen that morning; I probably showed no reaction at all, the impassive mask gripping my face with a vengeance. I stared at the article and read and reread it all the way from the nearby station to London on the train and by the time it pulled into Waterloo Station I knew that this was the man I wanted. His face was recognizably the face of the interrogator, his sunken cheekbones and eyes and mouth an older edition of that serious young man's features. He was speaking about me, and guardedly admitting that he had been there during my torture. I felt triumphant that I had found him, and that I knew his identity while he was unaware of my continued existence.

I had been haunted by what he described for half a century, but so, it now seemed, had one of my tormentors – the only one with a face and a voice, the only one I had ever been able to endow with a personality across the years. He too had nightmares, flashbacks, terrible feelings of loss. The article talked about Nagase atoning for guilt, about visiting Kanchanaburi many times since 1963, when the Japanese government deregulated foreign travel, laying wreaths at the Allied cemetery, and setting up a charitable foundation for the survivors of the Asian labourers who died in such vast numbers. In my moment of vengeful glory, triumph was already complicated by other feelings. This strange man was obviously drawn on in his work by memories of my own cries of distress and fear.

I had apparently found one of the men I was looking for and I had the near certainty, shadowed by only a tiny cloud of doubt, that I knew who he was and where he was. I was in such a strong position: I could if I wished reach out and touch him, to do him real harm. The years of feeling powerless whenever I thought of him and his colleagues were erased. Even now, given the information about what he had done since the war, and my own changing feelings about revenge, the old feelings came to the surface and I wanted to damage him for his part in ruining my life.

When I got back to Berwick much later that day, Patti said it was the first time I'd looked truly delighted for years. On my next visit to the Medical Foundation, liberally handing out photocopies of the *Japan Times* article, I was interested to be told that for the very first time in the staff's experience I could be described as 'animated'. Facial inscrutability was impossible now.

I still did not know what to do about Nagase. I made enquiries about him, writing to the British Ambassador in Tokyo and to experts on Japan's dreadful record of coming to terms with its past. Nagase's activities were well known, it seemed, to people concerned with the threat of a renewed Japanese militarism, but what I could not tell was whether his expressions of remorse were genuine or not. I needed to see that for myself. The thought was entering my head, distantly at first, that perhaps I should try to meet this man, to make up my mind with that face in front of me again. Many people could not accept the reality of our injuries after the war because they had not been there, because they could not make the leap of imagination out of their comfortable lives, but I wanted to see Nagase's sorrow so that I could live better with my own.

This half-thought desire took a long time before it could be expressed. One or two people suggested that perhaps it was time for me to forgive and forget. I don't normally argue openly about anything, but I began to argue just a little about this. The majority of people who hand out advice about forgiveness have not gone through the sort of experience I had; I was not inclined to forgive, not yet, and probably never.

Throughout the next two years I could not decide what to do with my information, which seemed the product of incredible and precious coincidence. Meanwhile, for the first time, and solely to benefit the Medical Foundation, I allowed myself to be interviewed by journalists. Hitherto, the prospect of anything resembling interrogation filled me with horror, but I managed to get through an interview with a woman from the *Sunday Times* and even, late in 1990, a television programme about the Medical Foundation, which was broadcast in January 1991.

I spent that year at my periodic meetings with Dr Turner discussing the effect of the discovery of Nagase on me and considering what I should do. I still thought often about striking him down, but Stuart helped me to see beyond murder. He thought that I should not try to meet my former interrogator at all, arguing that to do so would be to enter uncharted territory. Despite the range of their awful experience, not one of the Medical Foundation staff could find any precedent for a meeting such as I proposed. Helen Bamber could not recall a voluntary encounter between a person closely complicit with torture and his victim in the history of post-war Europe; while Stuart Turner more than once reminded me that there were many records of US veterans of the Vietnam War suffering traumatic flashbacks when confronted with strong reminders of their wartime experiences.

Still consumed by the desire to make Nagase suffer fully the consequences of his actions, I decided that I would like to surprise him, revelling in my superior knowledge and his ignorance of me. Aid for this vengeful plan came from an unexpected quarter. The director of the brief television film about the work of the Foundation and my own predicament, Mike Finlason, became so fascinated by the story which he saw unfolding that he decided to try to make a full-length documentary about Nagase and me. My intention was that a meeting should be arranged but that Nagase should be told only that I was a former Far East POW, and not be told that I had identified him as a member of the Kempei. At first Finlason acceded to my plan, but he became understandably and increasingly reluctant to stage a surprise assault on Nagase of the kind I wanted.

The ways of television were completely new to me, but I soon learned that there is many a slip between the full cup of excited plans for a film and the actual lip of the audience. Mike Finlason was then an independent director and this was his personal enthusiasm. Funding for the film proved elusive, and the early summer of 1991 passed without any of my plans nearing fulfilment – a delay that has almost certainly infinitely benefited at least two people's lives. Stuart Turner was warmly concerned about my intentions, and suggested that I should try to meet some Japanese people socially to prepare myself for the encounter which I was determined to arrange. Given that I had not spoken to a single Japanese person since 1945, this was no easy matter, but I agreed to try. Various schemes were canvassed: visiting a Japanese travel or airline office, for example, so that I could flee without difficulty if I found it necessary to do so.

No embarrassing meetings with startled Japanese ticket clerks had taken place when one day in early July 1991 I answered the phone at home, which I very rarely do; Patti has screened calls for a long time past, at my request, and she was out when the phone rang. The caller was a historian of my acquaintance, who asked whether I would be willing to meet a Japanese professor of history, a woman from Tokyo called Nakahara Michiko, who was researching the exploitation of POWs and Asian labourers by the Imperial Japanese Army on the Burma-Siam Railway. I said yes. My wife returned to find that I had arranged a meeting with a Japanese person at our own house. She was more than a little astonished.

For a few days before the meeting in late July I was frightened of my own response, but when the time came it was a revelation. It was a beautiful summer day, our best clear and light northern weather. Patti went to meet her at Berwick Station, and a little later I heard our garden gate clatter open. I saw my wife walk up the garden path beside a petite, smiling woman wearing elegant trousers and a black silk jacket, her hair a striking deep blue-black. We shook hands. Professor Nakahara spoke superb English, and within a few minutes I could tell that it was going to be all right. She is a considerate and learned woman, and after lunch we sat outside in the garden exchanging information and looking through papers, books and relics. Her husband, she told us, had been wounded at Hiroshima. She wanted to rescue the labourers from obscurity; dozens of books have been written about the POWs, but almost nothing about the *romusha*, as they were known to the Japanese. There were a quarter of a million of them: Malays, Indonesians, Chinese, Burmese, Tamils, a disorganized and starved multilingual army with no internal leadership or organization, unlike us. Michiko was interested in my memories of work in the railroad camps; I was fascinated by her as my first new link with Japan. She told me that she had once met Nagase.

The man who had crept under my skin and stayed there in 1943 seemed different through the eyes of others, and aspects of Japan began to interest me. Here, for example, was a historian unafraid of the truth, delving into her country's most shameful actions, and I liked her. Soon after her return to Japan, she wrote to us to say that she had received an invitation to the Akasaka

Palace to give the new Emperor Akihito a lecture on modern South-East Asian history, prior to his tour of the area. She accepted with the condition that she be allowed to speak freely.

In the month of Nakahara Michiko's visit I was given a copy of a small book by Nagase which he had published in Japan. All I knew was that it was called *Crosses and Tigers*, since my Japanese studies had not progressed much since my efforts with Bill Williamson in 1943, but I learned that an English edition had been published in Thailand in 1990. I ordered a copy and eventually a small package arrived. The book was a tiny paperback, with a picture of the railway bridge over the Kwae on its light green cover; it had less than seventy pages of text, roughly printed with bad type, but I sat down to read it as though it were a rare manuscript.

The book opens with a brief introductory account of Nagase's conscription in Tokyo, in December 1941, when I was waiting for his Emperor's army at Kuantan. He was classified B3, presumably an indication of low physical fitness, and the photograph he reproduces, taken on 20th December 1941 shows a very slender young man with a face I remembered too well – an intense, fine, timid and mournful face – dressed in Japanese Army uniform and forage cap, clutching a sword that looks too big for him. He describes how he was sent to Saigon to serve with the oddly-named 'Literal Intelligence Bureau' of the General Staff Office, and how he was then sent to Java to interpret for an intelligence officer collecting information at the end of the Indonesian campaign. By early January 1943, he was working in 'transport operations' at Singapore, snooping on POWs who were being sent up to the railway, and presumably searching their baggage for precious fragments of the kind that Fred Smith had taken with him on his way to Ban Pong. In March 1943, when we were already in Kanburi, he was assigned to Bangkok, to the headquarters of the Railway Construction Staff, and in September he received an order to serve with what he calls the 'military police platoon' at Kanburi. He acknowledges the terrible cost of the railway, and that a prisoner or labourer must have died for every sleeper laid; and that today it runs for less than a third of its original length.

The rest of the little book has three main sections: his memories of Kanburi; his reconstructed diary of his three-week expedition with the war graves group, including Padre Babb, in September-October 1945; and some brief remarks about his post-war experiences in Thailand.

The first section, and especially the first five pages of it, held me spellbound. Nagase arrives at Ban Pong in dark and cloudy weather. The scene as he recalls it is hellish, the sky overcast and grey, flocks of large black vultures perched on roofs and in the branches of tall teak trees. He thinks at first that vultures are native to this place, but then realizes that they are attracted to the smell of carrion around the prison camp.

The next day he goes to Kanburi. 'Again there were ghastly flocks of vultures when I walked across the field of tall weeds. The birds moved their heads back and forth every time they made a forward step.' Nagase meets a funeral procession of prisoners, carrying a body on a stretcher covered with a faded Union Jack, followed by a Japanese soldier with a gun and behind him four or five vultures nodding their heads to and fro. He sees the rough bamboo fence of the camp and is told by the sergeant accompanying him to pretend to be an inspector of the camp, since he is unknown and the prisoners may unwittingly give him information. He is shocked at the sight of the camp, and sees shabby roofless huts, sick prisoners shivering in soaking blankets, malaria victims rolling feverishly on their bedding or on the floor. The rain starts falling as a British officer comes up to him, pleading for improvements in their conditions, telling him that they have had no roof on their hut for over a week with malaria patients exposed to the rain. The 'weak dimmed eyes' of the malaria patients affect Nagase badly. He remembers seeing the same mournful gaze when prisoners were being packed thirty at a time into box cars in the scorching sun at Singapore railway station. There a blue-eyed British officer had persistently asked him where they were headed, over and over again, repeating the question, but Nagase was unable to answer. 'Why do blue eyes look so sad?' he asks.

He is assigned at Kanburi to the squad responsible for *Tokko*, intelligence and counter intelligence. He accompanies the head of the squad or a tall sergeant with a 'bluish, clean shaven face', at all times. Sometimes he is asked to impersonate a Thai and to talk with the prisoners in order to learn their thoughts and movements. I had not known that he also spoke Thai, or perhaps he was mimicking a Thai villager who knew a little English.

Some time before the opening of the railway in October they suspect that a radio is in operation among the prisoners, and that we are listening to Allied broadcasts. They discover the set when they inspect the prisoners' belongings without warning. When all the 'suspects' are brought to his intelligence squad, he writes, they have already been beaten badly. He thinks that one prisoner has been beaten to death.

Suddenly it's as though he steps out from behind a screen and I am looking at a scene familiar to me distanced as though in a dream. He writes:

Let me talk about a prisoner for whom I worked as an interpreter. It was found that he had a rough sketch of the Thai-Burma railway with the names of all the stations when the inspection of their belongings took place. He claimed that he was a railway fanatic and intended to take it home as a souvenir. His explanation was not convincing because the railway was a secret matter in those days.

Nagase says that they had to approve the charge of spying against this prisoner in order to commit him for court martial. He is interrogated but the POW stubbornly denies the charge, knowing that he will be condemned to death if he admits to being a spy.

The fierce questioning continued from morning till night for over a week, which exhausted me as well. The military policeman sometimes shouted at me because he got too excited to differentiate between the prisoner and me. The suspect looked weak and good natured, but he repeated his stubborn denials . . . The MP beat him with a stick. I could not bear the sight, so I advised him to confess to avoid further mental and physical pain. He just smiled at me. Finally, the policeman applied the usual torture. First they took him to the bathtub . . . Then his broken right arm was placed on his front and his left arm behind his back, tied with a cord. They laid him on his back with a towel loosely covering his mouth and nose. They poured water over his face. The soaking cloth blocked his nose and mouth. He struggled to breathe and opened his mouth to inhale air. They poured water into his mouth. I saw his stomach swelling up. Watching the prisoner in great torture, I almost lost my presence of mind. I was desperate to control my shaking body. I feared that he would be killed in my presence. I took him by the broken wrist and felt the pulse. I still remember clearly that I was relieved to feel an unexpected normal pulse.

With the prisoner screaming and crying, 'Mother! Mother!' I muttered to myself, 'Mother, do you know what is happening to your son now?' I still cannot stop shuddering every time I recall that horrible scene.

Nagase pauses to criticize the Imperial Rescript, the long oath of loyalty, which all recruits had to memorize, and the authoritarian system of absolute obedience that underlay it, which held a person's family responsible for his actions. He contrasts this system with the respect for fundamental human rights which seems, in his eyes, to be rooted in the minds of people in the West.

For the rest of the war Nagase spent six months in hospital, and was then returned to Kanburi, from which he set off with Padre Babb and his fellow officers on their special train in the search for abandoned graves. Nagase describes the quiet, restrained hostility of the big English and Australian men with whom he was forced to travel, the difficulties of persuading Japanese troops to co-operate with the search, and the sad state of the bewildered surviving romusha, clustering around the Allied officers and pleading to be sent home. Their plight moves him since the Japanese army units are by now attempting to clean up the POW graves, but the Asian labourers' graves are ignored by everybody. 'I feared that this contrast would make people think that the Japanese did not care about romushas' souls.' They find countless abandoned mounds of earth and wooden markers in the jungle, already strangled by vegetation. Nagase is disgusted by the fertility of the jungle, the myriad centipedes and worms, and comically afraid of tigers, which he imagines are lurking by the side of the track wherever he goes. He describes a tense confrontation with armed, desperate and 'awfully ferocious' Japanese troops at the end of the line in Burma, whose commanding officer at first refuses to salute the British captain leading the war graves party.

One evening, the Allied officers take him into their roofed wagon and sit him down, putting headphones around his ears. He hears a broadcast describing how the Japanese Railway Corps, the POW administration units and the 'special police' are suspected of being major war criminal groupings, and how a unit of the Allied forces is currently engaged in the collection of information about Japanese war crimes such as maltreatment of POWs along the railway. 'I was aware,' he writes, 'that all the officers' attention was focused upon me and my face turned pale, my throat and lips dried up and became frozen.' After a long silence he admits to them that he used to work for the special police. They ask him gravely if he has ever had any trouble with prisoners. 'Nothing in particular,' he answers, and they tell him that he will be all right, as long as he is with them, if he does his duty well.

Nagase notes that he began then to sense a breach between British and Japanese points of view regarding the value of human life and began to try to comprehend why GHQ in Tokyo should have pushed ahead with a railway line that British engineers had rejected 'because of the predicted large number of victims'. He concludes that it was the cult of absolute obedience and the absorption of the army leaders in 'an armchair plan' that made the difference. Later he decides, after seeing like a terrible revelation the thousands upon thousands of crosses behind the POW hospital at Chungkai, near Kanburi, that 'the refined civilization should be based upon humanity'.

Eighteen years after the war, when travel outside Japan became easier with the lifting of restrictions, Nagase and his wife went to Kanburi and stood in the large war cemetery, among the neat stone graves and the bronze plates with the name of each dead soldier.

In the center of the grand cemetery, a white cross stands against a blue sky. The cross is surrounded by approximately 7,000 officers and soldiers lying in the tropical serenity. They were the people who were searched and checked just after the war ended.

My wife and I moved forward to the white cross and offered a wreath at its base. The moment I joined my hands in prayer . . . I felt my body emitting yellow beams of light in every direction and turning transparent. At that moment I thought, 'This is it. You have been pardoned.' I believed this feeling plainly

. . . After I returned home I worked as an interpreter for the Occupation Army in Japan and a teacher at senior high school. After a year I had tuberculosis. When the tuberculosis took a turn for the better, I fell ill again. I suffered a most malignant cardiac neurosis. I had fits of palpitation . . . After the fit was gone, both my body and mind were worn out . . . Every time I had a fit, the torture scene in the military police flashed through my mind. I told myself that those prisoners suffered far more, and endured great pain.

. . . The sense of guilt had lain in my mind for a long time. The moment I visited the graves, I felt the sense of guilt vanish through my recognition that my wish finally came true. My health was getting better and my business went well.

Nagase visited Thailand many times after that, and did charitable work for the surviving Asian labourers, many of whom were unable to return home to India or Malaya after the war and dragged out miserable lives in villages near the railway; and he opened a temple of peace on the River Kwae Bridge, and spoke out against militarism.

It all seemed admirable, but I read about these things with a surprising sense of detachment. I had expected to feel some more powerful emotion, but apart from the eerie feeling of being present at my own torture as an onlooker I felt empty. And I wondered at his feeling that he had been forgiven. God may have forgiven him, but I had not; mere human forgiveness is another matter.

I put the book aside. After a few days, Patti picked it up and read it slowly one afternoon. The passages which I've quoted on Nagase's trip to the War Cemetery at Kanburi filled her with anger, much more than I had felt. She wanted to know how Nagase could feel pardoned. How could his sense of guilt simply 'vanish' if no-one, and me in particular, had pardoned him?

Patti's sense of indignation was such that she wanted to write to Nagase immediately and asked my permission to do so. She drafted a letter which was sent in late October 1991, enclosing a photograph of me. Now there could be no thought of a sudden confrontation between him and me.

Dear Mr Nagase

I have just finished reading your book Crosses and Tigers. This is of particular interest to me because my husband is the Royal Signals Officer who had been arrested, along with six others, in connection with the operation of a radio in the railway workshop camp near Kanchanaburi in August 1943. My husband also had with him a map of the railway. He is the man you describe on page 15 of your book, being tortured so terribly.

His mother did die at home in Edinburgh, one month after the fall of Singapore. A relative has told me that she died of a broken heart . . .

My husband already knew who you were, having recognized you from the article which appeared in the Japan Times of 15th August 1989.

He is most interested in having contact with you for he has lived with many unanswered questions all these years, questions to which perhaps only you can help him to find the answers. Maybe you also have questions about the Kanchanaburi Radio Affair? . . . If you are willing, perhaps you would agree to correspond with my husband?

My husband has lived all these years with the after effects of the cruel experiences he suffered and I hope that contact between you could be a healing experience for both of you. How can you feel 'forgiven' Mr Nagase, if this particular former Far Eastern prisoner-of-war has not yet forgiven you? My husband does understand the cultural pressures you were under during the war but whether he can totally forgive your own involvement remains to be seen and it is not for me, who was not there, to judge . . .

Yours sincerely

Mrs Patricia M. Lomax

* * *

On 6th November when Patti went downstairs to collect the mail which was lying on the floor just inside the front door she saw an express airmail letter from Japan. It was addressed to her but she brought it to me unopened. I sat in my pyjamas on the edge of our bed and opened the tissue-thin envelope.

Dear Mrs Patricia M Lomax

I am now quite at a loss after reading your unexpected letter. And I am thinking that it is very natural indeed for me to expect such this letter. The words you wrote to me 'If this particular former Far Eastern Prisoner of War has not yet forgiven you' has beaten me down wholely, reminding me of my dirty old days. I think having received such a letter from you is my destiny. Please give me some time to think it over and over again.

But please tell your husband that if I am a bit useful for him to answer any questions that he has had in his mind, I am willing to answer them.

Anyhow, I am beginning to think that I should see him again. Looking at the picture, he looks healthy and tender gentleman, though I am not able to see the inside of his mind. Please tell him to live long until I can see him.

Most sincerely yours

Nagase Takashi

p.s. Please let me know your Telepone number.

p.s. 2 Excuse that my mind has confused after reading your letter and I could only write what you read here. I will try to find out the way I can meet him if he agrees to see me.

And thank you very much for your taking care of him until today for a long time.

The dagger of your letter thrusted me into my heart to the bottom.

Patti thought this was an extraordinarily beautiful letter. Anger drained away; in its place came a welling of compassion for both Nagase and for me, coupled with a deep sense of sadness and regret. In that moment I lost whatever hard armour I had wrapped around me and began to think the unthinkable: that I could meet Nagase face to face in simple good will. Forgiveness became more than an abstract idea: it was now a real possibility.

As the days went by it seemed that Nagase's sincerity might be utterly genuine. I began to appreciate more fully how damaged he must be by what he had done, however unwillingly; an interrogator suffering in retrospect with his victims. Nor was his concern to make reparation some occasional thing; it was truly almost a way of life; I learned later that he had been back sixty-odd times to Thailand since 1963. He had also become a devout Buddhist, and his creation of a temple at the bridge was obviously a tremendous achievement for him.

He must have had a terrible fright when he received Patti's letter, a letter from beyond the grave. Patti replied later that week, and I took another step towards him. She enclosed a personal letter from me. Patti's letter was splendid and from the heart, setting out briefly what had happened to me since the war. My letter was brief, cool and formal; it was the best I could manage. My letters are always somewhat formal nowadays.

I asked him at first for information: were the searches made specifically to look for radio sets? What made the Japanese Army suspect that there were sets in the camps? And who gave the orders? I was still determined to establish an indelible historical record of what had happened.

Nagase's reply supplied little new information, for he had been briefly in Saigon at the end of October 1943 and by the time of his return we were already in 'the monkey houses', as he described those cages in the Kempei's back yard. He thought that they had not been tipped off, but that they were looking for radios, and that they were apprehensive that we were communicating with Thais outside the camp (their great fear was that there were so few of them to hold so many of us in subjection). He thought, finally, that Captain Komai, who was hanged after the war, gave the orders for the beating. He added: 'I know his son lives in the north of Japan, having dishonour.' He closed by saying that he wanted to meet me partly so that our meeting would explain 'the stupidity' to the world, especially to those Japanese 'who still want to have aggression toward foreign lands'.

It took us a year to arrange our meeting. Neither Patti nor I are wealthy, and we are both retired, and it is difficult to afford expensive air travel to South East Asia. (My arms and hips are in such a state that the cramped conditions of economy-class seats make long flights impossible.) We hoped that we might be able to obtain funding from the Sasakawa Foundation, which encourages understanding between Britain and Japan, but delayed doing so because there was still a possibility of the documentary film being made, and though I was now more sensitive to the danger of turning myself into an entertainment and wanted to meet Nagase independently of whatever our television friends wanted, I insisted that the film should be made for the Medical Foundation, which would play a large part in the documentary.

Nagase and I wrote to each other, but it is difficult to carry on a sustained correspondence with someone you have only recently stopped hating enough to kill, and sometimes all the old resistances welled up. I was frank with him, telling him that I found it difficult to write to him, and he was kind and understanding, always replying promptly to my letters. We wanted to meet in Thailand and afterwards he wanted me to come with him to Japan at the time of cherry blossoms in Kurashiki, which he assured me were very beautiful.

In the end, believing that Nagase and I could not wait much longer and that the world of film would wear us down, I went to the Sasakawa Foundation and they agreed to help to finance our trip. They also felt that the proposed documentary would have some effect in promoting their aims of reconciliation and understanding, and agreed to loan money for that too. I agreed, as long as the Medical Foundation could own the film when the costs were recovered. With these organizational contingencies at last out of the way, I was ready to face my old enemy eagerly and in good heart.

CHAPTER TWELVE

BANGKOK WAS NOT the city I remembered. After the nine-hour flight in refrigerated comfort the heat closed around us as soon as Patti and I emerged from the plane.

Escaping the heat was easy; this time I was an honoured guest, and they had sent an air-conditioned Rolls. Bangkok's skyline was now all semi-skyscrapers and glass buildings. I remembered a deathly emptiness in the streets and our prison truck making a great deal of noise; now there were six-lane freeways with an endless honking column of cars and lorries. It reminded me of TV pictures of Los Angeles. Everything seemed so hot and slow despite the busy rush of vehicles. It took us no less than three hours to reach our hotel from the airport.

Two days later, feeling tense and irritable as the moment came closer, we set off for Kanburi. Bangkok Noi Station is on the west side of the city, another once-great cavern from the steam age which, in its time of glory, linked Bangkok to Singapore. Those days ended in 1927, with the opening of a new bridge across the Menam River, and the station became a backwater – an appropriately stagnant place from which to send trains to the Burma-Siam Railway. The trains still run from here to Kanburi and beyond it to Nam Tok, but there the line peters out less than a third of the way to its original terminus in Burma, and Bangkok Noi has become a little more neglected. But a thriving market stretches alongside the station, women traders selling everything from fruit to pieces of vivid coloured cloth, and has expanded on to the old carriage sidings and the tracks themselves, where we browsed along the stalls. The last time I had walked through a railway station in Siam it was with a rope around my middle, my arms in splints and the possibility of a death sentence ahead.

The train to Kanburi, a big diesel locomotive pulling seven coaches in blue-and-white livery, runs through flat, fertile land crossed by irrigation ditches and green with rice, fruit and palm trees. I looked at the countryside intently, but it gave back little enough to help prepare me for what I was doing; I was remembering the past while hoping for a different future in the years that remained, and it was not easy to reconcile the two.

At Nong Pladuk, the train passes through a little station with one platform, very neat, tidy and bright: boxes full of red and yellow flowers and small shrubs in wooden barrels give it the look of a model station, a toy. There is no trace of the camp to the north of the line, behind the platform, where the first POWs from Singapore set up the first camp for the construction of the railway. But on the south side of the line, in sidings tattered with dry grass and weeds, there are rows of covered goods vans like those used for moving POWs up the line. Some of them have almost certainly survived and stand there in the heat with their doors open, as they used to when they were underway packed with thirty prisoners and their baggage.

Above the sidings there is an old-fashioned wooden water-tower on stilts. This is the original built by the Japanese Army for watering the engines, mainly those imposing C56s; here is where they were gathered, fuelled and repaired. I saw one of the first big fleets of them on my way to Bangkok for our trial.

To the west of Nong Pladuk near Ban Pong the single track divides in two; the line on the left is the old main line to the south, which ends at Singapore; the line to the right is the proper beginning of the Burma-Siam Railway. It looks peaceful today, a clean and well-kept track swinging off towards the wild uplands of Kanchanaburi Province and Three Pagodas Pass, the border with Burma. Just before the two tracks diverged I looked hard at the ground beside the railway on the north side. The railway stores and the temporary workshop camp were just beside the line. Thew made the first radio there, and brought back his stolen Buddha to our hut. There isn't a trace of the camp now; pleasant houses, gardens and a large school seem to occupy the same ground.

From Ban Pong to Kanburi for thirty miles the line runs through villages and more flat rich land, even a few factories with their own sidings: a use has been found for this section of the railway, at least. As the mountains rose up wooded and indistinct in the haze, we reached Kanburi. The big railway workshops have disappeared like everything else, and I stared at the nearly empty sidings as though I could make some evidence appear, but I saw none.

Out in front of the station, on a deserted piece of track, stood a magnificent old locomotive. It was a Garratt, an engine legendary for its mighty hauling power in the last decades of steam, a giant handsome workhorse with two sets of eight-coupled wheels; why it had been placed here I couldn't imagine, but it had the aura of a great piece of human effort and it awakened all the old passion in me. The big Garratt's iron strength looked fragile against the green of the trees and plants around it in this hot, damp weather, the sheer power of the forest which had so appalled Nagase when he was searching for graves in 1945. There is some fatal sadness about these machines in the tropics: they embody so much failure and tragedy, and decaying beauty.

A short run beyond Kanburi brought us to the platform at the River Kwae Bridge; the train was longer than the platform, so we got down on to the track itself and walked beside it, next to the dried and oil-stained timber of the sleepers. The heat was ferocious and the smell of diesel rose up from the track. We came to a broad area in front of an open level-crossing which leads on to the bridge. The engine, its siren blasting, growled across the bridge, the seven coaches slowly moving through the girders of the eleven spans set on their concrete piers, and then the train disappeared westwards towards the mountains. Silence rose up, and was gradually drowned by the noise of lorries and motor-cycles resuming their journeys as the level-crossing opened again. The bridge piers in the brown muddy water were cracked and pitted by the fragments of bombs dropped in 1944, when the US Army Air Force damaged the bridge. They looked as though they had not been touched for fifty years.

We booked into a hotel across the river from the town, and had lunch in the River Kwae Restaurant, where we met Tida Loha, its remarkable proprietor. She had had the generosity and im-agination to give Nagase a plot of land next to the bridge so that he could build his temple of peace, and she is an astute and diplomatic woman. She has met many ex-POWs and Japanese ex-servicemen over the years, and knows a great deal about the fierce hatreds that were played out between strangers in her town during the war.

Time was now running out. Nagase and I had arranged to meet in the morning, on the opposite side of the bridge near the little museum devoted to the railway, and I could not bear to alter the arrangement even a little, so that when he and his wife arrived at his hotel at six in the evening instead of at midnight, as planned, there was a kind of panic. Ian Kerr, an associate of the Medical Foundation who had come to the meeting in case there was a crisis, saved me from having to stay in my own room, a prisoner once again in Kanburi, by taking Patti and me out for dinner, to a floating restaurant where I played with a friendly cat and tried to forget about the next day. It was late when we went to bed.

In the morning we crossed to the other side of the river and walked up the steps to a broad veranda overlooking the bridge. I sat down to watch and wait. I was dressed rather formally in a shirt and slacks, and wore a Sutherland tartan tie – surely the only tie for miles around. The sun was climbing and the air was oppressively hot, though it was not yet nine in the morning.

From about a hundred yards away I saw him walk out on to the bridge; he could not see me. It was important for me to have this last momentary advantage over him; it prepared me, even now that I no longer wanted to hurt him. I walked about a hundred yards to an open square, a kind of courtyard overlooking the river, where we had arranged to meet.

A huge smiling figure of Buddha dominated the courtyard and as I sat down I realized that there was another benign presence throwing a shadow on to the wide expanse of terrace: a carefully preserved locomotive, a veteran of the Royal Siamese Railway, built in Glasgow, I noticed, in the year of my birth. This exquisite relic could have come from a brightly-lit dream, with me sitting on an empty square, a silent steam engine close at hand, waiting for something to happen.

He came on to the terrace, walking past the engine. I had

forgotten how small he was, a tiny man in an elegant straw hat, loose kimono-like jacket and trousers. From a distance he resembled an oriental carving, some benign wizened demon come to life. He carried a shapeless blue cotton shoulder bag. As he came closer I could see that he wore around his throat beads of dark red stone on a thick string. I remembered him saying to me again and again 'Lomax, you will tell us', other phrases he had recited in the voice I hated so much . . .

He began a formal bow, his face working and agitated, the small figure barely reaching my shoulder. I stepped forward, took his hand and said '*Ohayo gozaimasu, Nagase san, ogenki desu ka?*' 'Good morning, Mr Nagase, how are you?'

He looked up at me; he was trembling, in tears, saying over and over 'I am very, very sorry . . . ' I somehow took command, led him out of the terrible heat to a bench in the shade; I was comforting him, for he was really overcome. At that moment my capacity for reserve and self-control helped me to help him, murmuring reassurances as we sat down. It was as though I was protecting him from the force of the emotions shaking his frail-seeming body. I think I said something like 'That's very kind of you to say so' to his repeated expressions of sorrow.

He said to me 'Fifty years is a long time, but for me it is a time of suffering. I never forgot you, I remember your face, especially your eyes.' He looked deep into my eyes when he said this. His own face still looked like the one I remembered, rather fine-featured, with dark and slightly hidden eyes; his wide mouth was still noticeable beneath cheeks that had sunken inwards.

I told him that I could remember his very last words to me. He asked what they were and laughed when I said 'Keep your chin up.'

He asked if he could touch my hand. My former interrogator

held my arm, which was so much larger than his, stroking it quite unselfconsciously. I didn't find it embarrassing. He gripped my wrist with both of his hands and told me that when I was being tortured – he used the word – he measured my pulse. I remembered he had written this in his memoir. Yet now that we were face to face, his grief seemed far more acute than mine. 'I was a member of Imperial Japanese Army; we treated your countrymen very, very badly.' 'We both survived', I said encouragingly, really believing it now.

A little later, I'm sure he said: 'For what purpose were you born in this world? I think I can die safely now.'

He asked me if I remembered the 'bath house' where I was tortured. I had to admit I couldn't recall it; he said that there was an episode between the shouting in the room and the drowning with the hosepipe in the yard, when they took me into some sort of bathroom and filled a metal tub, and the Kempei Gunso held my head underneath the water. 'You remember big can?' Nagase asked, making a round shape with his hands. I had to take his word for it. I told him that I did certainly remember the Gunso's wooden ruler banging on the desk, and that I didn't like him very much. Nagase agreed that he was 'a very rough man'.

It's impossible to remember everything we talked about, but we sat there so long that the sun moved right around and we were no longer in the shade. (Patti told me later that she was having a sharp argument in the background with a journalist who spotted a story on the terrace and was trying to photograph us; I never heard a thing.) The content of our conversation hardly mattered. We laughed a lot, after a while, and were happy in each other's company. I can recall snatches of what we said quite clearly, especially some of his quaint phrases, and have an impression of the rest.

At one point Nagase suddenly began talking about my map. He reminded me that I'd tried to tell him I had a sketch of the line 'because you are mania of railway', as he put it. 'I tried to believe it,' he said, 'but at that time in Japan railway mania was not so popular.' Then he said that he knew we had every kind of 'mania' in our country and had tried to persuade the Gunso that I was not the leader of the group. I pointed out that the Gunso hadn't believed me anyway, and Nagase said that they had *wanted* a spy; they could not understand otherwise where we had found the makings of a radio, and were obsessed with preventing contacts between us and civilians. He himself had, as I suspected, searched prisoners' belongings at Singapore when they were leaving for Ban Pong and the north.

He asked where I had hidden the map in the Sakamoto Butai; it had always puzzled him why they failed to find it when they searched the huts. I explained that it was in a hollow bamboo in the wall of the latrine and that the American-speaking interpreter had only found it later when I'd been reckless enough to hide it in my kit. Nagase spoke of 'that fellow's' suffering as a 'minority man' in America before the war, and how he had a 'hard mind towards the white man'.

He told me what he had done in the last year of the war after he had recovered from his malaria: translating propaganda leaflets dropped by our planes, patrolling the perimeter of the camps searching for spies and parachutists, generally appeasing the futile hunger for information of a defeated empire; he spent a lot of time hiding from bombers and fearful of treading on delayed-action bombs.

He wanted to know if Captain Komai, who was held responsible for the deaths of Hawley and Armitage, had beaten us personally; he had met his son a few years earlier. I said that I thought he had probably done so, but I couldn't be sure. Nagase assumed that I had been tortured again at Outram Road, and I had to explain that there are rare occasions when overt torture is not the worst punishment. He was kind enough to say that compared to my suffering his was nothing; and yet it was so obvious that he had suffered too. 'Various sufferings, various sufferings in my heart and mind . . . ' He told me how he had studied history and become totally opposed to militarism; about his wife, Yoshiko, who was quite wealthy, about his English-language school and her teaching of the tea ceremony.

Later that morning we went into the museum next to the terrace. The long rooms were stiflingly hot. Laid out on the floor were rusty chains which had been used to move the wooden sleepers; a few spikes; some ropes and saws. There was a set of big rusty iron hooks – couplings for goods vans – and a few of the little four-wheeled bogies used to push more and more heavy timber and iron up the line and on to the backs of already-exhausted men. They looked insignificant lying there, the wheels jammed with rust and useless except to remind people what had been done with them. The big iron cooking vessels, called *kwalis*, of the kind we used for cooking rice when I was mess officer were laid out as though for offerings on a long table.

By then we had introduced Mrs Nagase and Mrs Lomax to each other, and they were finding a common language of sympathy and understanding. Nagase said he had often walked past the site of the Kempeitai house when he came to Kanburi, so we decided to go to visit it together. The building has of course been demolished and the site built over. We were driven by Tida Loha, who helps so many of the former POWs who visit Kanburi, and Patti sat in the front of the car with her. I sat in the back between Nagase and a Japanese friend of his, and my wife turned around while we were moving through the crowded streets and just looked at us. Our eyes met and we smiled: I knew she was thinking; there I was sitting between two Japanese men on my way back to that place, and all three of us smiling and laughing.

The Kempei house was well and truly gone. The yard where the 'monkey houses' were kept is now occupied by a family dwelling. Places where such things have been done can be wiped out so easily. Torture, after all, is inconspicuous; all it needs is water, a piece of wood and a loud voice. It takes place in squalid rooms, dirty back yards and basements, and there is nothing left to preserve when it is over. Marks on the body can fade quickly too, and it is thanks to people like Helen Bamber that the hidden traces which can't simply be built over are uncovered and brought back into the light.

After our inconsequential return to the place where we had first met, we visited the war memorials. To reach the Allied cemetery at Chungkai we took a long-tailed craft which ripped along the river like a speedboat past reed-beds, cultivated fields and green walls of trees. The heat was amazing. Even the river seemed to be sprouting under it – weeds, lily pads, trailing bits of vegetation. When we alighted we walked through the red-roofed portico and a cool gallery. The traditional legend is picked out on the entrance: 'Their Name Liveth For Ever More'. The vast graveyard is immaculately clean, gardened and swept. Bronze tablets are set into blocks of glittery limestone, shaped like lecterns. Some of the tablets are dedicated simply to 'A Soldier of the 1939-45 War, Known Unto God'. Might the vanished Bill Williamson be lying here unclaimed?

We walked around, Patti and I drifting off together and leaving Nagase and Yoshiko behind. We talked a little, and there was then a moment of doubt; I think I finally expressed, among those lines of graves, a resolution for which I had been searching for years.

The Japanese War Memorial, which POWs were forced to build some time in 1944, is a sadder and more neglected place. A cenotaph now showing blotches of weather and stress was erected in a compound surrounded by low trees; it is ill-kept and deserted. The cenotaph incorporates plaques to the dead of other countries, like an afterthought. Some ex-POWs, who can never forgive, throw stones at the memorial when they come here; the scars are visible on the stained concrete. Mrs Nagase told us that morning that her brother was killed in the last days of the war, somewhere in Burma, one of the many young men who were never given a chance.

Nagase and I talked a lot about the railway. The utter futility of it still astonished both of us. The Pyramids, that other great engineering disaster, are at least a monument to our love of beauty, as well as to slave labour; the railway is a dead end in the jungle. Most of the track in the border area was torn up after the war, the sleepers used for firewood or for building houses. The line had some strategic military value at the time, but only in the service of a doomed campaign that cost millions of lives. The line has become literally pointless. It now runs for about 60 miles and then stops. The rest of it is as abandoned as the little line which I found on Unst in the Shetland Islands in 1933.

As we walked and talked, I felt that my strange companion was a person who I would have been able to get on with long ago had we met under other circumstances. We had a lot in common: books, teaching, an interest in history, though he still found one of my 'manias' puzzling; and I warmed to him more and more as the time in Kanburi went by. We were due to fly to Japan together at the end of the week.

I still needed to consider the matter of forgiveness, since it so concerned him. Assuming that our meeting, in itself, constituted forgiveness, or that the passage of time had made it irrelevant, seemed too easy; once someone raises forgiveness to such a pitch of importance you become judicial. I felt I had to respond to Nagase's sense of the binding or loosening force of my decision.

A kind Thai woman who we met that week tried to explain the importance of forgiveness in Buddhism to me; I understood that whatever you do you get back in this life and if what you have done is tainted with evil and you have not made atonement for it, evil is returned to you in the next life with interest. Nagase dreaded hell, and it seemed that our first meeting had made parts of both our lives hellish already. Even if I could not grasp the theology fully, I could no longer see the point of punishing Nagase by a refusal to reach out and forgive him. What mattered was our relations in the here and now, his obvious regret for what he had done and our mutual need to give our encounter some meaning beyond that of the emptiness of cruelty. It was surely worth salvaging as much as we could from the damage to both our lives. The question was now one of choosing the right moment to say the words to him with the formality that the situation seemed to demand.

* * *

We flew to Osaka, surrounded by Japanese businessmen. I was separated from Patti until a very sophisticated gentleman, speaking excellent English, heard from her what we were about and gave up his seat so that we could be together. Mrs Nagase and some of her pupils, young professional women of great charm and courtesy, met us at the airport and within a couple of hours we were on the extraordinary bullet train from Osaka to Okayama; it was like riding a missile adhering to the rails. We sat on the top deck as we swept past the continuous spread of small houses and other buildings along the coast of the inland sea.

Kurashiki, where we went next, is a jewel, an Oxford or a Bath among Japan's devastated and rebuilt cities, almost untouched by the war and its old city later spared by developers. I loved the wide, clean canal running through it, the swans and the little bridges. Yoshiko took us to 'the old house', her family's pre-war residence which is maintained as a traditional Japanese dwelling. She comes from an old and substantial Kurashiki family, and she is proud of her city. The house is beautiful, with internal paper walls and graceful plain rooms furnished sparsely with low tables and hangings. We sat on cushions for the tea ceremony, though I was unable fully to concentrate on the intricate and graceful ritual because it was some time since I had attempted to sit cross-legged. I was struck, though, by the low doors of the tea-house in the yard, built small so that a man wearing a sword could not pass through them. This seemed a civilized precaution.

In the 'new house', where the Nagases live, I saw the same chaos of books and papers with which I am surrounded at home. One day I sat unwittingly in his study in the same chair, in almost the same position, in which Nagase had sat for his photograph for the *Japan Times* and in which I had rediscovered him.

Nagase was determined to show me the cherry blossoms at their finest, and it became a running joke. He would announce each morning that the cherry blossoms were 'open today 30 per cent', or 45 per cent, and that soon we would be able to see them as they were meant to be seen. He once took us to a park in Okayama, and was disappointed to find that in that particular garden the blossoms could only be judged to be 40 per cent open.

It was astonishing to be walking around this handsome town: a few years before I could not have imagined meeting a Japanese person voluntarily and now I was strolling in streets full of them, a tourist in my seventies, an honoured guest of two good people. Everyone we met was extremely courteous, and it was wonderful to me to see these crowds of smiling, well-dressed young people who are heirs to an economic superpower that leads the world in electronics, when I remembered my patient explanations of how a radio transmitter works in that wooden room in Siam in 1943!

Their command of engineering skill was displayed most beautifully in the bridges over the inland sea, connecting Honshu and Shikoku. I asked specially to see them, since the marvel of the Forth Bridge was one of my childhood wonders. They form the greatest span of bridges in the world, nine miles long, a sequence of bridges leaping off and disappearing gracefully over the horizon.

So we did what tourists are expected to do in Japan, and it was most enjoyable, but this is not a travel book and all the time I was aware of an unresolved question between Nagase and me. I found it hard to choose the right moment; there were always others around, and Nagase had a tendency to wish to make our encounter public, a symbol of reconciliation, and this gave some of our outings the character of official visits, with Japanese pressmen dogging our footsteps.

Meanwhile, we attended to things that were important to both of us, in different ways. We went to Hiroshima, and Patti and I laid a bunch of mixed flowers on the memorial. A director of the Peace Memorial Museum, himself deformed by radiation, showed us around. Terrible photographs of burnt children, of people with radiation sickness, of obliterated streets; we saw a man pointing out, with the stump of his hand, the image of a human figure preserved as if it had been photographed by the flash of the atomic blast.

The whole atmosphere of Hiroshima is like that of a shrine. Nagase and I were guilty of violating its respectful busy gravity rather disgracefully. We were walking around the museum together, Patti and Yoshiko in front of us with some of Nagase's friends. In the background there was a hubbub of chattering and commentary. Suddenly, as Patti later told me, she heard an outburst of unseemly hilarity behind her. There we were, two old gentlemen laughing our heads off in this sanctum of peace.

We had been talking about the last days of the war. Nagase asked me when I had heard about the nuclear attack on Hiroshima. 'On 8th August,' I told him. He was astonished: this was at least two days before he and his unit were told about it. He wanted to know how we could possibly have known, locked up as we were in Changi and deprived of contact with the outside world. Ah, I told him, but of course we had a radio. And for some reason that set us off, even in a place of such awful seriousness.

One day, to the surprise of our hosts, I asked to see a memorial of a very different kind, the Yasukuni Shrine in Tokyo, the centre of Japanese imperial tradition and the chief cult centre of what was once Japan's state religion, Shinto Buddhism.

Nagase and I had talked about historical truth and he was concerned – almost to the point of obsession – with ensuring that the Japanese should be aware of what their army did in the name of the Emperor before 1945. He believes that there must be a break with all vestiges of the cult of obedience to authority; he is a militant spiritual humanist. He often talked about how there was so little in the way of good history to put into Japanese schoolchildren's hands; so little encouragement to face up to the past and come to terms with it. Nagase's crusading spirit, which is courageous and laudable, can become a little wearing, as when he wished to publicize our outings; but the more he talked the more I could understand his zeal. His obsession had become atonement and reconciliation, which need publicity – whereas mine had been with private remembering and revenge. The positions he takes up arouse fierce hostility in Japan. He once said that he would not be surprised 'to wake up and find myself dead'.

A clearer picture of what he is fighting against cannot be seen than at Yasukuni, to which we were taken by Professor Nakahara, who we had the good fortune to meet again. The shrine is at one level a moving war memorial, dedicated to the worship of those who died for the Emperor, but at another it is an unashamed celebration of militarism. Cherry blossom trees are bedecked with little white ribbons with personal messages and requests. In the grounds you can find a monument to the Kempeitai – it is like seeing a memorial to the Gestapo in a German cathedral. In front of a museum building next to the shrine, and very much part of it, is parked a field gun, for all the world like the Imperial War Museum in London – except that this is a place of religious worship. And alongside the artillery-piece, there is an immaculate C56 steam locomotive, described by the shrine authorities as the first engine to pass along the Burma Railway. It stands proud, its smoke-deflectors polished and its great wheels pressing down into the gravel, its beauty a monument to barbarism.

Nagase told me how he had protested vigorously when the C56 was installed at Yasukuni in 1979. He wrote to the officials of the shrine, and reminded anyone who would listen that Tojo is reputed to have visited Siam when the construction of the railway was about to start, and said that it must be completed even though one prisoner should die for every sleeper on the line; and Nagase had pointed out that this particular engine demanded a sleeper for every metre of track. Both Tojo, as a soldier of the Emperor, and the machine are worshipped at Yasukuni.

* * *

In all the time I spent in Japan I never felt a flash of the anger I had harboured against Nagase all those years, no backwash of that surge of murderous intent I had felt on finding out that one of them was still alive. Indeed Nagase gave me the impression of having been prepared for a much more irritated and difficult encounter than ours turned out to be.

Perhaps that is why he seemed afraid, suddenly, when I asked to see him alone in his hotel room in Tokyo, where we were staying prior to our return to Britain. Days before, I had worked out what to do. I had decided to give him a piece of paper which I thought would meet both our needs, and had planned to give it to him in Kyoto; he had wanted very much to show me the great temples of the ancient former capital of Japan.

It rained heavily on the morning of our planned visit to Kyoto, and Nagase felt unwell, so we went with Yoshiko to that extraordinary place. In the rain, the glitter of the Golden Pavilion was softened, its image in the lake blurred. We walked around the stark, simple gardens and looked at everything we could, but I was worried about Nagase's brush with his old cardiac trouble and anxious now to make our final peace.

Looking out the window of our room in the nondescript, modern Tokyo hotel, I could see through a gap created by a building site the coming and going of trains in the huge Tokyo railway station. I sat waiting for Patti and Yoshiko to go out. My request to see Nagase on his own must have carried a charge of electricity, for it disturbed Yoshiko and she said to Patti, with a worried look on her face, 'Heart', and glanced pleadingly at me. I said that it would be all right, but she could not hide her distress.

After they had gone I went next door. There in that quiet room, with the faint noise of trains and the city streets rising up to us, I gave Mr Nagase the forgiveness he desired.

I read my short letter out to him, stopping and checking that he understood each paragraph. I felt he deserved this careful formality. In the letter I said that the war had been over for almost fifty years; that I had suffered much; and that I knew that although he too had suffered throughout this time, he had been most courageous and brave in arguing against militarism and working for reconciliation. I told him that while I could not forget what happened in Kanburi in 1943, I assured him of my total forgiveness.

He was overcome with emotion again, and we spent some time in his room talking quietly and without haste.

* * *

The next morning we saw Nagase and Yoshiko to their train back to Kurashiki. He phoned us from there that evening to make sure that we were all right. I thought that I had seen him for the last time, perhaps for the last time in our lives. The following day we ourselves made our way to the train for Osaka, from where we would fly to Britain. When after a journey of three hours, the train drew to a halt in Osaka, we stepped on to the platform. At the exact spot where our carriage door opened there was my friend Nagase standing with Yoshiko, smiling and bowing. They knew exactly which coach we were in, and they were like excited children, so pleased to have tricked us; it was good to see them.

They took us to the airport and we left Japan. As the plane tilted us over the bay of Osaka, I held my wife's hand. I felt that I had accomplished more than I could ever have dreamed of. Meeting Nagase has turned him from a hated enemy, with whom friendship would have been unthinkable, into a blood-brother. If I'd never been able to put a name to the face of one of the men who had harmed me, and never discovered that behind that face there was also a damaged life, the nightmares would always have come from a past without meaning. And I had proved for myself that remembering is not enough, if it simply hardens hate.

Back in Thailand, at the Chungkai War Cemetery, when Patti and I walked off on our own, she had had a moment of doubt as she looked at the rows and rows of graves, and wondered whether we were doing the right thing after all. It was only a moment, for we both knew we should be there. I said then: 'Sometime the hating has to stop.'

ACKNOWLEDGMENTS

I acknowledge with gratitude the work of my literary agent, Hilary Rubinstein, whose experience, wisdom and kindness have contributed so much to the completion of this work.

Two members of the staff of the Imperial War Museum, Roderick Suddaby, Keeper of the Department of Documents, and Dr Christopher Dowling, Keeper of the Department of Museum Services, must also be given special thanks for encouragement and help over a long period of time.

I also owe a special debt to Mike Finlason, film producer and director, for his belief in the special nature of the story, for organising the filming of the unique events in Kanchanaburi in 1993 and for making the documentary *Enemy My Friend*, first shown publicly in South Africa.

I am also grateful for support from Jonathan Uzzell.

From Jonathan Cape, I would like to thank Jenny Cottom for her editorial care and the clear design of the book; and Kirsty Dunseath for her much appreciated hard work.

Nothing could have been achieved without the help of three ladies in Berwick-upon-Tweed. First, Julie Wastling helped at the start of the project; Joan Scott later undertook the processing of most of the pre-war part of the book. Sabina Maule worked on the extensive wartime and post-war section, much of which was revised constantly, and produced faultless typescripts at top speed, often despite personal and domestic commitments.

To Helen Bamber, Director of the Medical Foundation for the Care of Victims of Torture, I extend my deepest thanks for compassion, advice and encouragement, despite the claims of an exceptionally busy working life and the demands of the organisation of which she was a co-founder.

To my dear wife Patti, special acknowledgment must be made for her constant trust, devotion and support through both difficult times and good times.

Eric Lomax

Joe Payne

About the Author

ERIC LOMAX was born in 1919. He lives in Berwick-upon-Tweed in the north of England.

pg 288
Slave Labor

Japanese Imperialism

pg. 272
273

Traidor, inconfeso y mártir

Letras Hispánicas

José Zorrilla

Traidor, inconfeso
y mártir,

Edición
de
Ricardo Senabre

QUINTA EDICIÓN

EDICIONES CÁTEDRA, S. A. Madrid

Ilustración de cubierta: Manuel Pereda de Castro

© Ediciones Cátedra, S. A., 1982
Don Ramón de la Cruz, 67. Madrid-1
Depósito legal: M. 7.557-1982
I.S.B.N.: 84-376-0064-2
Printed in Spain
Impreso en LAVEL. Los Llanos, nave 6. Humanes
Papel: Torras Hostench, S. A.

Índice

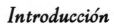

Introducción

Los años de formación

Infancia

José Zorrilla y Moral, hijo de José y Nicomedes, nació en Valladolid, el día 21 de febrero de 1817. A los diez años ingresó en el Real Seminario de Nobles, dirigido por los jesuitas. En las páginas iniciales de sus *Recuerdos del tiempo viejo* evocará el poeta aquellos años infantiles: «Halléme yo allí condiscípulo de los primeros títulos de Castilla, y recibí una educación muy superior a la que hasta entonces solían recibir los jóvenes de la clase media.» Pero muy pronto se revelará la auténtica vocación de Zorrilla: «En aquel colegio..., negligente en los estudios serios de la filosofía y las ciencias exactas, me apliqué al dibujo, a la esgrima y a las bellas letras, leyendo a escondidas a Walter Scott, a Fenimore Cooper y a Chateaubriand, y cometiendo, en fin, a los doce años, mi primer delito de escribir versos.» El niño actúa también en las representaciones teatrales que el colegio organiza periódicamente y que corren a cargo de los alumnos. En estas tempranas aficiones encontramos ya, sin duda —aunque prefiguradas y en embrión—, dos de las facetas esenciales del futuro literato: la lírica y la dramática.

El padre de Zorrilla fue desterrado de Madrid por motivos políticos, y obligó a su hijo a trasladarse a Toledo con objeto de estudiar leyes. Pero el muchacho no tenía vocación de jurista. Él mismo explica cómo en Toledo, «en vez de asistir asiduamente a la Universidad, me di a dibujar los peñascos de la Virgen del Valle, el castillo de San Servando y los puentes del Tajo; y vagando día y noche como encantado por aquellas calles moriscas [...], en vez de llenarme la cabeza de definiciones de Heinecio y de Vinio, incrusté en mi imaginación los góticos rosetones y las preciosas cresterías de la Catedral y de San Juan de los Reyes, entre las leyendas de la torre de don Rodrigo, de los palacios de Galiana y del Cristo de la Vega, a quien debo hoy mi reputación de poeta legendario». En *A buen juez, mejor testigo*, por ejemplo, tropezaremos con una visión crepuscular de Toledo —callejas estrechas y sombrías, rincones misteriosos— cuyas raíces se hallan en aquellas impresiones de los años mozos.

En Valladolid, Zorrilla siguió dedicando su atención a las «piedras, ruinas y tradiciones», mientras leía con entusiasmo el Romancero y admiraba crecientemente a Espronceda y a Víctor Hugo. A fines de 1836 encontramos a Zorrilla en Madrid, donde colabora en un periódico de vida efímera, cuyos redactores acabaron siendo perseguidos por la Policía. El poeta pudo escapar de la justicia gracias a un disfraz de gitano, y volvió a Madrid poco más tarde. Era el 12 de febrero de 1837, justamente un día antes del suicidio de Larra. El dato es importante, porque supone la revelación pública de Zorrilla como poeta. Cuando el cuerpo de *Fígaro* recibió sepultura en el cementerio de la puerta de Fuencarral, un joven de larguísima melena se destacó del grupo de asistentes y, con unas cuartillas en las manos, comenzó a recitar:

Ese vago clamor que rasga el viento
es la voz funeral de una campana:
vano remedo del postrer lamento
de un cadáver sombrío y macilento
que en sucio polvo dormirá mañana.

Ante un auditorio súbitamente fascinado fue surgiendo, verso a verso, el poeta. Aún no había cumplido Zorrilla los veinte años, y él mismo se encargó, andando el tiempo, de recordar aquella primera actuación pública:

Broté como una yerba corrompida
al borde de la tumba de un malvado,
y mi primer cantar fue a un suicida;
¡agüero fue, por Dios, bien desdichado!

El poeta

A partir de este momento, los hechos externos de la vida de Zorrilla quedan oscurecidos por su brillante y popular carrera literaria. En 1837 publica su primer tomo de poesías, avalado con un prólogo de Nicomedes Pastor Díaz. Los influjos de Calderón, Victor Hugo y Lamartine asoman inequívocamente en estas composiciones iniciales. El segundo tomo, que apareció poco después, iba encabezado con una dedicatoria a Juan Donoso Cortés y Nicomedes Pastor Díaz, en la que Zorrilla declaraba: «Al publicar el segundo [tomo] he tenido presentes dos cosas: la patria en que nací y la religión en que vivo. Español, he buscado en nuestro suelo mis inspiraciones. Cristiano, he creído que mi religión encierra más poesía que el paganismo.» *La Virgen al pie de la Cruz*, composición religiosa, es tal vez lo más notable de estos primeros volúmenes, en el segundo de los cuales aparecen ya dos leyendas: *Para verdades, el tiempo, y para justicias, Dios* y *A buen juez, mejor testigo.* Este género, mezcla de poesía lírica y épica, es característico de Zorrilla y, en ocasiones, constituye un indudable embrión teatral.

En sus años de vejez, el poeta evocó garbosamente aquellos escarceos iniciales:

> Yo era entonces un mancebo
> cuyo estro patibulario
> el libro y el escenario
> de sangre y sombras llenó.
> Era moda, era lo nuevo
> desenterrar las horrendas
> fantasmas de las leyendas
> que la Edad Media creó.
> La época era innovadora,
> audaz, revolucionaria,
> y un vago, un prófugo, un paria
> fui de su revolución.

El desafío del diablo (1845) y las conocidas *El capitán Montoya* —esbozo de un Don Juan que asiste alucinado a su propio entierro— y *Margarita la tornera*, son leyendas destacadas. Paralelamente, en el extenso poema *Granada* hay algunos de los fragmentos más inspirados y brillantes del poeta.

En 1839 Zorrilla contrae matrimonio con Florentina Matilde O'Really, dieciséis años mayor que él. En 1845 marcha a Francia, donde permanece un año. Volverá a París en 1850, definitivamente consagrado ya como poeta popular y dramaturgo de éxito. Después de residir cuatro años en París, Zorrilla cruza el Atlántico y marcha a Méjico. Allí disfruta de la protección del empera-

dor Maximiliano, cuya muerte, en 1867, le ins-
pirará el poema *El drama del alma*.

Cuando Zorrilla vuelve a España —1866—, su
mujer ha fallecido. Tres años más tarde, pasados
ya los cincuenta, el poeta se casa en segundas
nupcias con Juana Pacheco. Zorrilla, convertido
en poeta «oficial», sigue escribiendo y publicando
sin cesar, aunque en su producción se notan ya
ciertos síntomas de un prematuro agotamiento.
El 31 de mayo de 1885 ingresa en la Real Academia Española, con un discurso en verso que es,
en realidad, una melancólica autobiografía, que
concluye así:

> Excusad tan excéntrico discurso:
> no puedo ya cambiar naturaleza.
> ¿Qué más queréis de mí? Clara os he dicho
> mi verdad, y podéis o no creerla.
> Soy el más popular y el más famoso,
> pero el poeta soy de menos ciencia;
> miembro inútil a ser en vuestro cuerpo
> voy, si tal me aceptáis: tenedlo en cuenta.
> ¿Ya académico soy? Dios os perdone
> error tan grato para mí; sincera
> será mi gratitud cuanto me dure
> la vida... ¡lo que ya no es gran promesa!
> Pero aunque viva siglos, ya mi gloria
> no podrás revivir, ¡noble Academia!,
> ni en el cielo del arte hacer de nuevo
> brillar la luz de mi apagada estrella.
> No arrancarán del alma las espinas
> las coronas que nimben mi cabeza,
> ni me hará creer el pueblo que soy grande
> siendo, cual son, mis obras tan pequeñas.

En 1889, el Duque de Rivas, en sustitución de
la reina regente, corona solemnemente al poeta
en Granada (vid. M. Sancho: *Crónica de la co-
ronación de Zorrilla*, Granada, 1889). Pocos años
después, el 23 de enero de 1893, Zorrilla muere
en Madrid.

Zorrilla, dramaturgo

Características de su teatro

Varios rasgos fundamentales caracterizan la producción dramática de Zorrilla. En primer lugar, la perfecta asimilación de los modelos clásicos españoles del Siglo de Oro. Lenguaje, versificación y léxico hacen que, en ocasiones, el lector se sienta transportado sin dificultad al siglo XVII. Ante una obra como *Más vale llegar a tiempo que rondar un año*, por ejemplo, piensa Alonso Cortés (*Zorrilla*, I, 275) que se trata de una auténtica comedia de capa y espada, y, en efecto, sólo un análisis sumamente cuidadoso y sutil del estilo podría diferenciar esta obra de algunas de Calderón o Moreto.

El ejemplo clásico proporciona también a Zorrilla la materia de sus obras dramáticas, que, examinadas en conjunto, constituyen un verdadero recorrido a través de toda la historia de España. Desde el reinado de Wamba, en el siglo VII, revivido en·*El rey loco*, hasta el de Carlos II en *Ganar perdiendo*, Zorrilla ha reconstruido, en un amplio mosaico dramático, más de diez siglos de historia española. Don Rodrigo aparece en *El puñal del godo* y *La calentura*. Sancho el Mayor de Navarra, en *El caballo del rey Don Sancho;* el reinado de Pedro el Cruel sirve de fondo a *El zapatero y el rey* y *El molino de Guadalajara*; el Burgos de los Reyes Católicos es evocado en la comedia *Entre clérigos y diablos* o *El encapuchado*, mientras que *El alcalde Ronquillo* se desarrolla en Valladolid bajo Felipe II. La lista podría prolongarse aún mucho más, ya que este despliegue de fondos históricos comprende la mayor parte del teatro de Zorrilla.

El propio autor se encargó de recalcar su deuda con la historia:

> Era la historia del mundo
> compendiada en el rumor
> universal y solemne
> que en himno vital, perenne,
> el universo fecundo
> canta al Supremo Hacedor.
>
> ....
>
> Con don Pedro entré allí en tratos;
> allí el capitán Montoya
> vio cómo abrían su hoya,
> y ante un juez Cristo juró;
> allí eché al mar a Pilatos,
> resucité a don Rodrigo,
> y a ser de bronce testigo
> Jesús a la Cruz bajó.
>
> Allí me contó su historia
> Margarita la tornera,
> me habló allí una calavera
> y hablé al rey don Sebastián;
>
> allí Satanás la gloria
> cerró al alcalde Ronquillo,
> y allí por un postiguillo
> metí en el cielo a don Juan.

No es éste un rasgo exclusivo de Zorrilla, sino una característica de época. Mesonero Romanos, en su artículo «Rápida ojeada sobre la historia del teatro español. Época actual», publicado en el *Semanario Pintoresco Español* en 1842, señalaba que la comedia clásica había dejado de interesar al público, que pedía a los autores «sensaciones más fuertes, obras más análogas a la agitación exterior de la sociedad». Y añadía: «Muchos autores, todos jóvenes, todos ardientes apasionados de la nueva escuela, se presentaron en la palestra. El drama histórico, más o menos exagerado, se puso a la moda; y apenas quedó poeta que no tomase a su cargo el retratarnos *ab irato* y según la moda del día a uno por lo menos de nuestros augustos monarcas desde Ataulfo hasta la casa de Borbón.»

Naturalmente, en muchos de estos casos —y Zorrilla no es una excepción—, los elementos históricos presentes en las obras constituyen tan sólo el marco en que se insertan aventuras y lances legendarios, a veces inverosímiles. En el P. Mariana y en la crónica de Cristóbal Lozano *David perseguido* buscó Zorrilla por igual muchas de sus fuentes de información.

Otra característica destacable de este teatro es la imposición del verso como único vehículo dramático. Incluso la solución mixta de verso y prosa, que en 1835 parecía haber asentado definitivamente el Duque de Rivas con su *Don Álvaro*, se derrumba tras el impacto de Zorrilla, que solamente la utilizará una vez, en su breve drama *Los dos virreyes*. La obra procedía de una novela de Pier Angelo Fiorentino traducida poco antes al español por Ferrer del Río, con el título de *El gran Virrey de Nápoles*, y Zorrilla, envuelto en un compromiso, calcó casi literalmente los enfáticos diálogos de la novela.

Técnica dramática

El verso de Zorrilla es ágil, flexible, de seguro efecto sobre el espectador. Con cierta frecuencia, el poeta sobrepasa al dramaturgo y se detiene morosamente en tiradas líricas que interrumpen el curso de la acción y son, por tanto, inútiles desde el punto de vista teatral. En compensación, ningún dramaturgo romántico tuvo la habilidad de Zorrilla para plantear las situaciones con tan indiscutible eficacia. Desde el primer momento, el espectador se siente atraído por la acción, cuyos principales resortes aparecen cuidadosamente velados a fin de que el interés no decrezca. Esta habilidad falta, por lo general, en los desenlaces, donde el autor parece haber perdido ya todo entusiasmo por la obra y deja que ésta marche por sí misma hasta desembocar en un final visiblemente inferior al arranque. Sin duda, este rasgo procede, como las consabidas rimas fáciles que alguna vez salpican las páginas de Zorrilla, de su carácter de poeta nerviosamente improvisador y poco reflexivo.

Los ingredientes más habituales de esta técnica dramática pueden enumerarse así: la presencia del personaje romántico aureolado de misterio y movido por oscuros designios (don Ramiro, en *El caballo del rey don Sancho*; Van-Derken, en *El alcalde Ronquillo*; don Carlos, en *Lealtad de una mujer y aventuras de una noche*; Germano y Rodesinda, en *El rey loco*; Gabriel de Espinosa, en *Traidor, inconfeso y mártir*, entre otros muchos ejemplos); el colorido ornamental en los relatos y descripciones puestos en boca de algunos personajes (y bastaría, en este sentido, recordar ciertas tiradas popularísimas de *Don Juan Tenorio*); el despliegue de una escenografía típicamente romántica, en la que no faltan truenos, visiones espectrales, fantasmas y toques de ánimas, sobre los que el propio Zorrilla ironizó tres años antes de su muerte, en sus reveladores *Recuerdos del tiempo viejo*: «Yo tengo en mis dramas una debilidad por el toque de ánimas; olvido siempre que en aquellas épocas se contaba el tiempo por las horas canónicas; y cuando necesito marcar la hora en la escena, oigo siempre campanas, pero no sé dónde, y pregunto qué hora es a las ánimas del purgatorio.» Lo que importa, pues —y el dato no puede ser más característicamente romántico—, no es la verosimilitud de unos personajes en una situación determinada. Lo primordial es la complicación de la trama argumental y su resolución posterior mediante la intervención del azar y de las revelaciones y anagnórisis sorprendentes, como acontece en *El alcalde Ronquillo* o en *Traidor, inconfeso y mártir*. La consideración del arte como factor de embellecimiento lleva a Zorrilla con frecuencia a la composición de tiradas líricas, dramáticamente inútiles y hasta perjudiciales, en las que el predominio del poeta sobre el dramaturgo desequilibra la construcción. Tal vez las muestras más notables de esta proclividad se hallen en *Don Juan Tenorio*, como el mismo autor —severo juez de sus propias obras— reconoció paladinamente al referirse a una famosa escena: «Don Juan trae a los talones toda la sociedad, representada en el novio de la mujer por engaño desflorada, en el padre de la hija robada y en la justicia humana, que corren gritando justicia y venganza tras el seductor, el robador y el sacrílego; por el amor de doña Inés, va a matar a su padre y a don Luis, y tiene preparada su fuga y el rapto en un buque de que habla Ciutti; pues bien, en esta situación altamente dramática, a aquel enamorado, que por su pasión ha atropellado y está dispuesto a atropellar cuanto.hay respetable y sagrado en el mundo, cuando él sabe muy bien que no van a poder permanecer allí cinco minutos, no se le ocurre hablar a su amada más que de lo bien que se está allí donde se huelen las flores, se oye la canción del pescador y los gorjeos de los ruiseñores, en aquellas décimas tan famosas como fuera de lugar.»

Las tiradas líricas, herederas de las «relaciones» del teatro clásico, asumen en muchos casos, en el drama romántico, una función similar a la de las arias operísticas: destacan el personaje, permiten el lucimiento del actor y del poeta, pero se engastan difícilmente en la acción teatral e impiden su adecuada progresión. Las consecuencias extremas de tal estética se reflejarán, ya durante el período siguiente, en las más desafortunadas obras de Echegaray y sus seguidores.

Cronología

En cuarenta años de actividad, Zorrilla escribió un total de treinta obras dramáticas, si se cuentan por separado las dos partes de *El zapatero y el rey*. Para este cómputo hemos eliminado *Juan Dandolo* —escrita en colaboración con García Gutiérrez— y *El doctor Diógenes*, firmada —aunque no escrita— conjuntamente con Luis Pacheco, así como *La mejor razón, la espada*, por ser una simple y fidelísima refundición de *Las travesuras de Pantoja*, de Moreto. Con lo cual, las obras enteramente originales se reducen a las siguientes (salvo indicación en contrario, la fecha señalada es la del estreno): *Vivir loco y morir más* (escrita en 1837); *Más vale llegar a tiempo que rondar un año* (escrita en 1839, estrenada el 11 de enero de 1845); *Ganar perdiendo* (publicada en 1839); *Cada cual con su razón* (26 de septiembre de 1839); *Lealtad de una mujer y aventuras de una noche* (7 de marzo de 1840); *El zapatero y el rey* (1.ª parte, 14 de marzo de 1840; 2.ª parte, 5 de enero de 1842); *Apoteosis de Don Pedro Calderón de la Barca* (18 de abril de 1841); *El eco del torrente* (5 de febrero de 1842); *Los dos virreyes* (16 de abril de 1842); *Un año y un día* (12 de octubre de 1842); *Sancho García* (29 de noviembre de 1842); *El puñal del godo* (7 de marzo de 1843); *Sofronia* (íd.); *El molino de Guadalajara* (22 de octubre de 1843); *El caballo del rey Don Sancho* (11 de noviembre de 1843); *La oliva y el laurel* (1 de diciembre de 1843); *Don Juan Tenorio* (28 de marzo de 1844); *La copa de marfil* (10 de mayo de 1844); *El alcalde Ronquillo, o el diablo en Valladolid* (21 de enero de 1845); *El rey loco* (15 de enero de 1847); *La reina y los favoritos* (5 de abril de 1847); *La calentura* (5 de noviembre de 1847); *El excomulgado* (5 de septiembre de 1848); *La creación y el diluvio* (12 de octubre de 1848); *Traidor, inconfeso y mártir* (3 de marzo de 1849); *Amor y arte* (5 de abril de 1862); *Entre clérigos y diablos, o El encapuchado* (19 de marzo de 1870); *Pilatos* (14 de marzo de 1877); *Don Juan Tenorio* [zarzuela] (31 de octubre de 1877).

Como se observará, la producción dramática de Zorrilla es bastante regular entre 1839 y 1849. De todo este período, es la época de 1842 y 1843 —cuando el poeta tiene veinticinco y veintiséis años— la más fecunda y, en conjunto, la más sólida. Tras el estreno de *Traidor, inconfeso y mártir* se abre un largo paréntesis después del cual apenas hay nada considerable en el teatro de Zorrilla.

Traidor, inconfeso y mártir

Argumento

Acto I. En una posada de Valladolid, el dueño recibe a un misterioso personaje que le anuncia la inminente llegada de unos huéspedes y solicita para ellos el mejor alojamiento. Poco después llega don César de Santillana con idéntica recomendación, e inmediatamente el alcalde don Rodrigo, padre de don César, que repite análogas indicaciones (*escenas I-V*). Llegan a la posada Arbués, el criado, y doña Aurora. Don César confiesa al criado que trata de averiguar la verdadera identidad de su amo, el pastelero Gabriel de Espinosa (*escenas VI-X*). Don César declara a doña Aurora su amor, pero ella le rechaza (*escenas XI-XIII*). Aparece Gabriel. Los intentos de don César por averiguar su identidad fracasan (*escenas XIV-XV*). Surge inesperadamente el alcalde don Rodrigo con varios soldados y prenden a Gabriel, que se deja apresar con indiferencia (*escenas XVI-XVII*).

Acto II. Don Rodrigo sospecha que el supuesto pastelero es, en realidad, el rey Don Sebastián de Portugal, de quien se dice que no ha muerto en Alcazarquivir. Gabriel se muestra contradictorio en sus respuestas y hace sentirse perplejo a don Rodrigo (*escenas I-VI*). Un noble portugués identifica sin vacilar a Gabriel de Espinosa como el desaparecido rey Don Sebastián. Éste insiste en que es un simple pastelero. Se decide trasladarlo a Medina (*escenas VII-IX*). Por amor a doña Aurora, don César está dispuesto a dejarlo escapar. Pero Gabriel no acepta (*escenas X-XIII*).

23

Acto III. La cárcel de Madrigal. El rey ha aprobado la sentencia de muerte dictada contra Gabriel de Espinosa (*escenas I-IV*). Don Rodrigo decide ejecutar inmediatamente la sentencia. Don César insiste en su amor por Aurora. Pero Gabriel revela que ésta es hija natural de don Rodrigo y hermanastra, por tanto, de don César (*escenas V-IX*). Gabriel es ejecutado. Un documento revela que se trataba del auténtico rey don Sebastián. Doña Aurora maldice a su recién descubierto padre, ante la consternación de éste y de don César (*escenas X-XI*).

Fuentes

El 4 de agosto de 1578, el rey portugués Don Sebastián moría en la batalla de Alcazarquivir, soltero y sin sucesión. A pesar de haber sido reconocido su cadáver por algunos nobles prisioneros, comenzó a correr la leyenda de que no había muerto. Esto contrariaba las aspiraciones de Felipe II al trono de Portugal. Al amparo de la leyenda surgieron varios impostores que fueron rápidamente descubiertos y eliminados (vid. Michel d'Antas: *Les faux Don Sébastien*, París, 1866). Uno de ellos se mantuvo más tiempo: Gabriel de Espinosa.

El curioso suceso se narra en un librito que tuvo gran éxito: la *Historia de Gabriel de Espinosa, pastelero en Madrigal, que fingió ser el rey Don Sebastián de Portugal. Y asimismo la de Fray Miguel de los Santos, de la Orden de San Agustín, en el año de 1595.* Impreso en Xerez, por Juan Antonio de Tarazona. Año de 1683. Se trata de la refundición de alguna de las versiones del hecho que aparecieron en 1595 y 1596. Hay, además, todavía sin estudiar, multitud de manuscritos y noticias en torno a la impostura de Espinosa. Así, por ejemplo, el ms. que lleva el número 9.324 en la Biblioteca Nacional de Madrid, titulado *Noticias varias sobre el suceso del pastelero de Madrigal, prisión del arzobispo toledano Carranza...*, etc. O los mss. 1.493, 1.601, 2.527, 6.488 7.178, 7.448, 8.568 y otros muchos. En cuanto al libro impreso en Jerez, que contiene la presunta versión histórica de los hechos, narra cómo, en septiembre de 1595, un hombre llamado Gabriel de Espinosa, «con hábito y traje de hombre ordinario», regaló unas ricas joyas a una «mujercilla», la cual, sospechando que eran robadas, denunció el hecho ante don Rodrigo de Santillana, alcalde de la Chancillería de Valladolid. En sus indagaciones, el alcalde descubrió que Gabriel de Espinosa, que declaraba ser pastelero en Madrigal, tenía en su poder unas cartas dirigidas a él por doña Ana de Austria y por el fraile agustino portugués fray Miguel Dos Santos; en dichas cartas, Espinosa recibía el tratamiento de «Majestad». Averiguó también don Rodrigo que varios nobles portugueses habían visitado repetidamente al misterioso pastelero. Al tomar declaración a Espinosa, éste confesó ser «hombre común y bajo», y añadió que «había fingido ser el rey Don Sebastián» para «ser tan regalado y enriquecido» como de hecho era (*Historia de Gabriel de Espinosa...*, cap. VI, página 44). No obstante, la crónica añade que Espinosa hacía estas afirmaciones con «tal aire y desdén, que se echaba de ver querer deshacer lo que de palabra decía» (*íd.*, pág. 45), y que mantuvo la misma actitud contradictoria hasta el momento mismo de su ejecución.

Zorrilla no debió de conocer la *Historia* impresa en Jerez, porque sus informaciones acerca del tema proceden de otra fuente distinta, aunque, con toda probabilidad, apoyada en aquélla: la *Historia de España desde los tiempos primitivos hasta la mayoría de la reina Doña Isabel II, redactada y anotada con arreglo a la que escribió en inglés el doctor Dunham,* por don Antonio Alcalá Galiano (Madrid, imprenta de la Sociedad Literaria y Tipográfica, 1845). El ejemplar de esta obra que poseyó Zorrilla conserva una señal en el pasaje donde se habla del rey don Sebastián (vid. ALONSO CORTÉS: *Zorrilla*, II, 73). En el tomo V (págs. 87-88) se cuenta cómo el agustino portugués fray Miguel Dos Santos, confesor del prior de Crato —otro de los aspirantes al trono—, conoció a Gabriel de Espinosa, que «a la sazón estaba ejerciendo el pobre oficio de pastelero, y que era bastante parecido al rey don Sebastián», y le convenció para que se hiciese pasar por el difunto monarca. Esperaba así el astuto fraile favorecer las pretensiones del prior de Crato. Gabriel de Espinosa era «aunque de humilde origen, nada grosero en el lenguaje o en los modos», ya que «había adquirido gran trato de gentes y un modo de hablar y de portarse muy superior a su situación en el mundo». La citada *Historia* sigue informándonos de que Espinosa, durante el proceso, «se portó de un modo muy singular, ya afirmando con descaro que era un personaje importante, ya repitiendo que nunca había pretendido salir de su conducta humilde». Su comportamiento, en suma, fue tan contradictorio «que hubo de infundir en sus jueces dudas».

Estas líneas fueron la principal fuente histórica que Zorrilla utilizó para escribir su drama.

Repercusión literaria

La figura del joven rey portugués, muerto en combate, atrajo desde muy pronto la atención de poetas y dramaturgos. En el *Romancero General* de 1600 se recogen ya tres romances sobre el suceso. También puede recordarse la conocida can-

ción «Por la pérdida del rey don Sebastián», de
Fernando de Herrera:

Voz de dolor y canto de gemido
y espíritu de miedo, envuelto en ira,
hagan principio acerbo a la memoria
de aquel día fatal, aborrecido,
que Lusitania mísera suspira,
desnuda de valor, falta de gloria.

En el teatro, el testimonio más antiguo parece
ser una comedia de Lope de Vega, *La tragedia del
rey don Sebastián y Bautismo del príncipe de
Marruecos*, con toda seguridad anterior a 1604,
puesto que aparece citada en la lista de comedias propias que el Fénix insertó en la primera
edición de *El peregrino en su patria*.

En 1887, Adolf Schaeffer dio a conocer un vo-
lumen falto de portada, pero, al parecer, impreso
en el primer tercio del siglo XVII, que contiene
ocho comedias, entre las cuales figura *El rey don
Sebastián*, de Luis Vélez de Guevara. El único
ejemplar conservado, que utilizó Schaeffer para
su edición, se halla actualmente en la Biblioteca
de la Universidad de Friburgo. Por otra parte,
existe una versión del texto, con numerosos cam-
bios y variantes, en el manuscrito 15.291 de la
Biblioteca Nacional de Madrid, con el título
La jornada del rey don Sebastián en África; el manuscrito, no autógrafo, ha sido editado por Wer-
ner Herzog *(Comedia famosa del rey don Sebastián*, Madrid, 1972), quien conjetura que Vélez de
Guevara debió de escribir la comedia poco antes
de marzo de 1607.

En relación con el mismo tema existe también
una comedia de don Juan Bautista de Villegas
titulada *El rey don Sebastián y portugués más
heroico*, a la que resulta difícil asignar fecha de
composición, pero que fue recogida en la *Parte*

diecinueve de las comedias nuevas y escogidas de los mejores ingenios de España (Madrid, Pablo de Val, 1663), donde se atribuye erróneamente a Francisco de Villegas. Se tienen noticias de que, en octubre de 1622, la compañía de Cristóbal de Avendaño representó ante la reina la comedia *La pérdida del rey don Sebastián*. Puede tratarse de una obra distinta, hoy perdida, aunque también cabe la posibilidad de que sea una de las ya citadas, con una pequeña alteración del título.

El caballero toledano don Diego Duque de Estrada, en su curioso libro autobiográfico *Memorias del desengañado*, repleto de lances pintorescos, narra cómo tuvo que guardar reposo durante unas semanas, a consecuencia de un accidente, y añade: «El tiempo que vacaba de las muchas conversaciones de caballeros y aun damas que continuamente tenía, hice dos comedias: la una *El rey Sebastián fingido*, muy celebrada, y la otra *El forzado vencedor*» (edic. Gayangos, Memorial Histórico Español, XII, pág. 131). Como los sucesos narrados en este pasaje corresponden, según su autor, al año 1614, ésta sería la fecha de la comedia. Ciertamente, muchas afirmaciones contenidas en las memorias de Duque de Estrada han sido puestas en duda o refutadas por los historiadores con argumentos probatorios, lo que aconseja no aceptar sin cautela cuanto don Diego se atribuye. Pero nada impide suponer en este caso que el autor escribiera, en efecto, aquella obra, aunque luego se haya perdido sin dejar más huellas, como tantas otras de nuestro teatro clásico.

La primera versión teatral de la historia de Espinosa que se nos ha conservado es *El pastelero de Madrigal*, del dramaturgo madrileño Jerónimo de Cuéllar (1622-h.1665), impresa tan sólo tres veces y que no ha vuelto a editarse desde el siglo XVIII a pesar de ser obra de mucho interés. Cuéllar sigue con gran fidelidad la *Historia* impresa en Jerez. La comedia es, simplemente, el relato de una impostura cuyo plan conoce el espectador desde las primeras escenas. El personaje del supuesto rey no encierra, por consiguiente, misterio alguno, salvo para algunos personajes del drama: los criados, Leonor, don Sancho. Incluso el propio alcalde don Rodrigo, encargado por el rey de investigar el asunto, se encuentra perplejo ante las contradictorias respuestas de Espinosa a lo largo de los interrogatorios del acto III. Finalmente, la confesión de Miguel Alonso —trasunto del auténtico fray Miguel Dos Santos—, que ha urdido la suplantación, aclara el asunto:

> Andaba yo imaginando
> cómo una traza tuviera
> de usurparle al gran Felipe
> la corona portuguesa.
> ....
> Vino Gabriel de Espinosa
> al lugar, en cuyas señas,
> rostro, edad, costumbres, voz,
> gravedad, traza y presencia,
> hallé cuanto yo buscaba,
> pues parece que mi idea,
> por mi mal adivinando
> la docta naturaleza
> del perdido Sebastián,
> le hizo una copia perfecta.
> Al instante que le vi,
> propuse que el medio fuera
> de mi intención; empecéle
> a tratar, y entre las veras
> mezclando tal vez las burlas,
> le pinté las conveniencias
> que de fingir ser el Rey
> el seguírsele era fuerza.

La confesión de Miguel provoca la inmediata ejecución del pastelero, a pesar de que éste aún alega: «Más soy de lo que parezco». Por otra parte, resulta evidente que Cuéllar intenta rebajar la aureola mítica del personaje desde el principio. Así, por ejemplo, ya en el primer acto se nos descubre que Espinosa, que corteja a Leonor, ha sido amante de la criada de ésta, Clara, de la que tiene una hija. El pastelero es tan sólo, en suma, un suplantador habilidoso y lleno de ambición, a quien ayuda su extraordinario parecido físico con el difunto rey portugués. Hubiera sido impensable una actitud distinta por parte del dramaturgo. La obra de Cuéllar se estrenó cuando aún reinaban los monarcas de la Casa de Austria, y no era conveniente plantear en la escena dudas acerca de la legítima actuación de Felipe II en el asunto de Portugal. De este modo, *El pastelero de Madrigal* se inscribe —quizá voluntariamente, dada la vinculación de Cuéllar a la Corte como ayuda de cámara del Rey— en la extensa serie de obras que, a lo largo del siglo XVII, contribuyen a exaltar la figura de Felipe II y a sofocar los rescoldos del «sebastianismo». No deja de ser sintomático que, si medio siglo después de la derrota de Alcazarquivir hallamos todavía obras apologéticas, como la de Sebastián de Mesa (*Jornada de África por el Rey don Sebastián. Y unión del reino de Portugal a la Corona de Castilla*, Barcelona, Pedro Lacaballería. 1630), a finales del XVII aparezca el libro de Juan Baena Parada, *Epítome de la vida e feitos del Rei D. Sebastião de Portugal*: *para servir de desengaño aos sectarios que esperan pole sua vinda* (Madrid, Emprenta de Francisco Barrios, 1961), cuya versión castellana se publica, también en Madrid, el año siguiente, indicio de que el tema seguía suscitando interés.

El antecedente más inmediato de *Traidor, inconfeso y mártir* es una novela de Patricio de la Escosura: *Ni rey ni roque*, publicada en 1835.

Escosura, que conoció, según él mismo declara, la versión de Jerez, se sirvió de ella únicamente para la última parte de la novela, y aun eso en aspectos nimios. Si, por ejemplo, *la Historia* citada refiere que Espinosa tenía una hija de dos años, llamada Clara, de modales tan distinguidos que no aceptaba comer sin servilleta ni beber sin salvilla, Escosura recoge el detalle puntualmente, pero transforma el dato real —la niña era ilegítima— en otro más patético y acorde con su idea del personaje: Gabriel había enviudado algún tiempo antes y la niña es, por consiguiente, huérfana. La novela de Escosura ofrece, pues, un tratamiento nítidamente romántico del tema. El personaje de Espinosa se configura ya como un ser perseguido, marginado, aureolado por cierto misterio y enfrentado a la sociedad que representa la justicia real. Las numerosas peripecias de la obra son absolutamente ficticias, y sólo al final se ve el autor obligado a incorporar a la novela los datos de la historia real, aunque advierte: «Esta causa célebre está envuelta en un misterio impenetrable. Verdad es que, poco después de su fallo, se publicó en Jerez una relación de ella; pero está hecha, como es de presumir, para publicarse viviendo aún el tirano y acabadas de inmolar las víctimas.» Escosura no se atreve a falsear la historia —este paso decisivo corresponderá a Zorrilla—, aunque sus simpatías de narrador están más cerca de Espinosa que de sus jueces. Ajeno a las preocupaciones de Cuéllar, el novelista intercala en el relato frecuentes y violentas diatribas contra Felipe II: «Cobarde, como su padre valiente; cruel, como aquel generoso; y fanático, como religioso era Carlos, ningún crimen arredraba a Felipe cuando se trataba de su seguridad, de su venganza o de los mal entendidos intereses de su religión.» Este cambio de perspectiva anuncia ya ciertos aspectos del drama de Zorrilla, cuya versión, sin embargo, es muy personal, como luego se verá.

Después de *Traidor, inconfeso y mártir* existen todavía dos obras narrativas que inciden de nuevo en el tema. La primera es la novela *El pastelero de Madrigal* (1862), de Manuel Fernández y González. El autor cuenta ya con la obra de Zorrilla y desarrolla algunos de sus elementos. Así ocurre, por ejemplo, con la historia de Mari-Galana, que, enamorada de Espinosa y despechada por el rechazo del pastelero, lo denuncia ante el alcalde don Rodrigo de Santillana, de quien al final descubre ser hija ilegítima. De igual modo, la relación de sus andanzas por Europa y África que hace Espinosa en *Traidor, inconfeso y mártir* (acto II, escena 6.ª), se convierte en la narración de Fernández y González en una accidentada y truculenta novela de aventuras donde lo exótico y lo inverosímil se mezclan en una amalgama tumultuosa, muy del gusto de los folletinistas decimonónicos.

Para mostrar hasta qué punto la *Historia* impresa en Jerez fue aprovechada, tanto por Escosura como por Fernández y González, bastará un simple cotejo. La crónica narra así el momento en que Santillana localiza al pastelero:

Y en sintiendo *[Gabriel]* que había justicia en casa, se alborotó y comenzó a vestir; subió el alcalde y hallóle con una camisa de Holanda, cuello y puños de cadeneta, pegados a la camisa, a uso de más que de hombre común, unos calzones de Holanda muy delgada, y ya cuando el alcalde llegó tenía calzados unos borceguíes acuchillados [...]. Preguntóle *[el alcalde]* más, que por qué se había mudado de la posada el día antes. Respondió que porque la huéspeda era puerca; y replicándole cómo un pastelero reparaba en si la huéspeda era o no limpia, respondió con satírico donaire: «Antes por serlo he menester reparar más en la limpieza.»

Por su parte, Escosura sigue de cerca la fuente en *Ni rey ni roque* (libro IV, cap. 5):

El alcalde lo halló sin jubón ni otro vestido que una camisa de fina holanda, con cuello y vueltas de cadeneta pegados a ella, y unos calzones también de la misma tela [...]. Don Rodrigo le preguntó:

—¿Quién sois? ¿Cómo os llamáis?

—Mi oficio es el de pastelero en la villa de Madrigal; llámome Gabriel de Espinosa.

—¿Y por qué mudásteis de posada hace dos días?

—Era la huéspeda muy puerca, y gústame la limpieza.

—Mucho escrúpulo es ese para un pastelero, hermano.

—Antes por serlo, es menester reparar más en la limpieza.

En *El pastelero de Madrigal*, Fernández y González reproduce así la escena (II, I, 16):

El alcalde encontró a Gabriel de Espinosa, que había sentido justicia en la casa, vistiéndose apresuradamente. Cuando el alcalde llegó tenía calzados unos borceguíes o botines acuchillados [...]. Preguntó [el alcalde] a Gabriel de Espinosa, como si no le conociera:

—¿Quién sois?

—Soy pastelero de la villa de Madrigal [...].

—¿Por qué habéis mudado diez veces de posada en quince días?

—Porque en las unas temía ser robado y en las otras la huéspeda era puerca.

—¿Cómo repara en que la huéspeda sea puerca o limpia un pastelero?

—Antes por serlo debo cuidar más de la limpieza —dijo con sarcasmo Gabriel.

El último eco de la historia se halla en un breve, pero intenso relato de Francisco Ayala: «Los impostores», incluido en el libro *Los usurpadores* (1949), cuya idea central consiste, según el propio autor, en que «el poder ejercido por el hombre sobre su prójimo es siempre una usurpación». Para Ayala, cuya obra alcanza un extraordinario grado de depuración ideológica y estilística, Gabriel es un usurpador, no por suplantar al rey don Sebastián, sino porque el afán de dominio es ya una usurpación y una impostura. Si la mayor altura dramática de la historia la alcanza la obra de Zorrilla, el planteamiento intelectual más riguroso del problema se debe, sin duda alguna, a Francisco Ayala.

Obra predilecta

En sus *Recuerdos del tiempo viejo* escribe Zorrilla, a propósito de *Traidor, inconfeso y mártir*: «Es mi única obra dramática pensada, coordinada y *hecha* según las reglas del arte: sus dos primeros actos están *confeccionados* maestramente, y tengo para mí que por ellos tengo derecho a que mi nombre figure entre los de los dramáticos de mi siglo.»

La preferencia del autor está perfectamente justificada. La disposición de actos y escenas es más trabada y coherente que en cualquier otra obra, y la retórica expresiva se ha reducido merced a un esfuerzo de contención muy notable. Los diálogos hinchados y brillantes de otros dramas se transforman aquí en conversaciones de tono casi normal. Los personajes gesticulan menos que de costumbre y *hablan* más. Esta búsqueda de la sobriedad revela a un Zorrilla maduro, mucho más reflexivo que de costumbre. No deja de ser significativo que *Traidor, inconfeso y mártir* se sitúe, cronológicamente, en el ápice de la producción dramática de su autor, quien, después del estreno, dejaría voluntariamente de escribir para el teatro durante muchos años.

Técnica y estilo

Tratamiento del tema

La primera innovación de importancia que presenta la obra de Zorrilla frente a las de sus antecesores, es haber hecho del pastelero y el rey una misma persona. Esta circunstancia confiere al personaje central una grandeza dramática de que carecen los de Escosura o Cuéllar. Allí encontrábamos un hábil impostor que pretendía hacerse pasar por don Sebastián. Zorrilla, mucho menos preocupado por la verdad histórica, nos presenta un don Sebastián auténtico que prefiere fingirse pastelero y no darse a conocer. Con esta afortunada inversión, lo que era tan sólo un tema de leyenda adquiere consistencia y posibilidades dramáticas.

Caracteres románticos

De esta radical innovación se derivan algunas consecuencias de interés. Se potencia, en primer lugar, un elemento romántico que Zorrilla no podía desdeñar: el misterio que envuelve al personaje principal, llevado al extremo de que el espectador no conoce la verdadera identidad de este personaje hasta la escena última. Zorrilla, con una técnica habilísima, reveladora de un profundo sentido teatral, sabe lograr desde el principio este clima de misterio. En efecto; el autor ha distribuido las referencias a Gabriel de Espinosa y su inminente llegada a partir de la segunda escena (verso 13 de la obra), con tres parlamentos paralelos a cargo de otros tantos personajes: el Marqués, don César de Santillana y el alcalde don Rodrigo. No se trata, sin embargo, de explotar el endeble recurso teatral de los confidentes, que ofrecen al espectador información sobre el personaje que todavía no ha aparecido en escena. Lo notable en la organización de estos tres parlamentos sucesivos es, justamente, que no proporcionan información alguna sobre el enigmático viajero —tan sólo ciertos rasgos físicos—, sino que sirven para crear un estado de expectación. La contradicción entre la ausencia de detalles precisos acerca de los huéspedes y el encarecimiento con que éstos son recomendados al posadero, suscita en el espectador una creciente tensión, y envuelve las escenas iniciales en un clima de curiosidad que constituye un modelo de planteamiento dramático. Si los dos primeros visitantes entregan abundante dinero para sufragar los gastos del viajero y sus acompañantes, el tercero, que resulta ser el alcalde Rodrigo de Santillana, añade un dato nuevo:

> Hospedadles
> con mucho agrado y servidles
> sin dudar cuanto demanden:
> su gasto corre por cuenta
> del rey...

Con ello, la tensión crece, y el espectador se siente intrigado por la identidad de quien provoca hasta tales extremos la preocupación del rey. El resultado es que, a lo largo de estas tres escenas consecutivas, el viajero misterioso del que. tanto se habla asume la función de personaje central sin hacer siquiera acto de presencia. Pero el drama posterior se basará en el antagonismo entre Gabriel de Espinosa y sus perseguidores. Por eso Zorrilla monta la escena V, que sigue a la anterior, sobre un monólogo de Burgoa, el posadero, que aporta datos acerca de los Santillana y anticipa así el enfrentamiento posterior:

> Ya, ya están frescos los tales
> viajeros. Los Santillanas...
> Raza de réprobos; aves
> de mal agüero; golillas
> todos; búhos de las cárceles
> y de las horcas, que sólo
> pronosticar pueden males.

Las escenas siguientes entre Burgoa, Arbués, Aurora y don César prolongan el clima de expectación, ya que el tema básico de los diálogos continúa siendo la misteriosa personalidad de Espinosa y éste sigue sin aparecer. Las escenas XI y XII permiten, además, plantear otro tema —el amor de don César a Leonor—, que será factor decisivo en el desarrollo posterior del conflicto.

Con todo ello, Gabriel de Espinosa, evocado incesantemente a partir del verso 13 de la obra, no hará su aparición en escena hasta el verso 966, ya casi al final del primer acto, lo que permite a Zorrilla jugar hábilmente con la inquietud y curiosidad del espectador mientras van apuntándose los motivos más importantes del drama. A partir del momento de su aparición, la figura del pastelero se adueña por completo de la escena. Su enfrentamiento con el astuto alcalde don Rodrigo, en una escena situada sagazmente en medio del acto II —por consiguiente, en el centro de la obra—, es una de las muestras de dialéctica dramática más perfectas que puede ofrecer el teatro español del siglo XIX. Las dudas y temores de don Rodrigo, irritado y abrumado a la vez por las respuestas de Espinosa, resultan mucho más verosímiles que en la obra de Cuéllar; también la desdeñosa actitud de superioridad con que actúa el supuesto pastelero es psicológicamente más plausible, y todo ello porque el personaje posee una majestad no fingida, sino auténtica, aunque el espectador lo ignore aún. Paradójicamente, el falseamiento a que Zorrilla somete la historia confiere a los personajes mayor autenticidad y mayor coherencia psicológica. La historia se convierte en drama, y el Gabriel Espinosa histórico alcanza contextura de personaje trágico, condenado a un destino inexorable que no desea rehuir:

> Si yo fuera
> el rey Don Sebastián morir debía
> por la quietud del reino, y mi alma entera
> ser mártir a ser rey preferiría.
> Si soy un impostor y perjudico
> con mi existencia la quietud de España,
> debo morir también.

El rey don Sebastián, oculto bajo el disfraz de un sencillo pastelero, ha comprendido que los acontecimientos políticos provocados por su supuesta muerte, así como la subsiguiente anexión de Portugal por Felipe II, son hechos irreversibles, y que su destino como rey ha concluido en la derrota de Alcazarquivir. Por eso afirma:

> Morir debo
> si no por Sebastián, por Espinosa.

Y el mismo alcalde don Rodrigo, aun aterrado por la incertidumbre, reconoce:

> Por ser y por no ser perecer debe.

La intuición de Zorrilla al rehacer la historia del pastelero de Madrigal radica en haber advertido que las circunstancias políticas exigían la ejecución del impostor, e incluso del propio rey portugués, en el caso de que hubiese aparecido. Las dudas razonables del juez respecto a la justicia del proceso deben ser ahogadas en beneficio de la «razón de Estado». El Espinosa-don Sebastián de Zorrilla sabe esto y, en consecuencia, conoce de antemano su propio final; de ahí su grandeza, su superioridad dramática sobre todos los pasteleros de Madrigal literarios. Ahora bien: al crear un personaje que ha aceptado desde hace tiempo su fracaso y se ha oscurecido voluntariamente —en ningún momento consta que desee recuperar el trono—, Zorrilla necesitaba inventar una motivación que justificara las acciones del falso Espinosa, que se desplaza incesantemente de un lado a otro para llamar la atención de la justicia y dejarse aprehender. Y esta motivación, sin base real ya, es la historia de doña Aurora, cuya condición de hija natural de don Rodrigo descubre Gabriel en el último momento. Esta intriga secundaria, llena de componentes típicamente románticos —violación, matrimonio secreto, encierro en un convento, amor imposible, venganza y anagnórisis final—, crece desmesuradamente en el tercer acto y está a punto de desequilibrarlo. El propio Zorrilla reconocía que la escena final era endeble: «El mal gusto del tiempo me arastró a prolongar con veintiséis versos más tan repugnante escena», confiesa.

La historia de Aurora y de los anteriores atropellos de Santillana en Portugal son, pues, soportes necesarios para explicar el proceder del falso Espinosa, el cual, fracasada su misión como rey, asume la responsabilidad de proteger a Aurora y vengar el ultraje de don Rodrigo despertando en él un atroz sentimiento de culpabilidad y provocando el rechazo de su hija. El tinte caballeresco que de este modo adquiere el personaje central —reparador de agravios, defensor de doncellas, fiel a la amistad y a la justicia— acentúa así la concepción romántica de la historia.

Los ejes dramáticos

La intriga dramática se halla organizada, pues, sobre dos temas distintos que acabarán siendo convergentes: la historia del supuesto impostor acosado por la justicia y la del amor de don César a doña Aurora. Ambos temas generan relaciones entre las dos parejas de personajes: Gabriel y Aurora, por un lado, y don Rodrigo y don César, por otro. Se trata de dos parejas correlativas, cuyo rasgo distintivo común es una relación de parentesco: Don Rodrigo es padre de don César, y Gabriel es el presunto padre de Aurora. Esta distribución corresponde al planteamiento de un sistema binario que refleja las dos fuerzas en pugna: perseguidores y perseguidos, jueces y reos, autoridades y ciudadanos, poderosos y humildes.

La ruptura de este esquema consabido se anuncia en numerosas ocasiones; sustancialmente, cada vez que dos personajes invierten sus papeles y, por consiguiente, se altera el signo de la relación entre ambos; así ocurre cuando don César es desairado por doña Aurora (acto I, escena 11), o cuando soporta el desdén y la altivez de Gabriel (acto I, escena 15); paralelamente, también don Rodrigo se empequeñece frente a Espinosa (acto II, escena 6, y III, 2), e incluso ante doña Aurora, que mantiene una actitud despectiva hacia él ya antes de la anagnórisis final (por ejemplo, en el acto III, escena 6). Todos estos quiebros del esquema dual, que en principio parecía delinearse con nitidez, anuncian la ruptura final del mismo, que sobreviene en el momento en que se deshace el único elemento conectivo que facilitaba la agrupación: el parentesco. Cuando en el acto II, escena 11, el espectador descubre que Aurora no es hija del misterioso Gabriel de Espinosa, se produce en el sistema de relaciones inicial —padre-hijo/padre-hija— una «casilla vacía»: desde el punto de vista estructural, el hecho determina una reconstrucción del sistema, que se consumará en el desenlace del drama, cuando ya Gabriel ha de-saparecido: Aurora es también hija de don Rodrigo. La recuperación del equilibrio estructural produce alteraciones en el contenido, que en este caso afectan a la dramatización de la historia: el amor de don César es ya definitivamente imposible, y la hija recién descubierta se convertirá para don Rodrigo en la materialización de un permanente remordimiento.

De este modo, los dos temas básicos enunciados confluyen en un punto común y, a la vez, acarrean resultados negativos: la acción de la justicia repercute en las relaciones entre los personajes y embota la posible historia amorosa; pero, al mismo tiempo, el ejercicio de la justicia engendra la injusticia, ya que su peso recae en un inocente. Como consecuencia, todos los personajes acaban por ser víctimas de una especie de *fatum* inexorable: Gabriel es ejecutado: doña Aurora pierde al hombre a quien amaba; don Rodrigo ordena un homicidio que se suma a sus desafueros anteriores; don César debe renunciar al amor de Aurora y descubre al mismo tiempo la historia poco edificante de su propio padre. El drama se convierte en tragedia.

La compleja red de relaciones que enlaza a los personajes ha sido urdida por Zorrilla con especial cuidado. Obsérvese, por ejemplo, el desarrollo del «triángulo» Gabriel-Aurora-don César. La entrada en escena de Espinosa se produce mediante una entrevista con don César (I, 15) en la que el tema fundamental es doña Aurora. Esta escena es el correlato evidente de otra anterior (I, 11), entre don César y doña Aurora, cuyo tema básico ha sido Gabriel. El gozne entre ambas es-

41

cenas lo constituye, por tanto, la intervención en ellas de un mismo personaje —don César—, con el desarrollo de dos contenidos contiguos. La organización da forma dramática a la actitud dubitante de don César, que se debate entre el amor a doña Aurora y cierta indefinible atracción que ejerce sobre él la figura del enigmático pastelero:

> Confieso que el alma mía,
> del punto en que os llegó a ver,
> por vos empezó a tener
> misteriosa simpatía.
> Confieso, sí, que amo a Aurora
> con amor tan delirante
> que no hay acción que me espante
> por ella...

Si en la primera entrevista entre doña Aurora y don César (I, 11) éste declara su amor a la dama, en la segunda (II, 10) se ofrece para facilitar la huida a los prisioneros. Ambas escenas generan una inmediata (II, 11) entre Gabriel y doña Aurora, en la que se produce una transferencia de relaciones: doña Aurora confiesa su amor a Gabriel y, en consecuencia —como antes don César—, le propone huir. La negativa de Gabriel cierra el tema del enamoramiento de don César, que se ha apoyado en varias escenas enlazadas de los actos primero y segundo (I, 11, 15; II, 10), para dejar paso al desarrollo de la pugna entre Gabriel y don Rodrigo, sustentada en dos pasajes fundamentales y correlativos de los actos segundo y tercero (II, 6 y III, 2). Así, el tema amoroso predomina en la primera mitad del drama, mientras que el debate sobre la identidad del supuesto pastelero cubre la segunda mitad. Los planteamientos esbozados en el primer acto se completan en el segundo —escenas entre don César y Aurora (I, 11 y II, 10) o entre don César y Gabriel (I, 15 y II, 2)—, en tanto que los conflictos surgidos en el acto segundo se desarrollan y completan en el tercero, como sucede con los dos enfrentamientos entre Gabriel y don Rodrigo. Ambas historias, que en apariencia surgen independientemente, se encuentran, sin embargo, relacionadas, y de esta vinculación se ofrecen significativos anticipos, no aportados por deducciones del espectador, sino presentes en la superficie del discurso. Puede señalarse un ejemplo en la segunda entrevista de don César con Gabriel (II, 2):

GABRIEL. ... Pero tened desde aquí,
y para siempre entendido,
que es mujer que no ha nacido
para vos ni para mí.
CÉSAR. ¡Cielos!
GABRIEL. De toda esperanza despedíos.
CÉSAR. ¿Ofrecida está a Dios?
GABRIEL. No: está elegida
para prenda de venganza

El anuncio de que el amor de Aurora es imposible parece insertarse en la peripecia sentimental de don César, pero, en realidad, afecta al problema de la identidad de Gabriel y de su relación con don Rodrigo, tema especialmente matizado por Zorrilla en tres escenas (II, 6; III, 2 y 9) que vertebran la evolución psicológica del personaje del alcalde. Jactancioso y seguro al comienzo, don Rodrigo pasa por estados de exasperación, inquietud y terror hasta acabar abrumado y vencido. La historia real es la de un proceso que concluye con la condena del acusado, y, sin embargo, Zorrilla ha creado una historia paralela, de naturaleza psicológica, en la que las relaciones se invierten: mientras el acusado crece en dignidad y nobleza, el juez se envilece; y si la trayectoria de Gabriel es liberadora y fecunda, la de don Rodrigo se convierte en un penoso itinerario hacia el descubrimiento de la culpa y la expiación.

Métrica

La versificación de *Traidor, inconfeso y mártir* es variadísima y escasamente sujeta a normas rígidas. Algunos versos sueltos, de enlace, y ciertas combinaciones libres de endecasílabos dan idea de la autonomía con que Zorrilla versificó. Hay un notable predominio del octosílabo en redondillas, romances y quintillas. El endecasílabo aparece, también en formas variadas, cuando el tono lírico se acentúa (escena XI del primer acto y parte final del tercero). He aquí el esquema métrico:

Acto I.—Versos 1-376 (escenas I-VII): romance en *a-e* [con una alteración de la rima en los vs. 107-109]; vs. 377-1253 (escenas VIII-final de XVII): redondillas; vs. 1254-1263 (parte final, escena XVII): quintillas.

Acto II.—Vs. 1264-1287 (escena primera): quintillas [con una cuarteta intercalada, correspondiente a los vs. 1269-1272]; vs. 1288-1407 (escenas II-III): redondillas; vs. 1408-1511 (escenas IV-V): romance en *e-o*; vs. 1512-2064 (escenas VI-VIII): redondillas [con una quintilla intercalada en vs. 1992-1996 y un terceto octosílabo en vs. 2017-2019]; último verso suelto; vs. 2065-2176 (escenas IX-X): romance en *í-a*; vs. 2177-2189 (principio escena XI): serventesios [último verso (2189) suelto]; vs. 2190-2380 (resto de la escena XI): romance heroico en *e-e*; vs. 2381-2400 (escenas XII-XIII): redondillas.

Acto III.—Vs. 2401-2836 (escenas I-mitad V): redondillas; vs. 2837-2850 (fragmento escena V): romance en *e-e*; vs. 2851-3015 (resto escena V-principio escena VII): redondillas [verso 2879 suelto]; vs. 3016-3020 (fragmento escena VII): quintilla; vs. 3021-3512 (final escena VII-escena IX): silvas y combinaciones libres de endecasílabos [con tres heptasílabos intercalados, vs. 3108, 3109 y 3255].

El estreno

Traidor, inconfeso y mártir se estrenó en el Teatro de la Cruz, de Madrid, el viernes 3 de marzo de 1849, en el beneficio de la actriz Matilde Díez, que interpretó el papel de Aurora. El personaje del rey don Sebastián corrió a cargo de Julián Romea. Antonio Barroso y Florencio Romea se encargaron, respectivamente, de don Rodrigo y don César. La obra fue bastante bien acogida por el público, pero sólo permaneció siete días en cartel. En sus *Recuerdos del tiempo viejo*, Zorrilla hace responsable de esto a Julián Romea, cuya interpretación no dio el relieve necesario a su personaje. Romea era un actor sobrio, pero habituado a la comedia. Ya antes del estreno, Zorrilla estaba persuadido de que «iba a dejar pálida la figura del rey don Sebastián, de que no iba a pasar de' Espinosa el pastelero, de que iba a seguir su fatal sistema de presentar en el drama la verdad de la naturaleza en lugar de la del arte, y de que iba, en fin, a representar un rey don Sebastián de levita». Así ocurrió, en efecto: Romea «presentó y no representó su personaje», según expresión del autor. En la crítica que el temible Martínez Villergas publicó en *Don Circunstancias*, los elogios a Julián Romea eran sumamente tibios y desvaídos.

En cambio, los otorgados a la obra han sido siempre, por lo general, inequívocos. Recuérdense, a título de ejemplo, las penetrantes observaciones de *Clarín*:

«En pocas partes se parece menos Zorrilla a sí mismo que en *Traidor, inconfeso y mártir*; no porque falten aquí sus facultades poderosísimas, sino porque faltan sus defectos, tan suyos; por los que se le reconoce como si fueran un estilo. En punto a forma correcta, noble, eufónica, eurítmica el *Traidor* es una maravilla, y tratándose de su autor maravilla doble. El *Traidor* es a Zorrilla lo que *El castigo sin venganza* a Lope. Hasta en la composición sabia, ordenada, sobria y atenta al contrapunto dramático, Zorrilla parece otro; y eso que se debe notar que a pesar de haber escrito el gran poeta casi todas sus obras a *la diable*, como él mismo declara, el gran instinto dramático que tiene le da hechas casi siempre unas exposiciones, unos primeros actos que son obras maestras de lo que las reglas clásicas piden en esta materia para despertar el interés y atraer con la armonía. Sea ejemplo este mismo drama, el *Traidor*, y sea ejemplo el primer acto de *El zapatero y el rey*, 1.ª parte.»

La obra se ha representado mucho en España y en América con gran éxito. Zorrilla declaraba haber visto «actores muy medianos y sin pretensiones, y hasta de teatros caseros, que siempre se han hecho aplaudir en el papel del rey don Sebastián». Pedro Delgado, Antonio Vico, Rafael Calvo y casi todos los grandes actores de la escena española han dado vida al extraordinario personaje de Zorrilla.

NUESTRA EDICIÓN

Hemos seguido el texto de la 2.ª edición de Baudry (París, 1852) reseñada anteriormente, modernizando la ortografía y después de corregir las erratas de impresión más evidentes, para lo cual hemos tenido en cuenta, en varias ocasiones, la edición de Narciso Alonso Cortés.

Bibliografía

Ofrecemos a continuación una relación sucinta de las principales ediciones de Zorrilla y de *Traidor, inconfeso y mártir*, seguida de un resumen bibliográfico con las monografías y estudios más importantes.

1. EDICIONES

Obras (Colección de los Mejores Autores Españoles, vols. 39, 40 y 54); París, Baudry, 1837; 2.ª edic., 1852.

Obras completas. Corregidas y anotadas por su autor. Edición monumental y única auténtica. Tomo I: *Leyendas tradicionales.* Sociedad de Crédito Intelectual, Barcelona, 1884 (sólo se publicó este tomo).

Obras dramáticas y líricas. Ed. de M. P. Delgado, Madrid, 1895, 4 vols.

Galería dramática: Obras completas, Madrid, 1905, 4 vols.

Obras completas. Madrid, Sociedad Editorial de España, 1943, 4 vols.

Obras completas. Ordenación, prólogo y notas de Narciso Alonso Cortés. Valladolid, Librería Santaren, 1943, 2 vols.

Traidor, inconfeso y mártir. Colección «El teatro de obras dramáticas», Madrid, 1849 (reeditada en 1859, 1865, 1873, 1881 y 1882).

Traidor, inconfeso y mártir. En «Autores dramáticos contemporáneos y Joyas del teatro español del siglo XIX», Madrid, 1881, tomo I, páginas 169-252. Con un prólogo sobre Zorrilla de Isidoro Fernández Flórez.

Don Juan Tenorio, Traidor inconfeso y mártir y El puñal del godo, Madrid, Aguilar, 1946.

Traidor, inconfeso y mártir, Madrid, ed. Dédalo, 1961.

Traidor, inconfeso y mártir, edic. R. Senabre, Madrid-Salamanca, Anaya, 1964 (2.ª edic., 1970).

Traidor, inconfeso y mártir. La calentura, Madrid, Espasa-Calpe, 1964.

Traidor, inconfeso y mártir, edic. E. Torre Pintueles, Madrid, Taurus, 1966.

2. ESTUDIOS Y MONOGRAFÍAS

Prescindimos en este resumen de las obras generales, tales como historias del teatro y de la literatura española, y damos preferencia a los estudios sobre la faceta específicamente dramática de Zorrilla.

OVEJAS, I.: «Don José Zorrilla», en *Obras,* 2.ª ed., París, Baudry, 1852, I, págs. I-XLIV.

VALBUENA, A. DE: *J. Zorrilla. Estudio crítico-biográfico,* Madrid, Fernando Fe, 1889.

ALONSO CORTÉS, N.: *Zorrilla. Su vida y sus obras.* Valladolid, Impr. Castellana, 1916-1920, 3 vols.

MENÉNDEZ, J. F.: «Apuntes para la biografía del poeta Zorrilla», en *Bolet. de la Bibl. Menéndez Pelayo,* V, 1923, 117-141.

ADAMS, NICHOLSON B.: *The «Pastelero de Madrigal», in Nineteenth Century Spanish Literature,* University of California Press, 1925.

PEERS ALLISON, E.: «El teatro de Zorrilla» (en *Historia del movimiento romántico español*, II, Madrid, Gredos, 1954, 266-287).

GOENAGA, A., y MAGUNA, J. P.: «Traidor, inconfeso y mártir» (en *Teatro español del siglo XIX*, New York, Las Americas, 1971, 221-252).

MARÍAS, J.: «Dos dramas románticos: *Don Juan Tenorio* y *Traidor, inconfeso y mártir*» (en *Literatura y generaciones*, Madrid, Espasa-Calpe, 1975, 41-55).

Traidor, inconfeso y mártir

Drama histórico en tres actos
escrito expresamente para el beneficio
de Doña Matilde Díez

PERSONAS

DOÑA AURORA.
GABRIEL ESPINOSA.
DON RODRIGO DE SANTI-
  LLANA, *alcalde de casa
  y corte.*
DON CÉSAR DE SANTILLA-
  NA, *capitán de jinetes
  del primer tercio de
  Flandes.*

ARBUÉS.
BURGOA Y NAO D'AN-
  DRADE.
EL MARQUÉS DE TAVIRA.
EL DOCTOR N.
UN ESCRIBANO.
ALGUACILES.
SOLDADOS.
UN CRIADO DE BURGOA.
OTROS CRIADOS.

*La escena en los dos primeros actos pasa en una
posada de Valladolid; y el tercero, en Medina del
Campo en el año de 1594 de N. S. J. C.*

ACTO PRIMERO

Antesala en una posada de Valladolid. Puerta en el fondo, que da al exterior. Dos a la izquierda, que dan al interior. Ventana a la derecha.

ESCENA PRIMERA

BURGOA, *que aparece;* un CRIADO, *que sale por el fondo.*

CRIADO	Señor amo.
BURGOA	¿Qué hay?
CRIADO	Un hombre.
BURGOA	¿Qué quiere?
CRIADO	Veros.
BURGOA	Que pase.
CRIADO	Entrad aquí, seor hidalgo.

ESCENA II

BURGOA; EL MARQUÉS, *embozado.*

MARQUÉS	Buenas noches.
BURGOA	Dios le guarde.

---

³ *Seor*, 'señor'. Vulgarismo arcaico, aquí necesario para la medida del verso. Comp. Zorrilla, *El zapatero y el rey*, 1.ª parte, I, 6: «Seor soldado, guárdeos Dios.»

MARQUÉS	¿Eres tú el huésped?
BURGOA	Yo soy. ⁵
MARQUÉS	¿Luis Burgoa?
BURGOA	Y Nao d' Andrade.
MARQUÉS	¿Portugués?
BURGOA	Lo canta el nombre:
	de Alfontes, en el Algarbe.
MARQUÉS	Paisanos somos.
BURGOA	¿Sois vos
	también?...
MARQUÉS	Escúchame y cállate. ¹⁰
BURGOA	Callo y escucho.
MARQUÉS	Esta noche
	vendrá a pedir hospedaje
	en esta posada un hombre,
	cuyas señas voy a darte
	para que no le equivoques. ¹⁵
	Edad, cuarenta años; traje
	negro, cabello rapado,
	barba crecida, semblante
	pálido, mirada de águila,
	sonrisa triste, andar grave. ²⁰
BURGOA	Con tantas señas, señor,
	que le equivoque no es fácil.
MARQUÉS	Aún faltan más; una dama
	en su compañía trae
	de apenas diecisiete años, ²⁵
	y haciendo veces de paje,
	viene sirviéndoles a ambos
	un veterano de Flandes,

---

⁵ *Huésped*, 'posadero' (Covarrubias: «el forastero que viene a nuestra casa o a nuestro pueblo; y güésped el mesonero, o el que tiene casa de posadas... Díjose del nombre latino *hospes,-itis*»). Comp. Pineda, *Agricultura cristiana*, IV, VIII: «Que no está seguro el huésped de su huésped.»

²⁰ *Grave*, 'digno, mesurado'. «Significa también circunspecto, que tiene entereza y causa respeto y admiración» *(Dicc. Aut.)*. Comp. *Quijote*, II, 32: «Una dama... hermosa sin tacha, grave sin soberbia, amorosa con honestidad.» Zorrilla, *O.C.*, ed. N. Alonso Cortés, I, 349 *b*: «Entonces el capitán,/con paso medido y grave/en mitad del aposento/fue decidido a encontrarle.»

en quien, por más que se afana
por tosco labriego en darse,   30
se revelan a la legua
las costumbres militares.
Lo mismo sea sentirles
a tus puertas acercarse,
con luz y sombrero en mano   35
saldrás hasta los umbrales;
mandarás de sus caballos
cuidar, y sus equipajes
subir a los aposentos
mejores que puedas darles.   40
Los servirás a su antojo
los más sabrosos manjares
y los vinos más añejos,
y entre tanto que ocuparen
cuarto en tu posada, en ella   45
no recibirás a nadie.
Yo toda entera la alquilo
para ellos. Ahí va parte
del gasto que hacerte puedan.
Cuando esa suma se acabe   50
te rellenaré esa bolsa;
lo que sobre, para gajes
del huésped y de los mozos.
Adiós y silencio, Andrade.

BURGOA   Un momento, caballero.   55
     ¿Y si ese hombre preguntare
     quién paga su gasto?

MARQUÉS   Nada
     digas.

BURGOA   ¿Y si se obstinare
     en saberlo?

MARQUÉS   Guardarás
     silencio; y la cuenta al darme   60
     tu silencio y sus porfías
     pondrás como cantidades

---

[30] *Darse por*, 'declararse, aparentar ser'.
[41] *Los* por *les*, complemento indirecto.

                    en guarismos, y yo sólo
                    veré las sumas totales.
                    Pero ten cuenta, Burgoa,   65
                    porque el oro que aquí ganes
                    crecerá con tu prudencia
                    y te se irá con tu sangre;
                    porque indiscreciones de oro
                    con hierro es bien que se atajen,   70
                    y fortuna que se canta
                    siempre se la lleva el aire.
BURGOA   Señor...
MARQUÉS   Adiós, que no quiero
                    que aquí, si llegan, me hallen. *(Vase.)*

ESCENA III

BURGOA; *después,* DON CÉSAR

BURGOA   ¡Aventura más extraña!   75
                    Alguna apuesta; algún lance
                    de amor; pero ¿qué me importa
                    a mí? Lo que es indudable
                    es que el bolsillo está lleno
                    de doblillas: ¿para gajes   80
                    las que sobrcn? ¡Bah! Lo menos
                    ciento por veinte. Adelante.
CÉSAR   *(Saliendo.)*
                    Buenas noches.

---

⁶⁵ *Tener cuenta:* «Frase que explica tener adverten-
cia o cuidado de alguna cosa, para que no se caiga en
algún inconveniente. O tener atención o reflexión sobre
alguna cosa que ha pasado o se .ha dicho» *(Dicc. Aut.).*
Comp. Zorrilla, *El alcalde Ronquillo,* II, 2: «Ten mucha
cuenta: oirás / una serenata, ¿estás? / Entonces habrá
de sobra / tiempo y ocasión.»
⁶⁸ *Te se,* vulgarismo por 'se te'. (Obsérvese la amena-
za ante una posible indiscreción.) Comp. Zorrilla, *Sancho García,* I, 11: «Sutil, astuta, / cuanto emprendí y
fragüé no te se esconde.»
⁸⁰ *Doblilla,* 'dobla', moneda equivalente a unos veinte reales. Comp. Zorrilla, *Don Juan Tenorio,* I, 12: «Todo
mi caudal perdí / dobla a dobla, una por una.»

BURGOA	¿Qué se ofrece?
CÉSAR	Hablar con el dueño.
BURGOA	Habladle.
CÉSAR	¿Eres tú?
BURGOA	Yo mismo.
CÉSAR	¿Estamos solos?
BURGOA	Sí.
CÉSAR	Atento estame.

Tres personas a tu puerta
vendrán muy pronto a apearse:
un hombre galán, de pálido
rostro y de noble talante;   90
una dama tan hermosa
como pintan a los ángeles,
y un escudero que tiene
mezcla de asistente y paje.
Dales lo mejor que tengas;   95
como a príncipes regálales;
lo que no poseas, cómpralo
y en el precio no repares.
Ahí tienes doscientos pesos
en oro: cuando los gastes   100
en su servicio, me pides
más, y si sobran, por gajes
te los embolsas, con ceros
sumas y cuentas cabales.

BURGOA	Caballero, perdonad, 105
	pero habéis llegado tarde.
CÉSAR	No te entiendo.
BURGOA	Un embozado
	que salía cuando entrabais

---

[87] Nótese la semejanza de estos versos con los anteriores del marqués (23 y ss.).

[96] *Regalar*, «agasajar o contribuir a otro con alguna cosa, voluntariamente o por obligación» *(Dicc. Aut.)*. Comp. Zorrilla, *El caballo del rey don Sancho*, I, 4: «A esos que allá abajo esperan, / hospedaje da y regálalos / con todo cuanto apetezcan.»

[107] La rima en *a - e* se corta bruscamente en este verso y en el 109, para reanudarse en el 110.

```
                    os ha ganado la mano,
                    y para esos personajes                      110
                    por quien os interesáis,
                    con palabras semejantes
                    a las vuestras ha alquilado
                    y pagado el hospedaje
                    de mi casa con el oro                        115
                    de este bolsillo: miradle.
CÉSAR               ¿Y quién era ese embozado?
BURGOA              No le conozco.
CÉSAR                               ¿Su traje,
                    su porte ni sus palabras
                    indicios no pueden darte                     120
                    de quién sea?
BURGOA                              No, señor
                    militar; ni su semblante
                    vi jamás, ni haber oído
                    recuerdo en ninguna parte
                    su voz.
CÉSAR                         ¿Es joven o viejo?                  125
BURGOA              ¿No le habéis visto?
CÉSAR                                     En la calle
```

---

[109] *Ganar la mano,* 'ganar por la mano'. «Es anticipar-
se a otro en hacer alguna cosa» *(Dicc. Aut.).*

[111] *Quien* por 'quienes' sin diferenciación del plural,
como en la lengua clásica («Siglos dichosos aquellos a
quien los antiguos pusieron nombre de dorados», *Quijote,* I, 11). Aquí, necesario para la medida del verso, como
en Zorrilla, *El excomulgado,* I, 10: «Pero jamás hombre
alguno / afirmar ha de poder / qué hijos a quien yo di
ser / fueron hijos de ninguno.»

[116] *Miradle* por 'miradlo' (el oro). Para éste y muchos
otros casos de *le* complemento directo, téngase presente
que la alternancia *le / lo* perdura a lo largo del siglo XIX
y que en Castilla se prefiere *le.* Más adelante (1854), la
Academia, recogiendo una sugerencia de Vicente Salvá,
asignará el uso de *le* a personas y el de *lo* a cosas.

[119] *Porte,* «la buena o mala disposición de una persona, y la mayor o menor decencia y lucimiento con que
se trata» *(Dicc. Aut.).* Comp. Zorrilla, «La leyenda de
Don Juan Tenorio», canto IV: «Y aunque su traje y
su porte / son sencillos y severos, / se ve que son caballeros / de raza y gente de corte.»

	estaba ya cuando yo	
	llegaba a tu puerta, y casi	
	no puse atención en él.	
BURGOA	Es un señor respetable,	130
	de barba gris, noble y rico.	
CÉSAR	¿Noble y rico? ¿De qué sabes	
	que lo es si no le conoces?	
BURGOA	Dan en él lo muy bastante	
	a conocer la riqueza	135
	su oro y su modo de darle;	
	y la nobleza, además	
	de su tono y de sus frases,	
	el aroma que se exhala	
	de su valona y sus guantes.	140
CÉSAR	Pues, señor, ¡cómo ha de ser!;	
	dijiste bien: llego tarde.	
	Réstame, pues, solamente	
	mis ofertas reiterarte:	
	emplea ese oro a gusto	145
	de quien le da, y lo que falte	
	yo lo abono; y a otra cosa,	
	que el tiempo vuela.	
	(Asomándose a la puerta.)	
	Melquiades,	
	acomoda los caballos	
	en la cuadra.	
BURGOA	Dispensadme,	150
	capitán: no puede ser.	
CÉSAR	¿Por qué?	
BURGOA	Porque no hay vacante	
	un solo pesebre en ella.	
CÉSAR	Pues en ese caso dame	
	un cuarto a mí y una cama,	155
	y que se vaya Melquiades	

---

[134] Hipérbaton: 'dan a conocer sobradamente su riqueza'.

[141] *¡Cómo ha de ser!*, exclamación de conformidad, equivalente a '¡qué se le va a hacer!'. Comp. Zorrilla, *El rey loco*, I, 6: «¡Mas cómo ha de ser! Vivimos / con semejantes miserias.»

	con los caballos.	
BURGOA	Tampoco	
	puedo serviros.	
CÉSAR	¡Bergante!	
	¿Intentas burlas conmigo?	
BURGOA	¡Dios me libre de burlarme	160
	de tan gallardo mancebo!	
	Mas tengo orden terminante	
	de aquel embozado incógnito	
	de no recibir a nadie	
	por esta noche en mi casa	165
	más que a ellos. Excusadme,	
	pues, capitán.	
CÉSAR	*(Se sienta.)*	
	Pues entonces	
	dame un bocado que el hambre	
	me satisfaga, y un trago	
	que me remoje las fauces.	170
BURGOA	Señor, todo está comprado	
	y nos cansamos en balde.	
	Pues que por esos viajeros	
	os interesáis, dejadles	
	libre la casa, y no hagáis	175
	que yo a mi palabra falte.	
CÉSAR	El caso es que a mí me importa	
	en esta casa quedarme	
	por esta noche y es fuerza	
	que me quede.	
BURGOA	Pues en grave	180
	compromiso me ponéis	
	si os quedáis, y por mi parte,	
	por cuantos medios me ocurran	
	estoy dispuesto a evitarle.	
CÉSAR	¿De modo que te propones	185
	en la plazuela plantarme	

---

[177] *Importar*, «convenir y hacer al caso alguna· cosa, ser útil y provechosa para algo» *(Dicc. Aut.)*. Comp. Zorrilla, *El alcalde Ronquillo*, I, 9: «A mi castillo / de Fuensaldaña, que importa / que estén a distancia corta / las venganzas de Ronquillo.»

	en una noche como ésta,
	con frío tal, oro y hambre?
BURGOA	Sí, señor.
CÉSAR	¿Sin más razones?
BURGOA	Os llevo dadas bastantes. 190
CÉSAR	Pues, señor, lo siento mucho;
	mas fuerza es que te se alcance,
	pues no eres tonto, que cuando
	muestro empeño semejante 195
	en hospedarme en tu casa,
	no vine para marcharme
	de ella otra vez despedido
	como un buhonero errante.
BURGOA	Pues mirad cómo ha de ser.
CÉSAR	Así: toma *(le da un papel)*
	y lee si sabes. 200
BURGOA	¿Y qué es esto?
CÉSAR	Lee.
BURGOA	*(Leyendo.)*
	«Dará
	Luis Burgoa Nao d'Andrade
	alojamiento en su casa
	número dos de la calle
	de la Antigua, al capitán 205
	del primer tercio de Flandes
	don César de Santillana
	con seis jinetes.»
CÉSAR	Cabales.
	Burgoa, en nombre del rey
	vas a ofrecerme de balde 210
	lo que por oro me niegas.
BURGOA	La boleta haré que os cambien

---

[192] *Te se:* cfr. nota v. 68. *Se te alcance,* 'comprendas'.
[199] *Cómo ha de ser,* cfr. v. 141.
[212] *Boleta,* «cedulilla que se da hoy a los soldados cuando entran en algún lugar, para que vayan a alojarse a la casa destinada por la Justicia» *(Dicc. Aut.).* Comp. Alemán, *Guzmán de Alfarache,* I, II, 10: «En cada alojamiento cogía una docena de boletas, que ninguna valía de doce reales abajo...»

	a cualquier costa.	
César	Será	
	trabajo inútil: es tarde.	
Burgoa	No importa; tengo dineros	215
	y muy buenas amistades	
	hoy en el Ayuntamiento.	
César	Pues, Burgoa, no las canses	
	inútilmente esta noche;	
	porque, a más de que es mi padre	220
	juez de la chancillería	
	y de casa y corte alcalde,	
	tengo seis hombres abajo	
	y un escudero, incapaces	
	de obedecer otras órdenes	225
	que las que yo quiera darles,	
	que del umbral de la puerta	
	no permitirán que pases.	
	Conque cede a mis razones,	
	que son, a fe, terminantes,	230
	y dame luz, cena y cuarto,	
	que con ese personaje	
	misterioso, seré yo	
	solamente el responsable	
	de todo, en nombre del rey	235
Burgoa	Callo al rey.	
César	Y muy bien haces,	
	que contra el rey nadie es cuerdo	
	en oponerse. Melquiades,	
	toma luz y desensilla	
	a Bayardo; a acomodarme	240
	voy en algún cuarto bajo	
	para que cuando llegaren	

---

221 *Juez de la chancillería;* propiamente *oidor:* «cualquiera de los ministros togados destinados en los Con-
sejos, Chancillerías y Audiencias, para oír en justicia
a las partes y decidir, según lo que unas y otras alegan»
(Dicc. Aut.).

222 *Alcalde de casa y corte,* juez togado que entiende
en causas civiles; «tiene la jurisdicción ordinaria en la
Corte y cinco leguas en contorno» *(Dicc. Aut.).*

	esos huéspedes, en casa	
	ya pagada no me hallen.	
BURGOA	Capitán, pues no hay remedio,	245
	yo os ruego con la más grande	
	humildad que os alojéis	
	en una sala que cae	
	al huerto que tengo a espalda	
	de la casa.	
CÉSAR	Que me place	250
	te digo el alojamiento.	
	Vamos allá.	
BURGOA	*(Los dos a la puerta.)*	
	Hacia esta parte	
	y en el fin del corredor	
	veréis una puerta grande	
	que da sobre otra escalera.	255
	Tomad el farol que arde	
	en el descanso; bajadla,	
	y Andrés os dará la llave	
	de vuestro cuarto, y decidle	
	que a vuestras gentes os llame.	260
	Yo os enviaré buena cena	
	y fuego.	
CÉSAR	Dios te lo pague. *(Vase.)*	

ESCENA IV

BURGOA; *después*, DON RODRIGO

BURGOA	Santillana y capitán,	
	y de los tercios de Flandes	
	y con la boleta en regla	565
	y espada de gavilanes,	
	¿quién le resiste? El incógnito	
	se hará cargo del percance	
	y tendrá su compañía	
	que sufrir y resignarse.	270
	Contra el rey nadie es valiente.	

RODRIGO	*(Entrando.)*
	¡Ah de esta casa!
BURGOA	Adelante.
RODRIGO	¿Sois el dueño de ella?
BURGOA	Soy
	Luis Burgoa.
RODRIGO	Dios le guarde.
BURGOA	Mil gracias; lo mismo digo. ²⁷⁵
	¿Qué se ofrece?
RODRIGO	Que oiga y calle.

Esta noche a esta posada
vendrá un viajero a apearse
con una dama encubierta
y un escudero; hospedadles   ²⁸⁰
con mucho agrado y servidles
sin dudar cuanto demanden;
su gasto corre por cuenta
del rey; y desde el instante
en que vuestra casa ocupen,   ²⁸⁵
de ellos, de sus equipajes
y cuanto les pertenezca
seréis vos el responsable.
Dejaréis entrar a todos
los que por él preguntaren.   ²⁹⁰
A todos, quienquier que fueren;
mas no dejaréis a nadie
volver a salir. Abajo
tenéis unos militares
alojados, y las órdenes   ²⁹⁵
competentes voy a darles
para que os presten auxilio
y en caso de apuro guarden

---

²⁹⁰ *Por él.* En realidad, 'por ellos', ya que el pronombre se refiere a un triple antecedente: el «viajero», la «dama» y el «escudero». Pero esta aparente anomalía permite destacar realmente al primero de los tres personajes nombrados.

²⁹¹ Uso arcaico de *quienquier*, con apócope de *-a* y antecedente en plural. Comp. *Quijote*, I, 25: «¡Oh vosotros, quienquiera que seáis, rústicos dioses...!»

	las puertas; conque silencio	
	y adiós; volveré más tarde.	300
BURGOA	Señor, vuestra autoridad	
	sea cual fuere, excusadme	
	que os pregunte a quién la honra	
	tengo de hablar.	
RODRIGO	Al alcalde	
	Rodrigo de Santillana.	305
BURGOA	¡Jesucristo!	
RODRIGO	Dios le guarde.	

ESCENA V

BURGOA

¡Dios nos asista! Con un
Santillana era bastante
para su mal; pero ¿juntos
el capitán y el alcalde   310
pisándoles los talones?
Ya, ya están frescos los tales
viajeros. Los Santillanas...
Raza de réprobos; aves
de mal agüero; golillas   315
todos; búhos de las cárceles
y de las horcas, que sólo
pronosticar pueden males.
Santillanas..., ¡fuego en ellos
y en quien a casa los trae!   320
No hay portugués que no tenga
con ellos cuenta. Mas baste,
que Dios dirá. Gente llega.
¡Andrés!
(Al ir a entrar por el fondo, sale AR-
BUÉS de viaje, enlodado.)

---

[315] *Golillas,* jueces y magistrados que usaban golilla,
«cierto adorno de cartón, aforrado en tafetán u otra
tela, que circunda y rodea el cuello» *(Dicc. Aut.).*

[319] *Fuego en ellos,* fórmula registrada ya por Correas
(Vocabulario de refranes), para indicar prevención o des-
confianza. Comp. la expresión *¡Fuego en quien sube del*
fango al más elevado rango!

BURGOA, ARBUÉS

ARBUÉS   No hay que incomodarse,
patrón; somos gente llana   325
mis amos y yo, y a nadie
gustamos de dar que hacer.
¿Hay aposentos capaces,
limpios y con buenas camas
para una dama, su padre,   330
su escudero y dos criados?

BURGOA   Sí, señor, los hay, y tales
que no habrá en palacio muchos
que en lo limpio les alcancen.

ARBUÉS   Pues poned en uno luces   335
para la dama.

BURGOA   Que bajen
voy a mandar por los trastos
que traigáis.

ARBUÉS   Que no se cansen
vuestros mozos; ya los nuestros
suben con los equipajes   340
    (Suben los mozos con baúles.)
¿Dónde los pondrán?

BURGOA   Allí,
en esos cuartos.

ARBUÉS   *(A los mozos.)*
                        Llevadles,
pues.

BURGOA   ¿Y la dama?

ARBUÉS   Se está
despidiendo de su padre.

BURGOA   Pues qué, ¿no se queda en casa   345
con ella?

---

³³¹ *Alcancen,* 'igualen'.
³⁴² En Baudry, *llevadlos,* por evidente errata.

ARBUÉS	Sí; mas tiene antes
	que entregar unos breviarios
	a un primo suyo, que es fraile
	en San Pablo, y tardará
	tal vez; mas no hay que esperarle. ³⁵⁰
BURGOA	Marta, Ginés, a esa dama
	alumbrad.
	(Sale doña AURORA.)
ARBUÉS	Ya llegan tarde,
	patrón.
BURGOA	¡Qué! ¿Sin aguardar
	que la sirvan?...
ARBUÉS	Si es más ágil
	que un lancero, y nunca se anda ³⁵⁵
	con cumplimientos.

ESCENA VII

ANDRÉS, BURGOA, DOÑA AURORA

BURGOA	(Buen talle,
	garboso andar y ¡qué hermosa!
	Dijo bien cuando a los ángeles
	la comparó el capitán.)
AURORA	¿Sois el huésped?
BURGOA	Ordenadme, ³⁶⁰
	señora: yo soy.
AURORA	¿Hay fuego
	en mi aposento?
BURGOA	Y bujía;
	y puede vueseñoría
	disponer de él desde luego
	y de toda mi posada. ³⁶⁵
	Os mandaré a mi mujer
	que os sirva.

---

³⁶⁰ *Huésped,* cfr. v. 5.
³⁶³ *Vueseñoría,* contracción de 'vuestra señoría'.
³⁶⁴ *Desde luego,* 'inmediatamente, al instante'.

AURORA   No es menester;
yo me sirvo sola y nada
necesito. ¡Arbués!
ARBUÉS   ¿Señora?
AURORA   Cuando vuelva, aunque sea tarde, ³⁷⁰
me avisarás.
ARBUÉS   A la hora
en que llegue.
AURORA   *(A BURGOA.)*
                        Dios os guarde.
BURGOA   ¿Tomaréis un refrigerio,
un tentempié, para abrigo
del estómago?
AURORA   ¿No os digo   ³⁷⁵
que nada quiero?
            (Vase por la izquierda.)
BURGOA   ¡Qué imperio!

ESCENA VIII

ARBUÉS, BURGOA

BURGOA   ¿Y vos no cenáis?
ARBUÉS   Poco ha
que comimos y costumbre
no tenemos.
BURGOA   A la lumbre
podéis venir, que la habrá   ³⁸⁰
buena en el hogar.
ARBUÉS   No tengo
frío; podéis sin reparos
cuando queráis acostaros;
porque mi amo, os lo prevengo,
de que le sirva no gusta   ³⁸⁵
nadie más que yo, que sé
su mañas.
BURGOA   Tenéis, a fe,
buen trabajo.

ARBUÉS	¡Bah! Se ajusta
	cada cual al que le toca
	en esta vida; yo estoy 390
	a su servicio y le doy
	cumplimiento... y punto en boca,
	que tengo sueño. Dejad
	la llave a mano y a abrir
	bajaré, cuando venir 395
	le sienta; que echen mandad
	pienso a los caballos; yo
	de este sillón haré lecho.
BURGOA	¿Dormiréis ahí?
ARBUÉS	¿Pues no?
	Es costumbre y ya estoy hecho. 400
BURGOA	Pues para cuando me acueste
	ahí queda la llave, y vos
	os gobernaréis.
ARBUÉS	Adiós,
	pues.
BURGOA	Descansad. (¡Mala peste 405
	me coja si yo me acuesto
	sin ver a ese hombre quedar
	dentro de casa!) *(Vase.)*
ARBUÉS	Cerrar
	no está de más.
	(Cierra la puerta del fondo.)

ESCENA IX

ARBUÉS; *después*, DON CÉSAR

ARBUÉS	En mi puesto
	heme ya.

---

[400] *Estoy hecho*, 'estoy acostumbrado'. Comp. Zorrilla, *O. C.*, ed. N. Alonso Cortés, II, 56: «Que las órdenes del conde / a obedecer están hechos.»
[404] En Baudry, *descansar*.

(Se sienta en el sillón y llaman a la puerta del fondo.)
                                        Han llamado.

CÉSAR   *(Dentro.)*   ¿Arbués?
ARBUÉS ¿Por mi nombre? ¿Quién será?   410
CÉSAR   ¿Alférez Arbués?
ARBUÉS   ¿Quién va?
CÉSAR   Abre a un amigo.
ARBUÉS   ¿Quién es?
CÉSAR   El capitán Santillana.
ARBUÉS ¿Don César?
CÉSAR   Sí; date priesa,
        Arbués, que nos interesa.   415
ARBUÉS *(Abre.)*
        ¡Válame la soberana
        Virgen! ¡Vos, mi capitán!
CÉSAR   No malgastemos, Arbués,
        nuestro tiempo.
ARBUÉS   Hablad: ¿qué hay, pues?
CÉSAR   Las bocacalles están   420
        tomadas alrededor
        y conmigo hay seis soldados
        en esta casa apostados.
ARBUÉS ¿Y qué?
CÉSAR   Que es a tu señor
        a quien buscan. Si Gabriel   425
        los umbrales de ella pasa,
        Arbués, dentro de esta casa
        todos sois presos con él.
ARBUÉS No os dé pena, capitán;
        mi amo, que lo sabe todo,   430
        de hacer encontrará modo
        inútil todo este afán.

---

414 *Priesa*, 'prisa'. Arcaísmo exigido aquí por la rima.
Comp. Zorrilla, *El alcalde Ronquillo*, I, 2: «La paz está
ya firmada / con Francia, y con tanta priesa, / que nos
manda una princesa / por poderes desposada.»

416 *Válame*, 'válgame'. Arcaísmo popular. Comp. *Quijote*, I, 6: «¡Válame Dios! —dijo el Cura dando una gran
voz.»

CÉSAR El asunto no es materia
de chanzas; en la partida
sé yo que le va la vida.   435

ARBUÉS ¡Diablo!

CÉSAR   La cuestión es seria.
Registrarán su equipaje
y hasta su misma persona,
y si razón no le abona
terminante, aquí su viaje   440
concluye, porque al misterio
de su vida dar alcance
quiere el rey.

ARBUÉS   ¿El rey?

CÉSAR   El lance
ves que no puede más serio
ser. Mi padre don Rodrigo   445
me ha encomendado su guarda,
diciéndome que le aguarda
pronto y ejemplar castigo.
Hasta ahora, a lo que creo,
de sus poderes abusa   450
la justicia, pues le acusa
a ciegas su buen deseo.
Mas he oído una expresión
que, a probarse con certeza,
le va a costar la cabeza,   455
sea impostura o ambición.

---

442 *Dar alcance,* 'averiguar'. Comp. Avellaneda, *Quijote*, XXV: «Por cierto, señor estudiante, que la enigma es bonísima, y aun el serlo tanto debe de ser la causa de que no dé alcance a su significación.» Zorrilla, *O.C.*, ed. N. Alonso Cortés, I, 685 *a*: «Que es un misterio mi nombre/que a no descubrirlo yo/no hay quien lo alcance en la tierra.»

446 *Guarda,* 'custodia, amparo'. Comp. Cervantes, *El celoso extremeño:* «Les hizo Carrizales un sermón a todas, encargándoles la guarda de Leonora.»

452 *Su buen deseo,* sujeto de *acusa.*

454 *A probarse,* prótasis condicional. Comp. Zorrilla, *El caballo del rey don Sancho,* I, 2: «Vuestro amor, vuestras ofertas, / ni puedo admitirlas yo, / ni a poder, las admitiera.»

74

Óyeme ahora. El destino,
por su bien o por mi mal,
me une a su sino fatal
y me arroja en su camino.   460
Instinto y veneración
por él en mi pecho ruegan,
y por Aurora me ciegan
cariño y adoración.
En el nombre de la ley   465
a espiarle a Madrigal
me enviaron, y cumplí mal
con las órdenes del rey.
Desde Madrigal os sigo.

ARBUÉS   Lo sabíamos.
CÉSAR   Tiempo es   470
de que sepamos, Arbués,
a qué atenernos. Conmigo
es preciso que Gabriel
hable esta noche. Es forzoso
que este arcano misterioso   475
penetre a la par con él.
Hay de un misterio tremendo
en su existencia la duda;
siempre me tendrá en su ayuda,
mas que se explique pretendo.   480
Yo quiero de cualquier modo
salvarle; quiero que a prueba
ponga mi fe y que me deba
su porvenir; en fin, todo
quiero comprenderlo, y sea   485
quien fuere, noble o villano,
vil traidor o soberano
coronado, que en mí vea
un fiel amigo, un apoyo
presto a dividir con él   490

[477] y s. Hipérbaton: 'Hay la duda de un misterio tremendo en su existencia.'

[490] *Dividir*, 'compartir'. Comp. Zorrilla, *Un año y un
día*, III, 4: «Allí está virgen la tierra / esperando a su
señor, / y conmigo su conquista / dividirá el español.»

	desde el sitial de un dosel
	hasta de la tumba el hoyo.
ARBUÉS	Que os ciega amor bien se ve.
CÉSAR	Arbués, si su amor merezco
	y si mi mano la ofrezco...	495
ARBUÉS	No la admitirá.
CÉSAR	¿Por qué?
ARBUÉS	Porque es Espinosa un hombre
	que no quiere que se una
	ni hombre alguno a su fortuna,
	ni nombre alguno a su nombre.	500
CÉSAR	Yo los males que le afligen
	acepto y sus opiniones
	sin pedir de ellas razones.
	Y si ocultarme su origen
	les importa, nunca el nombre	505
	preguntaré de mi esposa;
	sea honrada y cariñosa
	y nada habrá que me asombre.
ARBUÉS	Estáis loco, capitán.
	¿Queréis con un pastelero	510
	emparentar?
CÉSAR	Arbués, quiero
	salir de una vez de afán.
	Te he dicho que mi destino
	me lleva tras de Gabriel.
ARBUÉS	Pues es fuerza que huyáis de él;	515
	echad por otro camino.
CÉSAR	¡Arbués!
ARBUÉS	Yo sé lo que digo.
	Vuestro ayo fuí; soy ya viejo
	y daros puedo un consejo;
	tomadle, que es de un amigo:	520
	cumplid vuestra obligación
	sin tropezar con Gabriel,
	y el misterio que hay en él
	dejad en su corazón.

---

495 *La*, complemento indirecto.
500 En Baudry, *ni hombre alguno*.
505 *Les importa*, cfr. v. 177.

76

	Para vuestro amor, de roca	525
	será su alma, y recelo	
	que no os dará ni consuelo	
	ni satisfacción su boca. ·	

CÉSAR   Pues qué, ¿hace ese hombre un
                              [agravio
                  impunemente?

ARBUÉS   Lo que hace   530
                  no sé, mas no satisface
                  jamás.

CÉSAR   Pues bien, si su labio
                  satisfacción no me da,
                  yo le haré que hable sin gana
                  con mi acero.

ARBUÉS   Santillana,   535
                  en silencio os matará.

CÉSAR   ¿A mí?

ARBUÉS   Tal creo en conciencia.

CÉSAR   ¿Tiene algún filtro Gabriel?

ARBUÉS   No, mas acaso con él
                  pelea la omnipotencia.   540
                  Don César, tened a raya
                  vuestra locura y tomad
                  mi consejo: abandonad
                  la senda por donde él vaya.

CÉSAR   No puedo.

ARBUÉS   Una indiscreción   545
                  muy sandia sé que cometo,
                  mas voy a ser indiscreto
                  porque os tengo obligación.

CÉSAR   Habla, habla.

ARBUÉS   Ese Gabriel
                  Espinosa, el pastelero,   550
                  tiene más de caballero
                  que lo que aparenta él.

---

[528] *Satisfacción*, «modo con que se sosiega y responde enteramente a alguna queja, sentimiento o razón contraria» *(Dicc. Aut.)*.
[548] *Obligación*, «la correspondencia que uno debe tener al beneficio recibido de otro» (Covarrubias).

Tres años ha que le sigo
de su favor obligado,
que honra y vida me ha salvado   555
y más que dueño es mi amigo.

CÉSAR   Pero ¿quién es?

ARBUÉS   Voy a ello.
Quién es... sábenlo él y Dios.
Cuanto sé yo de él vais vos
a saber; mas bajo un sello   560
guardadlo siempre.

CÉSAR   Concluye.

ARBUÉS   Escuchad, pues, lo que sé,
y vos veréis de él, a fe,
si en pro o en contra os arguye.
Él sabe todas las leyes,   565
cuenta todas las historias,
los desastres y las glorias
de los europeos reyes.
Él conoce los blasones
como un rey de armas; él mide   570
las noblezas; él decide
sobre razas y opiniones;
y tales fuerzas alcanza
que con precisión certera
monta un potro a la carrera   575
y hace astillas una lanza
en el aire.

CÉSAR   ¡Jesucristo!
Eso se cuenta también
de Don...
        (ARBUÉS *le tapa la boca con la
        mano.*)

ARBUÉS   No digáis de quién.
De él yo lo cuento, y lo he visto.   580
Y, en fin, os diré un secreto:

---

⁵⁵² Comp. Cuéllar, *El pastelero de Madrigal*, jornada III: «En cada paso que ofrece/averiguación tan nueva,/en ese hombre se comprueba/que es más de lo que
parece.»

⁵⁶⁴ *Os arguye*, 'os demuestra'. Comp. Zorrilla, *Cada cual
con su razón*, I, 5: «Venid con la luz del sol, / sin reser-
va, en claro día, / y no a la luz de un farol, / que eso no
arguye hidalguía / en un galán español.»

78

	¿conocíais a Quiñones,	
	el teniente de dragones?	
CÉSAR	Sí.	
ARBUÉS	Sabéis que era el respeto	585
	de los diestros en la esgrima,	
	porque jamás estocada	
	le hirió, mientras que su espada	
	veinte muertes le echó encima.	
CÉSAR	Sí.	
ARBUÉS	No ignoraréis que muerto	590
	en Madrigal se le halló;	
	pues bien, Gabriel le mató	
	riñendo.	
CÉSAR	¿Cierto?	
ARBUÉS	Tan cierto,	
	capitán, como es de noche.	
	De Gabriel en la hostería	595
	con el teniente comía	
	yo una tarde, cuando un coche	
	paró a sus puertas, y de él	
	un embozado bajando,	
	se entró hasta allí preguntando	
	si estaba en casa Gabriel.	600
	Salió éste; y el forastero,	
	que ser mostraba en su porte	
	un gran señor de la corte,	
	llevó la mano al sombrero	
	al ir a hablarle; Quiñones,	605
	de quien sabéis la insolencia,	
	con aquella impertinencia	
	peculiar de los matones,	
	dijo: «¡Hola! ¿Esas tenemos?»	
	Mas no bien le oyó Gabriel,	610
	cuando viniéndose a él	
	le asió por los dos extremos	
	del collarín del coleto	
	diciendo: «¡Hola, seor espía!	

---

[595] En Baudry y otras edics., se lee *alférez*, por evidente error.
[602] *Porte*, cfr. v. 119.
[614] *Seor*, cfr. v. 3.

¡Yo os haré, por vida mía,   615
que me guardéis el secreto!»
Y con muñeca de hierro
zarandeándole de un lado
a otro, le echó derribado
bajo el banco como a un perro.   620
El teniente, puesto apenas
en pie, echó mano al acero
yéndose hacia el pastelero,
quien con miradas serenas
y voz grave e imperiosa   625
nos dijo: «Echémonos fuera».
Y echamos por la escalera
los tres en pos de Espinosa.
Detrás de unos paredones
que hay debajo del camino   630
paróse; fue su padrino
el otro, y yo el de Quiñones.
Capitán, juro a mi honor
que no he visto tal destreza
jamás, ni tanta firmeza,   635
serenidad y valor.
Era un maestro el teniente,
pero a las cuatro paradas
tenía tres estocadas;
rugía de ira y valiente   640
atacaba; mas escrito
debió estar: tendióse a fondo
Gabriel y cayó redondo
Quiñones sin dar un grito.
¿Y Espinosa?

CÉSAR
ARBUÉS
                          Ni un rasguño   645
sacó; en silencio su espada
limpió, que estaba manchada
de sangre hasta el mismo puño,
y envainándola con calma
nos dijo: «Quede lo hecho   650
sepultado en nuestro pecho,
y que Dios perdone su alma.»

---

621 *Puesto apenas*, 'apenas se hubo puesto'.

80

	Y volviéndonos a entrar
	otra vez en la hostería,
	no ha vuelto desde aquel día 655
	a Quiñones a mentar.
	Ahora, señor Santillana,
	pues sabéis que hondo cariño
	os cobré desde muy niño
	y os guardo afición cristiana, 660
	creed a un amigo viejo:
	por delante de Gabriel
	pasad sin topar con él;
	y agradecedme el consejo.
CÉSAR	Es tarde, y retroceder 665
	no quiero. Resuelto a todo
	vengo y de uno u otro modo
	esta noche le he de ver.
ARBUÉS	Yo no os lo puedo impedir;
	pero hacéis mal, os lo advierto. 670
CÉSAR	Más quiero por él ser muerto
	que sin Aurora vivir.
ARBUÉS	Allá os las hayáis.
AURORA	*(Dentro.)*

¡Arbués!

ARBUÉS	Pronto, marchaos; es ella.
	(Dentro.)
AURORA	¡Arbués!

(ARBUÉS *quiere obligar a* DON CÉSAR *a irse.*)

CÉSAR	Déjame la huella 675
	besar de sus castos pies.
ARBUÉS	¡Capitán!

---

[660] *Afición*, «la propensión, amor o voluntad del ánimo con que nos inclinamos a querer y amar alguna cosa» (*Dicc. Aut.*). Comp. *Quijote*, I, 25: «La reina Madásima, a quien yo tengo particular afición.»

[671] En Baudry y otras edics., *mas*, adversativa.

81

ESCENA X

DOÑA AURORA, DON CÉSAR, ARBUÉS

AURORA   *(Saliendo.)*
                 Oyendo estoy
           a Arbués hablar ha una hora.
           ¿Es mi padre?

CÉSAR   No, señora.

AURORA   ¡El capitán!

CÉSAR   Sí, yo soy.   680

ARBUÉS   Ver al señor pretendía.
           Le dije que ausente estaba;
           insistía él, porfiaba
           yo, y por eso se oía
           hablar aquí, doña Aurora.   685

AURORA   Anduviste descortés
           con el capitán, Arbués.

ARBUÉS   Vuestro padre...

AURORA   Sin demora
           me debiste de avisar
           de su llegada, y al punto   690
           saliera yo.

CÉSAR   Sea asunto
           concluido; él atajar
           debió mi imprudente paso.

AURORA   Si vos salís en su abono,
           yo su falta le perdono.   695
           (A ARBUÉS, *que se va.)*
           Sal.

---

694 *Abono,* 'aprobación'; *abonar,* «aprobar y dar por buena alguna cosa, y asegurarla por tal» *(Dicc. Aut.).*

DON CÉSAR, DOÑA AURORA

AURORA   ¿Puedo saber acaso
la causa que aquí os obliga
a presentaros ahora?

CÉSAR   Es un secreto, señora;
perdonad que no os le diga.   700
Confiarle sólo debo
a vuestro padre.

AURORA   *(Retirándose.)*
                    En tal caso...

CÉSAR   *(Deteniéndola.)*
Aguardad.

AURORA   Decid.

CÉSAR   Acaso
vais a enojaros.

AURORA   Me atrevo   705
a esperar de vuestro honor
que no me osará decir
nada que no pueda oír
sin peligro o sin rubor.

CÉSAR   Nada, señora. ¡Yo os juro   710
por la honra en que nací
que nada oiréis de mí
que no sea noble y puro!

AURORA   Hablad, pues.

CÉSAR   Que fui sospecho
torpe por demás, señora,
si no habéis visto hasta ahora   715
el arcano de mi pecho

AURORA   ¿Cómo queréis que comprenda
secretos que en él guardáis
si no me los reveláis?

CÉSAR   Si en los ojos una venda   720
de indiferencia y rigor
no os hubierais puesto, Aurora,

	me ahorrarais hacer ahora	
	la relación de mi amor.	
AURORA	¿Conque amáis?	
CÉSAR	Con frenesí.	725
AURORA	Pues ¿y a quién?	
CÉSAR	A un ángel.	
AURORA	¡Oh!	
	¿Y os paga?	
CÉSAR	Creo que no.	
AURORA	¿Lo sabe?	
CÉSAR	Creo que sí.	
AURORA	¿Se lo habéis dicho?	
CÉSAR	Jamás.	
AURORA	¿Por qué?	
CÉSAR	Porque es mi pasión	730

      más que amor, veneración;
      idolatría quizás.
      Es un amor que no tiene
      en su vil naturaleza
      un átomo de impureza: 735
      amor que del cielo viene.
      Es un innato cariño
      tan casto como profundo,
      tan inmenso como el mundo,
      tan puro como el armiño.   740

---

[724] *Relación*, «la narración o informe que se hace de alguna cosa que sucedió» (*Dicc. Aut.*) Comp. Zorrilla, *Don Juan Tenorio*, I, 9: «Y en tanto que humedecemos / la garganta, verdadera / relación haznos de un lance / sobre el cual hay controversia.»

[727] *Pagar*, «significa también corresponder al afecto, cariño u otro beneficio» (*Dicc. Aut.*). Comp. Cervantes, *La ilustre fregona*: «Y a procurar que ella me quiera, pagándome con honesta voluntad lo que a la mía, también honesta, se debe.»

[740] El verso *tan puro como el armiño* aparece en todas las edics. antepuesto a *tan inmenso como el mundo*, sin duda por error, ya que altera la redondilla. El tópico es frecuente en Zorrilla: «Vuelve a su pecho el corazón de niño; / se le roba a la guerra y la venganza, / se le torna más puro que el armiño» (*O.C.*, ed. N. Alonso Cortés, I, 784 *a*); «la chica, eso sí, es muy bella, / y pura como el armiño» (*íd.*, 1700 *a*).

Sin otro bien, ni otro dueño,
ni más afán, ni más guía
en la tierra, noche y día
cón él vivo, con él sueño.
Un amor sublime, santo,   745
mas tan tirano, tan fiero,
que sus fuerzas considero
a mis solas con espanto;
porque no hay ley, no hay deber
que pueda mi corazón   750
al poder de mi pasión
con ventajas oponer.
Si la que amo me dijera:
«Sé traidor: véndete esclavo»,
mi fe llevando hasta el cabo   755
me infamara y me vendiera.

AURORA   ¡Jesús, qué amor tan horrendo!
    ¿Dónde adquirido lo habéis?

CÉSAR   ¿Os reís?

AURORA   ¿Pues qué queréis,
    si os estáis contradiciendo?   760

CÉSAR   ¿Dó está la contradicción?

AURORA   ¡Pues ahí es nada! ¿Un cariño
    tan puro como el armiño,
    una sagrada pasión
    de cuyo infernal poder   765
    creéis que os llegue a obligar
    vuestro rey a abandonar,
    la libertad a vender?

CÉSAR   Sin vacilar un momento.

AURORA   ¿Porque una mujer os ame   770
    consentís en ser infame,
    traidor y esclavo?

CÉSAR   Consiento.

AURORA   Haceos un poco atrás.

CÉSAR   ¿Por qué?

AURORA   Esa pasión que tanto
    ponderáis, más que amor santo,   775

| | es amor de Satanás. |
| CÉSAR | ¡Infeliz del corazón
que tal amor no comprende! |
| AURORA | Más lo es en el que se enciende
la llama de tal pasión. | 780 |
| CÉSAR | ¡No os mofarais de ella así
si la comprendierais, no! |
| AURORA | ¿Y quién os dice que yo
no guardo ese amor en mí? |
| CÉSAR | *(Sorprendido.)*
¡Vos! |
AURORA	Don César, sólo Dios	785
	amor tan ciego merece.
CÉSAR	Amor es Dios y enloquece.
AURORA	Y loco estáis.
CÉSAR	*(Se arrodilla.)*
¡Ah! Por vos.
AURORA	¡Insensato!
CÉSAR	Por vos, sí;
yo os amo, Aurora, os adoro.	790
AURORA	¿Pues creéis que yo lo ignoro?
CÉSAR	¡Cielos!
*(Álzase del suelo, acercándose
a AURORA.)*
AURORA	*(Apartándose.)*
No lleguéis a mí.
CÉSAR	¿Me rechazáis?
AURORA	¡A fe mía!
Yo acepto vuestro respeto,
mas no quiero ser objeto	795
	de una torpe idolatría.
No soy más que una mujer,
y del Criador hechura;
sólo como criatura
estimada quiero ser.	800
CÉSAR	Esas palabras, Aurora,
que una esperanza me dan...
AURORA	Si tal creéis, capitán,

---

779 'Más lo es *aquel* en el que se enciende'. En Baudry,
mas lo es.

86

	olvidadlas desde ahora.	805
CÉSAR	Me confundís y no sé	
	unir con vuestra bondad	
	vuestro rigor.	
AURORA	En verdad	
	que yo tampoco sabré	
	tal arcano descifraros.	
	Lo que sí os sabré decir	810
	es que no puedo admitir	
	vuestro amor; mas sin reparos	
	mi amistad toda os ofrezco.	
	Creedme: Dios me es testigo	815
	de que os quiero por amigo,	
	mas por galán no os merezco.	
CÉSAR	¡Cómo!	
AURORA	Os lo diré mejor	
	y no me guardéis encono:	
	vuestra amistad ambiciono;	
	vuestra pasión me da horror.	820
CÉSAR	Me asombráis.	
AURORA	Es un arcano	
	que penetrar no podemos.	
	Galán, jamás nos veremos;	
	amigo, aquí está mi mano.	

(Le tiende la mano.)

CÉSAR	¡Ah! Os entiendo. Compasión	825
	os causó mi amor y ahora	
	burlaros os plugo, Aurora,	
	con mi pobre corazón.	
	Mas esta mano que estrecho	
	sobre él y que llevo al labio...	830

---

816 *Galán*, «el que galantea, solicita o logra alguna mujer» *(Dicc. Aut.).* Comp. Zorrilla, *Cada cual con su razón*, II, 3: «¿Pues de qué sino de amor / pueden tratar los galanes?»

823 'Como galán'.

824 'Como amigo'.

827 *Os plugo*, 'os plació'. Indefinido arcaico. Comp. Zorrilla, *El alcalde Ronquillo*, V, 3: «Como queráis; mas ved de qué manera / vuestro sepulcro al rey labrar le plugo.»

(Va a besar la mano. DOÑA AURORA
se lo impide.)

AURORA   La boca le hará un agravio;
            no la levantéis del pecho.

CÉSAR   Ese tono...

AURORA   Es harto serio.

CÉSAR   No os comprendo. Si es capricho
            de vuestro humor...

AURORA   Ya os lo he dicho, 835
            capitán: es un misterio
            que yo no entiendo tampoco.

CÉSAR   Pues yo lo penetraré.

AURORA   ¿Cómo?

CÉSAR   A vuestro padre haré
            que me lo explique.

AURORA   Estáis loco. 840

CÉSAR   ¡En eso parar espero
            con vuestras contradicciones!

AURORA   Pues oídme unas razones
            terminantes, caballero.

CÉSAR   Hablad.

AURORA   Me habéis ponderado 845
            vuestra acendrada pasión,
            y vais en mi corazón
            a saber lo que hay guardado.
            Hay un amor casto, ciego,
            de mi pecho en la guarida, 850
            tan largo como mi vida,
            tan ardiente como el fuego.
            Amor de goces tan suaves,
            tan exento de dolores,
            como el olor de las flores, 855
            como el cantar de las aves.
            Este amor es un cariño
            tan ajeno de impureza,
            como el que a tener empieza
            naciendo a su madre el niño. 860
            Hoguera es de inmenso amor;

---

860 *Naciendo,* 'apenas nace'.

88

mas de su llama tranquila
no se extingue ni vacila
el constante resplandor.
En el duelo, en la ventura,   865
en la inquietud y en la calma
siempre en el fondo del alma
como una estrella fulgura;
y brilla su claridad
en su centro solitario   870
cual lámpara en un santuario,
cual faro en la tempestad.

CÉSAR   ¿Amáis?
AURORA   Amo a un noble ser
de quien ignoro hasta el nombre;
le amo todo cuanto a un hombre   875
puede amar una mujer.
Le amo desde que le vi;
le amo con toda mi fe,
y al sepulcro bajaré
con su amor dentro de mí.   880
Con él sueño, con él vivo;
lo que él desea apetezco,
lo que aborrece aborrezco,
y mi corazón, cautivo
de su sola voluntad,   885
a ella no más obedece.
Él me dice: «Ama, aborrece»,
y amo y odio sin piedad.
Me dijo: «De ese mancebo
serás amiga», y yo os digo   890
que vois sois mi único amigo,

---

881 Comp. Zorrilla, *O.C.*, ed. N. Alonso Cortés, I, 1004 *a*:
«No se aparta de mí noche ni día / su casta imagen: mi pasión, mi dueño,/con ella vivo, con su imagen
sueño».
883 Falta este verso en la edic. de Baudry.
888 Comp. Zorrilla, *El zapatero y el rey*, 2.ª parte, II,
8: «No hay nada para mí que vos primero,/ni ley, ni
amor; para serviros vivo./'¡Da, hiere!', me decís, y doy
y hiero,/y el pan aprecio que de vos recibo.»

porque él lo quiere y yo debo
quererlo; y si él me dijera
«véndete esclava», ¡por Dios
os juro que, como vos   895
por mí, por él me vendiera!
Ya mi secreto sabéis.
Respetad de él comedido
lo que no hayáis comprendido;
y si no os satisfacéis   900
con las razones que os dan,
haced cuenta, en conclusión,
que nací sin corazón.
Buenas noches, capitán.

CÉSAR   Esperad.

AURORA   Ni un solo instante.   905
El alma leal que abrigo
franca está para el amigo
y muerta para el amante.

*(Vase por la izquierda, cerrando
la puerta.)*

ESCENA XII

DON CÉSAR

¡Ama a un hombre cuyo nombre
no conoce! Fascinada   910
está su alma enamorada
por él. ¿Y quién es ese hombre?
Un año hace que los sigo
y a nadie he visto jamás
llegar ¡Un enigma más   915
de los que llevan consigo!
Con él sueña, con él vive;
lo que él desea apetece.
Él manda y ella obedece
y ser de su ser recibe.   920
¡Oh! Sí: lo expresaban bien
sus ojos, su voz, su gesto.

---

894 'Véndete como esclava'.

Sí, encierra un amor funesto
su corazón. Pero ¿a quién?
¡Ama a un hombre misterioso   925
de quien hasta el nombre ignora!
¿Ama y no a mí? ¡La traidora!
¡Sandio de mí! Estoy celoso.
Celoso y tal vez acecha
la muerte aquí a ese Gabriel   930
de Espinosa. ¡Cielos! ¿Si él?...
¡Él! ¡Estúpida sospecha!
Su padre... ¿Y si no lo es?
¿Si el misterio y soledad
que guardan de liviandad   935
fuera un velo infame? —¿Arbués?

ESCENA XIII

DON CÉSAR, ARBUÉS

ARBUÉS   Aquí estoy.
CÉSAR   Pronto, responde.
            Aurora a otro hombre ama.
            ¿Quién es? Di. ¿Cómo se llama?
            ¿Adónde está ahora? ¿Adónde   940
            le vio? ¿Cuándo?
ARBUÉS   Capitán,
            ya os previne que acercaros
            a nosotros era echaros
            en un abismo de afán;
            y ya lo veis: un instante   945
            nada más que habéis hablado
            con ella, os ha trastornado
            corazón, juicio y semblante.
CÉSAR   La amo, Arbués, y estoy celoso.
            Dime, por tu vida, Arbués,   950
            ¿sabes bien si Gabriel es
            su padre?

_____

934 y ss. Hipérbaton: '¿si el misterio y soledad que
guardan fueran un velo de infame liviandad?'.

ARBUÉS	¡Pues es chistoso!
CÉSAR	¡Ay! De la duda la hiel
	me emponzoña el corazón.
ARBUÉS	Pues no perdáis la ocasión 955
	de consultarla con él.
CÉSAR	¿Llega?
ARBUÉS	Le siento venir.
CÉSAR	¿Cómo?
ARBUÉS	Acostumbra a silbar
	recio.
CÉSAR	¿Y silbó?
	(Llaman: aldabonada.)
ARBUÉS	De llamar
	acaban.
CÉSAR	Ve, pues, a abrir. 960

(Vase ARBUÉS *por el fondo llevando la llave.)*

Es forzoso: le hablaré;
la vida en ello le va.
Si se obstina…, mas no, a fe;
primero le salvaré
y Dios amanecerá.   965

ESCENA XIV

DON CÉSAR, ARBUÉS; GABRIEL, *embozado*

GABRIEL	¡Hola, señor capitán!
CÉSAR	Os aguardaba.
GABRIEL	¿Qué hay, pues?
CÉSAR	Solos.
GABRIEL	Déjanos, Arbués.

---

956 *Consultarla* (la duda).

965 Variante de la locución *Amanecerá Dios y medraremos*, con que se expresa confianza en el porvenir.

DON CÉSAR, GABRIEL

GABRIEL	Podéis hablar.
CÉSAR	Tal vez van
	mis palabras a causaros 970
	extrañeza.
GABRIEL	No lo espero.
CÉSAR	Muy claro con vos ser quiero.
GABRIEL	Pues no os andéis con reparos.
	Con cuanta más claridad
	habléis vos, a mi entender 975
	os debo yo comprender
	con mayor facilidad
CÉSAR	Yo soy...
GABRIEL	*(Interrumpiéndole.)*
	Os conozco bien:
	adelante.
CÉSAR	En Madrigal
	me acantoné de orden real... 980
GABRIEL	Para guardarme; también
	lo sé. Adelante.
CÉSAR	Hoy en pos
	de vuestros pasos...
GABRIEL	Venís
	por lo mismo; me decís
	cosas que sé como vos. 985
CÉSAR	Pues bien: lo que según creo
	ignoráis vos todavía
	os diré.
GABRIEL	Por vida mía,
	capitán, que ya deseo
	que algo nuevo me digáis. 990
CÉSAR	Pues oíd.
GABRIEL	Estoy atento.
CÉSAR	La casa en este momento
	está cercada y estáis

preso en ella.

GABRIEL   Ya lo sé.

CÉSAR   ¿Conque sabiéndolo ya   995
entrasteis?

GABRIEL   Pues claro está.

CÉSAR   ¿Por voluntad?

GABRIEL   Ya se ve.

CÉSAR   ¿Luego confiáis?...

GABRIEL   En Dios
primero y después en mí.

CÉSAR   ¿Sabéis que os acusan?...

GABRIEL   Sí.   1000

CÉSAR   ¿De un delito?...

GABRIEL   (Interrumpiéndole.)
                              No, de dos.

CÉSAR   ¿Sabéis cuáles?

GABRIEL   Sí, por cierto.

CÉSAR   Pues, a lo que se murmura,
cualquiera de ellos...

GABRIEL   Segura
trae mi sentencia: soy muerto.   1005

CÉSAR   ¿Con ella os chanceáis?

GABRIEL   Sí tal.

CÉSAR   ¿Podréis probar?...

GABRIEL   Una cosa.

CÉSAR   ¿Que sois?...

GABRIEL   (Interrumpiéndole.)
                    Gabriel Espinosa,
pastelero en Madrigal.

CÉSAR   Podrán dudarlo tal vez.   1010

GABRIEL   ¿Por qué?

CÉSAR   Porque lo desmiente
vuestro gentil continente
y es muy receloso el juez.

GABRIEL   Dios me hizo así, y en mi mano

---

995 'Aun sabiéndolo', fórmula concesiva.

1012 *Continente*, «modo de proceder y portarse uno, y
lo mismo que compostura, modestia, aire y acciones»
(Dicc. Aut.). Comp. *Quijote*, II, 41: «Esto dicho, dejando
a Clavileño, con gentil continente se volvieron por donde
habían venido.»

	no está cambiar de figura.	1015
CÉSAR	Diz que andáis con mucha holgura	
	para ser sólo un villano.	
GABRIEL	Soy rico.	
CÉSAR	Querrán papeles	
	que os acrediten de tal.	
GABRIEL	Resmas tengo en Madrigal	1020
	de los de envolver pasteles.	
CÉSAR	¿Hay algunos con pinturas?	
GABRIEL	Mil.	
CÉSAR	¿Son estampas de santos?	
GABRIEL	Hay de todo.	
CÉSAR	Y entre tantos	
	¿hay conocidas figuras?	1025
GABRIEL	¿Echáis menos, capitán,	
	alguna?	
CÉSAR	No: mas ha un rato	
	que el juez buscaba un retrato	
	fiel del rey Don Sebastián.	
GABRIEL	Siento no tener ninguno.	1030
CÉSAR	Pues creo que el juez pretende	
	deteneros, porque entiende	
	que lleváis sobre vos uno.	
GABRIEL	¿Qué habría en que le llevara	
	para que en mí se encarnicen	1035
	los golillas?	
CÉSAR	*(Mirándole atentamente.)*	
	Es que dicen	
	que lo lleváis en la cara.	

[1016] *Diz,* 'dicen'. Apócope vulgar. Comp. Quevedo, *Buscón*, ed. F. Lázaro, I, 1: «Las damas diz que salían por verle a las ventanas»; Zorrilla, *O. C.*, ed. N. Alonso Cortés, II, 632: «Diz que el mundo es un teatro.»

GABRIEL	Ni es tan deforme la mía,
	ni osara yo andar, por cierto,
	con la cara que un rey muerto 1040
	usaba cuando vivía.
CÉSAR	Pues la justicia cree ver
	en vos semejanza tal
	con él, que de vos muy mal
	sospecha.
GABRIEL	¡Cómo ha de ser! 1045
	(Un momento de pausa.)
CÉSAR	Yo os cobré afecto; fiad
	vuestro secreto de mí,
	y al depositarlo aquí
	lo echáis en la eternidad.
GABRIEL	Mozo, si tuviera un día 1050
	que fiar algo a algún hombre,
	creedme, os juro a mi nombre
	que de vos lo fiaría.
CÉSAR	Fiadme ese nombre, pues.
GABRIEL	Gabriel; lo acabáis de oír. 1055
CÉSAR	¡Os obstináis en morir!
GABRIEL	Ley de los que nacen es.
CÉSAR	¡No me entendéis!
GABRIEL	¡Vive Dios!
	Ni vos me entendéis tampoco
	a mí.
CÉSAR	Parecéisme loco. 1060
GABRIEL	Y a mí mentecato vos.
	Porque a la verdad, mancebo,
	grima me da contemplaros
	así el seso devanaros
	por decirme algo de nuevo. 1065

1045 *¡Cómo ha de ser!,* cfr. v. 141.

1046 y s. *Fiad de* por 'fiad en', construcción arcaica con el valor de 'confiad en'. Comp. Cervantes, *El gallardo español,* jorn. I: «Respondedle cortésmente, / con el término prudente / que de vuestro ingenio fíd»; Zorrilla, *O. C.,* ed. N. Alonso Cortés, II, 64: «El conde, en su red cogido, / pero fiando a la par / de la gente de Vivar...»

1053 *Fiar de,* cfr. v. 1046.

Tras de tanto ir y venir,
¿no habéis echado de ver
que yo no quiero entender
lo que me queréis decir?
¿Os figuráis que viví   1070
entre el pueblo catorce años
sin percibir los extraños
cuentos que corren de mí?
¿Pensáis que es ésta la vez
primera que en mí repara   1075
el vulgo, y que cara a cara
me veo yo con un juez?
Venid acá, pobre niño;
¿pensáis que no conocí
que en vos germinó hacia mí   1080
un simpático cariño?
Yo como en un libro leo
claro en vuestro corazón,
y bien de vuestra afición
la causa escondida veo.   1085
Sé que a mí os atrae un nudo
cuyo mágico poder
os hace ante mí poner
vuestro pecho por escudo.
Pero su atracción oculta   1090
resistid, porque os advierto
que ese nudo con un muerto
os estrecha y os sepulta.
Resistid; porque un ser soy
que infesto el lugar que habito,   1095
que cuanto toco marchito
y asolo por donde voy.

CÉSAR   ¿Qué me importa? El horror mismo
del misterio que hay en vos
de sí me arrebata en pos,   1100
y ciego voy a su abismo.

GABRIEL   ¡Mancebo!
CÉSAR   Con vos iré

[1084] *Afición*, cfr. v. 660.

	por doquiera que vayáis.	
	Oídme: y cuando sepáis	
	mi secreto...	
GABRIEL	Ya lo sé.	1105
CÉSAR	¿Qué sabéis?	
GABRIEL	Cuanto ha pasado	
	por vuestro pecho hasta ahora.	
	No ignoro nada: de Aurora	
	sé que estáis enamorado.	
	Sé que por ella me habláis,	1110
	y que tras ella venís,	
	y que por ella vivís,	
	y que con ella soñáis.	
	¿Creéis que en vuestro semblante	
	no he conocido al entrar	1115
	que la acababais de hablar?	
	Y en vuestro mustio talante,	
	¿creéis que no entiendo acaso	
	que el amor de vuestro pecho	
	al declararla, no ha hecho	1120
	de vuestras palabras caso?	
CÉSAR	¡Caballero!	
GABRIEL	¡Qué demonio!	
	De todo estoy enterado:	
	hasta de que habéis pensado	
	pedírmela en matrimonio.	1125
CÉSAR	Sí, que mi amor...	
GABRIEL	(Interrumpiéndole.)	
	Sé que es grande,	
	profundo, honesto y leal;	
	pero es un amor fatal,	
	imposible.	
CÉSAR	Que os demande	
	por qué dejad.	
GABRIEL	Lo primero,	1130
	porque si mal no me fundo,	
	no os quiere ella: lo segundo,	
	porque yo tampoco quiero.	

1116 *La* compl. indirecto, como en el v. 495.
1120 *La*, compl. indirecto (cfr. v. 495).

CÉSAR	¡Me escarnecéis!
GABRIEL	¡No, por Dios!

¿Y a qué viene el enojaros?   1135
¿No queréis que hablemos claros?
Pues claro os hablo yo a vos.

CÉSAR   ¡Ea, pues! Claros hablemos
y sepamos de una vez
a qué atenernos.

GABRIEL   ¡Pardiez!   1140
No alcéis la voz, que podemos
a las gentes de la casa
despertar, y creer pueden
cosas que aquí no suceden,
capitán.

CÉSAR   Lo que aquí pasa   1145
es que quiero penetrar
el misterio que os rodea,
y que es fuerza que así sea,
porque no he de tolerar
en calma, como un villano,   1150
que tan sin razón los dos
despreciéis mi amistad vos
y vuestra hija mi mano.
Confieso que el alma mía,
del punto en que os llegó a ver,   1155
por vos empezó a tener
misteriosa simpatía.
Confieso, sí, que amo a Aurora
con amor tan delirante
que no hay acción que me espante   1160
por ella; mas me devora,
a par con el del amor,
el fuego de un justo antojo
ceder sin razón mejor.

[1136] El adverbio *claro* interpretado como adjetivo y so-
metido, por tanto, a concordancia. Comp. Zorrilla, *El zapatero y el rey*, 1.ª parte, I, 6: «Pero al caso, señor Diego: / dispuesto estoy a escucharos; / hablemos de prisa
y claros, / que he de partirme muy luego.»
[1155] *Del punto en que*, 'desde el momento en que'.

	Soy noble y cuando os ofrezco 1165
	mi raza unir con la vuestra,
	que me deis más noble muestra
	de lo que valéis merezco;
	porque si no, con derecho
	tendré por cosa segura 1170
	lo que de vos se murmura
	y lo que yo me sospecho.

GABRIEL   ¿Y qué es lo que sospecháis?
CÉSAR   Que sois...
GABRIEL   ¿Quién?
CÉSAR   Un impostor
          y que desecháis mi amor...   1175
GABRIEL   ¿Por qué?
CÉSAR   Porque vos la amáis.
GABRIEL   ¡Desdichado!
CÉSAR   Una de dos:
          satisfacedme al momento,
          o sepulcro este aposento
          es para mí o para vos.   1180
GABRIEL   Niño, dándoles gran precio,
          la mayor satisfacción
          que debo a tu protección
          y a tu amor, es el desprecio.
          Ve, pues, si te satisface   1185
          la de que no los admito,
          porque el amor no me place
          y el favor no necesito.
CÉSAR   ¿Eso a mí?
GABRIEL   Y antes que te abra
          sepulcro, entiende que puedo   1190
          abismarte con un dedo
          como con una palabra.
CÉSAR   Decídmela.
GABRIEL   No la esperes.
CÉSAR   Pues bien; quiero en mi despecho

1178 *Satisfacedme*, 'dadme explicaciones' (cfr. v. 528).
1186 'La [*satisfacción*] de que'. *Los admito*, catáfora:
'el amor y el favor'.

	ser o muerto o satisfecho. 1195

ser o muerto o satisfecho. 1195
*(Don César desenvaina su espada,
yendo contra Gabriel. Éste desenvaina la suya poniéndose en guardia,
en cuyo punto aparece Aurora.)*

GABRIEL   Sea, pues que tú lo quieres.

ESCENA XVI

GABRIEL, DON CÉSAR, DOÑA AURORA,
después DON RODRIGO

AURORA   ¡Teneos!
CÉSAR   Todo es en balde.
*(La puerta del fondo se abre de re-
pente y sale Don Rodrigo, detrás del
cual se ven cuatro soldados con mos-
quetes en la parte exterior de la puer-
ta. Gabriel baja su espada dando un
paso atrás, con tal rapidez que el juez
no pueda tener tiempo de apercibir-
se de que estaba en guardia.)*
RODRIGO   En nombre del rey.
GABRIEL   ¿Qué es eso?
RODRIGO   Gabriel Espinosa, preso
             sed.
GABRIEL   Lo estoy, señor alcalde.   1200
RODRIGO   ¿Cómo?
GABRIEL   Ese mozo, sintiendo
             que aún en vela andaba yo,
             por esa ventana entró
             que me fugara temiendo;
             hallándome en pie y armado   1205
             darme a prisión me intimaba,
             y mi espada le entregaba

1197 *Teneos*, 'deteneos'. Comp. Zorrilla, *El zapatero y
el rey*, 1.ª parte, I, : «Tente, Blas, no salgas, no.»
1206 *Me intimaba*, 'me ordenaba'.

	cuando vos habéis entrado.	
RODRIGO	Vuestras armas y equipaje	
	quedan embargados.	
	(A Don César.)	
	De él	1210
	y ellas te encargo.—Gabriel	
	Espinosa, vuestro viaje	
	no os es dado continuar	
	hasta que duda no quede	
	de quién sois.	
GABRIEL	Su merced puede	1215
	cuando guste comenzar	
	sus indagaciones.	
RODRIGO	Luego.	
	Interrogar me es preciso	
	testigos; mas ya, os lo aviso,	
	preso estáis.	
	(A don César.)	
	Con él te entrego	1220
	aquella mujer.	
GABRIEL	Señora	
	se dice, alcalde; esta dama	
	noble es cual vos y se llama	
	por buen nombre doña Aurora.	
RODRIGO	Si es dama y noble, después	1225
	lo sabremos.	
GABRIEL	¡Quiera Dios	
	que no os pese luego a vos	
	saberlo!	
RODRIGO	Excesiva es	
	vuestra arrogancia.	
GABRIEL	No tanta	
	como tener con vos puedo.	1230
RODRIGO	Nadie a mí me infunde miedo.	
GABRIEL	Pues a mí nadie me espanta.	
	Conque adelante.	

[1228] Comp. Cuéllar, *El pastelero de Madrigal*, jornada III: «Don Rodrigo,/id con tiento, pues a vos/de este juicio han de juzgaros.»

RODRIGO   Adelante.
Vos a ese cuarto, señora;
y vos dad la espada ahora   1235
al capitán.
GABRIEL   Al instante.
(Alargando la espada, sin soltarla.)
Ahí la tenéis; y os suplico,
joven, que si no os enoja
me la guardéis, que es la hoja
buena, y el puño muy rico.   1240
(GABRIEL entrega su espada a DON
CÉSAR, quien al mirarla exclama
asombrado:)
CÉSAR   ¡Jesús!
GABRIEL   Ved con atención
su primor.
CÉSAR   ¡Corona real
tiene el pomo!
GABRIEL   Y el tazón
las armas de Portugal.
RODRIGO   ¡Hola! Pondréis a mi alcance   1245
cómo hubisteis esa espada.
GABRIEL   Dadlo por cosa alcanzada:
la compré en Cintra de lance.
RODRIGO   *(Acercándose y viendo la espada*
que tiene DON CÉSAR.)
¡Prenda regia!
GABRIEL   ¡Por San Juan!
Yo lo creo; como que es   1250
prenda de un rey portugués:
fue del rey Don Sebastián.
RODRIGO   *(A don CÉSAR, aparte.)*
César, guárdale, por Dios:
porque si se huye perdemos
la cabeza ambos a dos.   1255

1245 *Pondréis a mi alcance,* en mi conocimiento.
1246 *Hubisteis,* 'conseguisteis'. Comp. Zorrilla, *Un año
y un día,* I, 6: «Yo estoy mal acostumbrado / a haber
cuanto necesito.»

CÉSAR   Ya lo sé.
                 (Vase DON RODRIGO *por la puerta
                 del fondo.)*

                      ESCENA XVII

                      GABRIEL, CÉSAR

                 *(Don César va a acercarse a Ga-
                 briel con precipitación; éste le con-
                 tiene con un gesto.)*
GABRIEL   No hagáis extremos,
                 que os perdéis.
CÉSAR   ¿Pero sois vos?...
GABRIEL   ¿Quién?
CÉSAR   Él.
GABRIEL   Porfiado estás.
CÉSAR   Pero...
GABRIEL   ¿Y si fuese quizás?
CÉSAR   Muriera por vos, señor.   1260
GABRIEL   Dormir un poco es mejor.
                 Dejad a Dios lo demás.
                 (Vase por la izquierda, dejando a
                 DON CÉSAR *estupefacto.)*

ACTO SEGUNDO *

La misma decoración del acto primero

ESCENA PRIMERA

DON CÉSAR, *sentado y meditabundo*

Dijo bien: no pertenece
a la tierra el ser de ese hombre.
Me fascina; me enloquece.   1265
¡Que en derredor de su nombre
gira el mundo me parece!
Sí; de cuanto le rodea
es el eje, el punto fijo.
Todo lo demás voltea   1270

---

* Las escenas quinta, sexta, séptima, décima y undé-
cima de este acto no hubieran podido ser terminadas
por mí sin el eficaz auxilio de mi amigo don José María
Díaz, que me ha ayudado a escribirlas, sacándome gene-
rosamente del atolladero en que me tenían metido las
dificultades de su empeño. Las variaciones, inversiones
y adiciones que después han sufrido, las han dejado tales, que ni el señor Díaz ni yo seríamos probablemente
capaces de distinguir en ellas los versos que a cada cual
pertenecen; yo no debo, sin embargo, apropiarme la parte que no me corresponde de estas escenas; y si por
ventura nuestra el público las aplaude, el señor Díaz
tiene derecho a sus aplausos, lo que se complace en decir públicamente su mejor amigo,

José Zorrilla.

** José María Díaz, autor teatral y fácil versificador,
compuso varios dramas de asunto histórico, como
La reina Sara, Juan sin tierra, Virtud y libertinaje o
La muerte de César.

105

en torno suyo. Me dijo
que iba a dormir, pero vela;
no he cesado de sentir
sus pasos, por más cautela
que puso al ir y venir   1275
por su aposento. Recela
que le sorprendan; previene
cauto el porvenir; y pienso
que entre su equipaje tiene
objetos que le conviene   1280
·no mostrar. ¿Es él? ¡Inmenso
riesgo corre!... ¿Y si no es?
¡Ay de mí! Siempre es de Aurora
padre, hermano... algo... A través
doy con todo; me devora   1285
la impaciencia... Llamo, pues.

*(Llama a la puerta por donde se
fue* GABRIEL *en la última escena del
acto primero.)*

ESCENA II

DON CÉSAR, GABRIEL

GABRIEL   ¿Qué me queréis?
CÉSAR   Advertiros
            de que mi padre el alcalde
            vendrá pronto.
GABRIEL   Será en balde.
CÉSAR   No lo será el preveniros   1290
            que toda la noche ha estado
            declaraciones oyendo
            de gentes que ha ido prendiendo.
GABRIEL   Pues el tiempo ha malgastado.
CÉSAR   Vuestra situación es grave.   1295
GABRIEL   ¡Lo sé!
CÉSAR   Quizás un proceso...

_____

1284 *Dar al través*, «metafóricamente vale destruir alguna cosa, abandonarla o perderla» *(Dicc. Aut.).*

GABRIEL	Vuestro padre anda ya en eso.
CÉSAR	¿Culpado saldréis?
GABRIEL	¿Quién sabe?
CÉSAR	Mi padre es hombre tenaz.
GABRIEL	¡Pues a buena parte viene! 1300
CÉSAR	Es que tal vez os condene.
GABRIEL	Cumplo la pena, y en paz.
CÉSAR	Mas si antes que vuelva él
	hacer prevención alguna
	os importa...
GABRIEL	¿A mí? Ninguna. 1305
CÉSAR	¡Señor!
GABRIEL	Llamadme Gabriel.
CÉSAR	Vos lo dijisteis: secreto
	nos liga un nudo a los dos
	y siento a un tiempo por vos
	inclinación y respecto. 1310
	Quisiera una prueba hallar
	irrecusable que daros
	de mi fe para obligaros
	sin recelo a confiar
	en mí.
GABRIEL	¡Vaya! ¡Estáis chistoso, 1315
	por Dios! En este aposento
	queríais hace un momento
	atravesarme furioso,
	¿y ahora mi confianza
	conquistaros pretendéis 1320
	con ofertas? Ya sabéis
	que la razón se me alcanza
	de esa simpatía oculta
	que me tenéis; y a respeto
	muéveos sólo mi secreto, 1325
	que vuestra aprensión abulta
	tanto, que seguís mi viaje
	vos y a atajarle se arroja
	el juez, porque se os antoja
	que soy un gran personaje. 1330

1305 *Os importa*, 'os conviene (cfr. v. 177).

CÉSAR	Las apariencias están
	por ahora en contra vuestra.
GABRIEL	Pues la verdad se demuestra
	con la verdad, capitán.
CÉSAR	Pues bien: antes que un proceso 1335
	entable el juez contra vos
	valiera más, ¡vive Dios!...
GABRIEL	¿Qué me diera por confeso
	yo mismo? Que haciendo justo
	del juez el empeño, diera 1340
	por supuesto yo que era
	no sé quién, y por dar gusto
	él al rey, y diversión
	al populacho, me ahorcara
	y Aurora por vos quedara? 1345
	¿Es ésa vuestra cuestión?
CÉSAR	No así abuséis imprudente
	de ese misterioso influjo
	que a respeto me redujo
	para con vos, e insolente 1350
	mi lealtad y mi amor
	ultrajéis. Ésta es sincera,
	y mi pasión verdadera,
	señor.
GABRIEL	¡Dale con señor!
	Vos sois noble y yo villano. 1355
	Vos sois gentil caballero
	y yo humilde pastelero;
	decid Gabriel liso y llano.
CÉSAR	Me vais a desesperar.
GABRIEL	Y vos me vais a aburrir. 1360
CÉSAR	¡Vos obstinado en fingir!
GABRIEL	¡Vos empeñado en hablar!
CÉSAR	¿Pronto a todo, fascinado
	que estoy por vos no miráis?
GABRIEL	¿Y os mando yo que tengáis 1365
	de mi porvenir cuidado?

1345 *Por vos*, 'para vos'
1346 *Cuestión*, 'propuesta'

108

CÉSAR	Una palabra tan sólo.
GABRIEL	¿Vais a volver a lo mismo?
CÉSAR	De esperanza en este abismo
	dadme un rayo.
GABRIEL	¿Cuál?
CÉSAR	Sin dolo, 1370
	prometedme responder
	a una pregunta.
GABRIEL	Si puedo,
	responderé.
CÉSAR	No hayáis miedo
	que os pueda comprometer
	la respuesta. ¿Sois de Aurora 1375
	padre?
GABRIEL	No conoció más
	que a mí por padre jamás.
CÉSAR	¡Oh! ¡No lo sois!
GABRIEL	En buena hora
	que no lo soy os diré;
	mas de este arcano la llave 1380
	tengo solo.
CÉSAR	¿Ella no sabe?...
GABRIEL	Nunca se lo revelé.
CÉSAR	¿Y la amáis?
GABRIEL	Mucho, quizá
	mucho más de lo que debo.
CÉSAR	¿Conque la guardáis?...
GABRIEL	¡Mancebo! 1385
CÉSAR	Sí, para vuestra.
GABRIEL	Jamás.
	Pero tened desde aquí,
	y para siempre entendido,
	que es mujer que no ha nacido
	para vos ni para mí. 1390
CÉSAR	¡Cielos!
GABRIEL	De toda esperanza
	despedíos.
CÉSAR	¿Ofrecida
	está a Dios?

GABRIEL	No: está elegida
	para prenda de venganza.
CÉSAR	¿Vuestra?
GABRIEL	Yo no voy en pos 1395
	de venganzas.
CÉSAR	¿Es quizá
	de su familia?
GABRIEL	De más
	arriba.
CÉSAR	¡Del rey!
GABRIEL	De Dios.
	(¡Imposible atar un cabo!
	¡Su ser parece que abarca 1400
	con la altivez del monarca
	la abnegación del esclavo!)

ESCENA III

DON CÉSAR, GABRIEL, *un* ALGUACIL

ALGUACIL	Su señoría el alcalde
	don Rodrigo.
CÉSAR	En el momento
	volved a vuestro aposento. 1405
GABRIEL	La entrevista será en balde.

ESCENA IV

DON CÉSAR, DON RODRIGO

RODRIGO	¿Seguros ambos?
CÉSAR	Seguros,
	señor.
RODRIGO	Todo lo recelo
	de él, que es audaz.

1404 *En el momento,* 'inmediatamente'.

CÉSAR	Sin embargo,
	no temáis ningún extremo. [1410]
RODRIGO	¿Le has hablado?
CÉSAR	Sí, un instante
RODRIGO	¿Y qué dice? ¿Muestra miedo
	de la justicia?
CÉSAR	Ninguno.
RODRIGO	Bravea, ¿eh?
CÉSAR	Nada de eso;
	tranquilo está; tal vez tiene [1415]
	de justificarse medios.
RODRIGO	Imposible: en contra suya
	tengo datos manifiestos.
CÉSAR	¿Sabéis ya?...
RODRIGO	Nada. Hilo a hilo
	voy la madeja cogiendo. [1420]
	Parece que hay en la vida
	de ese hombre tantos enredos
	que sólo a fuerza de maña
	y paciencia, deshacerlos
	es posible. Mas no es [1425]
	lo que me trae más inquieto
	lo intrincado del negocio,
	que el laberinto estoy hecho
	a recorrer de las leyes.
	Acósame el alma empero [1430]
	una agitación, que no
	sé distinguir con acierto
	si es afán o repugnancia,
	si es duda o presentimiento.
	Hay un punto de la historia [1435]
	de ese hombre cuyo misterio
	del tiempo de mi mayor
	pesar me trae un recuerdo.
CÉSAR	¿De cuándo?
RODRIGO	Tú no lo sabes:
	eras aún pequeñuelo. [1440]
	Luego, estas causas políticas

[1428] *Estoy hecho*, 'estoy acostumbrado', como en el v. 400

                    de Portugal me trajeron
                    siempre desgracias. Parece
                    que el destino, con empeño
                    fatal para mí, me pone   1445
                    portugueses siempre en medio
                    de mi camino. Seis años
                    anduve por aquel reino
                    en comisión especial,
                    los rebeldes persiguiendo,   1450
                    y como todos conspiran
                    contra el rey y su gobierno,
                    yo soy allí detestado.
CÉSAR   Fuisteis quizá muy severo.
RODKIGO   Fui de Felipe segundo   1455
                    leal servidor. Tan terco
                    como ellos en resistirse
                    fui yo en desplomar sobre ellos
                    todo el rigor de las leyes,
                    y a fe que no me arrepiento.   1460
                    Rebeldes eran: cumplí
                    con mi obligación; mas tengo
                    todavía que volverles
                    cierta partida, y si puedo,
                    quedarán tan bien pagados   1465
                    como yo bien satisfecho.
                    Mas· las horas vuelan. César,
                    déjame aquí con el preso.
                    Guarda esa puerta por fuera
                    y si llamo acude presto.   1470

                          ESCENA V

                        DON RODRIGO

                    Las diligencias primeras
                    terminaron, y el proceso
─────────────
    [1463] *Volver*, «restituir lo que se ha tomado o quitado»
(Dicc. Aut.). Comp. Zorrilla, *Vivir loco y morir más*, I,
5: «No, mi honra no te di; / tú, Román, me la quitas-
te. / Vuélvemela, que no es tuya.»

está entablado. ¡Malditos
portugueses!... ¡Qué de enredos!
Dieciséis, y gente toda   1475
de probidad, de respeto
y hasta de ciencia, declaran
que en el fondo de su pecho
existe la convicción
de que el trágico suceso   1480
es falso y que están seguros
de que en África no ha muerto.
Unos en Cintra le han visto,
y en Cintra fue donde él mesmo
dijo que compró su espada.   1485
Otros cruzando le vieron
el Tajo una tarde; el fraile
dice que en su monasterio
le rezó él mismo una misa
antes del alba, y a esto   1490
para obligarle, del Papa
le mostró bula, y que cierto
está de que él era. Y todos
afirman con juramento
que fueron a Madrigal   1495
y que le reconocieron.
Ahora bien, señor alcalde,
pise su merced con tiento,
que es la tierra escurridiza.
O es él, o no; en los decretos   1500
de Dios todo cabe y todo
cabe en los humanos yerros.

1484 *Mesmo*, arcaísmo necesario aquí para mantener la
rima en *e - o*. Comp. Zorrilla, *El zapatero y el rey*, 1.ª parte, IV, 13: «Y en los secretos / de nuestras gentes hablaba / como en sus negocios mesmos.»

1489 Comp. Cuéllar, *El pastelero de Madrigal*, jornada III: «Díjose públicamente/que el rey Sebastián ha-
bía/oído misa cierto día/en Cabo de San Vicente,/en un
descalzo convento;/y cuando de allí salió/un hombre pasar le vio...»

1501 Comp. Zorrilla, *O.C.*, ed. N. Alonso Cortés, II, 339 *b*:
«Eso dice el recuerdo legendario/y de Dios en los juicios
todo cabe.»

Si en verdad es él, alcalde,
no será en verdad muy cuerdo
ahorcarle sin dar al rey   1505
de todo aviso primero.
Si es un impostor... también
le avisaré, y a lo menos,

si se yerra, entre los dos
el error compartiremos.   1510

ESCENA VI

DON RODRIGO, GABRIEL

RODRIGO   ¡Hidalgo!
GABRIEL   Más alto pico.
RODRIGO   ¿Caballero?
GABRIEL   Todavía
más alto.
RODRIGO   Su señoría
me excuse si no le aplico
su título verdadero.   1515
Mas hablemos un instante
y de hoy para en adelante
no erraré en él, porque espero
que aquí y a solas los dos
me diréis la jerarquía   1520
que ocupáis.
GABRIEL   Su señoría
•   espera bien, pues ¡por Dios
que sabiendo yo quién es

1511 *Más alto pico*, 'tengo mayores pretensiones'. Comp.
Cervantes, *El coloquio de los perros:* «Más alto picaba
mi amo, otro camino era el suyo»; Quevedo, *Buscón*, ed.
F. Lázaro, I, 7: «Señor, ya soy otro, y otros mis pensamientos; más alto pico, y más autoridad me importa
tener.» Zorrilla, *O.C.*, ed. N. Alonso Cortés, I, 1875 *b*: «Yo
ceso aquí: hay situaciones/que por muy alto que pique,/
no hay pluma que las explique/cual las siente el corazón.»

114

	debo de hablar sin reparo!	
RODRIGO	Eso quiero, que habléis claro.	1525
GABRIEL	Ya veréis.	
RODRIGO	Decidme, pues,	

señor Gabriel.

(Va a sentarse a la mesa.)

| GABRIEL | Un momento, | |

señor don Rodrigo.

| RODRIGO | ¿Qué? | |

| GABRIEL | ¿Vais a sentaros? | |
| RODRIGO | Sí, a fe. *(Se | |

[*sienta.*)

(GABRIEL trae con mucha calma una silla y la coloca frente a la mesa de DON RODRIGO.)

¿Qué hacéis?

GABRIEL	Lo mismo; me siento.	1530
RODRIGO	Yo soy alcalde de corte.	
GABRIEL	Sí; mas no sabéis quién soy	

yo y si mal o bien estoy
sentado ante vos.

| RODRIGO | ¿Del porte | |

audaz de que usáis conmigo,   1535
buenas razones supongo
que me daréis?

| GABRIEL | Me propongo | |

hacerlo así.

RODRIGO	Pues prosigo.	
GABRIEL	Seguid.	
RODRIGO	La duda primera	

que al escucharos me asalta   1540
es la de que nombre os falta
digno de vuestra alta esfera.

GABRIEL	Lo tengo.	
RODRIGO	Pues no lo sé.	
GABRIEL	Gabriel Espinosa.	
RODRIGO	¿Un tal	

pastelero en·Madrigal?   1545

1534 *Porte,* cfr. v. 119.

GABRIEL   Sí.
RODRIGO   Pues poneos en pie,
            señor pastelero.
                (GABRIEL *se levanta*.)
                            Así:
            ante el juez sólo se sienta
            quien altos títulos cuenta.
GABRIEL   Como me sucede a mí.   1550
            (Se vuelve a sentar.)
RODRIGO   (Ir le tengo de dejar
            por donde quiera, y a ver.)
GABRIEL   (Pienso que mi proceder
            le empieza a desconcertar.)
RODRIGO   ¿Pues cómo oficio tan bajo,   1555
            siendo tan alto, elegís?
GABRIEL   Por vivir, cual vos vivís
            de la ley, de mi trabajo.
RODRIGO   Mas mi toga y aranceles
            no deshonran.
GABRIEL   No, a fe mía;   1560
            pero yo hacer no sabía
            otra cosa que pasteles.
RODRIGO   (No es lerdo el señor Gabriel.)
GABRIEL   (Astuto es el don Rodrigo.)
RODRIGO   (Por aquí nada consigo,   1565
            pero yo daré con él
            en tierra al fin.) ¡Caballero!
GABRIEL   Mandad.
RODRIGO   Una relación
            que os llamará la atención
            contaros quisiera.
GABRIEL   Espero   1570
            que será, por lo galana,
            lo discreta y lo curiosa,
            la invención más ingeniosa
            del señor de Santillana.
RODRIGO   Pues oíd. Buen capitán   1575
            más que rey, de fe tesoro,

[1568] *Relación*, cfr. v. 724.

	allá en las playas del moro	
	murió el rey Don Sebastián.	
	¿Supongo que de una historia	
	tan pública oísteis algo?	1580
GABRIEL	¡Si vierais qué poco valgo	
	en esto de la memoria!	
RODRIGO	En vuestro horno no me extraña	
	que estéis de noticias falto.	
GABRIEL	Sé que a su muerte de un salto	1585
	pasó Portugal a España.	
RODRIGO	Justo; mas hoy los noveles	
	vasallos, por sacudir	
	sus leyes, dan en decir	
	a los pueblos a ellas fieles	1590
	que ha sido una usurpación,	
	y pregonan de concierto	
	del rey en África muerto	
	la fausta resurrección.	
GABRIEL	¡Oiga! No está mal pensado.	1595
RODRIGO	No; mas la dificultad	
	era el dar en realidad	
	con el rey resucitado.	
	Buscósele con esmero	
	y hallóse, por toda cosa,	1600
	un tal Gabriel Espinosa,	
	en Madrigal pastelero.	
GABRIEL	Vamos, ya caigo; el error	
	de esta semejanza mía	
	hizo a vuestra señoría	1605
	creer que soy...	
RODRIGO	*(Interrumpiéndole.)*	
	Un impostor.	
GABRIEL	¿Quién lo dice?	
RODRIGO	Yo lo digo,	
	y el rey Felipe, y el mundo	
	entero.	
GABRIEL	Pues miente el mundo,	
	y el rey, y vos, don Rodrigo.	1610
RODRIGO	Inútil es vuestra audacia;	
	testigos tengo allá fuera	

que os acusan por doquiera
por impostor.

GABRIEL   ¡Vaya en gracia!
Mas permitid que os arguya: 1615

para llamarme impostor,
esa impostura, señor,
ha de ser mía y no suya.
¿Y dónde hay hombre capaz
de jurar que he dicho yo   1620
que era el rey?

RODRIGO   Vos mismo no.

GABRIEL   Entonces dejadme en paz.
Si yo me parezco a un rey
y el vulgo por rey me tiene,
citar al vulgo os conviene,   1625
pero no a mí, ante la ley.

RODRIGO   ¡Espinosa!

GABRIEL   Don Rodrigo,
aunque en leyes sois muy ducho,
os falta que aprender mucho
para habéroslas conmigo.   1630
¿Cree, buen juez, vuestra altiveza
que a ser yo el que habéis pensado
estaríais vos sentado
y cubierta la cabeza?

            (DON RODRIGO *se levanta y se descu-*
            bre conforme va hablando GABRIEL.)

1614 ¡*Vaya en gracia*! Expresión de desdén, equivalente, en este caso, a '¡qué me acusen!'.

1616 *Argüir*, «acusar convenciendo a alguno y hacién-
dole ver alguna cosa mala que ha ejecutado o defecto
que tiene» *(Dicc. Aut.).*

1631 «Altivo, el soberbio y levantado de pensamientos.
Altiveza, la tal soberbia» (Covarrubias). Comp. Lope de
Vega. *Lanza por lanza, la de Luis de Almanza,* acto I
(BAE, 212, p. 90 *a*): «Cogió a traición la furia impe-
tuosa /del andaluz soberbio la altiveza»; Zorrilla, *Ganar
perdiendo,* III, 7: «Que es ya mucha ceguedad, / osadía
y altiveza, / acosar vuestra nobleza / contra nuestra
voluntad.»

1632 *A ser yo,* fórmula condicional (cfr. v. 454).

118

	Rodrigo de Santillana,	1635
	a ser yo el que habéis creído
	hubierais vos ya salido
	¡vive Dios! por la ventana.
RODRIGO	(Por quien soy que me ha turbado.
	¿Si contarán con razón	1640
	lo de la resurrección?)
GABRIEL	(¡Pobre juez!)
RODRIGO	(No habría osado
	palabras tan arrogantes
	decir.) Señor... Si en mal hora...
GABRIEL	Ni tan bajo como ahora	1645
	ni tan alto como antes.
RODRIGO	(Tanta majestad me asombra.)
	Gabriel, quienquiera que seáis,
	manda en mí el rey que digáis
	quién sois en fin.
GABRIEL	Una sombra.	1650

Y porque acabemos voy,
y afanes para excusaros,
señor Santillana, a daros
cuenta exacta de quién soy.
Nací donde quiso Dios;   1655
si de noble raza, bien
se demuestra en mí; de quién
me importa callar, y a vos
saber de mí no os importa.
Prestadme empero atención,   1660
pues va a ser mi relación,
cuanto complicada, corta.
Apenas cumplí la edad
que se llama juventud,
con loca solicitud,   1665
con ciega temeridad
abandoné mis hogares

1649 Comp. la situación que se inicia aquí con otra
muy similar, en la leyenda «Las píldoras de Salomón»
(Zorrilla, *O.C.*, ed. N. Alonso Cortés, I, 685 *a* y ss.).

1661 *Relación*, cfr. v. 724.

1662 Tan corta como complicada.

y en más remoto hemisferio
dueño del mayor imperio,
pirata fui de los mares.   1670
En ellos, profundo osario
de cien bajeles, guerrero
alcé mi estandarte fiero,
de Asia y Europa corsario,
y amontoné más tesoros   1675
que guarda el mar en su centro
y arenas quemadas dentro
de sus desiertos los moros.

Ebrio con tanta riqueza
dejé mi gente y la mar,   1680
queriendo en tierra ostentar
mi valor y mi grandeza,
y con el nombre supuesto
de marqués de Mari-Alba,
al lado del duque de Alba   1685
gané en sus glorias un puesto
y en la cabeza esta herida; *(La mues-*
                                                  [tra.)
bien es que al que me la abrió
con mi espada le abrí yo
las puertas de la otra vida.   1690

RODRIGO   No os daría poca pena
               después,

GABRIEL   ¡Fue un fatal desliz!...
RODRIGO   *(Mirándole a la frente.)*
               No es mala la cicatriz.

GABRIEL   La cuchillada fue buena.
               No me tendió, sin embargo;   1695
               el furor me mantenía
               y combatí todavía
               hasta caer tiempo largo.

               Mas harto al fin del oficio
               de lidiar en tierra firme,   1700

1688 'Bien es [*cierto*] que', fórmula concesiva.
1700 *Lidiar*, 'luchar' (lat. *litigare*). Comp. Zorrilla, *El excomulgado*, I, 5: «Cayó del rebelde en manos / y sólo

licencia para salirme
por entonces del servicio
al duque de Alba pedí.
Diómela el duque cortés,
y vedla. *(Le da un papel.)*

RODRIGO   Su firma es: 1705
para el marqués...

GABRIEL   Para mí.
Di, pues, vuelta hacia la Corte,
sirviéndome mucho en ella
primero mi buena estrella,
después mi lujoso porte.   1710
Por ese tiempo de vos
nadie hablaba todavía
y a mí el rey me recibía
con grande amistad.

RODRIGO   (¡Gran Dios,
entonces fue cuando vino   1715
el monarca portugués
a Castilla! ¿Será, pues,
este hombre?) ¿Quién previno
más festejos a usarced?

GABRIEL   No hay por qué ocultarlo al fin;   1720
el conde de Medellín
con tantos me hizo merced
que corresponder no supe
como era mi obligación.

RODRIGO   ¿Y os tuvo tal atención   1725
en Madrid?

GABRIEL   No: en Guadalupe.

RODRIGO   ¿En ese pueblo?

GABRIEL   Sí tal.

---

salvarse pudo / por su lanza y por su escudo / lidiando
contra villanos.»

1710 *Porte*, cfr. v. 119.

1716 El rey Don Sebastián mantuvo conversaciones con
Felipe II en el monasterio de Guadalupe, a finales de
1576 (cfr. A. Rodríguez-Moñino, *Viaje a España del rey
Don Sebastián de Portugal*, Madrid, 1956).

1719 *Usarced*, contracción de 'vuestra merced'.

121

RODRIGO	No recuerdo de que allí...
GABRIEL	Al rey de España en él vi
	junto al rey de Portugal.	1730
	Después... abrid, Santillana,
	un paréntesis aquí,
	y poned en él de mí
	cuanto mal os diere gana.
	Basteos saber, don Rodrigo,	1735
	que perdí mi oro y·mi gloria
	sin que una buena memoria
	me quedara, ni un amigo.
	Por tierra extranjera anduve
	errante como un bandido,	1740
	y el pan que en ella he comido
	que mendigármelo tuve.
	Mas el desengaño, al fin,
	¿qué ánimo feroz no doma?
	Llegué arrepentido a Roma	1745
	remando en un bergantín.
	Visité a Su Santidad;
	confesión le hice de todo
	y el Santo Padre halló modo
	de absolverme en su piedad,	1750
	dándome por penitencia

1749 *El Santo Padre,* expresión censurada como «grosero galicismo» por Baralt (*Dicc. de galicismos,* 2.ª ed., 1890) y rechazada también por Mir y Noguera (*Prontuario de hispanismo y barbarismo,* 1908). Pero ya existe en el mismo sentido un dictamen anterior, del P. Isla, *Fray Gerundio de Campazas,* IV, 8: «Una mujer de manto /no ha de llamar al Papa el *Padre Santo,* / porque, cuadre o no cuadre, / es más francés llamarle el *Santo Padre.*» Vid. otro ejemplo en Zorrilla, El *excomulgado,* I, 3: «Y en vista / de esos datos, respondáis / al Santo Padre.»

1750 Comp. Zorrilla, en la leyenda «La azucena silvestre» (*O.C.,* ed. N. Alonso Cortés, I, 819 a): «Crucé veloz/ ríos y montes, y llegando a Roma,/del rebaño de Cristo ante el pastor/postrado de mis crímenes nefandos/hice entera y contrita confesión./El pontífice santo, del Eterno/en la tierra vicario, mi dolor/y mi arrepentimiento contemplando,/con estas condiciones me absolvió».

	de los pecados sin cuento	
	que abrasan mi pensamiento	
	y me abruman la conciencia,	
	que emprendiera el viaje entero	1755
	del Santo Sepulcro a pie.	
RODRIGO	¿Y lo hicisteis?	
GABRIEL	Por la fe	

lo juro de caballero.
Y aún fue más: Su Santidad
me ordenó que renunciara   1760
mi jerarquía y que echara
mi nombre en la eternidad.
He aquí por qué no os lo digo.
Penitente le arrojé
dentro de ella y le olvidé   1765
para siempre, don Rodrigo.

RODRIGO ¡Interesante proemio!
Y a ser cierto...

GABRIEL Lo es tanto
que tengo del Padre Santo
por testimonio y por premio   1770
esta bula. Me conviene
que la leáis. *(Le da otro papel.)*

RODRIGO Os la tomo.
No está vuestro nombre.

GABRIEL ¿Y cómo,
si a quien se dio no le tiene?

RODRIGO Proseguid.

GABRIEL Mi protector   1775
el Papa en sus santos juicios
utilizar mis servicios
imaginó, y fiador
constituyéndose mío,
me envió a un poderoso estado,   1780
que al verme tan bien fiado
fió un bajel a mi brío.

1752 *Sin cuento*, 'innumerables'. Comp. Cervantes, *El
amante liberal*: «Mis ojos han derramado, derraman y
derramarán lágrimas sin cuento.»

123

Venecia fue nuevamente
del corsario protectora;
ved de tan noble señora,   1785
don Rodrigo, la patente. *(Le da otro*
                              [papel.)
Volví al mar; del africano
las costas guardando anduve
y en un combate que tuve
los dos dedos de esta mano   1790
perdí; mas, su nave hundida,
cogí a mi enemigo preso.
La mano llevo por eso
siempre en el guante metida.
El rumbo a Venecia di   1795
contento, cuando topé
con un barco de no sé
qué argelino; resolví
abordarle, y por despojo
de esta sangrienta jornada   1800
rescaté una desgraciada
niña, a quien con noble arrojo
defendía un pobre anciano,
y a quien, según esperaba,
iba a vender por esclava   1805
el argelino inhumano.

RODRIGO   ¿Y esa niña es doña Aurora?
GABRIEL   Que pasa por hija mía.
RODRIGO   ¿Familia, pues, no tenía?
GABRIEL   Y tiene.
RODRIGO   ¿Por qué hasta ahora   1810
          no se la habéis vos devuelto?
GABRIEL   Necesito presentar
          documentos que probar
          puedan que es ella, y resuelto
          estoy conmigo a guardarla   1815
          mientras tanto.

[1786] *Patente*, «título o despacho que se da de orden del
rey para el goce de algún empleo» *(Dicc. Aut.).*

RODRIGO   ¿Y dónde están
los documentos?

GABRIEL   Vendrán
muy pronto, porque entregarla
mucho a su padre me importa.

RODRIGO   Pensáis que él os dé...

GABRIEL   Al contrario; 1820
las riquezas del corsario
son para ella.

RODRIGO   Porción corta
no será.

GABRIEL   ¡No habrá, a fe mía,
quien competirla pretenda!
Millones tiene en hacienda;   1825
millones en pedrería.

RODRIGO   ¿Dónde?

GABRIEL   En Venecia.

RODRIGO   ¿Estarán
en el poder?...

GABRIEL   Del Estado.
Es ahijada del Senado
serenísimo y tendrán   1830
que devolvérsela salva
sus parientes a Venecia,
rica y libre, cual la precia
el marqués de Mari-Alba.
Ya nuestra historia sabéis.   1835
A qué vine a Madrigal
y a qué voy a Portugal,
indagadlo si podéis.
Ni sabréis de mí otra cosa,
ni nadie más de mí sabe;   1840
sólo Dios tiene la llave
del corazón de Espinosa;

1819 *Me importa,* cfr. v. 177.

1842 Comp. Zorrilla, *O.C.,* ed. N. Alonso·Cortés, I, 1009 *a:*
«Sólo Dios tiene la llave/de su oscuro porvenir»; *íd.,*
I, 2117 *a b:* «La clave/de la inquietud de un alma que
necesita amar/la tiene Dios, que guarda del corazón la
llave.»

125

	y si más de lo que digo	
	saber importa a la ley	
	llevadme a Madrid; el rey	1845
	me conoce, don Rodrigo.	
RODRIGO	(Su altivez en confusión	
	me pone y su majestad	
	me asombra. ¿Será verdad	
	lo de la resurrección?	1850

y si más de lo que digo
saber importa a la ley
llevadme a Madrid; el rey   1845
me conoce, don Rodrigo.

RODRIGO   (Su altivez en confusión
me pone y su majestad
me asombra. ¿Será verdad
lo de la resurrección?   1850
Si miente lo hace con tal
aplomo y con tanta fe,
que a poco más le daré
por el rey de Portugal.
Mas no ha de quedar por mí.   1855
Yo he de apurar este arcano;
no dirán que de un villano
impostor juguete fui.)

(Llama DON RODRIGO *y habla en secreto con un alguacil, que se vuelve
a marchar.)*

GABRIEL   (¿Secretos con el ministro
de justicia? Estoy al cabo: 1860
tenemos careo; alabo
por sorprendente el registro.)

ESCENA VII

DON RODRIGO, GABRIEL, *el marqués de* TAVIRA

GABRIEL *se aparta a un lado y, sen-
tándose, se mantiene en toda esta
escena dando la espalda al marqués.)*

1846 Comp. Cuéllar, *El pastelero de Madrigal*, jornada III: «Rodrigo.—El rey, atento a la ley,/es fuerza que
justo sea. GABRIEL.—Pues lléveme a que me vea,/ que
bien me conoce el Rey». Escosura, *Ni rey ni Roque*, libro IV, capítulo 6: «Si el rey quiere enterarse de quién
yo sea, personas tiene a su lado que me conocen, y
muchas.»
1853 y s. *Dar por*, 'considerar'.
1862 *Registro*, 'investigación'. *Registrar*, «examinar y es-
pecular alguna cosa» *(Dicc. Aut.).*

126

RODRIGO   Señor marqués, perdonad
             si cumpliendo obligaciones
             de juez...
MARQUÉS   Vuestras atenciones   1865
             os agradezco en verdad;
             pero advertid que mañana
             quiero dejar a Castilla,
             y que el mesón de una villa
             no es el lugar, Santillana,   1870
             que me conviene; os prevengo
             que hombre soy muy principal
             y de todo Portugal
             la sangre más limpia tengo.
GABRIEL   (Si mi mente no delira,   1875
             ¡por Dios, que está en mi presencia
             la hinchada magnificencia
             del buen marqués de Tavira!)
RODRIGO   No os he de faltar en nada;
             mas quiero que me digáis   1880
             sin doblez cuanto sepáis
             de aquella fatal jornada
             de África; corre el rumor
             por ahí de que no es cierto
             que Don Sebastián ha muerto;   1885
             y aun hay algún impostor
             que usurpa su augusto nombre.
GABRIEL   (Y el gesto y el ademán.
                 (Mirándole.)
             ¡Pobre rey Don Sebastián
             si en manos cae de este hombre!)   1890
RODRIGO   Conque decid: ¿es verdad
             que en África el rey murió?
             Que allá estuvisteis sé yo
             con toda seguridad.
             Hablad, marqués de Tavira;   1895
             vuestra nobleza es notoria.
             No echéis en su ejecutoria
             el borrón de una mentira.
MARQUÉS   Inexperto capitán
             de mi edad en el vigor,   1900

127

	esclavo fue mi valor	
	de mi rey Don Sebastián.	
	Juntos un mismo bajel	
	a tierras del africano	
	nos llevó; como un hermano	1905
	al combate fui con él.	
	Un mar de sangre corrió.	
	Pero al partirse la suerte	
	sólo el baldón y la muerte	
	a nosotros nos tocó.	1910
GABRIEL	(No sé por qué la memoria	
	de ese lance me enternece	
	y me irrita; no parece	
	sino que cuentan mi historia.)	
MARQUÉS	El rey, que escudo y celada	1915
	tiró para más grandeza	
	de valor, en la cabeza	
	recibió una cuchillada	
	tal, que la frente serena	
	le rajó hasta la nariz.	1920
RODRIGO	*(A GABRIEL.)*	
	¡No es mala esa cicatriz!	
GABRIEL	La cuchillada fue buena.	
RODRIGO	*(Al MARQUÉS.)*	
	Seguid.	
MARQUÉS	El rey, nuevo Marte	
	de tan sangrienta jornada,	
	continuó, rota la espada,	1925
	defendiendo su estandarte,	
	hasta que el filo fatal	
	de un yatagán africano	
	segó de su izquierda mano	
	dos dedos.	
RODRIGO	*(A GABRIEL.)*	
	Si no oí mal	1930
	me habéis dicho...	

[1928] Yatagán, 'sable o alfanje usado por los orientales'
Comp. Zorrilla, *O.C.*, ed. N. Alonso Cortés, I, 1331: «Y
a tiempo fue. Su yatagán sangriento/Muley blandiendo,
apareció a sus ojos».

GABRIEL	*(Con calma y sin volverse.)*
	Que perdí
	dos dedos en un combate
	naval.
RODRIGO	Marqués, el remate
	de la batalla.
MARQUÉS	Caí
	bajo un hachazo a los pies 1935
	de mi rey... y no vi más;
	perdí el sentido.
RODRIGO	Quizás
	al recobrarle después...
MARQUÉS	Ya no le hallé; con la luna
	tomé del mar el camino, 1940
	maltratado peregrino,
	caballero sin fortuna,
	llevando en el corazón
	el recuerdo de una hazaña
	que será, no para España, 1945
	para su rey un baldón.
RODRIGO	¡Señor marqués de Tavira!
	Esa frase infamatoria...
MARQUÉS	No tendrá mi ejecutoria
	el borrón de una mentira. 1950
RODRIGO	Conque, en fin, ¿el rey murió?
MARQUÉS	No lo sé, ¡por vida mía!
	Si lo supiera os diría,
	señor alcalde, que no.
RODRIGO	*(Al marqués, llevándole aparte.)*
	¿Buena memoria tenéis? 1955
MARQUÉS	Buena.
RODRIGO	¿Y vista?
MARQUÉS	Perspicaz.
RODRIGO	Si vive y le veis, ¿capaz
	de conocerle seréis?
MARQUÉS	¡Si vive habéis dicho!
RODRIGO	Sí.
MARQUÉS	¿Tenéis, pues, noticias de él? 1960

1949 y s. Comp. con los vs. 1898 y 1899.

RODRIGO	¿Recibisteis un papel
	anónimo?
MARQUÉS	Recibí
	uno ayer.
RODRIGO	¿Y qué os decía?
MARQUÉS	Las señas de un personaje
	me daban que iba de viaje	1965
	y aquí a hospedarse vendría;
	mandábanme a un comerciante
	que me daría dinero
	para pagar del viajero
	el gasto, y que en el instante	1970
	fuera a cobrarlo y corriera
	con el pago, y tras el tal
	viajero hacia Portugal
	la vuelta sin falta diera.
RODRIGO	¿Y cobrasteis?
MARQUÉS	Sí, cobré.	1975
RODRIGO	¿Y pagasteis?
MARQUÉS	¿Pues cobrado
	por mí, no fuera pagado?
RODRIGO	Perdonad, ¿e iréis?
MARQUÉS	Iré.
RODRIGO	¿Luego sabéis de quién es
	el anónimo?
MARQUÉS	Aunque no	1980
	lo sé, jamás me engañó
	en uno.
RODRIGO	¿Os ha escrito, pues,
	otros?
MARQUÉS	Varios.
RODRIGO	Sobre asuntos...
MARQUÉS	Secretos.
RODRIGO	Mas ¿ciertos?
MARQUÉS	Sí.
	Siempre que salieron vi	1985
	ciertos en todos sus puntos.
GABRIEL	(¡Con famosos servidores

1987 *Famoso*, calificación irónica con la acepción 'co-

	cuenta el rey Don Sebastián!	
	¡Pobres reyes! ¡Siempre dan	
	con tontos o con traidores!)	1990
MARQUÉS	Si he concluido, no es cosa	
	de estarme aquí sin provecho.	
RODRIGO	Perdonadme que aún insista;	
	mas ya que memoria y vista	
	tenéis, de ese hombre en acecho	1995
	estad, y del rey en nombre	
	os mando decir, marqués,	
	si le conocéis, quién es.	
GABRIEL	(Santillana es todo un hombre.)	
MARQUÉS	(¿Qué diablos de juego es éste?	2000
	Posición más engorrosa!)	
RODRIGO	(A GABRIEL.)	
	Señor Gabriel Espinosa,	
	permitid que os manifieste	
	que habéis descortés andado	
	con el marqués de Tavira,	2005
	que está mirándoos con ira.	
GABRIEL	¿Se lo habéis vos ordenado?	
RODRIGO	Ved que son los portugueses	
	quisquillosos; despedidle	
	al menos; vamos, decidle	2010
	cuatro palabras corteses.	
GABRIEL	Voy, pues que vos lo queréis.	
RODRIGO	(Yo apuraré la mentira.)	
GABRIEL	¿Señor marqués de Tavira?	
MARQUÉS	¡Jesucristo!	
GABRIEL	¿Qué tenéis?	2015
MARQUÉS	Señor... ¿Sois vos?... ¿Aún vivís?	
GABRIEL	¡Si vivo! ¿Pues no lo veis?	
	¿Pero qué diablos decís?	
MARQUÉS	¡Ese gesto, ese ademán,	
	esa voz, ese semblante	2020
	que no olvidé ni un instante!	

---

sa buena y perfecta y que merece fama' (Dicc. Aut.).
Cfr. A. Rosenblat, *Buenas y malas palabras* [5], Caracas-
Madrid, 1969, págs. 15 ss.

(Cae de rodillas.)
Es el rey Don Sebastián.

GABRIEL   ¡Imbécil! A ser de cierto
Don Sebastián, ¿no reparas
que antes que me delataras   2025
a mis pies te hubiera muerto?

MARQUÉS   ¡Jesús!

GABRIEL   Señor Santillana,
¿que sé, daréis por supuesto,
que sois vos quien me ha
                    [dispuesto
una farsa tan villana?   2030

RODRIGO   ¡Yo! ¿Farsa?... ¿Y con que interés?

GABRIEL   Salta a los ojos; es fuerza
que ya la opinión se tuerza
del buen pueblo portugués.
Interesa a un impostor   2035
ahorcar porque más en él
no espere y soy yo, Gabriel,
el que os parece mejor.
Ya veis que os he comprendido.
Vos y ese hombre los traidores   2040
sois aquí y los impostores;
con él estáis convenido.

RODRIGO   ¡Yo!

GABRIEL   Traedme otro marqués.
como ese; aunque sean doce.
Ni ese sandio me conoce,   2045
ni es noble, ni es portugués.

(GABRIEL se mete desenfadadamente en su cuarto, dejando estupefactos al MARQUÉS *y a* DON RODRIGO.)*

RODRIGO VIII

DON RODRIGO, *el marqués de* TAVIRA

RODRIGO   Ese hombre me va a volver
el juicio a mí. ¡Por mi vida

que está buena la salida!
No me queda más que ver. 2050
Mas me pone en confusión
su aplomo, su majestad
y su audacia... ¿Habrá verdad
en esta resurrección?

MARQUÉS   Sandio dijo..., sandio soy, 2055
mas contenerme no pude.

RODRIGO   ¿Es él?

MARQUÉS   No habrá quien lo dude.

RODRIGO   ¿Estáis seguro?

MARQUÉS   Lo estoy.

RODRIGO   ¿Engañado no os habrán
vuestro error y su apariencia? 2060

MARQUÉS   No.

RODRIGO   ¿Jurarais en conciencia?...

MARQUÉS   Que es el rey Don Sebastián.
(Llamando.)

RODRIGO   El capitán Santillana.

ESCENA IX

DON RODRIGO, *el* MARQUÉS, DON CÉSAR

RODRIGO   Ruégoos que me perdonéis
señor marqués, mas me obliga 2065
mi deber a hacer que el viaje
suspendáis.

MARQUÉS   (Ya no podría
continuarlo; ya le he visto
y a verle nada más iba.)

RODRIGO   *(A* DON CÉSAR, *aparte.)*
Escucha, César.

CÉSAR   Decid. 2070

RODRIGO   Antes de que apunte el día
deben de partir los presos.

CÉSAR   ¿Adónde van?

RODRIGO   A Medina
del Campo.

CÉSAR	¿Pues qué razones
	hay?
RODRIGO	Dos: aquí la atrevida 2075
	audacia de algunos pocos
	que mucho a Gabriel estiman
	pudiera hacer un arresto
	y burlar a la justicia.
CÉSAR	¿Sabéis, pues?...
RODRIGO	Yo no sé nada. 2080
	La situación se complica
	de tal modo que no hay ciencia
	ni sagacidad que sirvan
	para dominarla. Doña
	Ana de Austria, sobrina 2085
	del rey y abadesa ahora
	de las monjas agustinas
	de Madrigal, y otras muchas
	personas como ellas dignas
	de respeto, es menester 2090
	que declaren. En la villa
	de Madrigal peligroso
	fuera instalarme. En Medina
	hay cárcel segura, estoy
	casi a la distancia misma 2095
	de aquí que de Madrigal,
	y hay algunas compañías
	de arcabuceros.
CÉSAR	¿Pues tantas
	precauciones son precisas?
RODRIGO	Todas son pocas tratándose 2100
	de una cabeza proscrita,
	que puede hacer la desgracia
	de toda una monarquía.
	Tú le escoltarás, y luego
	partirás a toda prisa 2105
	a la corte, para el rey
	con una consulta mía.

2078 *Arresto*, «resolución precipitada, arrojo y determinación» *(Dicc. Aut.).*

Voy a mandar las literas
traer, y estar prevenida
la escolta que has de llevar.   2110
César, la más exquisita
vigilancia ten; con ellos
vas guardando nuestras vidas.
Adiós. Seguidme si os place,
señor marqués de Tavira.   2115

ESCENA X

DON CÉSAR, *después* DOÑA AURORA

    *(*DON CÉSAR *aguarda a que se vayan*
DON RODRIGO *y el marqués. Escucha
un momento a la puerta del fondo y
va a abrir la primera de la izquierda,
donde está el cuarto de* DOÑA AURORA,
llamándola con precaución.)

CÉSAR   ¿Aurora?... ¿Aurora?... Cerráronla
en la cámara vecina
sin duda porque no oyera
lo que en ésta sucedía.
    (Entra y vuelve a salir con DOÑA
AURORA.)
Venid, Aurora.

AURORA   ¿Qué pasa,   2120
capitán, que así os obliga
a llamarme?
    *(*DON CÉSAR *cierra la puerta del
fondo.)*
              ¿A qué cerráis
las puertas con tanta prisa?

CÉSAR   ¡Aurora, Aurora! Esta casa
es ya una cárcel sombría   2125
para vosotros.

AURORA   ¡Dios mío!
¿Qué decís?

CÉSAR   De la justicia
en poder estáis. Gabriel
con pertinacia inaudita
se obstina en callar, e inútil   2130
todo es con él. Ni le obligan
las ofertas, ni le mueven
los ruegos, ni le dominan
las amenazas. Impávido
hacia el abismo camina   2135
con el semblante sereno
y en los labios la sonrisa,
cual si pudiera de un soplo
disipar la enfurecida
tempestad en que sin rumbo   2140
va la nave de su vida.

AURORA   Capitán, es inflexible;
sus acciones son siempre hijas
de una decisión resuelta
y de una convicción íntima,   2145
y no cede.

CÉSAR   Pues os lleva
esa condición altiva
hoy, antes que raye el alba,
a la cárcel de Medina
bajo mi custodia.

AURORA   ¿Entonces?...   2150

CÉSAR   Ya os he dicho que no había
ley ni deber que valiera
para mí lo que una mínima
insinuación vuestra. Habladle
vos que sois su amor, su hija;   2155
habladle y decidle: «Huyamos;
don César nos facilita
la fuga, huyamos...» y huid,
Aurora. Y ya que mi vida,
por un tenebroso arcano   2160
que vuestro padre no explica,
está ¡ay de mí! para siempre

de la vuestra dividida,
huid, y al menos debédmela
aunque pierda yo la mía.   2165
Huid. Nada hay que me espante:
seré traidor, si es precisa
la traición para salvaros.

AURORA   Dios hará que tal mancilla
sobre vuestro honor no caiga.   2170
        *(Mira por el hueco de la cerradura
del cuarto de* GABRIEL.*)*
Él va a salir... ¡Que me asista
rogad al cielo!... Y dejadme
con él.
        (Vase DON CÉSAR, *cerrando la
puerta.)*
                Trae embebecida
su alma en los pensamientos
de hiel que le martirizan.   2175
        (Sale GABRIEL, *sombrío, los brazos
cruzados, sin ver a* AURORA, *que se ha
retirado a un lado, y habla consigo
mismo.)*

ESCENA XI

DOÑA AURORA, GABRIEL

GABRIEL   A él solo, sí, desenredar le toca
la peligrosa red que se me tiende;
sólo el rey puede descoser mi boca;
él sólo; si me salva o si me vende,
él con Dios se verá; no es cuenta
                              [mía. 2180
Yo acepto mi fortuna, tal cual sea

---

²¹⁶³ *Dividida,* 'separada'. Comp. Cervantes, *El casamien-
to engañoso:* «Dos camas tan juntas que parecían una
a causa que no había espacio que las dividiese»; Zorrilla, *O. C.,* ed. N. Alonso Cortés, II, 406: «¡Qué importa
que nos divida / tanta tierra y tanto mar!»

137

la que el cielo me dé; mas vendrá
[un día
en que todo mortal con Dios se vea,
y en aquel día en que de Dios es-
[pero
temblar ante el semblante soberano, ²¹⁸⁵
yo, de cetro en lugar, tener prefiero
una palma de mártir en la mano.

AURORA   ¿Ni una mirada para mí?
GABRIEL   Mi Aurora,
único sol que en mi sombría frente

disipa con la luz de una sonrisa ²¹⁹⁰
las nubes del. pesar que la enne-
[grecen,
perdóname si en reflexiones tristes
abismado ante ti pasé sin verte.
Mas ¿por qué el llanto tu mirada
[enturbia?
¿Por qué la agitación que te con-
[mueve? ²¹⁹⁵
¿Qué te asusta, mi bien?
AURORA   Riesgos traidores
te acechan por doquier, tal vez la
[muerte,
¿y te admira, señor, de que mi llanto
copioso y triste mis mejillas rie-
[gue?
GABRIEL   Te engañas.
AURORA   Tú. La misteriosa nube ²²⁰⁰
que impenetrable tu existencia en-
[vuelve
es fuerza que hoy ante la ley se
[rasgue
de un juez, terror de cuantos nobles
[seres
asilo hallaron, nacimiento o nom-
[bre

---

²¹⁸⁴ y s. Hipérbaton: 'Espero temblar ante el semblante soberano de Dios.'

	de Tajo y Miño en las riberas fér- [tiles. 2205
GABRIEL	¿Quién te lo ha dicho?
AURORA	Yo lo sé.
GABRIEL	Pregunto quién te lo ha dicho.
AURORA	El capitán, que tiene más de leal, de noble y generoso que tú de franco con quien más te [quiere.
GABRIEL	¡Aurora!
AURORA	No receles que mis labios 2210 dejen salir palabras imprudentes que a impulso de un amor desati- [nado complique más la situación presente.
GABRIEL	¿De don César, al fin, ¡desventu- [turada!, al fuego dio tu corazón albergue? 2215
AURORA	Mi corazón entero es de otro hombre y me son los demás indiferentes... Ni te hablara yo de él en esta hora que habrá de ser para los dos so- [lemne. Yo quiero al capitán porque tú [mismo 2220 me viniste a decir: «Aurora, quié- [rele»; mas yo le quiero porque tú lo [mandas, porque quiero no más lo que tú [quieres.
GABRIEL	Quiérele, Aurora, porque ya es [acaso el solo amigo que tu padre tiene. 2225
AURORA	¡Mi padre, sí, mi cariñoso padre!... ¿No es éste el nombre que emplear en esta situación? [conviene
GABRIEL	Silencio, Aurora;

que es el encanto de mi vida ad-
                                    vierte
ese nombre feliz.

AURORA   Pero ese nombre, 2230
dímelo de una vez, ¿te pertenece?

GABRIEL ¿Quién te lo hizo dudar? ¿Quién te
                                    [lo dijo?

AURORA La que a tu lado y con placer mil
                                    [veces
y acaso en busca de la paz perdida
veló tu sueño y sorprendió inocente 2235
tu secreto.

GABRIEL   ¡Gran Dios! ¿Y nada dije
de mi vida anterior? ¿De otros pla-
                                    [ceres,
de otros tiempos, en fin?

AURORA   Nada dijiste,
nada, señor; mas aunque dicho hu-
                                    [bieres
en el pecho de Aurora lo enterraras, 2240
que en ti a sufrir como a callar
                                    [aprende.

GABRIEL (¡Miserable de mí! Porque el
                                    [misterio
que intentan aclarar oculto quede
siempre en mi corazón, ¿será pre-
                                    [ciso
que yo mismo la lengua me cercene?) 2245
(GABRIEL *escucha desde aquí como
distraído en sombrías reflexiones.*)

AURORA Padre...

GABRIEL   Explícate, Aurora.

AURORA   Oye: al impulso
de una curiosidad impertinente,
o de otro sentimiento inexplicable
que en mí se agita y que en mi alma
                                    [enciende
la misteriosa luz de una esperanza 2250

2241 *Que*, relativo cuyo antecedente es *Aurora*.

140

lejana, incierta, misteriosa, débil,
cedí, señor, y en la callada noche
mi lecho abandoné..., porque a mi
                              [mente
mil visiones de amor se amonto-
                              [naron
en confuso tropel, puras y alegres 2255
como las olas que la mar en calma
sobre sus lomos incansables mece;
como las aves que en el árbol saltan
trinando al son de la escondida
                              [fuente.

GABRIEL   Prosigue, Aurora.
AURORA   Abandoné mi lecho 2260
y al tuyo me acerqué, como quien
                              [teme
ser sorprendido en criminal intento
por un extraño que a su lado
                              [duerme.
Tu faz un punto contemplé y mi
                              [labio
un ósculo filial puse en tu frente. 2265
¿Me oyes, Gabriel?
GABRIEL   Prosigue, Aurora mía,
tu voz la voz de un ángel me parece.
AURORA   Al contacto sutil del labio mío
sonreíste, señor; y tu voz débil
oí que el nombre mío murmuraba 2270
entre esos ayes con que el mal
                              [divierte
de una pasión el que vivió en el
                              [mundo
secretos hondos ocultando siempre;
y entonces supe por la lengua
                              [misma
que hablar en sueños indiscreta
                              [suele, 2275

2271 *El mal de una pasión*, compl. directo de *divierte*,
'aparta'.

141

que si es la tuya misterioso arcano
espesa sombra mi existencia en-
                                    [vuelve.

GABRIEL ¿Y entonces?

AURORA   Me aparté ruborizada
de quien mi padre no es; sentí más
                                    [fuerte
latir mi corazón; sentí otra sangre 2280
circular por mis venas más ardiente;
sentí en presencia del mayor cariño
mi cariño filial desvanecerse,
y al apartarme de tu lecho
                                    [trémula
un ósculo de amor grabé en tu
                                    [frente. 2285

GABRIEL No lo digas jamás, Aurora mía.
Jamás a nadie tu pasión reveles.
Quema los labios que en mi frente
                                    [seca
pusiste; quema el corazón rebelde
que, el cariño filial de sí arrojando, 2290
dio a mi cariño en su lugar albergue.

AURORA Es ya tarde, Gabriel. Mi amor es hijo
de tu callado amor.

GABRIEL   Tú lo mereces;
tú eres la sola flor que brotar hizo
en mi camino Dios... Dios, que al
                                    [ponerme 2295
sobre la tierra, me alfombró de
                                    [espinas
la senda que mis pies recorrer
                                    [deben;
pero yo no merezco tu amor santo;
yo soy un árbol cuyo tronco
                                    [estéril,
despojado de vida por el rayo,   2300
ya ni sombra, ni flor, ni aroma tiene.

AURORA No, no; tú eres un árbol cuya
                                    [sombra
cobijó mi niñez; cuyo ámbar bebe

mi pobre corazón, de quien tú
[sólo
sombra, delicia y alimento eres. 2305
Dios me entregó a tus brazos en mi
[infancia,
porque Dios quiso que en tu pecho
[ardiente
brotase, para encanto de tu vida,
de esta pasión correspondida el
[germen.

GABRIEL   Tienes razón, Aurora; reconozco 2310
en tu amor la piedad omnipotente.
Tienes razón, Aurora, Dios del cielo
te envía…, un ángel de los cielos
[eres.

AURORA   Escúchame, Gabriel.
GABRIEL   Habla.
AURORA   En el nombre
de esa pasión que en nuestras almas
[hierve 2315
desaparezcan hoy esos misterios
que nuestras dos historias oscurecen.
GABRIEL   Imposible.
AURORA   No temas que me espante,
Gabriel, ni me arrepienta, cono-
[ciéndote,
de haberte amado nunca.
GABRIEL   Es imposible. 2320
AURORA   Habla. Dime quién soy; dime quién
[eres.
Si eres villano y en tus venas viles
la sangre impura y maldecida tienes
de raza hebrea o de morisca
[tribu,
yo te amaré, Gabriel; si reales
[puedes 2325
ostentar de tu estirpe en el escudo

2325-27 Hipérbaton: 'si puedes ostentar en el escudo de
tu estirpe coronados y espléndidos cuarteles reales'; es
decir, 'si eres rey'.

coronados y espléndidos cuarteles,
yo te amaré, Gabriel; si eres acaso
criminal fugitivo y por mí temes
de un patíbulo infame la deshonra, 2330
yo te amaré, Gabriel; llama si
                                    [quieres
a un sacerdote y que con lazo eterno
anude nuestras almas; y no pienses
que el deshonor de criminal me-
                                    [moria
me humille. Te amo con amor tan
                                    [fuerte 2335
que oraré mientras viva en tu se-
                                    [pulcro,
orgullosa del nombre que me dejes.

GABRIEL   ¡Calla, Aurora, deliras!

AURORA   Un momento,
Gabriel, óyeme aún, no te impa-
                                    [cientes.
Si eres un impostor, un ambicioso 2340
cogido al fin entre sus propias redes,
huyamos; tienes ocasión y tiempo.
Sí, nuestra fuga el capitán protege;
huyamos, nuestro amor y nuestra
                                    [infamia
arrastrando a remoto continente. 2345

GABRIEL   ¡Aurora!

AURORA   Hoy a la cárcel de Medina
rayando el alba trasladarnos deben,
y el capitán, que en nuestra guarda
                                    [parte...

GABRIEL   Silencio, Aurora, ¿deshonrarle
                                    [quieres
para salvarte tú?¿Sabes que si huyo 2350
cuando en su guarda el infeliz me
                                    [lleve
morirá en mi lugar y que al fugarme

2348 *Guarda,* cfr. v. 446.

me doy por criminal siendo ino-
[cente?
Yo no huiré jamás; ni sé, ni
[quiero,
ni nací para huir; ya muchas veces 2355
la he visto cara a cara, y en el pecho,
no por la espalda, me herirá la
[muerte.

AURORA   Hiéranos a los dos un mismo golpe.
GABRIEL   Tú no debes morir; aún que hacer
[tienes
sobre la tierra.

AURORA   ¿Qué sin ti?
GABRIEL   Llorarme. 2360
AURORA   ¿Lo mandas?
GABRIEL   Yo, no: Dios; obedece.
Dios me pone en los labios un can-
[dado;
no lo intentes romper. Pura, ino-
[cente,
noble eres tú; si a deshonrada
[tumba
mi silencio me lleva, Dios lo quiere. 2365
Inclina, Aurora, la cabeza humilde
bajo la voluntad omnipotente,
y ora en mi tumba sin vergüenza,
[Aurora.
Mártir me quiere Dios y obede-
[cerle
es fuerza. Vive; y si te dice el mundo 2370
que he sido un impostor, el mundo
[miente.
Yo no he dicho jamás que era el que
[buscan
y a morir me enviarán sin cono-
[cerme.
Ora en mi tumba sin vergüenza, y
[ora

2356 *La he visto,* catáfora: 'la muerte'.

145

mientras los hombres libertad te
[dejen; 2375
y si te culpan como a mí, en silencio
digna siempre de mí como yo muere.

AURORA   ¿Tú me lo mandas? Obedezco: sea,
Gabriel; digna de ti quiero ser
[siempre.

ESCENA XII

DOÑA AURORA, GABRIEL, DON CÉSAR *

CÉSAR   Don Rodrigo sube.
GABRIEL   (A DON CÉSAR.) Oíd   2380
antes. Si en algo apreciáis
a Aurora, ved cómo enviáis
ese papel a Madrid.·
           (GABRIEL da una carta a DON CÉ-
SAR, que la toma rápidamente.)
CÉSAR   Sabéis que mi fe la aprecia
en más que mi mismo honor.   2385
Yo lo llevaré.
GABRIEL   Al señor
embajador de Venecia.

ESCENA XIII

DICHOS, UN ALGUACIL, después DON RODRIGO

ALGUACIL   (Entrando.)
           Su señoría.
GABRIEL   Aguardamos
sus órdenes.

_____

    * Las acotaciones de Baudry, Alonso Cortés y otros
señalan «después don Rodrigo», aunque en realidad este
personaje no aparece hasta la escena siguiente, a continuación del «Alguacil».

146

RODRIGO	*(Entrando.)*
	Os espera
	allá abajo una litera, 2390
	señor Gabriel.
	(GABRIEL, tomando de la mano a DOÑA AURORA y dirigiéndose a la puerta, dice:)
GABRIEL	Pues partamos.
RODRIGO	¿Ni inquirís adónde vais
	ni tomáis vuestro equipaje?
GABRIEL	Vos que disponéis mi viaje
	sabréis cómo me lleváis. 2395
RODRIGO	Conmigo.
GABRIEL	Pues ya tardamos.
RODRIGO	Vuestros cofres van con sellos.
GABRIEL	Haced lo que os plazca de ellos.
RODRIGO	Pues cuando gustéis.
GABRIEL	Pues vamos.
	(Vanse: delante GABRIEL con DOÑA AURORA, luego DON RODRIGO y DON CÉSAR.)

ACTO TERCERO

Sala de juicio en la cárcel de Madrigal; decoración ochavada; puerta en el fondo; balcón a la derecha; al mismo lado, en la segunda caja, puerta del calabozo de GABRIEL; *puertas a la izquierda de otros calabozos; mesa con papeles plumas, etc.*

ESCENA PRIMERA

DON RODRIGO *y* EL ESCRIBANO, *sentados a la mesa.* GABRIEL, *al otro lado, en un sillón reclinado tranquilamente, y como ajeno a lo que pasa a su rededor.*

ESCRIBANO   Señor, no duerme.
RODRIGO   ¿Y qué mal   ₂₄₀₀
halláis en que esté despierto?
ESCRIBANO   Que escucha.
RODRIGO   Es un hombre muerto;
que escuche o no ya es igual.
Seguid leyendo.
ESCRIBANO   *(Tomando un papel de la mesa.)*
                   Un oficio
del doctor don Juan de Llanos.   ₂₄₀₅
RODRIGO   ¿Qué dice?
ESCRIBANO   Que siendo vanos.
interrogatorio y juicio,

148

	mandó dar a fray Miguel	
	el día cinco tormento.	
RODRIGO	¿Y qué dijo?	
ESCRIBANO	Que era invento	2410
	suyo lo de que Gabriel	
	fuese el rey de Portugal,	
	y que le movió a este engaño	
	el intento de hacer daño	
	al rey don Felipe.	2415
RODRIGO	Mal	
	salió. Leed.	
ESCRIBANO	(Otro papel.)	
	Petición	
	de la nominada Aurora.	
RODRIGO	¿Y qué pide esa señora?	
ESCRIBANO	Ver a su padre.	
RODRIGO	Ocasión	
	llegará de que le vea	2420
	cuando esté ya confirmada	
	su sentencia, y no haya nada	
	que temer de que así sea.	
ESCRIBANO	(Otro papel.)	
	Novena solicitud	
	del preso llamado Arbués.	2425
RODRIGO	¿Qué solicita?	
ESCRIBANO	Que, pues	
	vivirá poco, en virtud	
	de haberle dado tormento,	
	se quisiera despedir	
	de su amo antes de morir.	2430
RODRIGO	No ha lugar hasta el momento	
	de la real confirmación	
	de su sentencia, si vive	
ESCRIBANO	(Otro papel.)	
	Una carta que os escribe	
	un anónimo.	

2408 Alusión a Fray Miguel Dos Santos, que urdió la
historia del pastelero (cfr. *Introducción*). Zorrilla mezcla elementos históricos con otros de su propia inven-
ción.

RODRIGO   Cuestión   2435
                    diaria: amenazas, fieros
                    contra mí y contra los jueces;
                    juramentos y sandeces
                    de rebeldes o embusteros.
                    Adelante.
ESCRIBANO   *(Una carta.)*
                                Para el juez   2440
                    don Rodrigo Santillana;
                    llegó de Madrid.
RODRIGO   ¡Pardiez!
                    ¿Y así os estabais con ella?
                    Dadme acá.
ESCRIBANO   Tomad, señor.
RODRIGO   De César.
                    (Leyendo.) «Del portador   2445
                    mañana sobre la huella
                    partiré; media jornada
                    ante mí llegará a esa.
                    Ni puedo darme más priesa,
                    ni hasta hoy el rey hizo nada.»   2450
                    ¡Gracias a Dios que tocamos
                    en el fin de ese proceso!
                    Llevaos vos todo eso,
                    escribano.
ESCRIBANO   ¿Os esperamos?
RODRIGO   Afuera; y si algún correo   2455
                    de la corte de Madrid
                    llega, que suba decid
                    al punto.
ESCRIBANO   Está bien.
                    (Vase el escribano.)

2436 *Fieros,* «bravatas y baladronadas con que alguno
intenta aterrar a otro» *(Dicc. Aut.).* Comp. Cervantes, *La
guarda cuidadosa*: «No me afrentan tus razones, / pues
has perdido en el juego, / que siempre un picado tiene / licencia para hacer fieros.»
2448 *Ante mí,* 'delante de mí, antes que yo'.
2449 *Priesa,* cfr. v. 414.

GABRIEL, DON RODRIGO

RODRIGO
(Deseo
salir de este laberinto
de una vez y de ese hombre   2460
a quien no hay nada que asombre.
Me repugna por instinto.
Su faz sombría, su calma
imperturbable, su irónica
conversación, su sardónica   2465
sonrisa eterna. en el alma
me infunden honda inquietud.
No me acusa la conciencia
de nada; di la sentencia
con severa rectitud,   2470
conforme a ley; mas presiento
que hay en todo esto un arcano
que sondar pretendo en vano
y deja sin complemento
la obra de la justicia.   2475
Exhala ese hombre satánico
no sé qué de frío y pánico...
Creo que me maleficia.
En fin, poco resta ya.
Si el rey la sentencia envía   2480
firmada, el último día
es hoy que calor le da.)
¿Dormís, señor Espinosa?

GABRIEL   Casi, casi, señor juez.

RODRIGO   ¿Cansado estáis?

GABRIEL   ¡Pse!

RODRIGO   ¿Tal vez   2485
sufrís dolor?

GABRIEL   Poca cosa.

RODRIGO   Aquí estaréis menos mal
que en la torre.

GABRIEL	Así, así.
RODRIGO	Que apreciarais más creí mi caridad.
GABRIEL	Me es igual. ²⁴⁹⁰
RODRIGO	¿Tal vez me guardáis rencor por la cuestión?
GABRIEL	¡Brava pena, por Dios!
RODRIGO	La prueba fue buena.
GABRIEL	Pudo haber sido mejor.
RODRIGO	Confieso que fue cruel ²⁴⁹⁵ el tormento.
GABRIEL	Pero inútil.
RODRIGO	¿Lo creéis prueba tan fútil?
GABRIEL	Ya lo veis.
RODRIGO	Volver a él podemos aún.
GABRIEL	Volvierais a ver lo que visteis ya. ²⁵⁰⁰
RODRIGO	La segunda vez quizá vuestro silencio rompierais.
GABRIEL	Sería inútil fatiga; y ahora que hablamos de esto, de hoy para entonces protesto ²⁵⁰⁵ contra todo cuanto diga; y ya podéis calcular que si en negar doy después lo dicho, el tormento es cuento de nunca acabar. ²⁵¹⁰
RODRIGO	¡Por Dios que sois hombre fuerte y gastáis bizarro humor!
GABRIEL	Soy terco y sufro el dolor;

---

²⁴⁸⁹ *Apreciarais* por 'apreciaríais'.

²⁴⁹⁵ Léase *crüel*, con diéresis, para completar el octosílabo.

²⁵¹² *Bizarro*, 'sorprendente, caprichoso'. Comp. Zorrilla, *El zapatero y el rey*, parte 1.ª, I, 6: «En verdad / que sois un hombre bizarro / y siempre con buen humor.»

²⁵¹³ *Sufro*, 'soporto'. Comp. *Quijote*, I, 25: «¿Dónde se ha de sufrir que un caballero andante como vuestra merced se vuelva loco?...» Zorrilla, *El puñal del godo*, 6:

soldado soy, y a la muerte
voy como iba a la pelea.   2515
Más despacio o más aprisa
hallarla es cosa precisa,
mas temerla es cosa fea.

RODRIGO   Vuestra fortaleza envidio;
mas noto en vos ha un momento   2520
tristeza y decaimiento.
¿Qué tenéis?

GABRIEL   Que me fastidio.

RODRIGO   ¡Que os fastidiais!

GABRIEL   Sí, a fe mía!
Tres meses ha que aquí estoy
y lo mismo hacemos hoy   2525
que hicimos el primer día.
«Traed ante mí a Gabriel.»
Vuelta vos a preguntar,
vuelta yo a no contestar.
«Al calabozo con él.»   2530
Vuelve a amanecer el día,
y vuelta a sacar al preso,
y vuelta a leer el proceso,
y vuelta a nuestra porfía.
«Hablad, señor Espinosa.   2535
—No quiero, señor alcalde.
—Qué habéis de hablar. —Que es
                        [en balde.»
Y siempre la misma cosa.
No hubo más que la semana
en que me disteis tormento   2540
que variara…, y ya me siento
casi bueno, Santillana.

RODRIGO   Me amedrenta, ¡vive Dios!
vuestra eterna sangre fría.

───────────
«Mas no soy hombre que a sufrir me avengo / razones
de tamaña altanería.»
    2522 *Me fastidio*, 'me aburro'. Comp. Zorrilla, *O.C.*, ed.
N. Alonso Cortés, I, 1309: «¿Te fastidias, sultana? ¿Te
impacientas?/¿De tu infeliz alméh con las historias/va-
cías de interés no te contentas?»

GABRIEL	También me amedrentaría	2545
	a mí si fuera que vos.	
RODRIGO	Vuestra osada impavidez	
	cada día toma creces.	
GABRIEL	Sí; parecemos a veces	
	el reo vos y yo el juez.	2550
RODRIGO	Es que a veces hallo en vos	
	un misterio que me espanta.	
GABRIEL	Es que tal vez se levanta	
	tras mí la sombra de Dios.	

(Pausa.)

RODRIGO   Yo creo, señor Gabriel,   2555
             que no es Dios, es Satanás
             quien de vos está detrás
             y os dejáis llevar por él.
             ¿A qué hombre de sano seso
             no hartaran vuestras pesadas   2560
             continuas baladronadas
             que llenan vuestro proceso?
             ¿Qué son, pues, vuestras preñeces
             y siniestras reticencias?

GABRIEL   Tembladlas si son sentencias;   2565
             reídlas si son sandeces.

RODRIGO   Pues bien: hablad de una vez;
             si ese secreto fatal
             existe en vos, hacéis mal
             de ocultarlo a vuestro juez.   2570
             Si sois quien juzgan, decid:
             «Yo soy»..., probadlo y mañana...

GABRIEL   *(Variando de tono.)*
             ¿Cuándo vendrá, Santillana,
             el capitán de Madrid?

2546 *Si fuera que vos*, 'si estuviera en vuestro lugar'.

2553 y s. Comp. Zorrilla, *El zapatero y el rey*, 2.ª parte, I, 13: «Pues eso os digo yo a vos: / que el rey don Pedro es tan hombre, / que no hay cosa que le asombre / siendo él la sombra de Dios.»

2563 *Preñez*: «metafóricamente vale confusión, dificultad, oscuridad incluida en alguna cosa que la da a conocer de algún modo» (*Dicc. Aut.*).

2571 *Juzgan*, 'piensan'.

154

RODRIGO	Hoy mismo.
GABRIEL	¡Gallardo mozo! 2575
	¿Le queréis mucho?
RODRIGO	¿Pues no,
	si es mi hijo?
GABRIEL	También yo
	le quiero bien y me gozo
	con su vista. ¿No tenéis
	más hijos que él?
RODRIGO	Nada más. 2580
GABRIEL	¿Ni los tuvisteis jamás?
RODRIGO	Las preguntas que me hacéis,
	Espinosa...
GABRIEL	Son sencillas.
RODRIGO	No sé qué se me figura
	que hay en ellas...
GABRIEL	¿Por ventura 2585
	os pregunto maravillas?
	Tenéis un hijo mancebo
	y si hubisteis os pregunto
	más que él; no hay en el asunto
	de mi cuestión nada nuevo. 2590
RODRIGO	¡Jamás podré conseguir
	arrancar de vuestra faz
	ese sarcasmo tenaz!
	¿Qué me tenéis que decir?
	Acabemos, Espinosa. 2595
	Esa burlona altivez
	que excita en mí alguna vez
	una duda misteriosa,
	¿qué significa? Parece
	que no os habéis convencido 2600
	de que juzgado habéis sido,
	de que ya no os pertenece
	vuestra acotada existencia,
	y de que según la ley
	no falta sino que el rey 2605

2588 *Hubisteis*, arcaísmo por 'tuvisteis'.
2590 *Cuestión*, 'pregunta', término censurado como galicismo por Baralt (*Dicc. de galicismos*).

confirme vuestra sentencia.
¡Parece que en vuestro pecho
hay una firme esperanza
que os da audacia y confianza
contra esa ley!

GABRIEL   Es un hecho.   2610

RODRIGO   ¿Creéis que no firmará
el rey?

GABRIEL   Esa es cuenta suya.
Dios por sus obras le arguya.
¿Le habéis vos escrito ya
que pido verle?

RODRIGO   Y respuesta   2615
aguardo; ¿mas si apeláis
al rey en vano?

GABRIEL   Me ahorcáis,
y se concluyó la fiesta.

(DON RODRIGO *mira a* GABRIEL *con
asombro*; GABRIEL *permanece sereno.*)

RODRIGO   Sospéchome que estáis loco.

GABRIEL   Tal vez.

RODRIGO   Aunque más bien creo   2620
que es otro vuestro deseo.

GABRIEL   ¿Cuál creéis?

RODRIGO   Ir poco a poco
dilatando la sentencia,
dando a entender que aún hay más
que esperar de vos.

GABRIEL   Quizás.   2625

RODRIGO   Pues os protesto en conciencia
que hoy tendrá fin vuestro afán;
si el rey no manda otra cosa
morís hoy por Espinosa,
o por rey Don Sebastián.   2630
Basta ya de dilaciones;

[2613] *Le arguya*, 'le acuse'.

[2626] *Protestar*, «asegurar con ahínco y eficacia» (*Dicc.
Aut.*). Comp. Zorrilla, *La reina y los favoritos*, III, 7:
«A fe mía, / señor conde, que os protesto / que no espe-
raba tan presto / veros, ni aquí.»

harto estoy de toleraros
y me es ya en mengua trataros
con tales contemplaciones.
Vos sois un villano artero,   2635
un taimado embaucador
que esperáis suerte mejor
dándoos por un caballero.
¡Un necio que aguarda en vano,
negándose a confesar,   2640
que nunca le han de matar
como a un infame pagano
sin confesión! Mas caéis
en un miserable error:
si no queréis confesor,   2645
sin confesión moriréis.
Y no tenéis que cansaros;
no me habéis de aventajar;
si os obstináis en callar,
yo me obstinaré en ahorcaros.   2650
¿Ahora os reís?

GABRIEL   *(Riéndose.)*

                                ¡Sí, por Dios!
Y no he muerto ya de hastío
porque, como ahora, me río
mil veces.

RODRIGO   ¿De qué?

GABRIEL   De vos.

RODRIGO   ¿De mí? En vuestra audacia loca 2655
os olvidáis, a mi ver,
que os puedo mandar poner
una mordaza en la boca.

GABRIEL   Verme mudo os diera pena;
de que es estoy persuadido   2660
mi voz para vuestro oído
el cantar de la sirena.

[2633] *Me es ya en mengua,* es una deshonra para mí'.
Comp. Zorrilla, *Más vale llegar a tiempo que rondar un
año,* III, 4: «¡Oh! ¡Sobre ellos caiga un día / su vili-
pendio y su mengua!»
[2638] *Darse por,* cfr. v. 30.

¡Mordaza! De vuestros fieros
a pesar, si lo procuro
de veras, estoy seguro,   2665
señor juez, de adormeceros.
Ya me parece, ¡pardiez!,
que comenzáis a turbaros
y no he hecho más que miraros.
Os voy a decir, buen juez,   2670
lo que pasa en vuestro pecho:
a fuerza de ir y volver
sobre quién soy, de mi ser
un fantasma os habéis hecho.
Ser superior me imagina   2675
vuestra razón exaltada,
y mi voz y mi mirada
os deslumbra y os fascina.
Todo se os vuelven antojos;
si os miro fijo a la cara,   2680
os turbáis como si echara
fuego o sangre por los ojos.
Si en paz llevando mi suerte
alejo de mí el pesar,
creéis que voy a evitar   2685
con algún filtro la muerte.
Si de vuestros hijos hablo
y por ellos os pregunto,
no parece sino asunto
de vendérselos al diablo.   2690
Si levanto un poco más
estando solos la voz,
cual de una bestia feroz
teméis, y os echáis atrás.
Y si al hablarme con saña   2695
vos, os hablo con violencia,
os dobláis en mi presencia

2663 *Fieros*, cfr. v. 2437.
2679 *Antojo*: «Se llama también el juicio que se hace
de alguna cosa sin fundamento» *(Dicc. Aut.).* Comp. Zorrilla, *Sancho García*, III, 8: «Moros, Sancho, enemigos
tus antojos / te pintan por doquier.»

como ante el viento la caña.
Tan hondo y siniestro influjo
he adquirido sobre vos,   2700
que, ¡no os lo demande Dios!,
me estáis suponiendo brujo.
No parece, Santillana,
sino que sabéis que puedo
haceros temblar de miedo   2705
cuando me diera la gana.
¿Y no es verdad, don Rodrigo,
no es verdad que mi semblante
os está siempre delante;
que andáis, que soñáis conmigo? 2710
¿No es verdad que se os alcanza
que tendrá alguna razón
al mostrar mi corazón
tan osada confianza?
¿No es verdad que todo cabe   2715
en hombres y que tal vez
en vuestra vida de juez
hay algún secreto grave
que creéis hundido vos
en la eternidad oscura,   2720
y que teméis por ventura
que me lo revele Dios?
¿No es verdad que cuando a solas
hablo con vos, don Rodrigo,
va vuestra alma en lo que os digo 2725
como nave entre las olas,
esperando de un momento
a otro verse sumergida
por la mar embravecida
de mi airado pensamiento?   2730
¿No es verdad que habéis cruzado
una vez el Portugal
y cerca de Setubal
en mitad de un despoblado
un monasterio habéis visto   2735
cuya sagrada vivienda
fue teatro de una horrenda

	profanación?	
RODRIGO	¡Jesucristo!	
GABRIEL	¿No es verdad que cuando clavo	
	mis ojos en vuestro rostro	2740
	os hielo el alma y os postro	
	a mis pies como un esclavo?	
	¡De rodillas, Santillana!	
	Vuestra vida está en la mía;	
	viviréis más que yo un día;	2745
	si yo muero hoy, vos mañana.	
RODRIGO	¡Dios me valga!	

(DON RODRIGO *se arrodilla.*)

GABRIEL	¡Calla! ¿Y vos	
	lo tomáis como os lo digo?	
	Si esto es farsa, don Rodrigo;	
	serenaos, ¡vive Dios!	2750
RODRIGO	¿Conque es decir?...	
GABRIEL	Que divierto	
	mi fastidio, Santillana.	
RODRIGO	*(Furioso.)*	
	No haréis lo mismo mañana.	
GABRIEL	*(Con calma.)*	
	Ahorcándome hoy, no por cierto.	

ESCENA III

DICHOS, EL ALGUACIL

ALGUACIL	Su merced el capitán	2755
	Santillana.	
GABRIEL	Que nos cae	
	del cielo.	
RODRIGO	Y que el fallo trae	
	del rey.	
GABRIEL	Fin de nuestro afán.	

---

²⁷⁵² *Fastidio*, 'tedio'.

Escena IV

Don Rodrigo, Gabriel, Don César

RODRIGO ¿Traes tú los despachos?

CÉSAR Sí.
Mas ¿qué tenéis, padre?

RODRIGO Nada.   2760
¿Traes la setencia aprobada?

CÉSAR Sí.

RODRIGO ¿Dónde está?

CÉSAR *(Dándole un papel.)*
Vedla aquí.
*(Don Rodrigo toma, abre y lee el
pliego que le da Don César y dice
llamando:)*

RODRIGO ¡Hola!
*(Entran algunos alguaciles y el es-
cribano.)*
Cúmplase la ley.
Avisad al confesor   2765
y al verdugo ejecutor
de las justicias del rey.
Escribano, evacuad vos
la postrera diligencia:
intimadle la sentencia,
y que se encomiende a Dios.   2770

CÉSAR Señor...

RODRIGO ¡Silencio! Leed.

ESCRIBANO *(Empezando a leer.)*
Vista y fallada...

RODRIGO *(Interrumpiéndole.)*
Adelante.
La aprobación es bastante;

2767 *Evacuad,* 'cumplid'.
2769 «Intimar a uno la sentencia, leérsela por mandado
del juez» (Covarrubias). Comp. Zorrilla, *El zapatero y el
rey,* 2.ª parte, II, 2: «Vengo a intimarle una ley/de su
natural señor.»

ESCRIBANO fórmulas a un lado, haced.
(Leyendo.)

«Y en atención a que en los cofres
de dicho Gabriel Espinosa han sido
halladas muchas prendas y joyas de
valor, pertenecientes a la persona de
nuestro difunto sobrino Don Sebastián, rey de Portugal, sin que haya
podido probar Espinosa la legitimi-
dad de su adquisición y posesión;
y en atención a que el marqués de
Tavira y fray Miguel de los Santos
y otros señores castellanos y portugueses han declarado, unos en juicio
y otros en tormento, que le tienen y
han tenido desde que le vieron por
el rey Don Sebastián; y habiéndose
probado que muchos nobles portugueses le han visitado en Madrigal
para reconocerle, y que en su nombre se han escrito cartas, contraído
empréstitos y armado gentes para
concitar a la rebelión a los pueblos
en favor suyo; y teniendo en cuenta
que dicho Gabriel Espinosa no ha
negado nunca ser él el mismo rey
Don Sebastián, antes ha contribuido
a hacer creer a los incautos que lo
es efectivamente, no declarando jamás quién sea en realidad, dándose
ya por una persona, ya por otra, y
aparentando el gesto, las acciones y
las señales exteriores que, a su parecer, pueden convenir mejor con
los recuerdos y las pinturas que de
Don Sebastián se conservan entre
los que en vida le conocieron; y con-
siderando, en fin, que el cuerpo de

[2774] *Haced,* 'actuad'.

dicho rey fue por Nos rescatado del
poder de Muley Mahamet y traído
de África al monasterio de Belén,
donde yace sepultado; aprobamos y
confirmamos la sentencia contra él
dada, y le declaramos impostor infame, traidor a su rey y usurpador del
nombre del rey Don Sebastián. Por
cuyas razones le condenamos a ser
arrastrado y ahorcado y descuarti-
zado, y puesta su cabeza en una lanza a una de las salidas del pueblo
de Madrigal, en donde vivió, para
desengaño de incautos y escarmien-
to de traidores. Yo EL REY.» *

GABRIEL   *(Con ira.)*
               ¿Traidor yo, impostor infame?   2775
               ¿Muerte a mí con tal afrenta?
               (Serenándose.)
               Que Dios me la tome en cuenta
               cuando a su juicio me llame.
               (Al escribano.)
               ¿Tenéisme más que leer?
ESCRIBANO   Nada más.
GABRIEL   Pues despachemos   2780
               y tiempo no malgastemos.
               Sea lo que haya de ser.
CÉSAR   (¡Indomable corazón!)
RODRIGO   (¡Incomprensible fiereza!

---

* «Por traidor al rey nuestro señor, y embustero, y
porque siendo hombre vil y bajo se había querido
hacer persona real, le mandan arrastrar, y que sea
ahorcado en la plaza pública de esta villa, y su cabeza
puesta en un palo.» «Escosura, *Ni rey ni Roque*, libro
IV cap. VI).

2775 Comp. Escosura, *Ni rey ni Roque*, libro IV, cap. VI:
«—¡Traidor! —exclamó—. ¡Eso no!»

2780 *Despachemos*, 'abreviemos'. Comp. *Don Juan Tenorio*, I, 5: «Quiero / hablar con el hostelero. / —Con
él habláis; decid, pues. / —¿Sois vos? —Sí, mas despa-
chad, / que estoy de priesa».

	Ni aun inclinó la cabeza	2785
	para oír la intimación.)	
GABRIEL	Alcalde, estáis demudado,	
	trémulo…, ¡por vida mía!	
	Cualquiera imaginaría	
	que erais vos el sentenciado.	2790
RODRIGO	*(Airado.)*	
	Pronto lo viera. Tenéis	
	de vida tres cuartos de hora.	
GABRIEL	Son las cinco y cuarto ahora.	
RODRIGO	Encerradle.	
GABRIEL	*(A* DON RODRIGO.)	
	Hasta las seis.	
RODRIGO	Despejad.	

(Llevan a GABRIEL *a su encierro y vanse el escribano y los alguaciles por el fondo.)*

ESCENA V

DON RODRIGO, DON CÉSAR

CÉSAR	Padre, ¿qué es esto?	2795
RODRIGO	Que es fuerza que ese hombre	
CÉSAR	Dadle un día [muera.	
RODRIGO	Ni siquiera	
	una hora.	
CÉSAR	Que dispuesto	
	muera al menos cual cristiano.	
RODRIGO	Muera, y sea como fuere.	2800
CÉSAR	¡Sin confesión!	
RODRIGO	No la quiere;	
	es un hereje, un pagano.	

2795 *Despejar*, «salirse la gente, dejando libre y desembarazado el sitio que ocupaba» *(Dicc. Aut.).*

CÉSAR	Padre, estáis ciego de ira.
RODRIGO	Ira es lo que aparento,
	ira, César; pero miento, 2805
	es terror lo que me inspira
	ese hombre de Satanás.
	Y yo, ¡imbécil!, que le daba
	tormento porque no hablaba;
	no, no: que no hable jamás. 2810
	Que le lleven al cadalso
	con una mordaza puesta;
	que no hable con nadie; en esta
	hora cuanto diga es falso.
CÉSAR	Padre, sospecho ¡ay de mí! 2815
	que se os desvanece el juicio.
RODRIGO	Es obra de un maleficio.
CÉSAR	¿Os maleficiaron?
RODRIGO	Sí.
CÉSAR	¡Superstición!
RODRIGO	Ya lo ves;
	Gabriel me maleficó 2820
	y él ha de morir o yo.
	Ya firmó el rey; muera, pues.
CÉSAR	¡Padre!
RODRIGO	¡César!... ¡Hijo mío!
CÉSAR	¿Estáis delirando?
RODRIGO	¿Alguno
	me escuchó acaso?
CÉSAR	Ninguno. 2825
RODRIGO	(De mí propio desconfío.)
CÉSAR	Padre, algún mal os acosa;
	tembláis..., estáis demudado.
RODRIGO	Algún vértigo; he velado
	tantas noches de Espinosa 2830
	con el proceso maldito,
	me ha dado tanto que hacer,
	que en mí no estoy hasta ver
	que de en medio me lo quito.
	Mas no fue nada; pasó 2835

2831 Hipérbaton: 'con el proceso maldito de Espinosa'.

ya, César. Veamos, pues,
los despachos de la Corte.

CÉSAR   Tomad: aquí los tenéis.

RODRIGO   Esta es la consulta mía,
ésta la aprobación del   2840
consejo; ésta la carta
de su majestad el rey;
¿y este otro pliego sellado
de quién es?

CÉSAR   Yo no lo sé;
me fue entregado en palacio   2845
con todos ellos.

RODRIGO   ¿Por quién?

CÉSAR   Por el rey mismo.

RODRIGO   A ver: ábrele.

CÉSAR   Una real orden.

RODRIGO   Pues lee.

CÉSAR   *(Leyendo.)*
«En nombre del rey.—Por la presente, pondréis en libertad en la hora
en que la recibiereis, y sobreseyendo
en su causa, si hubiereis procedido a
formarla contra ella, a doña Aurora
Espinosa, detenida y a vuestras órdenes en la cárcel de Madrigal; dejando disponer libremente de sí misma a dicha doña Aurora, como fuere
su voluntad.—Madrid, etcétera.—A
don Rodrigo de Santillana.»

RODRIGO   ¿En libertad? No comprendo
tal orden del rey.

CÉSAR   Y está   2850
bien terminante.

RODRIGO   Y será
cumplida. Sigue leyendo.

CÉSAR   Otro pliego para mí.

RODRIGO   Rompe la nema y aparta
la cubierta. ¿Qué hay?

CÉSAR   Aquí   2855
viene un papel y otra carta.

RODRIGO	Lee.
CÉSAR	Dice el papel así:

(Lee.)

«En nombre del rey.—Otorgamos licencia para dejar el servicio de Su Majestad temporal o absolutamente, como más le conviniere, al capitán del primer tercio de Flandes, don César de Santillana.»

RODRIGO	¿Y para qué?
CÉSAR	¿Qué sé yo?
RODRIGO	¿Tú no la has pedido?
CÉSAR	No.
RODRIGO	Sigue. (¿Qué es esto? ¡Ay de mí!) [2860]
CÉSAR	*(Lee.)*

«Y ordenamos al dicho capitán don César, por ser así del agrado de Su Majestad, conducir con todo honor y escoltar con toda seguridad, durante su viaje por tierra de sus dominios y mares guardados por su real marina, a doña Aurora de Espinosa, hasta ponerla sana y salva en estados de Venecia, por cuyo embajador ha sido reclamada, como hija adoptiva de la República Serenísima.»

RODRIGO	¡Ira de Dios! Todo ahora lo comprendo.
CÉSAR	¿Qué es, señor, lo que comprendéis?
RODRIGO	Tu amor, ¡desventurado!, a esa Aurora.
CÉSAR	Es cierto: un amor profundo; [2865] mas no os traiga con cuidado, que es el más desesperado que hubo jamás en el mundo.
RODRIGO	¿Lo ves? ¡Ah! También a ti te han maleficiado; pero [2870]

[2862] Comp. Cuéllar, *El pastelero de Madrigal*, jornada III: «Y a quien de cerca le mira *[a Gabriel],*/encoge, turba y admira.»

167

	responde, César. Yo quiero
	saberlo ya todo; di.
	Tú con ella en connivencia,
	huir con seguridad
	queriendo, su libertad 2875
	conseguiste y tu licencia.
César	No, a fe mía.
Rodrigo	Sí, arrastrado
	por sus sortilegios has
	trabajado en contra mía
	con temeridad impía 2880
	y en favor suyo.
César	Jamás.
	Que tuve siempre confieso
	simpatía misteriosa
	e interés por Espinosa,
	pero no obré en su proceso. 2885
	Amé a Aurora, la amo aún;
	mas mi pasión despechada
	es imposible y no hay nada
	entre los dos de común.
	Mientras viva la amaré, 2890
	pero este amor solitario
	de mi pecho en el santuario
	sólo yo conservaré.
Rodrigo	¡Otro misterio!
César	Tremendo
	sin duda, padre, mas puede 2895
	conmigo, y mi brío cede
	a su poder.
Rodrigo	No lo entiendo.
César	Ni yo sé decir más de él
	sino que Aurora, señor,
	no nació para mi amor. 2900
Rodrigo	¿Quién te ha dicho eso?
César	Gabriel.
Rodrigo	¡Infeliz! Es su manceba.
César	Quien tal os dijo ha mentido,
	señor.
Rodrigo	Ella misma ha sido.

CÉSAR	¿Ella?
RODRIGO	En la primera prueba 2905
	del tormento.
CÉSAR	¡Cielo santo!
	¿La habéis puesto en el tormento?
RODRIGO	Es débil y habló al momento.
CÉSAR	¡Me paralizo de espanto!
	¿Qué abismo es éste de males 2910
	que por doquier nos circunda?
	¡Qué trama ésta tan fecunda
	de misterios!
RODRIGO	Los fatales
	hilos de esa negra trama
	tan sólo puede romper 2915
	la muerte, y hoy ha de ser.
	Que mueran él y su dama.
CÉSAR	¡Imposible! Mintió.
RODRIGO	¿Quién?
CÉSAR	Ella; no puede tampoco
	ser de Gabriel.
RODRIGO	¿Quieres loco 1920
	volverme?
CÉSAR	No. Sé muy bien
	lo que digo: esa mujer
	es prenda de una venganza;
	sólo con esa esperanza
	la conserva en su poder. 2925
RODRIGO	¿Ella de venganza prenda
	y en su poder? ¡Dios me asista!
	De este arcano ante mi vista
	se aclara la sima horrenda.
	¡Hola!
	(Toca la campanilla y entra un al-
	guacil.)
	En libertad a Aurora 2930
	poned al punto y aquí
	traedla. Escucha, ¡ay de mí¡,
	escucha, César, ahora
	un secreto horrible; ese hombre
	que no es nada y que lo es todo, 2935

de quien de saber no hay modo
religión, patria ni nombre;
ese hombre a quien nada espanta,
cuya altivez nadie doma,
penitente humilde en Roma,   2940
peregrino en Tierra Santa,
soldado en Flandes, marqués
en Madrid, corso en Venecia,
que alma y vida menosprecia
como al polvo de sus pies;   2945
a quien no rinde el tormento
y cuyo espíritu fuerte
ve a un paso de sí la muerte
y se sonríe contento,
no es criatura, es fantasma;   2950
no es vivo, es aparición,
quimera, ensueño, visión,
mas que de terror me pasma.
Es un hombre de otra edad;
un hombre que estando muerto   2955
halló su sepulcro abierto
y huyó de la eternidad
mis pasos para seguir;
es la sombra de otro ser
que sale a la tierra a ver   2960
nuestra sepultura abrir.

CÉSAR   ¡Ay de mí! El continuo afán
          del proceso de Gabriel
          os hizo concebir de él
          esas quimeras que están   2965
          trastornándoos la razón.

RODRIGO   Dices bien…, sí…, no comprendas
          jamás las causas horrendas
          de mi ruin superstición

DON RODRIGO, DON CÉSAR, DOÑA AURORA

AURORA	¡Libre!... Jamas esperé	2970
	que nos olvidara Dios;	
	(A don César.)	
	ni de haber fiado en vos	
	jamás me arrepentiré,	
	pues duda no queda en mí	
	de a quién debo, capitán,	2975
	la libertad que me dan,	
	cuando os vuelvo a ver aquí.	
RODRIGO	Despeja. Escuchad, Aurora.	
AURORA	¿Por qué le mandáis salir?	
RODRIGO	Porque nadie debe oír	2980
	nuestras palabras ahora.	
AURORA	¡Dios mío! ¿Qué extraño afán	
	os agita? ¿Es por ventura	
	mi libertad impostura?	
	¡Ah! No os vayáis, capitán;	2985
	quiere volverme tal vez	
	al tormento.	
RODRIGO	Oíd os digo:	
	sois libre, y yo vuestro amigo.	
AURORA	¿Cabe entre el reo y el juez	
	amistad? ¿Entre el verdugo	2990
	y la víctima? Jamás	
	os conoceré por más	
	que por juez.	
RODRIGO	¡A Dios no plugo	
	que fuese de otra manera!	
	Mas acaso desde ahora	2995
	variéis de opinión, Aurora.	

2978 *Despejar,* cfr. v. 2797.

2993 *Plugo,* cfr. v. 827.

(Vuelve a DON CÉSAR, *que perma-*
nece en pie junto a la puerta.)
¿Qué esperáis vos? Idos fuera.
(Vase DON CÉSAR.)

ESCENA VII

DON RODRIGO, DOÑA AURORA

RODRIGO   Nada receléis de mí,
pobre niña. En libertad
estáis; vuestra voluntad   3000
no tendrá ya coto aquí.
Serenaos, pues; oídme,
Aurora, y por cuanto améis
ruégoos que me contestéis
la verdad.

AURORA   Pues bien, decidme   3005
vos en conciencia primero:
¿mi libertad se me dio
con la de Gabriel? Si no
es así yo no la quiero.

RODRIGO   Sólo depende de vos   3010
la libertad; si un secreto
me aclaráis vos, os prometo
la libertad de los dos.

AURORA   ¿Es mío sólo el secreto
que me pedís?

RODRIGO   Sí, en verdad.   3015

AURORA   ¿Y vale la libertad
de Gabriel?

RODRIGO   Me comprometo
a dársela.

AURORA   Preguntad.

RODRIGO   ¿Qué tiempo hará que de Gabriel al
                              [lado
vivís?

172

AURORA   Desde muy niña.

RODRIGO   ¿Y qué memoría 3020
de vuestra infancia conserváis?

AURORA   Apenas
una vaga memoria me ha quedado
de aquellas horas al pesar ajenas.

RODRIGO   No espero yo que recordéis la
                                [historia
de vuestra infancia, cuya edad se ol-
                                [vida 3025
pronto y muy fácilmente con las pe-
                                [nas
o los placeres de la inquieta vida;
mas del lugar en donde habéis na-
                                [cido,
donde pasasteis los primeros años,
tendréis alguna idea.

AURORA   Muy confusa; 3030
tal, que puedo decir que la he perdido
mezclándola después con mil extra-
recuerdos posteriores.   [ños

RODRIGO   ¿De manera
que imposible os será, pues lo rehúsa
vuestra memoria ya, la más ligera   3035
noticia dar de vuestra edad primera?

AURORA   Tan imposible no. ¿Quién en su mente a un recuerdo infantil no da gua-
                                [rida?
¿Quién no vuelve los ojos tierna-
                                [mente
hacia las puertas de oro de la vida? 3040
¿Quién no recuerda en ocasión al-
                                [guna
el pobre hogar o la lujosa estancia
cuya techumbre guareció en su in-
                                [fancia

3021 Comp. esta situación con la que se plantea entre
Aurora y don Félix en el poema «Historia de tres ave-
marías», cuya versión definitiva apareció en 1859 (*O.C.*,
ed. N. Alonso Cortés, I, 1680 y ss.).

	el dulce sueño que gozó en la cuna?
RODRIGO	¿Vos recordáis ese lugar?
AURORA	Sin duda; 3045

mas no por la virtud de mi memoria
sola; tan fiel en esa edad no cabe
tenerla. Sé de mi infantil historia
lo que fui recordando con ayuda
de la voz de Gabriel, que es quien la
[sabe. 3050

RODRIGO   ¿Gabriel la sabe?
AURORA   Sí.
RODRIGO   ¿Y os la ha contado?
AURORA   Incompleta.
RODRIGO   (También la habrá engañado.)

Mas yo quiero saber sólo la idea
que hayáis vos en la mente conser-
[vado.

AURORA   Tengo, aunque muy confuso, algún
RODRIGO   ¿De qué?   [recuerdo. 3055
AURORA   De mil objetos.
RODRIGO   Aunque sea

en confusión, decídmelos.

AURORA   Me acuerdo

de una ribera donde yo cogía
yerbezuelas y conchas; del rugiente
mar, que sus ondas sin cesar mecía; 3060
de un monasterio triste y solitario
fundado al pie de un monte, y va-
[gamente
me acuerdo de la iglesia, con su
[coro
enverjado, sus techos con pinturas,
su altar lleno de flores, su sagrario 3065
iluminado con mecheros de oro;
y me acuerdo también, porque me
[daban
miedo, de las inmóviles figuras
de mármol que tendidas reposaban

3062 *Fundado,* edificado'.
3067 Comp. con una de las primeras composiciones del

encima de sus anchas sepulturas. 3070

RODRIGO   ¿Qué monasterio era ese?

AURORA   Era un convento
de monjas.

RODRIGO   ¿Qué país?

AURORA   No lo he sabido
nunca.

RODRIGO   ¿Jamás Gabriel os ha contado
lo que hacíais allí? ¿Quién conducido
os había a aquel claustro?

AURORA   No ha querido 3075
decírmelo jamás; sé que aposento
tenía allí mi madre y que he pasado
los tres primeros años de mi vida
allí.

RODRIGO   ¿Con ella?

AURORA   Sí.

RODRIGO   ¿De vuestra madre
os ha hablado Gabriel?

AURORA   Mil y mil veces. 3080

RODRIGO   ¿La recuerda a menudo?

AURORA   No la olvida
jamás; y sé que en sus nocturnas
                              [preces
le reza como a mártir.

RODRIGO   ¿Sabéis de ella
la historia, el nombre, la familia?

AURORA

Sé que fue un día festejada y bella 3085
y luego escarnecida y ultrajada.
Sé que el relato de su triste historia
es una horrible e infernal leyenda
que conserva Gabriel en su memoria
de expiación y de venganza prenda. 3090

autor, publicada doce años antes, en que se describe el
interior de una catedral: «Se van mostrando despacio/
las verjas de oro amarillas,/canceles de aquel palacio,/
que dividen el espacio/de la nave y las capillas./Se ven
en turbios colores/detrás de los altos hierros,/entre
marmóreas labores,/cumpliendo así sus destierros/dor-
midos los fundadores.»

RODRIGO   ¿Y qué es lo que sabéis de ese relato
            vos?

AURORA   Yo, nada tal vez y acaso todo;
            porque sus hechos sé, mas nunca
                                    [supe
            ni las personas, ni el lugar, ni el
                                    [modo.

GABRIEL   Pero, en fin, ¿qué sabéis de vuestra
                                    [madre? 3095

AURORA   Sé que era noble dama; que vivía
            en la corte de un rey a quien la unía
            una amistad profunda y verda-
                                    [dera;
            que era para aquel rey casi una her-
                                    [mana,
            pues juntos cuando niños se criaron 3100
            y fraternal amor constantemente
            uno a otro los dos se conservaron.
            Sé que èra cuanto rica generosa,
            y que el encanto de las gentes era
            por su virtud y ciencia prodigiosa; 3105
            que el vulgo la quería,
            la corte la admiraba
            y con ella secretos no tenía
            el rey, que como hermana la trataba.

RODRIGO   ¿Mas ese rey?...

AURORA   Murió.

RODRIGO   ¿Cómo?

AURORA   En la guerra; 3110
            y concluyó con él su dinastía,
            y otro rey vino a gobernar su tierra,
            y a otras manos pasó su monar-
                                    [quía.

RODRIGO   ¿Y vuestra madre entonces?...

AURORA   Fue mirada
            como enemiga del monarca nuevo, 3115
            y al fin de algunos meses acusada

3103 'Tan rica como generosa.' Comp. v. 1163.

176

	de traición; por diabólica su ciencia
	tomaron y la dieron por culpada,
	diciendo que hizo creer que el rey
	[vivía
	no sé a quién, a favor de un sortilegio 3120
	mostrando a sus conjuros evocada
	la aparición de su fantasma regio.
RODRIGO	¿Y después?
AURORA	¡Oh! Después..., eso es lo
	[horrible
	de la historia, señor. Se apoderaron
	de ella, de su palacio, de su hacienda, 3125
	los vendieron, sus armas infamaron,
	y ocupó un extranjero su vivienda,
	y su nombre y su raza se olvida-
	[ron.
RODRIGO	¿Y ella?
AURORA	Como las hojas del otoño
	desapareció de encima de la tierra, 3130
	y en ella más los hombres no pen-
	[saron,
	sólo pensando en libertad y guerra.
RODRIGO	¿Pero vos?...
AURORA	No lo sé... Sé que mi madre,
	pobre, triste, ofendida y no vengada,
	en aquel solitario monasterio 3135
	tejía su existencia desdichada,
	y yo existía ya, bajo el misterio
	de aquellas santas bóvedas velada.
RODRIGO	¿Y luego?
AURORA	No sé más.
RODRIGO	¿Gabriel no os dijo
	nada de vuestro padre?
AURORA	Le tenía 3140
	siempre por padre a él, y él me
	[quería

3120 *A favor de*, 'merced a'. Comp. Zorrilla, *Ganar perdiendo*, III, 9: «Ya ha salido mi hermano, / y a favor de
la noche tenebrosa / saldré también...»
3134 *Sólo pensando*, fórmula causal.

más que el padre mejor quiere a su
[hijo.

RODRIGO   ¿Pero cómo supisteis?...
AURORA   En su sueño
sorprendí su secreto; y como era
necesario su amor de una manera 3145
u otra, el amor filial hallé pequeño,
y del amor de la mujer y el niño
formé para Gabriel solo un cariño.

RODRIGO   Pero al saber que vuestro padre no
[era,
¿no preguntasteis vos?...
AURORA   Quién era el mío. 3150
RODRIGO   ¿Y qué dijo Gabriel?
AURORA   Que él lo sabía,
mas que de él a acordarme no vol-
[viera,
porque mi amor filial no merecía.

RODRIGO   Siempre merece un padre...
AURORA   No·lo ha sido
jamás el mío para mí.

RODRIGO   ¡Aurora!   3155
AURORA   ¿Creéis que una razón me fue bas-
[tante
para echar su memoria en el olvido?
Insistí, porfié, lloré, y ahora
sé que nunca mi amor ha merecido.
Sé que me echó a la vida despojada 3160
de su nombre, y sin pan y sin abrigo.

Sé que dejó a mi madre deshonrada,
en medio de la tierra abandonada
para llorar y perecer conmigo.

RODRIGO   ¿Y creéis a Gabriel?
AURORA   ¿Que si le creo? 3165
Es la verdad del cielo descendida;
su palabra es mi fe, y en esta vida
por su fe juzgo, por sus ojos veo.

RODRIGO   ¿Nunca os dijo Gabriel nada en
[abono

3169 *Abono* 'defensa, justificación'. Comp. Zorrilla, *El*

	de vuestro padre?
AURORA	Nada; y si lo hubiera, 3170
	yo sé bien que Gabriel me lo dijera.
RODRIGO	¿Es decir?...
AURORA	Que es mi padre y le perdono
	como amor exigir de mí no quiera.
	Mi madre, que al dolor ha sucum-
	[bido,
	de Dios le aguarda ante el excelso
	[trono. 3175
	Yo a quien sólo dio el ser nada le
	[pido;
	pero como él nos olvidó le olvido;
	como él me abandonó, yo le aban-
	[dono.
RODRIGO	¿Vive, pues?
AURORA	No lo sé.
RODRIGO	¿Mas si viviera?
AURORA	Como él no me buscó, no le buscara. 3180
RODRIGO	¿Y si una vez en la vital carrera
	con él os encontrarais?
AURORA	Le mirara
	sin ira, mas la espalda le volviera.
RODRIGO	¿Y si al veros partir él os llamara?
AURORA	De su paterna voz no hiciera caso. 3185
RODRIGO	¿Y si llorando el mísero os siguiera?
AURORA	Apresurara sin volverme el paso.
RODRIGO	Pero ¿y si os alcanzara y os asiera
	de los vestidos él?
AURORA	Los rasgaría
	dejándole en la mano los pedazos. 3190
RODRIGO	¿Y si os tendiera sus paternos
	[brazos?
AURORA	Su abrazo paternal rechazaría.

---

eco del torrente, II, 11: «Tiembla del [*puñal*] mío, esclava; / porque si tu conducta no te abona, / a la menor
sospecha en ti se clava.»

3173 *Como no quiera*, 'a menos que quiera'.

3177 y s. *Como*, 'de igual modo que'.

RODRIGO   ¿Por qué?
AURORA   Porque mi padre todavía
no ha ido a orar sobre la tumba os-
                              [cura
de mi madre, y Gabriel me dijo un
                              [día ³¹⁹⁵
que al querer abrazarnos se abriría
entre mi padre y yo su sepultura.
RODRIGO   ¡Fatal superstición!
AURORA   Tal es la mía.
RODRIGO   (Tal es la ira de Dios. Es un misterio
impenetrable. Satanás me ciega   ³²⁰⁰
sin duda y nunca a comprenderlo
                              [llega
mi corazón ansioso.)
AURORA   He respondido
a cuanto preguntarme habéis que-
                              [rido,
señor; a vos os toca.
RODRIGO   ¡Sí, a fe mía!
Vais a ver a Gabriel. (¡Oh! , sí; yo
                              [quiero ³²⁰⁵
apurar este cáliz de agonía.)
        (Abre la puerta que da al encierro
        de GABRIEL, *mientras* AURORA *dice:)*
AURORA   Libres al fin... Para Gabriel ahora
libre será mi corazón entero.

ESCENA VIII

DOÑA AURORA, DON RODRIGO; GABRIEL

RODRIGO   *(A Gabriel.)*
               Espinosa.
GABRIEL   Heme aquí.
AURORA   *(Viendo a Gabriel.)*
                              ¡Gabriel!

GABRIEL	*(Abrazándola.)*
	¡Aurora!
	¡Infeliz! ¿Quién aquí te ha condu-[cido? 3210
AURORA	La libertad, Gabriel: libres estamos,
	y cual juntos aquí nos han traído,
	juntos espero que de aquí par-[tamos
GABRIEL	*(Pidiendo explicación de estas palabras de Aurora.)*
	¡Santillana!
RODRIGO	*(Dándole la orden de su libertad.)*
	Leed.
AURORA	¿Ves?
GABRIEL	Lo comprendo
	todo: la agitación de don Rodrigo, 3215
	de mi Aurora infeliz la fe tranquila...
	¡He aquí el instante para mí tre-[mendo!
	La hora del martirio y del castigo.
	Señor, Señor..., mi espíritu vacila:
	sostenedme hasta el fin..., ¡sed vos [conmigo!) 3220
AURORA	¿Qué te agita, Gabriel?... Tu faz [sombría,
	tu palidez...
GABRIEL	Un poco conmovido
	estoy, y es natural, Aurora mía.
	Y también vos estáis descolorido,
	Santillana...
RODRIGO	Espinosa, concluyamos. 3225
	Yo os llamé...
GABRIEL	No os canséis: el por-[qué entiendo.
	¿A solas con Aurora habéis hablado?
RODRIGO	La historia de su madre me ha con-[tado.
GABRIEL	Sólo para que a vos os la contara
	se la he contado yo.

RODRIGO   Toda pretendo   3230
            saberla, pues.
GABRIEL   ¡Curiosidad avara!
RODRIGO   Pero que vos satisfaréis.
GABRIEL   Sin duda:
            Mas puedeos ser satisfacción muy
                                    [cara;
            porque os advierto, juez, que he ob-
                                    [servado
            que mis satisfacciones y respuestas, 3235
            por más que yo riendo os las he
                                    [dado,
            han sido siempre para vos funestas.
RODRIGO   Hablad... hablad.
GABRIEL   ¡Si os empeñáis en eso!
            Mas después de tres meses de pro-
                                    [ceso
            no sé cómo no estáis escarmentado 3240
            de interrogarme ya.
RODRIGO   ¡Siempre lo mismo!
            Acabemos, Gabriel.
GABRIEL   Sí, concluyamos;
            hora es de penetrar en este abis-
                                    [mo.
RODRIGO   Descender quiero a él.
GABRIEL   Y yo os prometo
            que lo haréis; el momento es opor-
                                    [tuno. 3245
RODRIGO   Decid, pues.
GABRIEL   Esperad, que este secreto
            os pertenece a tres, y falta uno.
            Llamad al capitán, que con vos
                                    [debe
            penetrarlo también.
            (Llama RODRIGO *y sale un alguacil.)*
                          ¡Hola! Don César.
AURORA   ¿Qué tienes, Gabriel mío? En tu
                                    [semblante 3250

_____
3235 *Satisfacciones*, cfr. v. 528.

182

	en tus palabras y ademanes noto
	siniestra agitación.
GABRIEL	Aurora mía,

tu corazón amante
por mí no tenga la inquietud más
[leve;
a mis pesares Dios hoy pondrá coto 325!
y ambos tendremos libertad en breve.
¿Tú no te olvidarás desde este día
de tu Gabriel?

AURORA   Jamás. ¿Eso preguntas?
Juntas caminarán nuestras dos vidas,
nuestras almas a Dios subirán juntas. ₃₂₆₀

GABRIEL   Sí; ni la muerte las podrá un ins-
[tante
mantener una de otra divididas.

AURORA   ¡Dios! ¿A qué mientas la muerte
[ahora?

RODRIGO   Ya está aquí el capitán.

GABRIEL   Silencio. Aurora.

[3262] *Divididas*, 'separadas', como en el v. 2164. Comp.
Zorrilla, *La copa de marfil*, II, 7: «Porque sería / con-
vencerte no más del muro inmenso / que nos divide.»
[3263] Evítese la sinalefa entre *muerte* y *ahora* para no
acortar el endecasílabo.

ESCENA IX

DOÑA AURORA, DON RODRIGO, GABRIEL, DON CÉSAR

GABRIEL   ¡Hola! Sed, capitán, muy bien ve-
                                                   [nido. 3265
                Voy muy pronto a emprender un
                                  [largo viaje
                y un encargo dejaros he querido.
CÉSAR   ¡Un viaje!
GABRIEL   Sí; estoy libre; me parece
                que el portador de la orden habéis
                                    [sido.
CÉSAR   (¡Ay de mí! La infeliz aún nada
                                      [sabe.) 3270
GABRIEL   Decidme, capitán, ¿me habéis traído
                un pliego de Madrid?
CÉSAR   Tomadle.
GABRIEL   Bueno;
                guardadlo por ahora. En esa carta
                de un gran misterio encontraréis la
                                  [llave.
                (A DON RODRIGO.)
                Vos sois algo curioso y no me fío   3275
                de vos; sois padre y juez; os la
                                    [confío,
                capitán, sólo a vos. Cuando yo parta,
                dádsela a vuestro padre y que la
                                    [lea.
                ¿Me entendéis? Cuando parta: que
                                  [no sea
                ni un solo minuto antes.
CÉSAR   Os lo juro. 3280
GABRIEL   Vuestra palabra sola es buen seguro.
                Además, por si acaso no volvemos
                a vernos, pues yo parto con Aurora
                del mundo terrenal a otros extremos,

quiero un regalo haceros en me-
                                    [moria 3285
de nuestro buen encuentro en esta
                                    [vida,
que os será complemento de mi his-
                                    [toria
y prenda de amistad y despedida
        *(Saca del pecho un relicario que
        lleva al cuello con una cadena.)*
RODRIGO   (Esa calma satánica me aterra.)
AURORA   (Tiemblo no sé por qué.)
CÉSAR   (No es ser humano 3290
quien así se despide de la tierra.)
GABRIEL   Tomad. Es, capitán, un amuleto
sagrado; don del Papa: un reli-
                                    [cario
que un *lignum crucis* venerado en-
                                    [cierra
y guarda como el pliego otro secreto. 3295
Con el respeto mismo que a un sa-
                                    [grario
contempladle, y lo mismo que la
                                    [carta
se le daréis al juez... cuando yo
                                    [parta.
        (A DON RODRIGO.*)*
Abridlo sólo vos: es mi conciencia
y Dios sólo con vos sondarla debe; 3300
en ella echad una ojeada breve
y reconoceréis la omnipotencia.
(Mas si un soplo hay en vos de fe
                                    [cristiana,
esperad a que muera, Santillana.)
¡Ea! Ya que se acerca mi partida,
escuchad, señor juez, el cuento ex- 3305
                                    [traño
que queríais saber, y por mi vida
que oiréis una historia divertida.
RODRIGO   (Yo tiemblo.)
GABRIEL   Oídme, pues. La escena pasa

no importa el día, la estación, ni el
[año, 3310
de noche, en Setubal, y en una casa.

RODRIGO   (¡Cielos!)
GABRIEL   Temblando estáis si no me
Santillana.   [engaño,
RODRIGO   Seguid.
GABRIEL   En hora buena.
En una alcoba cómoda, alumbrada
por una lamparilla perfumada   3315
con asiático aroma, bien ajena
el alma de inquietud y bien guardado
por leales domésticos, el dueño
de aquella rica estancia descuidado
yacía en brazos de agradable sueño. 3320
Era un hombre harto noble y po-
[deroso
para que no tuviera por asilo
muy seguro su casa, y al reposo
se entregaba en su cámara tranquilo.
Una noche creyó sobresaltado,   3325
a pesar de lo doble de la alfombra,
pasos del lecho percibir al lado.
Abrió los ojos y miró espantado
trazarse en la pared movible sombra:
volvió la faz y con la faz de seda   3330
se tropezó de un hombre enmasca-
[rado.
Frío quedó, ¡como el cadáver queda!
«Levantaos», le dijo con acento
imperioso el incógnito; y vistióse
la bata que él le daba. «A este apo-
[sento 3335
salid.» Obedeció y enfrente hallóse
de dos hombres plantados a la
[puerta,
una dama como ellos encubierta
y un sacerdote pálido, y tenaces

3327 'Al lado del lecho.'

186

sintió pesar sobre su frente yerta   ₃₃₄₀
las miradas ardientes y voraces
lanzadas a su frente descubierta
a través de los negros antifaces.
Entonces de estos hombres el pri-
[mero,
de la sombría dama el velo alzando, ₃₃₄₅
«¿la conocéis?», le dijo; y él tem-
[blando
«sí», respondió. «Pues bien, sed ca-
[ballero»,
repuso el disfrazado; y avanzando
el grave sacerdote se dispuso
a unirle con la dama en matrimonio, ₃₃₅₀
mientras el de la máscara se puso
a escribir en silencio el testimonio.
El despertado resistirse quiso,
pero su daga el disfrazado al pecho
le presentó y ceder le fue preciso; ₃₃₅₅
firmó, y el matrimonio quedó hecho.
Partió la dama y los demás con ella.
Mas quedóse el primer enmasca-
[rado
y dijo gravemente al despertado:
«Tenéis una mujer ilustre y bella, ₃₃₆₀
gracias a mí y a vuestra buena es-
[trella,
que os hizo viudo para ser casado;
le quitasteis la honra y habéis
[dado
nombre a sus hijos; mas seguid su
[huella
y morís, ¡os lo juro!, asesinado.» ₃₃₆₅
Dijo así el de la máscara y partióse
con los demás; y de la casa el dueño
en medio de la cámara quedóse

---

³³⁴⁹ *Grave*, cfr. v. 20.
³³⁶⁴ *Seguid su huella,* 'si seguís su huella', prótasis con-
dicional.
³³⁶⁷ En Baudry, *de la casa dueño.*

	dudando si era realidad o sueño.
RODRIGO	Tremenda realidad.
GABRIEL	*(Apartándole a un lado.)*

                         Sí, don Rodrigo; 3370
la dama, doña Inés, vos el casado.

RODRIGO   ¿Y vos, señor?...

GABRIEL   El hombre enmascarado.

RODRIGO   Tal vez Dios permitió...

GABRIEL   Lo habéis soñado.

RODRIGO   ¿Y si el sueño es verdad?

GABRIEL   Silencio, digo.
Que ellos no os oigan, que la faz no
                    [os vean; 3375
sueño o verdad, que sepultados sean
con vos el sueño, la verdad conmigo.

RODRIGO   Pero mi alma concibe en este
                    [punto
que ese arcano fatal guardar podría
una verdad.

GABRIEL   Os dije que era asunto 3380
concluido. Escuchadme: si yo fuera
el rey Don Sebastián, morir debía
por la quietud del reino, y mi alma
                 [entera
ser mártir a ser rey preferiría.
Si soy un impostor y perjudico   3385
con mi existencia la quietud de
                [España,
debo morir también, debo una
                [hazaña
de mi impostura hacer y sacrifico
mi vida a sostener esta patraña
que mi historia desde hoy hará
                [famosa. 3390
¿Me comprendéis?

RODRIGO   Señor, yo no me atrevo
dudando...

GABRIEL   Ahogad la duda; morir debo
si no por Sebastián, por Espinosa,
y deben sepultarse, don Rodrigo,

con vos el sueño, la verdad conmigo. 3395
No lo olvidéis.
(Vuelven al centro de la escena.)

AURORA   ¿No sigues tu leyenda,
Gabriel? No está acabada.

GABRIEL   No por cierto;
para leer su conclusión horrenda
de vuestros ojos quitará una venda
el juez cuando haya el relicario
                              [abierto. 3400

ESCENA X

GABRIEL, DOÑA AURORA, DON CÉSAR, DON RODRIGO,
el DOCTOR N, *alguaciles. A la parte exterior de la
puerta, soldados. Después,* EL VERDUGO

ALGUACIL   Las seis.
GABRIEL   Partamos, pues.
AURORA   ¡Virgen María!
Gabriel, ¿qué es esto?
GABRIEL   Mi destino, Aurora.
AURORA   ¡Tu destino!... ¡Mi mente se ex-
ALGUACIL   *(Anunciando.)*   [travía!
El verdugo del rey.
                    (Se presenta EL VERDUGO *con el
                    dogal en la mano.)*
AURORA   ¡Dios mío! ¡Ahora
lo comprendo! ¡Ay de mí!...
                    (Se desmaya en los brazos de DON
                    CÉSAR, *que la coloca en el sillón.)*
CÉSAR   ¡Mísera!
GABRIEL   El día 3405
concluye. Vamos pues; me faltaría
valor para dejarla si volviera
en sí. Pronto, marchemos.
DOCTOR   *(A* GABRIEL, *poniéndose a su lado.)*
                              Vos conmigo.
GABRIEL   Es inútil.

189

DOCTOR	Mirad.
GABRIEL	Todo es en vano.
DOCTOR	¿Sin confesión iréis?
GABRIEL	Ha que os lo digo 3410
	cuatro semanas ya.
DOCTOR	¿No sois cristiano?
GABRIEL	Porque le soy, si a confesarme
	[accedo
	os tendré que decir lo que no
	[puedo.
	Velad por ella, capitán; se encierra
	en ella sola cuanto amé en la tierra. 3415
RODRIGO	Señor...
GABRIEL	No os fatiguéis; empresa es vana.
	Llegó, rey o impostor, mi último día
	y moriré cual debo, Santillana.
	Si impostor, con impávida osadía,
	y si rey, con fiereza soberana. 3420

(Vase, y todos tras él.)

ESCENA ÚLTIMA

DON RODRIGO, DOÑA AURORA, DON CÉSAR

RODRIGO	A concebir mi mente no se atreve
	de la verdad el espantoso arcano.
	Por ser y por no ser perecer debe,
	sí; pero no mi desdichada mano
	a ciegas al patíbulo le lleve. 3425
	César, dame esa joya.
CÉSAR	Cuando muera.
RODRIGO	Sepamos antes la verdad entera,
	César.
CÉSAR	Padre, excusad vana porfía;
	con su secreto perecer quería
	y he de cumplir su voluntad pos-
	[trera. 3430
RODRIGO	¡César!

CÉSAR   Se lo juré.
AURORA   (*Volviendo en sí.*)
                              ¡Ay! ¿Quién hablaba
aquí? ¿Sois vos, don César? ¡Qué
                                        [terrible
pesadilla!
CÉSAR   (¡Infeliz!)
AURORA   Sí, yo soñaba
sin duda... ¡Eran quimeras! Mas...
                                        [qué horrible
sospecha! Ese silencio... Esa
                                        [tristeza... 3435
¿Qué sucede? ¡Ay de mí! Los pen-
                                        [samientos
no acierto a combinar en mi cabeza.
¿Y Gabriel? Aquí estaba unos mo-
                                        [mentos
hace. ¿Y Gabriel? Decid: ¿dónde
                                        [está ahora?
¿Dónde está? Yo he soñado que
                                        [venían 3440
por él. Mas ¡qué rumor!
          (*Ruido de voces dentro*; DOÑA AU-
          RORA *se abalanza a la ventana, que
          abre, a pesar de* DON CÉSAR, *que in-
          tenta impedírselo.*)
CÉSAR   Tened, Aurora:
tened, no os asoméis.
AURORA   ¡Ah! Me querían
engañar.
          (*Se asoma.*)
                    Allí va.—Luces, soldados,
gente... ¡Ay! Yo veo, pero no
                                        [concibo
lo que veo... Me envuelve el pen-
                                        [samiento 3445
una niebla, un vapor calenturiento,
y no sé comprender lo que percibo.
_____
[3441] *Tened,* como en el v. 1199.

Allí va. ¿Pero dónde se le llevan
sin mí? Se paran... ¡el afán me
                        [ahoga!
¿Qué palos son aquellos que se
                        [elevan ³⁴⁵⁰
allí? ¿Quién es aquel que con él
                        [sube?
¿Qué le ponen al cuello?... Es una
                        [soga.
¡Dios mío! Rasga la sangrienta
                        [nube
que me ofusca la mente... Un
                        [sacerdote.
¡Ah! Le van a matar... ¡Desven-
                        [turados, ³⁴⁵⁵
deteneos!... ¡Gabriel!... ¡Y yo,
                        [insensata,
que lo miraba estúpida! Malvados,
tened... Las manos sin oírme le
                        [ata...
(Volviéndose de repente a DON RO-
DRIGO.*)*
Pero vos, ¡miserable!, que sois
                        [hombre,
venid... gritad... gritad, alma co-
                        [barde, ³⁴⁶⁰
conmigo... ¡Deteneos! Santillana,
gritad; a mí no me oyen, ¡en el
                        [nombre
de Dios! Gritad... le quitan la es-
                        [calera...
Gritad.

RODRIGO   Sí, que se salve aunque yo muera.
       (Se acerca a la ventana y grita.)
       ¡En el nombre del rey!...

AURORA   *(Cayendo de rodillas junto a la
ventana.)*

               ¡Ay! ¡Es ya tarde! ³⁴⁶⁵

---

³⁴⁵⁸ *Tened*, cfr. v. 1199.

CÉSAR   *(Dando el relicario a* DON RODRIGO.)
             Tomad: sepamos la verdad postrera.
             *(*DON RODRIGO *toma y abre con an-*
             sia el pliego y el relicario que le da
             DON CÉSAR. *El relicario contiene un*
             papel y un retrato envuelto; el plie-
             go varios papeles. Lo primero que
             lee DON RODRIGO *es el papel del reli-*
             cario; después registra con ansia los
             papeles del pliego, y después desen-
             vuelve el retrato; todo con la mayor
             agitación y ansiedad. DOÑA AURORA
             permanece unos momentos de rodi-
             llas y se acerca después al grupo que
             forman DON RODRIGO *y* DON CÉSAR.)
RODRIGO   *(Leyendo.)*
             «En el nombre de Dios. Quienquier
                                   [que fueres,
             juez, sacerdote o asesino, pena
             de excomunión, después que lo
                                   [leyeres
             arroja al fuego este papel. El muerto ³⁴⁷⁰
             ha sido el rey Don Sébastián.»
AURORA   ¡A buena
             hora lo ves, imbécil asesino!
RODRIGO   *(Registrando el pliego.)*
             Mi firma. Una escritura..., mi
                                   [contrato
             de boda...
             (Desenvuelve el retrato.)
                         Y ésta, doña Inés Aldino.
AURORA   *(Quitándoselo.)*
             ¡Mientes! Es de mi madre ese
                                   [retrato. ³⁴⁷⁵

---

³⁴⁶⁸ y s. *Pena de excomunión,* 'bajo pena de excomunión' (ya que la identidad del muerto debe permanecer
secreta). Comp. Gallardo, *Ensayo...,* col. 1357: «Manda-
ban que el verdugo no entrase en la cárcel sin ser llamado de la justicia, pena de duzientos azotes.»

RODRIGO   (Teniéndole los brazos.)
               ¡Hija mía!

AURORA   (Rechazándole.)
                        ¿Tu hija?... Eso tan sólo
               me faltaba. ¡Hija tuya! ¡Alucinarme
               quieres con ese nombre! Mas el
                                        [dolo
               miserable comprendo. No lo in-
                                        [tentes.
               Tú no has podido la existencia
                                        [darme. 3480
               Mientes, viejo feroz; dime que
                                        [mientes.
               Tú para que su muerte te perdone
               me llamas hija tuya; mas te
                                        [engañas;
               nada hay en mí que tu maldad
                                        [abone;
               para ti sólo hay odio en mis en-
                                        [trañas. 3485

RODRIGO   (De rodillas.)
               ¡Hija mía!

AURORA   ¡Otra vez! No me lo digas,
               no me lo expliques; comprender no
                                        [quiero
               que el ser infame que en tu seno
                                        [abrigas
               me pudo dar el ser. Muerta primero.

RODRIGO   (Asiéndola del vestido.)
               ¡Calla, hija mía!

AURORA   Suelta, no me sigas.   3490

RODRIGO   ¡Huyes de mí!

AURORA   Por siempre.

RODRIGO   ¿Me abandonas?

AURORA   Como a mi madre tú.

RODRIGO   ¿Nada en mi abono

3484 *Abone*, cfr. v. 3171.
3485 Con este verso terminaba la primera redacción del
drama (cfr. *Introducción*: «Caracteres románticos»).
3492 *Abono*, cfr. v. 694.

te dice el corazón? Que me per-
[donas
dime.

AURORA   Mi madre contra ti ante el trono
de Dios venganza pide.

RODRIGO   ¡Horrendo encono! 3495
AURORA   Si eres mi padre tú, ¿por qué te ex-
[trañas
del infernal rencor que arde en mis
[venas?
La que tiene tu sangre en sus en-
[trañas
sólo puede tener sangre de hienas.
Suéltame, pues, de tu sangrienta
[mano. 3500
Mi padre era Gabriel, y su asesino
y el de mi madre, tú.

RODRIGO   Pero el destino
te une hoy a mí.

AURORA   *(Desprendiéndose de él.)*
Lo intentarás en vano.
Muerta mejor que a tu existencia
[unida.
Reniego, huyo de ti; mi ser olvida 3505
y el nombre de hija que tan mal
[empleas;
y ¡ojalá que infeliz como yo seas!
Y ¡ojalá en mi lugar, fiero homi-
[cida,
de mi madre y Gabriel junto a ti
[veas
la doble aparición toda tu vida! 3510
*(DON RODRIGO cae desplomado. DO-
ÑA AURORA se va por la puerta del
fondo. DON CÉSAR la sigue triste-
mente. Cae el telón.)*

<hr>

3505 *Olvida,* imperativo.
3510 Comp. con los versos finales del soneto de Espronceda a la muerte de Torrijos: «Y los viles tiranos, con
espanto/siempre delante amenazando vean/alzarse sus
espectros vengadores.»

Indice de voces y construcciones anotadas*

---

* Los **números** remiten a los **versos**.